Money and government
in the Roman Empire

Rome's conquests gave her access to the accumulated metal resources of most of the known world. An abundant gold and silver coinage circulated within her empire as a result. But coinage changes later suggest difficulty in maintaining metal supplies. By studying Roman coin-survivals in a wider context, Dr Duncan-Jones uncovers important facts about the origin of coin-hoards of the Principate. He constructs a new profile of minting, financial policy and monetary circulation, by analysing extensive coin evidence collected for the first time. His findings considerably advance our knowledge of crucial areas of the Roman economy.

This book will be an essential reference work for Roman historians and numismatists and will also be of interest to economic historians.

Money and government in the Roman Empire

RICHARD DUNCAN-JONES

Fellow of Gonville and Caius College, Cambridge

CAMBRIDGE
UNIVERSITY PRESS

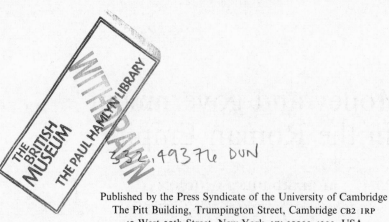
Published by the Press Syndicate of the University of Cambridge
The Pitt Building, Trumpington Street, Cambridge CB2 IRP
40 West 20th Street, New York, NY 10011-4211, USA
10 Stamford Road, Oakleigh, Melbourne 3166, Australia

First published 1994

Printed in Great Britain at the University Press, Cambridge

A catalogue record for this book is available from the British Library

Library of Congress cataloguing in publication data

Duncan-Jones, Richard.
Money and government in the Roman empire / Richard Duncan-Jones.
p. cm.
Includes bibliographical references and index.
ISBN 0 521 44192 7 (hardback)
1. Coinage–Rome–History. 2. Monetary policy–Rome–History.
3. Money–Rome–History. I. Title.
HG237.D79 1994
332.4'9376–dc20 93–31989 CIP

ISBN 0 521 44192 7 hardback

To Julia

CONTENTS

PLATES

FIGURES

TABLES

PREFACE

Although it is so remote in time, the Roman Empire has left a gigantic amount of coin. The amount from relatively modern discoveries must run into millions, even without allowing for finds in earlier centuries which were mostly melted down. Survival on this scale has its own interest, and seems to have a specific explanation, which is discussed in Part II. This book seeks to use coin evidence to study Roman minting policy, monetary organisation, and the monetary economy. For these purposes, co-ordinated analysis of a large amount of data has clear advantages over piecemeal study. Coin hoards of the Principate provide a rich source material whose potentialities as historical evidence are only slowly being exploited, partly because so many hoards remain unpublished. But the material available is now increasing rapidly, thanks partly to discoveries by metal detector, and has grown substantially while this book has been in preparation.

As a preliminary, the early chapters consider the Empire's finances and financial structure. And an initial economic chapter discusses the role of currency, the availability of coin, and monetary inflation. In the main part of the book, the evidence mainly comes from physical survivals of coin. The period examined ends at AD 235, close to the point at which written sources sharply diminish. The invaluable survey by J.-P. Callu takes up from AD 238.[1] Some evidence from the Late Empire is also used, particularly in the discussion of taxation in chapter 4.[2]

The book could have been extended by reproducing evidence more fully, but at the risk of overburdening it with technicality. Incorporating statistical analysis in a general historical work has not always been easy. To reduce the burden on the reader, the early chapters are relatively wide-ranging, and chapter 7 summarises much of the analysis of coin material.

The book is primarily intended as an essay in economic history. But its research has taken me much further into the world of numismatics than I could have foreseen. I have depended heavily on the advice and encouragement

---

[1] J.-P. Callu, *La politique monétaire des Empereurs romains de 238 à 311* (Rome 1969).
[2] For discussions of money and coinage in the Late Empire, see C.H.V. Sutherland, *The Roman imperial coinage* 6 (London 1967); P. Bruun, *The Roman imperial coinage* 7 (London 1966); J.P.C. Kent, *The Roman imperial coinage* 8 (London 1981); M. Hendy, *Studies in the Byzantine monetary economy c. 300–1450* (Cambridge 1985); G. Depeyrot, *Le Bas-Empire romain: économie et numismatique* (Paris 1987); G. Depeyrot, *Crises et inflation entre antiquité et Moyen Age* (Paris 1991).

of professional numismatists over the past ten or twelve years. Warmest thanks are offered to Monsieur M. Amandry, Dr M.A.S. Blackburn, Dr K. Butcher, Professor T.V. Buttrey, Dr I.A. Carradice, Professor P. Grierson, Dr C.J. Howgego, Dr C.E. King, Professor H.B. Mattingly, Dr R. Reece, Mr T. R. Volk, the late Mr David Walker and, most of all, to Dr A.M. Burnett and Dr R.F. Bland, with both of whom I have had many valuable discussions. Dr Burnett persuaded me to embark on die-studies, and gave generous access to the British Museum photofile. He has since kept me supplied with details of new imperial coin-hoards, including the important Belgian gold hoard. Dr Bland has also been a constant source of bibliographical help. Dr Burnett, Dr Bland, Dr Blackburn, and Mr Volk each at some stage cast an expert eye over sections of the die-dossiers, for which they deserve further warm thanks. Professor Buttrey, Professor Callu, Dr Kunisz, Dr Reece and Mr Walker also kindly gave me copies of numismatic works.

I wish to express special thanks to Professor M.H. Crawford for his help, advice and encouragement over a long period, which included the extended loan of his collection of auction catalogues, and early access to his listings of Imperial coin-hoards. His now classic work on Roman Republican coinage has also provided valuable stimulus, especially in its use of hoard evidence.

I have had stimulating correspondence with Professor E. Lo Cascio, Professor G.F. Carter and Dr W.E. Metcalf. I should like to thank Dr S. Balbi di Caro and Dr Metcalf for providing me with access to numismatic material in Rome and New York on several occasions. Mr W. Scheidel very kindly obtained and transmitted material from the coin photofile in Vienna. I was helped in writing about taxation by comments on an early draft of chapter 4 from Dr K.A. Worp and Dr J.D. Thomas. Dr Bland produced acute criticisms of drafts of three numismatic chapters. I have also received welcome help from Dr S. Banaji, Professor A.J. Graham, Professor J.H. Humphrey, Mr H.R. Hurst and Miss H. White.

Distinguished statistical colleagues contributed the initial diagnosis for the estimates of die-population in chapters 10 and 11, and the essentials of effective estimating techniques, without which these parts of the book could not have been undertaken. Dr A.W.F. Edwards suggested the statistical format for analysing the largest body of coin-data. My greatest thanks go to Mr R.A. Kempton, now Director of the Scottish Agricultural Statistics Service. He identified the statistical configuration of this material, as well as introducing me to unfamiliar techniques and to an advanced computer program for implementing them. He also gave considerable time to discussing my statistical efforts, and provided expert criticism at many stages. Dr P.M.E. Altham has also given kind help with statistical analysis. Naturally, none of those thanked are responsible for the uses to which their advice has been put, and all responsibility for errors and shortcomings remains the author's. By coincidence, two further publications discussing use of the negative binomial for modelling Roman coin-populations came to hand after this book had gone to press.[3]

Further warm thanks are offered to my College, for allowing me a sabbatical year, providing computer equipment, and above all for creating an intellectual environment in which I could draw on the help of colleagues from other disciplines. Besides Dr Edwards, scientific colleagues at Caius who gave substantive help include Dr P. Robinson, who at an early stage sorted a very large dataset on the University mainframe computer and provided graphics tools; Dr J.G. Robson, who gave me much invaluable help with microcomputers and software; and Dr R.J. Butcher, who explained programming in BASIC. At Caius I have also had the great privilege of discussing numismatic problems with Professor Philip Grierson, who also kindly provided innumerable loans of rare numismatic publications.

Chapters 12 and 13 are later versions of articles, whose technical content has been shortened (Duncan-Jones 1987 and 1989). I have relied for numerical and graphic analysis on excellent computer software in the shape of SYSTAT and SYGRAPH.[4] The statistical modelling in chapter 10 uses the more specialised program MLP, together with short programs by the author which are printed in Appendix 8.[5] The coin illustrations are reproduced by kind permission of the Syndics of the Fitzwilliam Museum and the Trustees of the British Museum.[6]

The book has taken a long time to research and write. I would like to dedicate it to my wife, with heartfelt thanks for the support and encouragement which have made a heavy task very much lighter.

---

[3] W.W. Esty, G.F. Carter, 'The distribution of the numbers of coins struck by dies' *AJN* 2.3–4 (1991–2). 165–86; A. J. Stam, 'Statistical problems in ancient numismatics' *Statistica Neerlandica* 41 (1987) 151–73.

[4] Leland Wilkinson, SYSTAT & SYGRAPH (Evanston, Ill 1988): SYSTAT, Inc. The diagrams were drawn using SYGRAPH.

[5] G.J.S. Ross, *Maximum Likelihood Program*, Copyright Rothamsted Agricultural Research Station (Rothamsted 1980).

[6] Fitzwilliam Museum: plates 1,2,5,7,8 and 9; British Museum: plates 3, 4, 6, 10 and 11. Photographs of Fitzwilliam coins were taken by the author, those from the British Museum by Dr R.F. Bland, to whom warmest thanks are given.

ABBREVIATIONS

Modern publications are cited by short title in the notes and by long title in the Bibliography (p. 269). Coin hoards are cited by name or by catalogue number (index p. 284; numbered hoard-listing, p. 261). Papyrological abbreviations, which mainly occur in chapters 2 and 4, follow standard forms (J.F. Oates, R.S. Bagnall, W.H. Willis, K.A. Worp, *Checklist of editions of Greek papyri and ostraka*[3], BASP Supplement 4 (1985); or E.G. Turner, *Greek papyri* (Oxford) (1968)). *Année philologique* abbreviations are used for journals.

The abbreviations for a few frequently cited works are shown below.

AE	*Année épigraphique*
ANRW	H. Temporini, W. Hase (edd.) *Aufstieg und Niedergang der römischen Welt*
ASR	A.S. Robertson *An inventory of Romano-British coin hoards* (forthcoming)
Barbieri	G. Barbieri 'Liberalitas', in E. de Ruggiero *Dizionario epigrafico di antichità romane* (1895–)
Blanchet	A. Blanchet *Les trésors de monnaies romaines et les invasions germaniques en Gaule* (1900)
BMCRE	H. Mattingly, R.A.G. Carson (edd.) *Coins of the Roman Empire in the British Museum* (1923–62)
Bolin	S. Bolin *State and currency in the Roman Empire to 300 AD* (1958)
Carradice	I.A. Carradice *Coinage and finances in the reign of Domitian AD 81–96* (1983)
CH	*Coin hoards*
Chalfont	R.F. Bland *The Chalfont hoard and other hoards* (1992) (*CHRB* 9)
CHRB	*Coin hoards from Roman Britain*
CIL	*Corpus Inscriptionum Latinarum*
Cohen	H. Cohen *Description historique des monnaies frappées sous l'empire romain*[2] (1880–1908)
CTMAF	X. Loriot, D. Nony (edd.) *Corpus des trésors monétaires antiques de la France* (1982–)
Dembski	G. Dembski 'Die antiken Münzschatzfunde aus Österreich' *NZ* 91 (1977) 3–64
Dig.	*Digesta Iustiniani*
ESAR	T. Frank (ed.) *Economic survey of ancient Rome* (1933–40)
FMRD	*Die Fundmünzen der römischen Zeit in Deutschland* (1960–)
FMRÖ	*Die Fundmünzen der römischen Zeit in Österreich* (1970–)

Gerov	B. Gerov 'Die Einfälle der Nordvölker in den Ostbalkanraum im Lichte der Münzschatzfunde', *ANRW* 2.6 (1977) 110–81
HA	*Historia Augusta*
HS	Sesterces
IGRR	*Inscriptiones Graecae ad res Romanas pertinentes* (1901–27)
ILS	H. Dessau *Inscriptiones Latinae Selectae*
Johnson	A.C. Johnson *Roman Egypt* (1936) (*ESAR* 2)
Kienast	D. Kienast *Römische Kaisertabelle: Grundzüge einer römischen Kaiserchronologie* (1990)
Kunisz	A. Kunisz 'Udzial zlotego pienadza w cyrkulacji na terytorium Egiptu w I–III w n.e.', *Wiadomisci Numizmatyczne* 27 (1983) 121–65
Mihailescu	V. Mihailescu-Birlibà *La monnaie romaine chez les Daces orientaux* (1980)
Milne	J.G. Milne *Catalogue of Alexandrian coins* (1933)
Mirnik	I.A. Mirnik *Coin hoards in Yugoslavia* (1981)
MLP	G.J.S. Ross *Maximum Likelihood Program* (1980)
MSR	F. Hultsch (ed.) *Metrologicorum scriptorum reliquiae*
Normanby	R. Bland, A. Burnett *The Normanby hoard* (1988) (*CHRB* 8)
OGIS	W. Dittenberger *Orientis Graeci Inscriptiones Selectae*
Protase 1	D. Protase *Problema continuitatii in Dacia in lumina arheologici si numismaticii* (1966)
Protase 2	D. Protase *Autohtonii in Dacia: I Dacia Romana* (1980)
RE	Pauly-Wissowa-Kroll *Real-Encyclopädie der Klassischen Altertumswissenschaft* (1894–)
Regling	K. Regling 'Der Schatz römischer Goldmünzen von Diarbekir (Mardin)', *Blätter für Münzfreunde* 66 (1931) 353–81
RG	*Res Gestae Divi Augusti*
RIC	H. Mattingly, E.A. Sydenham and others *The Roman imperial coinage* (1923–)
RIC I²	C.H.V. Sutherland *The Roman imperial coinage* I² (1984)
Sel. Pap.	A.S. Hunt, C.C. Edgar *Select papyri* (1932)
Strack	P.L. Strack *Untersuchungen zur römischen Reichsprägung des 2. Jahrhunderts* (1931–7)
Thirion	M. Thirion *Le trésor de Liberchies* (1972)
Walker	D.R. Walker *The metrology of the Roman silver coinage* (1976–8)

PART I

THE ECONOMICS OF EMPIRE

I

SURPLUS AND DEFICIT

1. INTRODUCTION

When chance winds drove a Roman tax-collector from the Red Sea to Ceylon, the island's king was said to be much impressed by the consistent weight of the silver coins that he brought with him.[1] But an observer meeting it in the twentieth century would be more likely to notice the diversity of Roman coinage, not merely its varied coin-types, but also the inconsistent weights, differing standards, and irregular shape.[2] Some of this diversity obviously reflected mass production in a traditional society with pre-industrial technology. But there are other features of the Empire which throw light on Roman minting policy and the monetary role of coin.

The Empire of the Principate was not fully monetised, and the state collected much of its revenue in kind.[3] Big private estates, like small peasant farms, were said to aim at self-sufficiency and to avoid the market place where they could.[4] But at the centre, there is little sign that the government could do without money, except when it distributed some of its grain revenue to a privileged elite. Money was of the utmost importance for the state's biggest spending commitment, maintaining a large army. Budgetary problems showed themselves in the form of shortage of money. A state which functioned in this way was almost bound to turn some of its regular revenue in kind into cash through the market-place.[5]

But in its fiscal operations, the Roman government seems to have done without credit.[6] There was no public debt to fill any gap between income and spending. Despite occasional government lending, government borrowing was practically unknown.[7] There were no resorts to large banks at times of crisis, and from what we can see, no large banks to resort to.[8] The state was

---

[1] Pliny *NH* 6.85. This was in the time of Claudius.
[2] This is partly because standards declined after the date referred to. For multiple standards in a single reign, see Table 15.4 (Augustus), Tables 15.6–9 (Nero, Domitian, Commodus, Severus, Caracalla).
[3] Duncan-Jones 1990, chapter 12.
[4] Duncan-Jones 1982, 37–8; Veyne 1990, 131–62.
[5] As it certainly did with the property of the condemned (section 2.1). See also section 2.4.
[6] For taxes in kind, see pp. 47–50.
[7] For lending see pp. 22–4. For borrowing, see p. 8. Pertinax as Emperor was said to have borrowed money and paid it back before his three-month reign had ended (*HA Pert.* 9.1).
[8] See Andreau 1987. For temple banking, see section 2.3 below.

more or less excluded from the active flow of credit between individuals.[9] Thus through its lack of financial sophistication, any cushioning of deficits had to come from the government's cash reserves. If money could not be found, the state would default on its obligations, with painful results for some of its employees.[10]

The pattern of financial management set by Augustus was one of extreme openhandedness. Augustus prided himself on the vast sums which had passed through his hands and been spent on distributions, games and buildings. His gold temple offerings could be seen as a marginal form of saving.[11] But consecrated temple treasure could not be drawn on under normal circumstances.[12] The amounts Augustus bequeathed were small by comparison with what he had spent.[13]

Any serious departure from this pattern of openhandedness by later Emperors ran the risk of unpopularity. Tiberius was almost the only ruler to put that to the test. Thus Emperors were committed to heavy public spending in the capital and in the army camps. Coupled with this was the need to show princely generosity towards individuals.[14]

Other features of government policy ignored economic rationalism. Willingness to assign tax burdens in accordance with political privilege rather than capacity to pay emerges in different ways. Ancient rights were allowed to persist, protecting some communities from the rigours of taxation.[15] New anomalies and exemptions showed little respect for economic constraints.[16] Fresh tax-immunities went on being created.[17] And by the Late Empire, privilege seems to have hardened, with the concentration of tax-burdens on

---

[9] For loans among the aristocracy, see the perceptive account by Frederiksen 1966; also pp. 23–5 below. Much Republican lending was lending to provincials to enable them to pay their taxes (cf. Broughton *ESAR* 4.541–54; Wilson 1966, 4–7, 156–7, 176–88). This continued in new provinces under the Principate: see Dio 62.2.1. Most mercantile lending is hidden from view, but see Duncan-Jones 1990, 42, 46–7, with *SB* 9571, studied by Casson 1986. Cf. Bogaert 1987, 72. Lending by an Imperial freedman in the Sulpicius archive from Puteoli may show funds of the Emperor being deployed in the money market (*AE* 1973, 157).

[10] For suspension of *praemia* under Augustus and Tiberius, n. 84 below; for suspension under Nero, Suet. *Nero* 32.1; for interruption of alimentary payments, Duncan-Jones 1982, 384.

[11] See n.59 below.   [12] For temple treasure, see pp. 8–9 below.

[13] Suet. *Aug.* 101.3; *RG* Appendix 1.   [14] See pp. 42–3 below.

[15] For example, a sizeable part of northern Tunisia apparently shared fiscal privileges with Carthage: Duncan-Jones 1990,178; *Consularia Const.* 30 BC, T. Mommsen ed. *Chron. Min.* 1, 217. In Egypt, land of Alexandria and the Menelaite nome remained tax-exempt, Alexandrians paid no poll tax, and paid little tax on garden-land (Châlon 1964, chapters 59–62; Delia 1991, 30–1).

[16] Titus, depicted as generous to a fault, is said to have promised petitioners more than his advisers said he could afford (Suet. *Titus* 8).

[17] Thus Claudius gave immunity to Cos, home of his physician, and Hadrian gave it to Selinus, where Trajan had died (Tac. *Ann.* 12.61; Broughton *ESAR* 4.708). Antoninus Pius gave tax-freedom to Pallantium in Arcadia, fancifully believed to be connected with the founding of Rome (Paus. 8.43.1–2). Nero gave tax-freedom to Greece, while Caligula refunded Commagene all its tribute (Suet. *Vesp.* 8.4; *Gaius* 16.3). Septimius Severus gave freedom to a number of African cities (*Dig.* 50.15.8.11; *ILS* 1430, 2911, 6792, 6796; see Jacques 1991). For some lists, *Dig.* 50.15.1; 50.15.8. Cf. Jones 1939; Bernhardt 1980.

the rural population, and away from urban populations.[18] But deliberate inequity is already obvious under the Principate, in the heavier poll-taxes on rural inhabitants in the one province which we can study in detail.[19]

The pattern of financial generosity passed down by Augustus probably militated against the building up of large reserves, as did spending increases by his successors. That left the State relatively vulnerable to short-term deficit, whether through overspending or through tax shortfalls. This makes oscillation between deficit and surplus easier to explain.[20] When it emerges that the successors to spendthrift Emperors could go on spending heavily, that suggests deficits which could be cured by waiting for tax-revenue to come in. Thus some deficits, even if accompanied by crisis measures, may indicate short-term difficulties, rather than the failure of long-term financial strategy. It is not clear how much long-term planning took place, despite the regular tax-cycles.[21]

The Empire's ability to recover quickly from intermittent bouts of overspending suggests a healthy underlying fiscal position, even if shortage of funds could frequently bring injustices such as seizure of large fortunes. Another fiscal device was manipulation of the coinage, which is discussed in later chapters.[22] Its importance should not be exaggerated, since the projections below suggest that under normal conditions only a fraction of state expenditure would come from newly minted coin. The armoury of financial expedients is worth exploring further, before attempting a brief review of fiscal events.

2. FINANCIAL EXPEDIENTS

2.1. PROPERTY OF THE CONDEMNED (*BONA DAMNATORUM*)

A recurrent theme is the condemnation of the rich for treason or social dereliction. The classic account is Tacitus's narrative of the later years of Tiberius. But that tends to explain too much in terms of intervention by the Emperor.[23] In practice, legislation which allowed substantial rewards for successful accusers left opportunities which were rarely neglected for very long.[24] The initiative might come from the accusers themselves. From time to

[18] Jones 1964, 1.63.
[19] See also n.10 above. Rates of personal taxation are almost a blank in other provinces, and Egypt should not be set aside as an exception to some imaginary norm.
[20] Finances at the start of the Principate were probably very disjointed, and Josephus even shows Herod giving Augustus some financial help at a time when he needed money for shows and handouts (*AJ* 16.128).
[21] For tax-cycles of 5 and 15 years, see pp. 59–63.
[22] Chapters 7, 14–16.
[23] For the Emperor as beneficiary, cf. Millar 1977, 167. A detailed examination of economic and fiscal evidence suggests that Suetonius treats similar episodes in different ways under different Emperors (Reekmans 1977).
[24] Emperors could choose to influence these things, and Domitian was said to have repressed *fiscales calumniae* early in his reign before changing his policy (Suet. *Dom.* 9.3; 10; 12.1). For the fall of the two richest men in Greece under Domitian, see Plutarch, *de frat. amore* 487F–488A (the example in Dio Chrysostom, *Or.* 7.12 may well also be Domitianic).

time, professional or self-appointed *delatores* were declared outcasts, to be scourged and driven from Rome by Titus, or cast adrift by Trajan.[25] The impact of accusations could be as great in the provinces as in Rome.[26] Since extortion from provincials was apparently the cornerstone of many great fortunes at Rome, absorption of private wealth by the state could be seen as one means of compensating for low provincial tax-rates.[27]

There seem to be cases where prosecutions were instigated from the throne. Nero's execution of six men reputed to own 'half of Africa' may be one example.[28] Another is Caligula's convictions of Gallic nobles, said to have brought in HS600 million.[29] Periods of civil war certainly brought the downfall of many rich families. Thus Augustus is said to have taken two-thirds of the property of all wealthy Egyptians after the battle of Actium, and in Italy many senatorial families failed to outlive the Republic, as a result of proscriptions and warfare.[30] Vespasian took funds from rich men in the East both during and after the civil war of 69.[31] Under Septimius Severus, supporters of Niger and Albinus were proscribed and executed.[32] This made sizeable inroads into the membership of the Senate, and the fiscal proceeds must have been enormous. Procurators of the *res privata* and *ad bona cogenda* appear at this time (likewise those *ad bona damnatorum* and *ad bona Plautiani*).[33]

These spectacular transfers from private wealth were supplemented by private legacies to the Emperor.[34] The great men of the late Republic could expect legacies from all sides, and Cicero claimed to have acquired HS20

---

[25] Suet. *Tit*.8.5; Pliny *Pan.* 34-5. Cf. Dio 68.1.2. The punishments, which included amphitheatre parades, were for criminals of low status. The bloodthirsty Claudius had already thrown to the lions the slaves and freedmen who had informed against their masters under his predecessors (Dio 60.13). Cf. Zijlstra 1967.

[26] See the excellent discussion by Brunt 1990, 30–1. As an example, the decree of Ti. Iulius Alexander (Châlon 1964, ll.35–45) suggests that the rich in Alexandria had been disastrously affected by the activities of accusers under Nero, and shows sales of property by the state in Egypt (ibid., ll.29–32; also Pliny *Ep.* 6.31.3). For soldiers as *agents provocateurs*, see Epictetus 4.13.5; cf. Tac. *Hist.* 1.85. For other *agents provocateurs*, Philost.*v.Apoll.* 7.27; 36.

[27] For extortionate governors, cf. Brunt 1990, 53–95. Early Roman tax-rates could be reckoned low: the Jews petitioned for Judaea to become a Roman province after Herod's death, saying that their king had taxed them too heavily (Josephus *AJ* 17.300–14). In the second century BC, Rome halved the tribute of Macedonia when making it a province (Livy 45.18.7). In Commagene it was the rich who wanted their kingdom to become a Roman province, and the poor who were against it (Josephus *AJ* 18.53).

[28] Pliny *NH* 18.35; cf. Tac. *Ann.* 16.2.; Duncan-Jones 1990, 141 n.54. Nero's seizure of estates to finance building in Rome: Dio 61.5.3–6; 62.18.5. His seizure of private fortunes in Greece, Rome and Italy: 63.11–12.

[29] Dio 59.22.3–4. For property seized by Gaius: 60.6.3. For Domitian, see n.24 above.

[30] Dio 51.17.7. The numbers were clearly large, but cannot be specified. Appian *BC* 4.5 gives a figure of about 300 defunct senators. Suet. *Aug.* 15 gives 300 as the number of senators and knights executed on one notorious occasion in 40 BC. But 300 was a proverbial number (Weinstock 1971, 398 n.10, with Seneca *de ira* 2.5.5; *HA Aurel.* 7.1 and other instances; see p. 17 below). For the embarrassingly large amounts of money produced by the sale of *bona damnatorum* under Augustus, see Suet. *Aug.*41.1.

[31] Tac. *Hist.* 2. 84.   [32] Dio 75.8.4–5; *HA Sev.*12.1.

[33] *HA Sev.* 12.4; *ILS* 1421; Millar 1977, 171, and n.65; Pflaum 1950, 90; Nesselhauf 1964.

[34] Bequests to the Emperor: Millar 1977, 153–8; Rogers 1947 remains a useful discussion in detail.

million in this way.[35] Augustus reputedly received the prodigious sum of HS1.4 billion in legacies in the last twenty years of his reign.[36]

Exceptional though that might be, legacies to the Emperor remained widespread. When Cassius's widow, although immensely rich ignored Tiberius in her will, that could be seen as a direct slight.[37] Tiberius let it pass. But under a coercive Emperor, the famous general Agricola felt obliged to make Domitian co-heir with his own wife and daughter.[38] Other coercive rulers, Caligula and Nero, responded to being left out of wills by seizing property.[39] In general, reluctance to accept money from testators with surviving children, or from testators they did not know, came to be regarded as an important Imperial virtue.[40] Nevertheless, childlessness among the aristocracy always brought wealth to the Emperor, providing it in a form which social etiquette obliged him to accept.[41]

2.2. SPECIAL LEVIES AND PAYMENTS

The most recurrent of the other forms of payment was *aurum coronarium*. Originally a perquisite of successful generals under the Republic, *aurum coronarium* became more frequent under the Empire.[42] Though still attached to military triumphs, it also celebrated the accession of a new Emperor, soon becoming a regular event. Augustus refused 35,000 pounds of *aurum coronarium* offered by the towns of Italy after Actium.[43] At his British triumph, Claudius received crowns of 9,000 and 7,000 pounds from two prime gold-producing areas, Gallia Comata and Hispania Citerior.[44] Under Hadrian, *aurum coronarium* was offered at the Emperor's accession and to celebrate the adoption of Antoninus Pius as heir. But in both cases, the payment from Italy was refused, and the payment from the provinces scaled down.[45] By the time of the Severi, *aurum coronarium* was being paid both at accession and on a more regular basis.[46] Documentary evidence for payment of the tax mainly belongs to the time of Commodus and the Severi, with a concentration under Elagabalus.[47]

Occasionally there were other forms of special payment. At the end of the Republic, various short-term taxes were introduced after Caesar's assassination,

[35] *Phil.* 2.40. Pliny's complacent comment suggests the same regularity under the Principate, *Ep.*7.20.6

[36] Suet. *Aug.* 101.3.   [37] Tac. *Ann.* 3.76.   [38] Tac. *Agr.* 43.4.

[39] Dio 59.15.1; Suet. *Gaius.* 38.2; Suet. *Nero* 32.2.

[40] Rogers 1947, 158. Pliny *Pan.* 43. Antoninus Pius even closed a loophole which benefited the Emperor, which had prevented children who were Greeks from inheriting if their parents had become Roman citizens (Pausanias 8.43.5).

[41] For childlessness, cf. e.g. *RE* Supp. Bd. 6.227–32 (Schiller); Syme 1988; Syme 1991, 235.

[42] See more fully Millar 1977, 140–2. The practice spread to Rome from the Hellenistic world.

[43] *RG* 21.3; Dio 51.21.4.   [44] Pliny *NH* 33.54.

[45] *HA Had.* 6.5; *Pius* 4.10.

[46] Bowman 1967, 59. Brunt 1990, 537 (*PYadin* 16, showing *aurum coronarium* as a payment to which estates in Arabia were liable).

[47] Wallace 1938, 470 nn.13–16 with *OBod* 1105–15.

to raise money for the coming wars. In 43 BC a capital tax of 4% on citizens, and a property tax on senators based on roof-tiles were brought in.[48] There was also a tax corresponding to a year's income on leased property and six months' income on owner-occupied property and on agricultural land.[49] In 31 BC Octavian levied a further tax of three months' income on agricultural property.[50] He also imposed taxes on the number of slaves owned in 42 BC, and on wealth owned by freedmen in 31 BC.[51]

Some of this fiscal innovation re-emerged during the dire financial crises of the late 60s AD. In what proved to be the closing months of his reign, Nero demanded a year's rent from tenants in Rome, to be paid in new gold or silver.[52] In 69 Vitellius introduced a tax on freedmen based on the number of slaves owned.[53] In 70, soon after the Flavian capture of Rome, the Senate proposed to float a public loan of HS60 million, recalling the loans during the Second Punic War.[54] Such initiatives are not seen later on, but the narrative becomes much less detailed.

2.3. PRECIOUS METAL FROM TEMPLES AND STATUES

Much of the precious metal of the ancient Mediterranean was housed in temples. A great deal took the form of cult statues and votive offerings. But there were also private or secular deposits, and in some large temples in the East, what amounted to a system of temple banking. At Ephesus, the great temple of Artemis accepted deposits from foreign individuals and governments, as well as from local citizens, and lent out funds.[55] Similarly, at Cos large sums were deposited in the temple by Queen Cleopatra and by the Jews.[56] And in Egypt under the Principate, some temples had substantial funds to lend for mortgages.[57] Herodian mentions funds, public and private, held in temples at Rome under the Severi, while Appian lists the Capitol at Rome and the temples at Antium, Lanuvium, Nemi and Tibur as having the largest consecrated funds in his day.[58]

---

[48] Dio 46.31.3.

[49] Dio 47.14.2. Caesar had recently presented all tenants in Rome and Italy with a year's rent, Suet. *Iul.* 38.2.; see Frederiksen 1966, 133–4.   [50] Dio 50.10.5.

[51] Appian *BC* 5.67; Dio 50.10.4.

[52] Suet. *Nero* 44.2. The insistence on new coin may have been an attempt to enforce the use of current coin, shortly after currency changes which gave older coin a premium value. Sutherland suggests that it was an effort to make those holding on to older coin surrender it for minting, but although Suetonius mentions furious protests, he suggests nothing of this kind (Sutherland 1987A, 106).

[53] Tac. *Hist.* 2.94.   [54] Tac. *Hist.* 4.47. Cf. Livy 24.11, 26.36.

[55] Dio Chrysostom 31.54 ff., a Trajanic source; Caesar *BC* 3.33. Cf. Acts 19.27–8: 'Great is Diana of the Ephesians.'

[56] Josephus *AJ* 14.112.

[57] Big temples also still had property and revenues from which a full-time priesthood was maintained, despite a partial confiscation of hieratic lands in 20 BC. (Johnson 639 ff.; mortgages: no. 404).

[58] Herodian 1.14.2–3; 3.13.4; 4.4.7. Appian *BC* 5.24.

By themselves, pious offerings were enough to ensure that the amounts of precious metal in temples steadily grew: Augustus's gold offerings to Apollo exemplified a practice which was socially very widespread.[59] Temple treasure inevitably attracted attention at times of war or upheaval. Rome's funds at the start of Sulla's war with Mithridates consisted of 9,000 pounds of gold raised from temple treasure.[60] Sulla took treasure from temples in Greece.[61] Caesar likewise plundered much temple gold when conquering Gaul in the 50s BC.[62] Cassius took the precious-metal statues from Rhodes, leaving only Apollo's chariot.[63] In 41 BC Octavian's forces took precious-metal votive offerings from the temples in Rome and Italy and turned them into cash.[64] And after Actium, Octavian took almost all the temple offerings from Egypt, happily without sacrilege, because Cleopatra had already removed them from the temples.[65]

A century later, Nero took votive offerings from temples in Rome and Italy, as well as hundreds of cult statues from temples in Greece and Asia, after the fire of Rome in AD 64.[66] Vespasian in his turn took large sums from Alexandria and its temples.[67] In the early fourth century, temple treasure confiscated by Christian Emperors provided material for the abundant new gold coinage.[68] The amounts of temple treasure are rarely specified, but Josephus indicates totals for the Jewish Temple in Jerusalem in the time of Crassus of 2,000 talents in money and 8,000 talents in treasure, about HS240 million.[69] But within our period, the sacred treasure of temples, while clearly of very great size, remained out of reach of the State under most circumstances.[70]

Perhaps surprisingly, precious-metal statues of the Emperor were much less

[59] *RG* 24.2: Dio 53.22.3; Suet. *Aug.* 52; about 80 silver statues of Augustus went into the melting pot to pay for them. Augustus also laid up about HS100 million from booty in a number of temples, which presumably included the 16,000 pounds of gold that Suetonius mentions (*RG* 21.2; Suet. *Aug.* 30.2). Pompey had similarly made offerings to Minerva, of 12,060 gold coins and 307 talents of silver, taken from sacred statues and images in the lands that he conquered (Diodorus 40.4). [60] Appian *Mith.* 22. [61] Larsen *ESAR* 4.365. [62] Suet. *Iul.* 54.
[63] Val.Max. 1.5.8; Plutarch *Brut.* 32; Dio 47.33.4.
[64] Suet. *Iul.* 54.2; Dio 48.12.4; Appian *BC* 5.24. Throughout Asia however, Octavian/Augustus restored the temple offerings plundered by Antony (*RG* 24.1). When dining at Bononia, Augustus found himself eating from gold plate cast from a statue which his host had plundered from a temple in Parthia, Pliny *NH* 33.82–3. For a prosecution for turning a silver statue of the Emperor into dinner plate, see Tac. *Ann.* 3.70.
[65] Dio 51.17.7. Pausanias could use the unpleasant deaths of Sulla, Caligula and Nero as divine vengeance for their theft of statues from Greek temples (9.33.6, 9.27.3), but had to excuse Augustus for similar actions (8.46).
[66] Tac. *Ann.* 15.45; Suet. *Nero* 32.4; Dio Chrysostom 31.148. Pausanias mentions 500 bronze statues that Nero took from Delphi alone (10.7.1; also 5.25.8, 5.26.3, 9.27.3, 10.19.2). But here Nero's aim seems to have been to acquire choice statues, not raw metal.
[67] Dio 66.8.3–4.
[68] Jones 1964, 1.108, 3.13 n.33; Anon. *de rebus bellicis* 2.1. For the increasing importance of gold in the course of the fourth century, see Depeyrot 1987A, 113–15. For gold finds from the Late Empire, see Callu 1983, Iluk 1985, Fagerlie 1967, and Adelson 1957.
[69] *AJ* 14.105. For cryptic details of the gold and silver taken from the *aerarium* by Caesar in the Civil War, see Pliny *NH* 33.56; cf. Crawford 1974, 639. For the treasure in the Capitol of two African cities, see Duncan-Jones 1982, 110 nos. 381–2. For a gift of 10 talents of gold to the great temple at Philae in 251/3, see Johnson, 641.
[70] But Commodus, like Nero, was said to have plundered temples (n.133 below).

sacrosanct. His official statues were always numerous and, like the Emperor's image on the coinage, they were an essential weapon of propaganda.[71] Dio nevertheless makes Maecenas criticise the institution because the statues are 'not only costly, but also invite destruction and last only a brief time'.[72] Augustus had eighty of his own silver statues melted down, and used the proceeds for gold offerings to Apollo.[73] Nerva, and no doubt others, went further and turned metal statues from the previous reign into coin.[74] In the Severan period, statues of Plautianus were melted down after his fall in 205, and gold lions were melted under Elagabalus.[75] Under Macrinus there had been a general outcry for all gold and silver statues to be melted down, from a citizen body whose taxes had just been increased. Macrinus at least limited his own statues to miniatures with a weight of 3 pounds of gold or 5 pounds of silver.[76]

2.4. SALES OF GOODS

The state's use of sale mechanisms is shown in the sale of conquered populations as slaves and in the constant sales of the goods of the condemned.[77] Less predictable are the sales of palace goods which took place at times of fiscal stress. They are attested under Caligula, Nerva and Marcus Aurelius.[78] In a different financial context, Pliny shows Trajan selling off sizeable numbers of houses and gardens acquired by Domitian.[79] These are akin to the sales of imperial land seen at other times.[80] Caligula had palace furniture brought from Rome to Lugdunum because prices were good there, while his successors sold furniture at Rome. Pertinax sold off palace goods, slaves, carriages and arms belonging to Commodus, after inheriting a virtually empty treasury.[81] Severus Alexander reputedly sold off the palace dwarves.[82]

---

[71] A sign of the importance attached to statues of the Emperor is the purported letter from Macrinus, a new ruler with no dynastic claims, ordering the Senate to commission six statues of his predecessor (*HA Macrinus* 6.8).

[72] 52.35.3. Pliny *Pan.* 55.10–11.

[73] See n.59 above. The episode is still surprising, and may show a need at the time to tap new sources of silver for minting. Some successors placed restraints on statues, or even refused them altogether (Claudius, Nerva, Macrinus; Dio 60.5.4, 68.2.1, 78.12.7). Pliny said that Trajan's statues were few and made of bronze (*Pan.* 52.4; 55.6), while the young Nero refused statues of solid gold and silver (Tac. *Ann.* 13.10).

[74] Dio 68.1.1. Statius shows a procurator's wife adding a new 100-pound gold statue of Domitian to those already on the Capitol (*Silv.* 5.1.188–93). For the destruction of Domitian's many gold and silver statues, see Pliny *Pan.* 52.3–5. *Damnatio memoriae* consistently brought destruction of the Emperor's images, and metal statues of Caligula, Nero, and Commodus must thus have gone into the melting pot, providing a potential source of new coin. Occasionally, as with Nero's Colossus, a statue was too good to lose, and a new head was substituted (Pliny *NH* 34.45; replaced a second time under Commodus, Jerome, *Chronicon*, Helm p.209).

[75] Dio 75.16.2, 80.12.2.   [76] Dio 78.12.7, 78.18.1.

[77] Harris 1979, 59–60, 81–2; Tac. *Hist.* 1.68; goods of the condemned, pp. 5–6 above.

[78] Dio 59.21.5; Suet. *Gaius* 39.1; Dio 68.2.2; *HA Marcus* 17.4.

[79] *Pan.* 50.5–6.   [80] P. 48 n.5.

[81] Dio 74.5.4–5; *HA Pert.*7.8–8.7. Septimius Severus afterwards reproached senators with having bought goods of Commodus, Dio 75.8.3.   [82] *HA Sev. Alex.* 34.2.

3. IMPERIAL FINANCES

In broad terms, the Empire moves from a very early phase under Augustus and Tiberius when funds were sometimes short, to a phase when the Emperors were able to spend much more freely. A further phase of financial constraint follows in the late Antonine period, succeeded by a period of heavy spending and new financial conditions under the Severi. The four phases are easy to identify, although points of transition and reasons for change cannot always be established.[83]

3.1. PHASE 1: THE JULIO-CLAUDIANS

Shortage of funds under Augustus and Tiberius is implied in the well-known difficulties in funding army discharge bonuses (*praemia*), which led to virtual mutiny.[84] Suetonius writes of Tiberius paying few discharge bonuses.[85] Arguably the amount fixed by Augustus, about thirteen years' pay, was too ambitious. Tiberius was also slow to pay the legacies of Augustus, and those of Livia, gave few shows and built few buildings.[86] His gifts to senators were criticised for being too small.[87] To modern eyes all of that might suggest prudent management rather than personal meanness. Tiberius's large surplus is mentioned only in order to criticise his successor (Table 1.2). Tiberius was able to reduce the sales tax from 1% to $\frac{1}{2}$% after new revenues became available from Cappadocia.[88] But he rapidly cancelled the four-year reduction in military service introduced in response to army unrest: it would have meant paying more discharge bonuses.[89] The credit crisis of 33 emphasised the shortage of liquidity at Rome; Tiberius's seizure of gold mines that year, apparently accompanied or followed by higher mint output, may have been in part a response to this.[90]

Caligula's short reign is depicted in terms of breathtaking extravagance, followed by desperate attempts to obtain funds. It offers little clue to the State's financial position under normal conditions, although Caligula reputedly began with a very large surplus and seems to have ended with a deficit.[91] Claudius's reign of thirteen years was long enough to allow some recovery; it includes heavy spending on two aqueducts for Rome (Table 1.2, no. 8), on the harbour at Ostia, and on an attempt to drain the Fucine lake.[92] Thirty-five senators and many knights died in this reign, and some funds, presumably substantial, came from the goods of the condemned.[93]

---

[83] For the chronology of minting policy, see chapter 7 below.
[84] Tac. *Ann.* 1.17; 26; 31; 35; *RG* 18.   [85] *Tib.* 48.2.
[86] Dio 57.14; Bodei Giglioni 1974, 153–4; Levick 1976, 122–3.
[87] See p. 43 n.49.   [88] Tac. *Ann.* 2.42.   [89] Tac. *Ann.* 1.78
[90] Tac. *Ann.* 6.19; see pp. 23–5.
[91] Building and spending: Bodei Giglioni 1974, 157–60. For money-raising, see n.29 and n.78.
[92] Suet. *Claud.* 19. In general, Bodei Giglioni 1974, 160–4.
[93] Suet. *Claud.* 29.2 ('300' knights, cf. n.30 above); Dio 60.15.5–16.1; Tac. *Ann.* 13.43; Seneca, *Apocol.* 10–11. For *bona damnatorum*, see pp. 5–6 above.

Financially, Nero's reign in some ways reverts to the pattern of Caligula, with early popularity, followed by immense expenditures, and a resort to large-scale seizure of property.[94] This again has little normative value. Nevertheless, there are possible suggestions of underlying financial strength in Nero's cancellation of 2% and $2\frac{1}{2}$% taxes, although this was followed by the introduction of new taxes. The Emperor's claim to have paid HS60 million into the *aerarium* each year suggests a surplus in patrimonial revenues, which by now presumably included the proceeds of expropriation, and a deficit in state revenues proper.[95]

3.2.   PHASE 2: AD 69–161

As Nero's successor, and heir to a legacy of civil war, Vespasian faced critical financial problems (Table 1.2, no. 3 below). In response, taxes were increased, and sometimes doubled.[96] Dio explains that at the start of his reign, while still in Egypt, Vespasian 'renewed many taxes that had fallen into disuse, increased many that were customary, and introduced still other new ones, later (doing the same) in the rest of the subject territory, in Italy and in Rome itself'.[97] Repercussions can be seen from stray survivals in Egypt (p. 56 below). Under Vespasian, Statius complimented a governor on enlarging the tribute paid by Africa.[98] Privileged provinces and cities in the East now lost tax-immunity, while Trachian Cilicia and Commagene began to pay tribute.[99]

Although Vespasian inherited a critical financial position, he could still be notably generous in his gifts, and he initiated large-scale rebuilding in Rome, including a new Capitol, and the Colosseum.[100] Thus, however surprisingly, state finances seem to have been largely restored during the ten years of his reign. Court and ceremonial costs were probably now much lower.[101]

The next three major reigns all show important new spending initiatives.[102] Domitian was able to increase army pay early in his reign, and even revived the coinage standards of earlier days.[103] But the pay-increase of one-third, roughly an extra HS150 million per year, soon proved difficult to sustain.[104] Some attempt was made to reduce army numbers, and the year after the pay

---

[94] For expenditures, see e.g. Suet. *Nero* 30–32; Bodei Giglioni 1974, 164–70; Frank *ESAR* 5.42–4. For seizures of property, n.28 and n.39 above; seizure of statues, n.66; forced contributions, n.52.

[95] Tac. *Ann.* 13.51; Dio 61.5.5; Tac. *Ann.* 15.18.

[96] Suet. *Vesp.* 16.1.   [97] Dio 66.8.3–4.

[98] *Silv.* 1.4.83–8; inscriptions show the same Rutilius Gallicus redrawing city and provincial boundaries in Africa (Thomasson 1984, 377 no. 49). For Vespasian's boundary revisions and absorption of unallocated land (*subseciva*) in Italy, see Frank *ESAR* 5.47 n.33.

[99] Suet. *Vesp.* 8.4.

[100] Suet. *Vesp.* 17–19; 8.5–9.1. Bodei Giglioni 1974, 177–9; Frank *ESAR* 5.44 ff.

[101] Cf. Tac. *Ann.* 3.55. Suet. *Vesp.* 19.2.

[102] It is conceivable that the more favourable financial climate was partly due to increases in the supply of precious metal (see chapter 7, section 4).

[103] Coinage: Carradice (Rogers 1984, 74–5 is completely misleading about the coinage). Finances: Syme 1979; Robathan 1942. Jones 1992, 72–9.

[104] For army costs, see pp. 33–7. For the date of the increase, see p. 87 n.8.

increase, the coinage experiment was scaled down.[105] Domitian nevertheless left a series of impressive buildings (Table 1.2, no. 18), at the cost of a reputation for rapacity towards the rich.[106]

Trajan's reign saw the start of the alimentary scheme in Italy which was to spread all over the peninsula.[107] The *alimenta* represented another important spending initiative, and one which was evidently sustainable despite the heavier bill for army pay. The scheme had begun by AD 101, before war in Dacia had brought booty.[108] Financial strength is again suggested. A very erratic sixth-century author attaches immensely high figures to Dacian war booty.[109] Trajan's lavish expenditure on baths, on a new Forum complex in Rome and on shows may have owed something to booty.[110] But the coinage does not suggest any especially high input of new metal until later in the reign.[111]

Hadrian dramatically increased government spending outside Italy.[112] He also carried out grandiose building in Rome, some of which survives.[113] Expenditure on handouts shot up, approximately doubling in this reign.[114] Dio mentions subsidies paid to Rome's neighbours as a reason for peace.[115] Hadrian's tax-policies were liberal, and included the biggest cancellation of tax-arrears up to that time (Table 1.1, no. 4).[116] Abandoning Trajan's new eastern provinces presumably economised on garrison costs. But Hadrian's ambitious and wide-ranging spending suggests a favourable financial position.

Nevertheless, his policies also imply underlying economic problems. Hadrian chose to be portrayed on the coinage as 'restorer of the whole world' (*restitutor orbis terrarum*) and of many individual provinces.[117] This rhetoric may have been meant to exalt the Emperor's concern for the provinces, rather than to advertise economic difficulties. Nevertheless, Hadrian's edicts on leasing and taxation show a clear awareness of financial strain in Egypt.[118] And his various measures to improve the fiscal and economic performance of the provinces tend to reinforce this. One effect of his initiatives was to unleash a new building boom in the provinces.[119] But Hadrian's travels all over the

---

[105] Army reduction: Dio 67.3.5; Suet. *Dom.* 12.1. Coinage: pp. 131, 216, 221ff.

[106] Plut. *Public.* 15.3–5; Suet. *Dom.* 5; 12.1; Dio 67.4.5–6; Bodei Giglioni 1974, 196–8. See p. 42 below.

[107] Duncan-Jones 1982, chapter 7. For the scale of the *alimenta*, see Jongman forthcoming. For an attempted reinterpretation, Woolf 1990.

[108] *CIL* IX 1455; see Duncan-Jones 1982, chapter 7.   [109] P. 129 n.11.

[110] Cf. p. 129 n.11. Dio 68.7.1, 68.15, 68.16.3;. Paus. 5.12.6; Bodei Giglioni 1974, 199–204.

[111] P. 129.

[112] Dio 69.5.3, 69.16.2; *HA Had.* 9.6, 10.1, 12.3, 13.4, 13.6; *IGRR* 4.1431 with Millar 1977, 421; Bodei Giglioni 1974, 205–7. For imperial building in the provinces, see MacMullen 1959.

[113] Boatwright 1987.   [114] P. 41 Table 3.6.   [115] 69.9.5.

[116] Duncan-Jones 1990, 66.   [117] *BMCRE* 3, clxxiii–clxxiv.

[118] Johnson nos. 35,319, pp.108,522.

[119] For economic measures, and building boom, see Duncan-Jones 1990, 66. For the mechanics of Hadrian's provincial building programme, see Arrian *Peripl.* 1.2 ff., with its criticisms of new building which included an inadequate statue of Hadrian.

empire, although they made him unique among peacetime rulers, probably created burdens as well as benefits.[120]

Perhaps significantly, the next reign was the first for more than half a century to show no major spending initiative. Nevertheless, Antoninus Pius spent generous amounts on building or rebuilding in Italy and the provinces.[121] He also made a small extension to the child alimentary scheme, and maintained handouts at Hadrianic levels.[122] Deterioration in the silver coinage in the 150s suggests the beginnings of serious metal shortage, or ineffective management.[123] The report that Pius left a very large surplus to his successors is at least coherent with their enormous expenditure on handouts immediately afterwards (Table 1.1, no. 5; but for the amount, see p. 17).

3.3. PHASE 3: AD 161–192

The reign of Marcus Aurelius, soon beset by military crisis, plague and revolt, started with the largest burst of spending on handouts seen so far. Five distributions took place within eight years.[124] The first was prodigious, bringing the Praetorians HS20,000 per head.[125] But from 165 onwards, plague had a very serious impact, and probably affected payment and collection of taxes.[126] The crisis measures which included sale of palace furniture presumably belong to the second half of the reign.[127] This did not prevent further handouts in 175 and 177, the second on a generous scale.[128] Marcus's wars showed the military initiative as lying outside Rome for the first time for many decades, and they probably brought little financial gain. But near the end of the reign the margin was apparently enough to allow the cancellation of a tax on gladiators.[129] Even so, financial resources seem to have been much smaller than at Marcus's accession.

The reign of Commodus seems to revert to the pattern of Caligula and Nero, with a sequence of early popularity, overspending, and expropriation and new taxes. Commodus's heavy spending is reflected in his handouts, which almost doubled the average seen in the mid-Antonine period.[130] Spending on games was also heavy. Commodus imposed new customs dues on rivers, harbours and main roads, and a poll-tax on senators and town-

---

[120] Indirectly stated in *HA Pius* 7.11; cf. Pliny *Pan.* 20.3–4. Reports of disfavoured Emperors make buildings constructed for their visits an unwanted burden (Dio 77.9.6–7, cf. Suet. *Nero* 35.5; see also Tac. *Ann.* 14.39). The imperial statues with which the empire soon proliferated after Hadrian's visits were evidently a charge on local funds (Paus. 1.18.6: Athens excelled by building a colossus; cf. 1.3.2, 1.24.7, 5.12.6, 8.19.1).

[121] Paus. 8.43.4; *HA Pius* 8.1–4; 9.1–2. Bodei Giglioni 1974, 208–10.

[122] The *puellae Faustinianae*: Duncan-Jones 1982, 319n. Handouts: p. 41.

[123] Table 15.8.   [124] Kienast 1990, 139.   [125] *HA Marcus* 7.9; Dio 74.8.4.

[126] P. 104.   [127] *HA Marcus* 17.4.   [128] P. 248.

[129] *ILS* 5163 (loosely dated to 177/80, but perhaps contemporary with the cancellation of tax-debt in 178: see Table 4.8).

[130] Table A. 1 p. 249.

councillors.[131] Dio, himself a senator at Rome for part of this reign, writes that the funds Commodus gave to his jesters equalled what he had killed many senators to obtain.[132] The accusations against Commodus in the Senate's ritual chant after his death included murder of innocent senators, use of *delatores*, setting aside of wills and plunder of temples.[133] His payments to barbarian tribes were significant, and continued to the end of the reign.[134] The treasury is said to have been virtually empty at the time of Commodus's sudden death (Table 1.1, no. 6), and his short-lived successor Pertinax resorted to selling off Imperial property, including Commodus's favourites.[135]

3.4. PHASE 4: AD 192–235

The civil war which followed lasted longer than the war of 68–70, and must have consumed immense resources. But Septimius Severus was still able within a few years to take the dramatic step of increasing army pay, probably by one-third (p. 33). He also maintained average spending on handouts at Commodus's very high level (p. 41). Clearly new funds had been obtained.

Enormous expropriations and heavier taxes seem to be the explanation.[136] The wealth of the opposing factions was taken over wholesale, and led to what was probably the largest single influx of private wealth into state coffers since the start of the Principate. New civil service departments were created as a result.[137] Cities and individuals who had supported Niger financially were made to pay up four times what they had given Niger.[138] Through his funds acquired by such means, Severus was able to go down as a generous ruler who left very ample reserves, reputedly more than any predecessor.[139]

Severus's son Caracalla raised army pay for the second time within two decades: he increased it by half, raising expenditure on handouts by even

---

[131] Herodian 2.4.7; Dio 72.16.3. For expropriations, Dio 72.16.2, Herodian 1.8.8.

[132] 73.6.2. There are obvious echoes of Nero's prodigious personal gifts (Table 1.2, 12).

[133] *HA Commodus* 18–19, citing Marius Maximus. Amidst the picturesque vituperation are brief words of welcome to Pertinax. Senatorial chants (*adclamationes*) were already regular practice in the first century, but Pliny explains that those at Trajan's accession were the first to be immortalised on bronze (*Pan.* 75.1–3; for their continuation in the Late Empire, see Roueché 1984 and Jones 1964, 331).

[134] Herodian 1.6.9; Dio 74.6.1.

[135] See n.81 above.

[136] Expropriations: Herodian 3.8.7; Dio 75.8.4–5, 75.14.3, 75.16.2–3; *HA Sev.* 12.1 (but the specific details in this life include invented names, Jacques 1992). The tax-changes are not well documented, but see chapter 4, p. 56.

[137] See p. 6 n.33 for the *res privata*. The move was foreshadowed by the post of *procurator kalendarii Vegetiani* in Baetica, set up to deal with an enormous private resource which became state property under the late Antonines (Manacorda 1977; Duncan-Jones *JRS* 71 (1981) 129).

[138] Dio 75.8.4.

[139] Dio 76.16.4; *HA Sev.* 12.3; Herodian 3.15.3. But the historians do not seem well informed about the size of government surpluses (see section 1.4, pp. 16–17).

more.[140] Caracalla's building included grandiose baths put up in Rome.[141] But his tax-changes clearly showed that Severus's surplus was not enough to finance all of this new expenditure. Caracalla doubled the 5% taxes on manumissions and bequests, and introduced new taxes, according to Dio's hostile but contemporary account. His conferment of citizenship brought more of the free population within the scope of these taxes.[142] Dio also shows Caracalla demanding crown money for supposed victories, as well as *ad hoc* payments in kind.[143] It is clear that the reign was financially unstable, and that the enormous new commitments were more than existing revenues and reserves could support.

But the last two major reigns in the period, those of Elagabalus and Severus Alexander, remain difficult to assess, and the sources provide almost no financial detail.[144] Under Elagabalus spending on handouts rose to even greater heights, with an increase of almost 50% in the mean level. Silver minting also increased dramatically.[145] About Severus Alexander the tradition is more benign. There was apparently some reining back, but his financial policies are quite indistinct.[146] Beyond the 230s, imperial finance becomes difficult to follow until a later stage. It may be significant that the faltering literary sources are not much helped by papyri or inscriptions in what has been called 'the dark tunnel' between AD 238 and 284.[147]

4. PROBLEMS OF THE SOURCES

Surviving historical sources offer very little guidance about the balance-sheet of the Empire. The literary tradition is typically more concerned with moral stereotypes than with systematic description. Nevertheless, where they exist, references to amounts spent should still be useful. But the figures that have come down contain particular problems of their own. Amounts are shown in Tables 1.1 and 1.2.

These figures are generally taken literally, but they have obvious limitations. Virtually every total is in very round figures. However, their stereotyping goes further. Two figures for large treasury surpluses are the same, although at different dates (HS2,700 million).[148] And Tacitus's two figures for great fortunes acquired by imperial favour are also identical (HS300 million for

---

[140] Army pay: Table 3.1 p. 34. Handouts: p. 249 Table A.1.

[141] For an estimate of their cost, see the forthcoming work by Janet DeLaine. A figure running to several hundred million sesterces is indicated.

[142] Dio 77.9.4–5.   [143] Dio 77.9.2–3.

[144] 'It is not easy to reach, or even approach, an adequate estimate of the reigns of the two boy princes (from 218 to 235).' (Syme 1971, 146).   [145] Cf. *HA Elag.* 27.7.

[146] Although full of detail, the life of Severus Alexander in the *HA* has very little historical value; it is nevertheless defended by Soraci 1974, 172 n.10.

[147] Jones 1964, 23, cited by Rathbone (1991, 5) in a book on the Heroninos archive which illuminates one of the most important exceptions. For third-century trends in the sources, cf. Duncan-Jones 1990, 68, fig.14. and 168 n.72.

[148] Accepting the earlier source where there is any choice (Table 1.1 nos. 2 and 9, with note).

Pallas and for Seneca).[149] The number 300 is known to have been a proverbial, and it occurs frequently.[150] To denote great wealth, Petronius repeats HS30 million five times in different contexts, implying that it too was proverbial.[151] The totals 30 and 60 million account for four out of seven figures between 20 and 99 million in Tables 1.1–1.2. In a further case, the archetypes 300, 3,000 and 3 million all appear in non-numerical contexts in Marcus Aurelius.[152]

Table 1.1 *Surpluses, receipts, deficits and tax-remissions*
(figures in millions of sesterces)

	Amount	Date	Sources
1. Four payments to the *aerarium*	150	31 BC–AD 14	*RG* 17.1
2. Funds in treasury	2,700	37	Suet. *Gaius* 37.33.
3. Gain from proscriptions in Gaul	600	39–40	Dio 59.22.3-4
4. Emperor's payment to the *aerarium*	40	57	Tac. *Ann.* 13.31
5. Annual payments to the *aerarium*	60	62	Tac. *Ann.* 15.18
6. Proposed public loan	60	70	Tac. *Hist.* 4.47
7. Deficit	[4,000]	70	Suet. *Vesp.* 16.3
8. Remission of unpaid taxes for past 15 years	900	118	*ILS* 309; Dio 69.8; *HA Had.* 7.6; *RIC* 2, Hadrian 590–3
9. Funds in treasury	2,700	161	Dio 74.8.3
10. Funds in treasury	1	193	Dio 74.8.3
11. Money taken from Albinus's followers in Gaul	70	196–7	Dio 75.5.2

Notes: 2. Dio gives this figure as 2.3 or 3.3 billion (59.2.6). 6. The transmitted text gives 40 billion, an impossible figure which is presumably a manuscript error for 4 billion (cf. Sutherland 1987A, 127). 8. For a fifteen-year cycle see pp. 59–61).

The repetitions of HS300 million for great fortunes in Tacitus seem to have a proverbial character.[153] So do Caligula's claimed benefit of HS600 million from proscriptions (300 × 2), the HS900 million which Vitellius's extravagance was reputed to have cost (300 × 3), and the HS2,700 million claimed for treasury surpluses at different dates (900 × 3).[154] The likelihood is that amounts within this family of stereotypes were often purely conventional, and not specific historical data in their own right.

---

[149] *Ann.* 12.53; 13.42. Tacitus even uses 300 million a third time to denote private wealth (*Dial.* 8, referring to Q. Vibius Crispus).
[150] See n.30.
[151] Duncan-Jones 1982, 241.   [152] *Meditations* 6.49; 2.14.   [153] N. 149.
[154] Tables 1.1 no. 3; 1.2 no. 13; 1.2 nos. 2 and 9.

Table 1.2 *State expenditures*
(figures in millions of sesterces)

	Amount	Date	Sources
1. Payments to treasury, and handouts	2,400	43 BC– AD 14	*RG* Appendix 1
2. Emperor's legacy to people and troops	c.100	14–15	Suet. *Aug.* 101; Tac. *Ann.* 1.8
3. Earthquake relief for Sardis	10	17	Tac. *Ann.* 2.47
4. Loan to victims of credit crisis	100	33	Tac. *Ann.* 6.17
5. Payment for fire damage in Aventine district	100	36	Tac. *Ann.* 6.45
6. Legacy to citizens and troops	c.100	37	Dio 59.2.2–3
7. Reimbursement of 20 years' tax to king of Commagene	100	37–41	Suet. *Gaius.* 16.3
8. Cost of two aqueducts for city of Rome	350	38–52	Pliny *NH* 36.122
9. Payment for fire damage to Bononia	10	53	Tac. *Ann.* 12.58
10. Payment to Lugdunum after fire	4	65	Tac. *Ann.* 16.13
11. Gifts to king of Parthia	200	66	Dio 62.6.5
12. Emperor's gifts to individuals	2,200	54–68	Tac. *Hist.* 1.20
13. Vitellius' spending on dinners	900	69	Dio 65.3.2; Tac. *Hist.* 2.95
14. Allocation for work on the Domus Aurea	50	69	Suet. *Otho* 7.1
15. Gilding of Capitol in Rome	288	82	Plut. *Public.* 15.3
16. Land-grants to poor	60	97–8	Dio 68.2
17. Donative & congiarium for adoption of Aelius Caesar	300– 400	137	*HA Had.* 23.12–14; *Ael.* 3.3; 6.2
18. Annual cost of 50% army pay-increase	280	211–17	Dio 78.36.3; Herodian 4.4.7
19. Poison from Upper Germany	30	217	Dio 78.6.3
20. Payment for peace with Parthia (Macrinus)	200	217	Dio 78.27.1

Notes: 2. The payments were HS43.5 million to people and tribes, and per capita amounts of HS1,000 for Praetorians, HS500 for the urban cohorts, and HS300 for legionaries. 6. Tiberius's public legacies seem to have been a virtual duplicate of those of Augustus, except that the civilian total was 45 million, and the praetorians received HS500 per head. 10. This payment reimbursed an identical payment by Lugdunum to Rome after the great fire in 64.

The stereotypes are so frequent that they were evidently part of common usage. That makes them a general cultural feature rather than one which reflects unfavourably on individual historians.[155] But their existence depletes the stock of figures for expenditure, and may leave doubts about other amounts. Even if the whole dossier were meaningful, it would still fall far short of a complete picture of imperial profit and loss,

[155] Here a specific reason for ignorance might be the cessation of Augustus's practice of publishing the accounts of the Empire (cf. Tac. *Ann.* 1.11; Suet. *Gaius* 16.1 is apparently the last reference). But in general even the simplest information, such as the birth-year of an Emperor, could face imprecision and conflicting claims by historians (Snyder 1964). Private individuals likewise could often mistake elementary details, such as the day of the week for a given date: 46% of such statements in papyri, and 26% in Latin inscriptions are erroneous (N = 26 and 43; Worp 1991, from late Roman evidence).

2

MONEY, PRICES AND INFLATION

1. BARTER AND NON-MONETISED EXCHANGE

Limited monetisation can take two obvious forms. One is pre-monetary exchange based on barter.[1] The other is monetary deprivation, where the market-place expects money, but too little coin is available. Both phenomena seem to exist in the Roman world. Barter may be a survival from a pre-monetary era, or an indication of metal shortage, or a sign that although there was enough coin, the State was not concerned to distribute it efficiently. What seems clear in the Roman world is that where money was available, it was used.[2] The wear-rate of low-denomination coin was quite high, even if by modern standards valuable coin wore out slowly and circulated slowly.[3] The ready market for counterfeit coin vividly suggests that more money was needed than was actually circulating.[4] Barter can be difficult to detect, and there is a strong likelihood that it was widespread in many less urbanised areas.[5]

Some documents from a much earlier society give interesting insights into types of exchange characteristic of the pre-modern world. In the Babylonian Code of Hammurabi, which is further from the time of Augustus than Augustus is from today, payment in grain was specified for hiring oxen or farm-labourers. But silver was specified for paying surgeons, brickmakers and tailors. This showed a demarcation between a countryside which used exchange in kind, and non-rural occupations which used money or proto-money.[6] In Babylon, precious metal was also a source of units of account, and could be used to facilitate transactions in kind. Thus in one case, eight slaves sold for 58 shekels of gold were paid for in a combination of grain, oxen, donkeys and wool, to the value of 58 shekels. Another document shows slaves

---

[1] Pausanias noted *à propos* of pre-monetary exchange in ancient Sparta that traders in his own day reported the continuing use of barter in India, even though the inhabitants had the gold and bronze needed for striking coin (3.12.4).
[2] Two important commercial archives from southern Italy in the first century AD show monetary transactions (Andreau 1974; Bove 1979; Casson 1980; Duncan-Jones 1982, 120 n.1; Frederiksen 1984, 327–8). Puteoli and Pompeii were both active ports, Puteoli among the most important in Italy.
[3] See chapter 13: bronze coin wore out rapidly, precious metal coin much more slowly (pp. 187–190 and 191).
[4] In the fourth century, Libanius writes as if producers of illicit coin were a recognised social category, from whom corrupt officials made large profits (*Or.* 18.138).
[5] For monetary stipulations settled in kind in evidence from the European Dark Ages, see Cipolla 1956, 4–5.
[6] Einzig 1966, 204. The Code of Hammurabi belongs to the twenty-second century BC.

being sold in advance for immediate settlement in oil, or later payment in metal.[7]

Surviving Roman evidence does not parallel this fully, but payments in wheat, loans in wheat, and wheat-payments as rent for other crops are all found in Egypt, the one significant source of documentary evidence.[8] An inscription from Phrygia of the mid-first century AD shows assessment of the main land-tax in grain, and other provinces paid taxes in kind.[9] Pliny mentions a tree-product which provides poor people in Spain with some of what they need for tax, presumably poll tax.[10] In a similar way, poll taxes in Syria in the eighth century were assessed in money but could be paid in kind if that was easier for the taxpayer.[11] Sixth-century evidence suggests that sudden shifts from taxing in kind to taxing in money could be onerous or even disastrous for the taxpayer.[12]

2. LIQUIDITY

In currency terms, the Roman world was above all things under-monetised. Single economic events could greatly affect its economic stability. Sudden releases of new metal might have immense repercussions. There was a big fall in the price of gold after Caesar's Gallic conquests, and a 60% drop in interest-rates after Augustus brought back treasure from Egypt. Caesar's spending evidently increased prices, since he allowed debtors to scale their debt to what their property had been worth before the Civil Wars.[13] If the money in circulation was suddenly drained off through too many government property-sales, or through a general calling-in of debts, the resulting crises could force the government to intervene.[14] New rules about senatorial investment could drive land prices up in Italy and down in the provinces.[15]

---

[7] Einzig 1966, 204, 206.

[8] Foraboschi, Gara 1982 list Roman documents recording payments in kind on p.81 (p.70 for a finding that 20% of transactions were wholly in kind in the Roman and Late Roman period, compared with 60% under the Ptolemies). For rents paid in wheat for non-wheat crops, see *POxy* 2188, 2351, 2776. For Egyptian taxation in kind, see chapter 4. Under Diocletian taxes were paid in wheat and barley for land sown with other crops (*PCair Isid* p. 105). For Egyptian banking transactions in kind, see Bogaert 1988.

[9] Duncan-Jones 1990, 200–1, 187–98. The modern assumption that Sicily, whose taxation in wheat Cicero's *Verrines* describe at length, was taxed in money under the Empire seems to be ill-founded (189–90).

[10] Pliny says of scolacium from the holm-oak 'pensionem alteram tributi pauperibus Hispaniae donat' (*NH* 16.32).

[11] From a contemporary source, Abou Yousouf Ya'koub 1921, 187; only non-Muslims paid the tax. Monetary transactions in kind can still be seen in recent societies. For example a study of a south Tunisian village in the 1960s showed that most villagers were in debt to the grocer for significant sums of money, but their debts were generally discharged by services. The objects and services could be definitely classified in value. 'Thus a unit of water is equivalent to an errand at the pharmacy . . . , a certain number of hours work in the oasis [equals] five or six cigarettes, [and] assistance at childbirth [equals] several measures of oil.' (Duvignaud 1970, 98–103 and 102).   [12] John Lydus, *de mag.* 3.61; Hendy 1985, 295.

[13] Suet. *Iul.* 42.2; *Aug.* 41.1; Dio 51.21.5. For his spending, see e.g. chapter 1, n.48. For Caesar's debt legislation, see n.32 below.   [14] Pp. 23–5 below.

[15] This was Pliny's obviously well-founded expectation, in a letter of uncharacteristic commercial advice (*Ep.* 6.19).

Local monetary shortage is suggested by private foundations set up to pay tax on behalf of the inhabitants of small Mediterranean islands in the second century.[16] Another symptom is the high incidence of forged Roman coinage in northern provinces such as Britain and Gaul.[17] Imperfect coins of all kinds were still tolerated. Dwarf coins and genuine coins chopped in two, which survive in significant numbers, suggest that the need for small change could override all questions of what was legal tender.[18] British evidence also suggests specific shortages of bronze coin. The inflow of bronze coin can be divided into a period of sporadic supply (AD 43–96); a period of regular supply (97–197); and a period of minimal supply from 197 onwards, when the bronze coin that was still being minted in Rome hardly reached provinces north of the Alps.[19]

Evidence for monetary deprivation is found in France as late as the post-Revolutionary period. In some country places, almost any coin was accepted as small change. Most surprising was the Roman bronze coin unearthed in bulk at Yzeure in the Moulinois in the early nineteenth century, which was pressed into service as pieces of 1 and 2 liards, and 1 and 2 sous. 'Until around 1870, many peasants bought only iron and salt, paid for all else in kind, and were paid the same way, [and] husbanded their money for taxes or hoarded it to acquire land.'[20] Even in the early twentieth century, wages of harvesters went on being paid in kind or in cash and kind in some places.[21] What finally changed all this was mainly an enormous expansion in the supply of cash, paper money increasing tenfold in volume between the 1880s and 1913.[22]

3.   STATE LENDING

In the speech credited to him by Dio, Maecenas urges Augustus to sell the public lands and lend out the proceeds, so that the lands would be cultivated while at the same time the money would make people more prosperous.[23] Imperial estates continued nevertheless to be directly exploited by the Emperor's servants on his behalf. But unproductive State land at least was being sold off in Egypt from Augustus's time onwards.[24] And Augustus lent money free of interest from surplus funds provided by sales of the property of

---

[16] Duncan-Jones 1964. The islands are Tenos and Ebusus. For tax safety-nets in other local benefactions, see MacMullen 1987, 739 n.9.

[17] Boon 1988 (for Gaul, 116, 126, 166).

[18] Boon 1988, 114–15, 126; Boon 1978.

[19] Walker 1988, 281–2. For clear parallel evidence in Severan Gaul, Buttrey 1972; Bompaire, Turckheim-Pey 1986, 473–6.

[20] Weber 1976, 33.

[21] Weber 1976, 35,36.

[22] Weber 1976, 40.

[23] Dio 52.28.3–4. For *ager publicus*, see Duncan-Jones 1990, 121–2, 124–6.

[24] Johnson pp. 150 ff.; chapter 4 n.5 below. For sale of imperial *praedia* by Antoninus Pius, see *HA Pius* 7.10.

the condemned.[25] The monetary crisis under Tiberius in AD 33 was exacerbated by the sales of *bona damnatorum* which had locked up much of the available coin in the treasury.[26] From this it seems that Augustus was careful to reduce the monetary impact of State property sales by putting the surplus proceeds back into the market, whereas Tiberius merely let events take their course.[27] When monetary crisis eventually came, Tiberius responded with interest-free loans like those of Augustus, lending out HS100 million for three years (section 4 below). Similar loans under Nero are suggested by Tacitus's mention of a transfer of HS40 million to the *aerarium* 'ad retinendam populi fidem'.[28]

The capital sums made available for loan were not very large in empire-wide terms, suggesting that crisis and remedy were essentially limited to the propertied class at Rome.[29] They say little about the state of liquidity or the need for credit elsewhere in the empire. State property-sales in Rome may at times have drained off liquidity in Rome in a quite artificial way. But it is still unlikely that supplies of coin were greater anywhere else. In fact liquidity at Rome benefited uniquely from Imperial spending on *congiaria* and building, and from spending by the political elite. And the high price-levels at Rome which contemporaries recognised were an obvious result of the concentration of much of the wealth of the Roman world in one place.[30]

4. THE TIBERIAN CREDIT CRISIS

The financial events of AD 33 provide the only description of a monetary crisis that survives from our period, and this gives them a special interest.[31] But we have to ask whether they illustrate a general problem, or merely short-term contingencies. Tacitus's account, the main source, seems to be dominated by stereotypes such as the evils of moneylending.[32]

The main events can be briefly summarised.

1. During the period of Tiberius's reign when accusers were already bringing down members of the aristocracy on other charges, the year 33 saw opportunist attacks which invoked Caesar's law about moneylending and

---

[25] Suet *Aug.* 41.1. This presumably refers to Augustus's interest-free loan of HS60 million for 3 years to private individuals (Dio 55.12.3a). For loans paid off by Augustus, see Dio 51.17.8, 51.21.4. .

[26] Tac. *Ann.* 6.17.

[27] Tiberius was no longer living at Rome by this date, and the mint was not at Rome either (p. 121). The remoteness of the mint might also be a reason for the unpopular delay in paying Augustus's public legacies (Dio 57.14.1–2). Only gold was struck at the beginning of the reign (Appendix 2), but the amounts could have been paid in gold coin (see p. 40).

[28] *Ann.* 13.31, AD 57.

[29] HS60 million under Augustus, HS100 million under Tiberius, HS40 million under Nero (see above).

[30] Duncan-Jones 1982, Appendix 8.

[31] Cf. Frank 1935; Rodewald 1976; Bellen 1976, 217; Demougin 1988, 117–23.

[32] Tac. *Ann.* 6.16–17; Dio 58.21.1–5; Suet. *Tib.* 48.1. Tacitus does not describe Caesar's legislation. For a reconstruction of its background and content, see Frederiksen 1966, 133 ff. In the parallel liquidity crisis of 49 BC, Caesar seems to have allowed the use of property to repay loans, and placed a low ceiling of HS60,000 on the amount of cash that could be held privately.

property-ownership in Italy. This law was almost a century old, and in abeyance.

2. The charges were found to be genuine, and the Senate, which certainly included interested parties, obtained an 18-month stay of execution to allow those affected to put their affairs in order.

3. This resulted in a general shortage of coin, firstly because of the suddenness with which debts were called in, and secondly because too much coin was locked up in the treasury as a result of property-sales following recent condemnations of the wealthy.

4. In response, the Senate then required that two-thirds of every loan should be invested in Italian land, and that two-thirds of every outstanding debt should be paid off.

5. This only made matters worse, because the loans were actually called in in full, and the property-market became glutted with estates of debtors desperate to sell, to the point where land-prices collapsed.

6. The problems were not resolved until the Emperor made available loan-funds of HS100 million interest-free for three years.

A cautious interpretation can still argue that the crisis resulted from political contingencies, not from economic or monetary malfunction. Suppression of credit by legal process at any date would always have produced drastic results, because loans underpinned aristocratic life to an extraordinary degree.[33] In fact any society where loans are widespread which suddenly discontinues lending curtails the available resources in a way that is bound to claim victims.

The crisis undoubtedly highlights reliance on borrowing by the upper classes, to sustain their heavy social commitments to building, luxury spending, social display, office-holding and munificence. But their preference for land rather than cash was probably a deliberate economic choice, which would have been made whatever the availability of coin.[34] Upper-class reliance on borrowing to finance expenditure suggests a primary reluctance to sell land, and a deliberate concentration of assets in this area, rather than an extremity dictated by shortage of coin.[35]

The fact that these sudden events overloaded the market for land shows either reluctance on the part of purchasers, or inability to absorb more than a certain amount of property in a short time. That suggests a limitation in the market mechanism, since a glut leading to low prices would have presented attractive buying opportunities which an efficient market would have taken

---

[33] For loans within the Roman aristocracy, see Frederiksen 1966, emphasising their importance within the social and political nexus, which could be separate from any economic function. Individuals can be seen simultaneously as borrowers and lenders (for an explicit example, Procopius, *Anecd.* 15.31).

[34] For parallels to this in the late Roman aristocracy, Hendy 1985, 218–20.

[35] It is symptomatic of the same attitudes in the provinces that when Pliny as governor in Bithynia tried to invest newly gathered municipal funds in land, no one wanted to sell land (*Ep.* 10.54.1). Pliny's own resources as a well-to-do senator were almost entirely in land, and he wrote of borrowing from a relative to finance a further land-purchase (*Ep.* 3.19.8).

up. The land-market at Rome may have been too small at that time to be able to absorb many upper-class landholdings on the vast scale on which these now existed. The treason-trials emphasised by Tacitus had been running for a number of years by AD 33, and had already brought down many leading members of the propertied class. Sales of their land must have reduced the amount that the market could absorb by the time of the debt crisis.[36]

But the events may have been exacerbated by a specific shortage of liquidity at Rome, which would in any case have been artificially increased by the restrictions on lending. One unfavourable feature was the location of the main mint at Lugdunum at this time, which reduced the circulation of new coin in Italy.[37] Another was the relatively modest scale of Tiberius's spending on building and spectacles in Rome.[38]

The scale of coin-output under Tiberius can hardly be assessed from available evidence.[39] But whatever its absolute quantity, the relative amount of precious-metal coin appears to have risen very substantially at about this point in his reign. Average denarius output seems to have increased almost eightfold, and average aureus output almost threefold, in the last six years of the reign, compared with the previous fourteen (Appendix 2). Thus even if the crisis cannot be explained by monetary events, subsequent monetary events were probably a response to the crisis.[40]

5. INFLATION

The only clear evidence for inflation in this period comes from the East. In the West, despite many costed gifts in surviving inscriptions, little is known about inflation before the time of Diocletian.[41] Spending on gifts unfortunately does not reveal underlying price levels.[42]

[36] Under the Principate, the property of the condemned was usually absorbed by the *fiscus*, or re-allotted by the Emperor to someone else (Millar 1977, 163–72). Tacitus makes it one of Tiberius's shortcomings that he took some private gold and silver mines for the *fiscus*, which may argue that this was not yet normal practice (*Ann*.6.19). See p. 6 above.

[37] See pp. 120–2.   [38] Cf. Suet. *Tib*. 46–8; Frank *ESAR* 5.36–9. See also p. 11 above.

[39] The suggestion that Tiberius's bronze was produced on a scale that made it comparable to silver in face value seems implausible (Rodewald 1976, 55). For later coin-output, see pp. 119–24 below.

[40] Mint activity was also resumed at Caesarea, where the Tiberian issues fall c.AD 25 and in 33/4 (Burnett, Amandry, Ripolles 1992, 7 ff.)

[41] Most of the impressive price-rise shown in Diocletian's Price Edict of AD 301 took place in the three preceding decades, making it irrelevant to the period studied here (Duncan-Jones 1982, 374–5). For comparisons between Diocletianic price-levels and those of the early Empire, see Corbier 1985.

[42] For misconceptions, cf. Duncan-Jones 1965, 306, discussing Szilágyi 1963. The alleged threefold increase in dining costs for the Arval Brothers between AD 183 and 213 would not prove inflation by a corresponding amount, even if genuine. But 100 denarii per head per occasion was almost certainly meant in both cases (*CIL* vi 2099; 2086; Pekáry 1959, 460). For levels of spending on public gifts in cities in Italy and Africa, see Duncan-Jones 1982, chapters 3 and 4. Some of the evidence refers to private tomb-costs, but these are normally undated. Grain-prices known outside Egypt tend to be artificially low (controlled prices at a time of famine) or artificially high (famine prices).

Table 2.1 *Average wine prices*

Date (AD)	Price in drachmas (per keramion or equivalent)	Source
45/6	c.3	Drexhage 1991, 61; *PMich* 127
45/7	c.4.4	Drexhage 1991, 61; *PMich* 123v
247/8	c.9.4	Rathbone 1991, 466
250/4	c.10.4	Rathbone 1991, 466
260/4	c.16.6	Rathbone 1991, 466

Note: For measures, see Rathbone 1991, 468–71.

Some of the market-magistrates at Ephesus, the first city of Asia, recorded on inscriptions how much bread had cost during their year of office.[43] The figure must have been creditably low to be mentioned at all. The rate under Trajan was 2 obols for a 1-pound loaf.[44] In an inscription of about AD 220, the price had risen to 4 obols for a 12-ounce loaf, or $5\frac{1}{3}$ obols per pound.[45] The annual compound increase over approximately 120 years is 0.83%.

This comparison clearly implies a substantial price increase of about 166% over a period of a century. If these figures were creditable, typical bread prices at Ephesus must often have been higher. That has its own interest, because even the prices stated are well above those from Italy or Egypt.[46]

Roman Egypt has left numerous commodity prices, many dated by year.[47] The obvious basis for an index is wheat prices. But as so often, the chronology is very uneven. Nevertheless, some inflation is obvious here. The clearest indication is the compulsory purchase price of 24 drachmas per artaba of wheat in AD 246, which compares with a standard compulsory purchase price of 8 drachmas in the second century, last attested in 162.[48] The compound increase per year is 0.61%.

Further measures of inflation are provided by prices for wine, and for donkey-hire, and wages for digging and harvesting (Tables 2.1–2.5). The amount of data is always small, and the results vary. To align Egyptian data with the Ephesus bread prices, linear regression is used in Table 2.5 to express

[43] For active municipal price-control, see *POxy* 1454, and Apuleius's parody of the activities of market-magistrates in *Met.* 1.24–5.

[44] *Inschriften von Ephesos,* 923 with 3010 and note; 1 pound 2 ounces for 2 obols in 924.

[45] *Inschriften von Ephesos,* 3010 with note; see also 938 for a price-tariff with four different grades.

[46] The other bread prices are not stated by weight, but the loaves probably weighed a pound or more (2-pound loaves are referred to in Egypt). At the dinners of working-class colleges in Lanuvium and Rome the loaves cost 2 and 3 asses per diner, compared with a low Ephesian price of 2 obols equalling $5\frac{1}{3}$ asses (Duncan-Jones 1982, 381). In Egypt, bread prices of 1 Egyptian obol are recorded, equalling $\frac{4}{7}$ or $\frac{2}{3}$ of an as per loaf (in 45/6; Johnson, 316). This is obviously well below the western levels and far below the price at Ephesus.

[47] See Drexhage 1991; D. Foraboschi, *PMil Vogl* 7, pp. 27–35; Rathbone 1991, 464–71; Johnson *passim.*

[48] Duncan-Jones 1990, 147. The wheat prices from the Heroninos archive are 20, 20 and 24 drachmas in AD 250–2, and 12 in three cases from AD 254–60 (figures in Rathbone 1991, 464).

Table 2.2 *Daily pay for harvesting*

Date (AD)	Rate (obols)	Place	Source
78/9	2	Hermopolis	*PLond* 131r, col.27
169/70	10	—	*PMil* Vogl VII, 33
169/70	12	—	*PMil* Vogl VII, 33
169/70	14	—	*PMil* Vogl VII, 33
258	20	Euhemeria	*PFlor* 322

Note: For the first papyrus, see Swiderek 1960.

Table 2.3 *Daily cost of donkey-hire*

Date (AD)	Rate (obols)	Source
78–9	2–3	*PLond* 131r, col.14
78–9	7	*PLond* 131r, col.15
109	4	*PMil* Vogl 212r 2.6
117	4	*PSI* 688r
152	7	*PMil* Vogl 302, 10
152	10	*PMil* Vogl 302,9
166	14	*PMil* Vogl 304, 4
166	14	*PMil* Vogl 304,6
167	8	*PMil* Vogl 152, 56
215	28	*BGU* 362
255	28	*BGU* 14
260	28	Rathbone 1991, 158
269	28	*PErl* 101, 2

Table 2.4 *Daily wages for digging*

Date (AD)	Rate (obols)	Source
28/23 BC	3	*PCorn* 25
78/9 AD	3	*PLond* 131r, col. 3
78/9	3–4	*PLond* 131r, col. 13
121/2	7	*PColl Youtie*, 1.24
251/2	16	Rathbone 1991, 157 and 456

Table 2.5 *Chronological cost-comparisons using linear regression*

Notional date (AD)	Wine price	Wage for digging	Wage for harvesting	Donkey-hire	Median
100	100	100	100	100	100
220	165	192	361	528	277

Note: Source: Tables 2.1–4 (wine data from co-ordinates up to AD 247–8). The figures represent the fitted price for AD 220 as a multiple of the fitted price for AD 100. The result is indexed to a base of 100. The equations from the co-ordinates shown in Tables 2.1–4 are: wine price = (date × 0.028) + 2.382; digging = (date × 0.050) + 1.529; harvesting = (date × 0.101) − 5.451; donkey-hire = (date × 0.147) − 10.580.

average costs over the period 100–220. The median increase in the four series is shown as 177% over this period. This Egyptian figure is closely comparable to the 166% already seen at Ephesus.[49] The compound increase per year is 0.86% per year, higher than for Egyptian wheat prices.

6. THE IMPLICATIONS OF THE PRICE-EVIDENCE

Egypt had its own silver currency struck in Alexandria, while Asia mainly depended for silver on a mixture of western denarii and locally struck drachmas.[50] In both places, any gold coin circulating was struck in the West, but the two provinces otherwise belonged to different currency zones. Yet inflation which was probably currency-based is seen in both areas and runs at similar rates (section 5). Presumably this indicates an increase in the volume of currency in circulation, either absolute or relative. A relative increase would mean that the exchange system became more fully saturated with existing coin, without the absolute volume of coin increasing.[51]

A simple quantitative paradigm appears closest to the truth. Other diagnoses have assumed sophisticated monetary awareness. Thus Hirschfeld interpreted the payment of 720 aurei by Septimius Severus to emissaries from the Senate as a sum of 1,000 aurei discounted by 28% to allow for silver debasement.[52] His hypothesis did not really explain why change in the denarius should affect payments made in other coin, and the close monetary

---

[49] Rathbone comments that in the Heroninos archive 'there is no trace of monetary inflation until the 270s' (Rathbone 1991, 5). But even there, average wine prices increase between the 240s and the 260s (Table 2.1), and other Egyptian evidence shows clear signs of inflation before this period (Tables 2.2–2.4). For some suggested composite figures for increases in personal costs between the first and third centuries, see Drexhage 1991, 453.

[50] The bronze coin in circulation was also local (Sartre 1991, 93). For occasional denarius-finds in Egypt, see p. 91.

[51] Denarii are slow in reaching full saturation of the exchange system in Britain, see p. 205.

[52] Domaszewski 1898–1900, 311–12, citing Hirschfeld on *HA* Sev. 6.4. Shifts in the price of gold remain largely cryptic. See *PBaden* 37, with text and discussion in West, Johnson 1944, 181, 90–92 (proposing a detailed chronology which is incompatible with the dates now known for prefects of Egypt under Trajan, cf. Bastianini 1988, no.24).

awareness that it would imply is not borne out elsewhere. The hoards suggest that monetary anomalies of a moderate kind were usually ignored.[53] This makes it unlikely that price-rises in this period were mainly due to discounting of debasement in the silver coinage.[54] In any case, gold was important if not dominant in the monetary pattern, and gold was not being debased.[55]

Can we assume that inflation could have been confined to the East, and that the West as a different currency zone could have remained unaffected? On paper the East had more sources of coin because of its local coinage. But the powerful Rome mint disseminated a tri-metallic coinage very widely, and part of its output, gold and some silver, also circulated in the East. The quantities produced were evidently large and in terms of silver, the volume of coin in circulation apparently grew during the second century.[56]

This suggests that liquidity in the West was no lower than in the East. If currency circulation in the East led to slow inflation, the same was probably true in the West. This argument, although indirect, suggests that the average monetary environment was slightly inflationary all over the empire. Local circulation-anomalies no doubt altered its effects in some regions. But the annual inflation-rate suggested is very low, of the order of 1% per year.

The army pay increases are worth considering in the context of inflation of about 170% between AD 100 and 220. Indexing the rate of pay under Domitian to 100, the likely rate under Severus is 133, and that under Caracalla 200.[57] This 100% increase seems to be below contemporary inflation, especially since Domitian's increase took place as early as AD 84. Thus in monetary terms, the Severan pay increases seem modest in the context of prices of their day. But additional payment in kind had been introduced by then (rations for the Praetorians had already appeared under Nero). The combined result was enough to restore the attractions of army service.[58]

7. COIN-OUTPUT AND PRICE-MOVEMENTS

Connections between coin-output and prices can only be studied in Egypt, the main source of documentary prices. Even in Egypt, none of the dated series is very big, and most of them do not refer to a standard article. Commodity-prices may vary so much with the seasons that price-levels would emerge fully only if there were many more examples.

Nevertheless, in a few cases the patterns seem to be more than random. One

---

[53] Chapter 14 n.20. In Continental Europe in the Renaissance period there seems to have been more awareness of the metal content of silver coin, and some active discounting of the effects of debasement by the market. But there are also indications in sixteenth-century England that debased coin could circulate at par (Miskimin 1987, 699).
[54] Mattingly commented that '[In the hoards] the increasing debasement of silver has no influence at first; only at the complete breakdown under Gallienus do we find a clear line drawn . . .' (Mattingly 1960, 179).
[55] See pp. 70–2.   [56] See pp. 193–4.   [57] Table 3.3.   [58] See p.33 n.3.

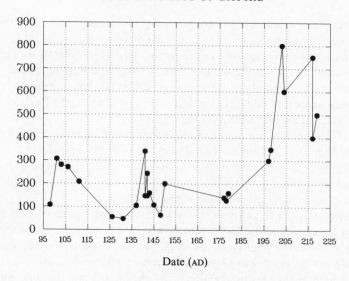

Figure 2.1 Prices for donkeys in Roman Egypt (in Egyptian drachmas).

example is prices for donkeys, on which the Egyptian peasant vitally depended for transportation. Their price is probably not heavily seasonal, unlike the price of wheat. Figure 2.1 shows the prices for donkeys between Trajan and the Severi.[59] There is a very clear peak under Septimius Severus and Caracalla, when prices more than double. Much smaller peaks occur earlier, under Trajan and Antoninus Pius, with troughs under Hadrian and Marcus Aurelius.

A comparison with the profile of mint-output indicated by a very large hoard (fig. 2.2) shows that the peaks in donkey prices do not belong to periods of high coin-output.[60] Thus little minting evidently took place under Trajan, little under Antoninus Pius, and almost none under Septimius Severus and Caracalla.[61] Since there is no doubt that Egypt's coin came from the Alexandria mint, this result is at first sight either paradoxical, or it suggests that there was no correlation between prices and minting.

But slow circulation of money is important here. Alexandrian mint-output was far higher under Commodus than under Marcus (fig. 2.2). Yet in an Egyptian hoard which ends in 191, just before Commodus's death, his coin is

---

[59] Drexhage 1986. Where a single figure is given for two animals, the average is used here. There are almost no first-century prices for donkeys.

[60] For hoard profiles and coin-output, see chapter 8, pp. 113–16. The prime source used here is Milne hoard 17, which has over 2,000 dated coins, and does not show the steep gradients in other large hoards of its period. This hoard is chosen because its coverage extends into the Severan period. But in percentage terms, its internal ratios between Nero, Vespasian, Trajan and Hadrian are almost exactly those of the median hoard, hoard 6, in the three largest second-century hoards summarised by Milne (hoards 2, 3 and 6). For year by year consistency between Egyptian hoards, see p. 113 below.

[61] For studies of Alexandrian minting under Trajan and Septimius Severus, see Christiansen 1988 (for his Trajanic results, see p. 169 n.32).

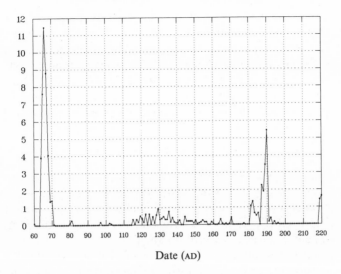

Figure 2.2 Annual percentages of coin in an Egyptian tetradrachm hoard, AD 60–220 (Milne no. 17).

only slightly more numerous than coin of Marcus.[62] This and other examples clearly show that diffusion of new coin to the hinterland was very slow.[63]

If circulation was so slow, that would mean that any impact of coin-output on prices in Middle Egypt would refer to coin struck some years earlier. This suggests a specific reason for the mismatch between figure 2.1 and figure 2.2. The dramatic price-surge under the Severi in figure 2.1 follows the heavy minting under Commodus, which was evidently the heaviest for more than a century. In the same way, the peak under Antoninus Pius follows the increase in minting under Hadrian. Trajan's small price-peak does not correspond to any obvious minting peak, although Nero's output was so enormous that its impact may have lasted for several decades (fig.2.2).

It is reasonable to ask whether the donkey-prices are enough to show the link suggested. If, for example, the Severan peak instead reflected increased requisitioning of pack animals in Egypt as part of a harsher tax-regime at that time, the evidence for a link between minting and prices would be much less. But such a wholesale effect is relatively unlikely, and the mechanism of price response to increased mint-output can be plainly identified in the fuller European evidence of the late Middle Ages.[64]

If minting and prices were interrelated in the relatively closed monetary system in Egypt, such relationships are also likely in the parts of the Empire

[62] Seventeen coins compared with 13 (Milne hoard 6, N = 2309). By contrast, in hoard 17 (n.60 above) the ratio of Commodus to Marcus is 37:1, or 347:19.
[63] For the rest of the empire, see p. 86. Similarly, second-century coin of a given reign struck in Rome reached its effective peak in Britain several decades after the reign had ended (p. 205).
[64] Miskimin 1987; Miskimin 1984, chapter 3; Munro 1984; Day 1987.

which depended on the Rome mint. But minting peaks at Rome did not follow those in Egypt, and output at Rome varied much less in the medium and long term.[65] The level of monetisation also inevitably differed from province to province. The fact that price-change in Egypt seems so dramatic may in itself suggest that the province was drastically under-monetised. The very low wastage-rates seen in Egyptian coinage point to exceptionally sluggish monetary circulation, and transactions in kind were very common in Egypt.[66]

8. CONCLUSIONS

In the Roman Empire the level of monetisation was restricted and uneven, and liquidity was generally low. Many tax-payments were payments in kind, and exchange based on barter was probably widespread below the surface. In evidence from other periods, it is clear that barter might still be the reality behind some exchanges described in money.

Restricted monetisation seems to have affected the wealthiest sector of Roman society. But crisis due to interruptions in the flow of credit between individuals throws light on the economic behaviour of the Roman upper class rather than on monetary shortage as such. The Tiberian credit crisis may nevertheless have been exacerbated by low public spending and restricted minting. The government lending on this and other occasions for which security in land was required was by definition lending to the propertied class.[67]

Price change in the empire at large remains elusive for lack of evidence. But commodity prices and wages slowly rose in Egypt, and their movement is paralleled by changes in bread prices in Ephesus, the leading city of Asia. This slow inflation probably existed in the Empire as a whole, and against its background the Severan army pay increases seem small in real terms. Nonetheless in conjunction with payments in kind, the new rates made army service more attractive.

Some interaction between minting and price-movements probably took place. In Egypt, short-term price-peaks seem to follow peaks in mint production, but might easily lag behind by as much as a decade. This mechanism, seen also in Renaissance Europe, probably existed in the rest of the Roman Empire. Its effects are characteristic of an economy in which liquidity and monetisation were very uneven.

[65] See pp. 126–42.
[66] It would be difficult to find matching ratios in hoards more than a century apart (n.60 above) if Egyptian currency was subject to rapid wastage. For transactions in kind, see n.8 above.
[67] Twofold security: Suet. *Aug.* 41; Tac. *Ann.* 6.17.

3

THE IMPERIAL BUDGET

INTRODUCTION

Before approaching coinage and currency, we need to look in more detail at the empire's financial position. The next two chapters consider the scale of spending and tax revenue. No complete figures for income or expenditure have survived, but large areas of expenditure can be estimated in some detail. Expenditure can then be compared with indications about revenue, to arrive at a rough figure for turnover. The scale of public spending provides a valuable backdrop against which estimates of the scale of monetary output can be assessed.

1. ARMY COSTS

1.1. SALARY COSTS

Army costs can be assessed by two routes. One is a detailed calculation based on number of units and rates of pay, while the other is based on Dio's figure for the cost of Caracalla's increase.[1] The results can be tested against each other.

If total salary-cost was equal to paying half a million legionaries (Table 3.1), the cost of army pay would be roughly that shown in Table 3.2, assuming an increase of one-third in 202.[2]

Set against Dio's HS280 million for the actual cost of Caracalla's increase, the estimate of its paper cost as HS400 million in Table 3.2 would make the army seriously below strength, at a time when Severus's pay-increase should have been making army service more attractive. The shortfall would be 30% ($\frac{400-280}{400}$). The recent large pay-increase makes that implausible. Arrius Menander, a member of Severus's *consilium*, explicitly contrasted voluntary recruitment in his own day with conscription at an earlier date.[3]

Thus the figures as they stand contain a serious contradiction. Since most

---

[1] Dio 78.36.3, with Herodian 4.4.7. For an earlier argument based on these co-ordinates, see Develin 1971, written before the work by Speidel and Holder used for the present estimates.
[2] From references to his declared policy of enriching the soldiers, Severus's pay increase (Herodian 3.8.5) must have been substantial (Dio 75.2.3; 76.15.2). But placing it above $\frac{1}{3}$ makes the discrepancies noted here even greater (for $\frac{1}{3}$, see Develin 1971, 692; cf. Duncan-Jones 1990, 115 n.28). According to the life of Severus, the increase took place in AD 202, the tenth year of the reign (*HA Sev.* 16.9). For his army policies in general, see Birley 1969 and Smith 1972.
[3] *Dig.* 49.16.4.10; Brunt 1990, 189–90.

Table 3.1 *The number of troops c.AD 200 and their cost*

	Number of legionary salaries (monetary equivalent)
1. 33 legions at 5,500 men	181,500
2. 47,900 *alares* at legionary rate	47,900
3. 176,240 *cohortales* at $\frac{5}{6}$ legionary rate	146,867
4. Rome units plus fleets (rough estimate)	40,000
5. Further 20% for higher ranks, and *numeri*	83,253
Total	499,520

Note: For pay, Speidel 1973 with Speidel 1992, showing a 5:6 ratio between *cohortalis* and legionary. The size of the legion is taken as 5,500 (Wierschowski 1984, 287). The legionary total includes new units raised under Marcus Aurelius and Septimius Severus. The figures for auxiliary strength come from A. R. Birley's estimates for AD 150, using Holder 1980 (Birley 1981B, Table 5; Holder 1980. See also Frere, Wilkes 1989, 118). Birley's estimates omit the cohorts now known in Asia, but 23 of his auxiliary units are not assigned by region (Speidel 1984). The fraction for officers is taken as roughly 20%, following estimates by Frank and Domaszewski, where officers add 21% to the rank-and-file cost for legionaries and Rome troops (Frank *ESAR* 5. 4–5; cf. Develin 1971, 691 where officer cost in the legions adds 20%).[4]

Table 3.2 *Provisional cost of army salaries*
(millions of sesterces)

Period (AD)	Army cost	Additional cost	Legionary pay per head
Before 84	450	—	900
84–202	600	150 million	1,200
202–212	800	200	(1,600)
212–	1,200	400	(2,400)

Source: Table 3.1.[5]

[4] For another estimate, based on Domitianic strengths, see Wierschowski 1984, 213. Hopkins (1980, 125), modifying figures from Frank, estimates 420,000 in legionary equivalent for the first century, when there were fewer legions. Estimates of army cost by MacMullen (1984, 579–80) use a much lower rate of auxiliary pay ($\frac{1}{3}$ the legionary rate, from Watson 1969, already superseded by figures in Speidel 1973). Estimates for the third century by Campbell, who discounts Dio's evidence for the size of the Caracallan pay-increase (1984, 162 n.2), assume that Severus raised pay by 66%, relying on doubtful arguments by Domaszewski from the benefits paid by military clubs at Lambaesis (Campbell 1984, 161 ff.).

[5] The size of establishment varied slightly. For the legions, see Dio 55.23.4.

of the unit and unit-strength estimates are straightforward, it seems that Caracalla's pay-increase and Dio's figure for its cost must refer to less than the whole army. Most of the discrepancy disappears if it is assumed that Caracalla's increase applied to the rank and file, but not to officers. The prospective cost would then be 312 million, making the shortfall between estimated and stated figures 10% ($\frac{312-280}{312}$). That difference may be unreal, since Dio's figure of 'over 70 million denarii' could mean an actual cost as high as 75 million (HS300 million).

1.2. DISCHARGE COSTS

In addition to army salaries, there were discharge-bonuses (*praemia*) for those who survived the quarter century of army service. Augustus fixed the amount at HS12,000.[6] Several group-dedications by legionaries discharged after serving their full term of 25–6 years survive in the second century; although 25 was the official limit, discharge in alternate years meant that some men served an extra year. These lists show totals of approximately 120 survivors per year, in two cases out of four, a third case being clearly exceptional.[7] If typical, that would imply mortality of about 44% over 25–6 years of service, from an average intake for a legion of 5,500 men of about 216 ($\frac{5,500}{25.5}$). The typical age of recruitment to the legions was about 20, and the implied survival-rate is below even the lowest standard demographic projections.[8]

But mortality would reduce the number during the years of service. From the closest fit in model life-tables, the reduction by the halfway point, year 13, would be about 20%.[9] Thus on average about 80% would survive as serving legionaries at any given time. In order to maintain full unit-strength under this regime, the intake would need to be 270 ($\frac{100}{80} \times 216$). The mortality then implied, already below the 'worst case' in model life-tables, would be 55% over 25 years of army service, instead of 44%. That might still be plausible for a very high-risk group in the pre-modern world. But the sample of legionary registers is very small, and its results cannot be pressed.

Taking 120 as the mean number of survivors per legion, the number of *praemia* required annually for an average complement of 30 legions would be 3,600 (2.18% of establishment). This would cost HS43 million per year at the Augustan rate of HS12,000 per head, rising to HS47 million under the Severi

---

[6] Dio 55.23.

[7] See Mann 1983, 59: about 120 per year in *ILS* 2302 and *CIL* III 6580; just over 100 in *CIL* III 6178; about 230 in *CIL* III 14507, but in this case probably reflecting exceptional recruitment in AD 169 due to plague or battle-losses.

[8] Figures for age of recruitment summarised in Forni 1953; for stylisation in the age-data, see Scheidel 1992. The survival-rate is below the lowest seen in the Princeton Tables (South), where 61% of males survive from age 20 to age 45 in a population with an expectation of life at birth of 19.9 years.

[9] The proportion of males alive at 20 who survive to $32\frac{1}{2}$ is 80% in the South Model 1 projections: Coale, Demeny[1], 656.

Table 3.3 *Annual cost of army salaries and* praemia: *schematic estimates* (millions of sesterces)

	Salaries	*Praemia* for legionaries	Total	Total if *praemia* also paid to auxiliaries
31 BC–AD 84	450	43	493	554
84–202	600	43	643	704
202–212	800	47	847	908
212–	1,080	47	1,127	1,188

Source: Table 3.2 and text. The figures do not allow for variation in the size of establishment (n.15).

when there were 33 legions. Caligula had halved the amount of the *praemium* for legionaries assembled for a German campaign, but Suetonius does not indicate that this had any long-term result.[10]

Auxiliaries, who received civil privileges such as citizenship at retirement are not explicitly known to have received *praemia*. Nevertheless, auxiliary service seems to have competed with legionary service; this would have been difficult if remuneration were much less.[11] Assuming that all *praemia* were roughly proportioned to salary, the mean number of legionary-equivalent *praemia* for the auxiliary numbers indicated by Table 3.1 is 4,245 per year (at the factor of 2.18% already calculated). That would cost a further HS51 million per year. A further 40,000 legionary-equivalent shares for other units in Table 3.1 could add a further HS10 million on the same footing.

Thus a rough calculation of the cost of *praemia* could put it at about HS104 million if payments were made to auxiliaries and other units, or about HS43 million if legionaries were the only beneficiaries.[12] Whether praemia can have been increased in step with salary remains very uncertain.[13] Apart from salary, the main vehicle for increased payment seems to have been the donative.[14]

The potential implications of *praemia* for total army cost are shown in Table 3.3.[15] Under the Principate some veterans were still granted land, when new colonies or land-assignments were made. Thus veteran colonies were founded at Antium and Tarentum under Nero in AD 60, and under Nerva

[10] *Gaius* 44.1.   [11] *Sel. Pap.* 149.

[12] The disputes over non-payment of *praemia* in Tacitus's *Annals* depict legionaries as the aggrieved parties, but auxiliaries are rare in the literary record (*Ann.* 1.17, 26, 31, 35).

[13] Domaszewski took it that Dio 77.24 showed that the legionary *praemium* under Caracalla was HS20,000 (cf. also Brunt 1950, 58). But this brief fragment seems to refer to one of Caracalla's donatives. The transmitted figures for Praetorians and legionaries are out of line with each other (1,250 denarii for Praetorians, 5,000 for legionaries).

[14] For donatives, cf. pp. 80–1 below.

[15] The estimates could be refined by allowing for variations in the number of units, but these cannot always be determined for auxiliary units.

Table 3.4 *The cost of citizen procurators*
(millions of sesterces)

	AD 192	Cost	AD 211	Cost
Trecenarii	1	0.3	10	3.0
Ducenarii	36	7.2	37	7.4
Centenarii	48	4.8	56	5.6
Sexagenarii	51	3.1	71	4.3
Total		15.4		20.3

and Trajan at Cuicul, Sitifis and Thamugadi in North Africa.[16] Land-grants were presumably easier to fund than cash payments, especially in provinces where they could be made from *agri captivi*.[17] But after Trajan, new veteran colonies ceased, possibly suggesting that difficulties in funding cash *praemia* had ended.[18]

2. CIVILIAN EMPLOYEES

Civilian salary-costs were another significant part of the Empire's budget. The most conspicuous are the citizen procurators whose grades specify their salary level. But there were also provincial governors, legionary commanders and lesser procurators.

2.1. CITIZEN PROCURATORS

A reconstruction from career inscriptions makes the total number of equestrian procurators 136 at the death of Commodus, and 174 at the death of Severus. These should represent minimum levels, assuming that posts once established remained in existence.[19] The totals are shown in Table 3.1. The great prefectures (Egypt, the Praetorians, the *annona*) were presumably trecenarian and would add almost another million to these figures.

2.2. SENATORIAL EMPLOYEES

Senatorial governors received payment under the Principate as under the Republic. The one definite fact is Dio's statement that the proconsulship of

---

[16] Mann 1983, 56–63.   [17] Tac. *Ann.* 12.32, and Mann 1983, 61.

[18] Government spending in the wake of Vespasian's tax-increases, including Domitian's substantial increase in army pay, Nerva's land-grants, and Trajan's child-support grants all suggests that the Empire had more funds by this time (pp. 12–13, 18).

[19] Pflaum 1950, 78, 96. The number missing should not be large, since most of the procuratorships are attested several times. But individual salaries can sometimes be uncertain (cf. Duncan-Jones *JRS* 71 (1981) 130).

Africa was worth HS1 million under Macrinus.[20] This high figure, and the obvious signs of hierarchy, imply that senators received substantially more than equestrians.[21]

A simple reconstruction might thus give consular governors HS1 million and praetorian governors HS500,000. Representative figures for the second century show 14 consular and 21 praetorian governors.[22] Their annual cost on this basis would be HS24$\frac{1}{2}$ million. A further 14 legates presumably paid at a rate similar to that of other praetorian employees might increase that to HS31$\frac{1}{2}$ million.[23]

Senators of praetorian rank also provided the legionary commanders. That leads to another HS12 million for a representative total of 24 legions with their own legates.[24]

2.3. NON-EQUESTRIAN PROCURATORS

Their important fiscal and administrative tasks meant that procuratorial departments required a sizeable infrastructure. This consisted of imperial freedmen and slaves.[25] As with equestrian procurators, some inscriptions illustrate their careers. But the inscriptions are too few for the number of posts to be reconstructed. The one salary definitely known, that of *proximi*, was HS40,000.[26] Even though individual salaries must have been below those of equestrians, in view of the numbers involved, their combined cost was probably at least comparable to that of the equestrian procuratorships. A pre-Severan estimate of HS15 million is conservative.

2.4. SUMMARY

The estimated civilian costs for a second-century date before changes under the Severi are shown in Table 3.5.

3. THE EMPEROR'S HOUSEHOLD COSTS

The cost of building and staffing imperial palaces and villas was probably not known to the rest of Roman society, and even speculation on this subject is rare. Picturesque details about the cost of Tiberius's pictures, Caligula's

---

[20] 78.22.5. Cf. Tac. *Agric.* 42.
[21] Some impoverished senators of good standing were paid HS500,000 a year by the Emperor, essentially for doing nothing (cf. Duncan-Jones 1982, 4 and 18 n.7).
[22] Marquardt 1881–5, 1, 494. For fuller details, showing the various changes that took place, see Birley 1981A, 16–17 and 26.   [23] Birley 1981A, 16–17.
[24] Birley 1981A, 16: in several small provinces the governor was also the legionary legate. This does not exhaust the list of salaried staff (even the *comites* of a legate received salaries, *Dig.* 1.22.4): but further estimating is difficult.
[25] Weaver 1972; Boulvert 1974. For named posts, Boulvert, 1974, 151–4; for salaries, Weaver, 1972, 229 and n.4 (cf. Boulvert, 1974, 154–5).
[26] *CIL* VI 8619.

Table 3.5 *Estimated civilian salary-costs*

Category	Salary-cost
Senatorial governors and legates	31.5
Legionary legates	12.0
Equestrian procurators	15.4
Prefects	0.9
Freedman and slave staff	15.0
Total	74.8

dinner parties, or Nero's tableware, reveal little of the Emperor's domestic spending.[27] The Emperor was richer by several magnitudes than his wealthiest subject. His way of life outshone everyone else's, and his domestic staff was much bigger even than that of the city-prefect with 400 slaves in his townhouse.[28]

Positions in the imperial household could carry immense power, and gave access to great wealth.[29] Holders include notorious figures such as Augustus's freedman Licinus, said to have made HS200 million as procurator in Gaul, Claudius's freedman Pallas, rich enough to refuse the Senate's grant of HS15 million, and Nero's freedman Polyclitus, sent to oversee the policy of consuls in Britain.[30] Imperial slaves could buy themselves out of slavery (there was a *fiscus libertatis et peculiorum*). Thus they owned a *peculium*, and posts of any significance were presumably salaried.[31]

4. HANDOUTS TO CIVILIANS AND SOLDIERS

An important touchstone of Imperial generosity was the cash handout to army and people.[32] The civilian handout was called a *congiarium* and the military handout a *donativum*. Already emphasised by Augustus in the *Res Gestae*, the handout soon became an inescapable public ritual, growing bigger and more frequent. Like the *sportulae* of municipal benefactors, the imperial handouts were nominally attached to specific events, in this case occasions

---

[27] Pliny *NH* 35.70; Seneca *Helv.* 10.4; Pliny *NH* 37.20.
[28] Tac. *Ann.* 14.43. Under Claudius and Nero an inscription at the imperial villa at Antium lists several imperial freedmen and freedwomen each year with their job-titles (*topiarius, structor, tegularius, nummularius*, among others: *CIL* x 6637).
[29] For their power, see Pliny *Pan.* 88.1.
[30] Duncan-Jones 1982, 343; Pliny *Ep.* 8.6.10; Tac *Ann.* 14.39.
[31] This *fiscus* is discussed in Jones's excellent study of clerical and subclerical grades in the civil service (Jones 1960, 160; cf. 109). High manumission payments, as high as HS13 million in the case of the *dispensator* of Nero's Armenian campaigns, were presumably 'earnings-related' in some way (Pliny *NH* 7.129). For proportioning of manumission payments to earnings, see also Duncan-Jones 1984. For manumission, cf. Jones 1960, 159–60, Weaver 1972, 97–104.
[32] For the army, see chapters 5 and 6. For the total cost, see also Appendix 1.

such as accessions, betrothals, or the naming of heirs. The average amount spent usually remained stable or increased.

The handouts went to privileged recipients who were already receiving regular payments.[33] The citizen recipients, the *plebs frumentaria* of Rome, were also paid every month in corn. Membership of this group could be purchased: Dionysius Halicarnensis shows slaves being freed in order to benefit from the corn-dole.[34] Soldiers received regular salaries paid partly in cash and partly in kind.[35] The handouts, at first every five to ten years, then roughly every three years on reign average, were a sizeable extra benefit.[36]

Congiaria totals per reign are known, and the amounts spent can be estimated reasonably well (see Appendix 1). The scale of donatives is more obscure, because written sources rarely report such details. But the sources suggest that handouts for the *plebs* typically meant money for the troops as well, and the two are unmistakably linked in Pliny's account of what was expected from a new ruler.[37] Quite different evidence, the surviving coin-hoards, shows strong overall dating correlations with the handouts to the *plebs*. This coincidence is difficult to explain except by recognising the hoards, distributed over most of the empire, as remains of the army handouts which typically accompanied *congiaria* in Rome.[38] That gives donatives approximately the same frequency as *congiaria*.

The relative size of expenditures on *congiaria* and donatives is indicated early in the period. In the legacies of Augustus, the citizens received HS260 per head, with a little more for the tribes, and the legionaries HS300. Here civilian and military entitlements were roughly the same, even though the few troops in Rome received higher rates, the Praetorians HS1,000, and the urban cohorts HS500. The main allocations under Tiberius's will in AD 37 were similar: HS300 for the citizens, HS300 for the legionaries, and HS500 to the Praetorians.[39]

Later evidence for a combined *congiarium* and donative under Hadrian suggests a high military allocation, with a capital cost perhaps twice that of the civilian handout.[40] That might indicate that by this date or on this occasion, Aelius's designation as heir, the auxiliary troops were being given donatives as well. It can be assumed that the cost of army donatives at least matched the

---

[33] Almost the only chance the unprivileged had of receiving anything was when the Emperor gave *missilia* or *sparsiones*, which meant money or gift-vouchers thrown down from on high on festive occasions in Rome (Millar 1977, 137).

[34] 4.24; see also *Dig.* 32.35.pr. Tacitus suggests a predominance of slaves in the city *plebs* (*Ann.* 4.27); and under the Principate, people of servile origin or immediate servile descent predominate overwhelmingly in tombstones from Rome (Taylor 1961).

[35] For payment in cash with stoppages for items in kind, see Rom. Mil. Rec 68–9. For payment in kind, see Dio 78.34.3; Suet. *Nero* 10.1; Tac. *Ann.* 15.72; *ILS* 2163.

[36] For comparability between donatives and *stipendium* in the fourth century, see Duncan-Jones 1990, 115–17.

[37] P. 87 n.4 below.

[38] For detailed argument, see chapters 5 and 6 below. The hoards contain other distinctive features which mark them out from ordinary private savings.

[39] Table 1.2, nos. 2 and 6. Suet. *Gaius* 17; Van Berchem 1939, 146–7.

[40] See p. 88 below.

Table 3.6 *The cost of* congiaria *and donatives: schematic estimates* (millions of sesterces)

Reign	*Congiaria* cost per reign-year	*Congiaria* and donatives combined
Augustus	9	18
Tiberius	7	14
Claudius	7	14
Nero	4	8
Vespasian	5	10
Domitian	9	18
Trajan	12	24
Hadrian	22	44
Antoninus Pius	22	44
Marcus Aurelius	25	50
Commodus	39	78
Septimius Severus	41	82
Caracalla	70	140
Elagabalus	113	226
Severus Alexander	42	84

Note: Reigns of four years or more are shown. The estimates in the second column assume equal costs and identical occasions for *congiaria* and donatives. Schematic totals are used, in the absence of exact reporting of the number of recipients. For sources and arguments, see above and Appendixes 1 and 7.

cost of *congiaria* in Rome. A series of amounts can be calculated on this assumption (Table 3.6).

5. BUILDING

The few extant cost figures are enough to show the vast scale of Imperial building expenditure, without offering any real guidance to the ordinary level of spending. Thus in the first century, two aqueducts cost HS350 million and the gilding of the Flavian Capitol HS288 million (Table 1.2, nos. 8 and 15). Some imperial buildings can be reconstructed from their physical remains. Their approximate construction costs could potentially be worked out by analogy with smaller Roman buildings whose size and cost is known.[41] But such reconstructions face considerable difficulties.[42] One is the problem of allowing for the luxury component of imperial building in Rome, which is very

[41] Thus unpublished work by the writer analysed a dossier of 11 public buildings in North Africa in this way, using inscriptions and archaeological remains.
[42] For some estimation for the Julio-Claudian period, see Thornton, Thornton 1989. The coefficients proposed do not always give convincing results.

substantial and cannot be gauged from provincial analogies. Enormous quantities of the most recondite marbles were brought from imperial quarries in the eastern Mediterranean, under non-market conditions.[43] A further difficulty is the lack of parallel data for the imperial palaces.

Nevertheless, Domitian's reign may offer some crude guidance to the overall pattern. The gilding of the Capitol cost 12,000 talents (HS288 million) according to Plutarch, a keen contemporary observer.[44] High though the figure is, it need not represent more than a third of the building costs of the reign. These also included the structure of the Capitol, the final tier of the Colosseum, a big stadium (whose site is now the Piazza Navona), and a palace whose immensely high gilded ceiling impressed visitors including Plutarch and Statius. If Domitian's building expenditure during a fifteen-year reign was roughly three times Plutarch's figure for one part of it, thus about HS900 million, the yearly average would be about HS60 million.

The scale of Domitian's building evidently stood at one end of a spectrum whose opposite end might have been as little as HS20 million per year. In default of anything better, these annual estimates of HS20–60 million can be taken as a rough order of magnitude for imperial building outlays.[45]

6. GIFTS AND PUBLIC SPENDING

When the traveller Ibn Battuta visited the Sultan of Delhi in 1334, he found ritualised gift exchange at the heart of court etiquette. No visitor could arrive empty-handed. But the Sultan's response was always so generous that suitable gifts could be had on credit. Ibn Battuta was thus able to equip himself with horses, camels and white slaves as his entrée to the palace. The presents showered on him in return included 5 villages and their revenues, 10 infidel slave-girls, the post of *qadi* of Delhi, very large sums of money, and vast amounts of flour and meat for his servants.[46]

Gifts had a similar importance at the Roman court, and there is little here that a Roman Emperor could not have given, whether that meant estates, preferment, revenues, money or payments in kind.[47] Emperors, like Sultans, were expected to give more than they received, a fourfold tariff applying to

---

[43] Some of this came from Mons Claudianus and Mons Porphyrites in Egypt: see Klein 1988. For other supplies, see Fant 1989A. See also Gnoli 1988; Anderson, Nista 1990. For further discussion, Fant 1988 and Fant 1993.

[44] *Publ.* 15.3–4. It grated on Plutarch that the Capitol's imported columns, which he had seen in Greece, were reworked and spoiled by Roman masons. See also p. 13 n.106

[45] Some of the building took place in the provinces: MacMullen 1959.

[46] Ibn Battuta, a cleric of distinguished family from Tangier, was being welcomed in Delhi as a fellow Muslim (Gibb 1971, 595–6, 738, 741, 745, 749).

[47] For gifts of slaves, note Titus's disposition of prisoners after the Jewish revolt, some of whom were used in building works in Egypt, and others given to different provinces (Josephus *BJ* 6.417–18). In Lucian *de salt.* 64, Nero granted a petitioner the right to make any request, and was then asked for a pantomime dancer (Millar 1977, 467). For a gift of corn by Augustus, see Millar, 135. For estates, cf. Pliny *Ep.* 10.58.5, where Domitian buys a small farm for a Bithynian philosopher.

New Year gifts in one source.[48] Members of the Senate who fell on hard times could sometimes expect a large capital payment, or even a princely salary for life.[49] Handouts to the people of Rome and to the troops were common events, and an obvious drain on resources.[50] But the outgoings for personal gifts could also be enormous. Tacitus's total of HS2.2 billion for the cost of gifts by Nero to his favourites is one of the largest figures recorded.[51]

The fact that a senatorial commission was set up to retrieve the funds spent by Nero shows that they could not all have come from the Emperor's purse. But even contemporaries found it difficult to distinguish between spending from the *aerarium*, the traditional state treasury, and spending from the *fiscus*, or Emperor's treasury. Clearly there was no real barrier to what the Emperor could spend.[52] In practice his financial position tended to coalesce with that of the state, even if Emperors varied in their willingness to exploit this fact.

Some other customs worked financially in the Emperor's favour. One was the crown gold traditionally given by each province at his accession. Another was the extremely widespread practice of remembering the Emperor in private wills.[53] Nevertheless, gift-obligations represented an open-ended economic commitment for the Emperor, because of the need to spend heavily on social encounters whose frequency could not easily be controlled.

7. FOREIGN SUBSIDIES AND GIFTS

The Empire's foreign policy involved monetary outlay in two main ways.[54] The first was a version of the gift exchange familiar in Roman society itself. Thus under the Julio-Claudians, contacts with foreign rulers meant large gifts or ceremonial outlays, in dealings with eastern kingdoms such as Parthia, Commagene and Armenia.[55] These gifts were semi-reciprocal, intended to

---

[48] See Millar 1977, 139–44, and especially 142–3 (gifts to the Emperor); 135–9, 467–8, 491–500 (gifts by the Emperor).

[49] See Duncan-Jones 1982, 4, 18 n.7. This applied only to socially worthy cases, not to spendthrifts, who were sometimes ejected from the Senate (Tac. *Ann*. 2.48). Generosity in this area was perceived as an imperial virtue very early on. Writing as a contemporary, Velleius could praise Tiberius's gifts to senators, which the hostile Tacitus afterwards condemned for their meanness (Velleius 2.129.3; Tac. *Ann*. 2.37–8; Suet. *Tib*. 47.2).   [50] See pp. 39–41

[51] Tac. *Hist*. 1.20; Suet. *Galba* 15.1. After Nero's death there were attempts to claw this money back, leaving the recipients with a token 10%.

[52] Millar 1977, 189–201, 167, with Dio 53.22.2–4, quoted by Millar, 190. In his account of Tiberius, Tacitus suggests that the dividing line between *fiscus* and *aerarium* was slight (*Ann*. 6.2; 6.17); see also Levick 1987. Nevertheless, Nero's claim to have given the *res publica* HS60 million from his resources each year indicates a continuing conceptual distinction between the finances of Emperor and state (*Ann*. 15.18). Hadrian reportedly insisted on all proceeds of property of the condemned going into the *aerarium*, not into the *fiscus* (*HA Had*.7.7).

[53] Crown gold: Millar 1977,140–2. The crowns offered to Claudius at his British triumph show really substantial payments (9,000 pounds of gold from Tres Galliae, 7,000 from Hispania Citerior, altogether about HS67 million; Pliny *NH* 33.54). For bequests to the Emperor, see pp. 6–7 above.

[54] For a valuable discussion, see Gordon 1949, based on his Michigan thesis which the writer has also consulted; for Germany, Wolters 1991, 116–21.

[55] Gordon 1949, 62. According to Chinese sources, the first Roman embassy to China, in AD 166, brought presents of ivory, rhinoceros horn and tortoise shell (Hirth 1885, 42 and 94).

mark out the importance of the occasion, and were not paid on any regular basis.

More important was the payment of foreign subsidies. Today these might represent foreign aid, but in the Roman world they were mainly a diplomatic bribe to unruly neighbours. Subsidies were one of the techniques of foreign policy which also included making client kingdoms, and granting border land to tribesmen.[56] Although subsidies are rare in extant Julio-Claudian evidence, the practice seems to have existed from a very early date.[57] From the time of Marcus Aurelius onwards, they are emphasised increasingly in the sources.[58]

Tacitus mentions regular payments to the Germans in contexts referring to the Flavian period.[59] Frontinus indicates that Domitian actually paid for revenue lost by the Cubii on land added to Roman territory.[60] His inconclusive campaigns led to the payment of annual subsidies to Decebalus which soon became a pretext for the invasion of Dacia by Trajan.[61] Eulogy of Trajan, like that of Pertinax, could claim that here was an Emperor so strong that Rome no longer needed to pay subsidies.[62] Such claims were of course unreal, and complaints from the Roxolani soon showed that regular payments were still being made.[63] Hadrian, after relinquishing Trajan's eastern conquests, followed a policy of military preparedness, coupled with heavy subsidy to peoples across the frontier.[64] Named recipients include the Roxolani, the Iberi and the Albani.[65] Hadrian gave the Iberi an elephant, a band of 50 men and large presents.[66]

Under Marcus Aurelius, large-scale frontier warfare returned to the Empire. Money payments were among Marcus's strategies towards barbarian petitioners, which also included grants of citizenship and tax exemption in individual cases.[67] But Marcus's biggest concession was paid in land: he gave foreign tribes rights of settlement in Dacia, Pannonia, Moesia, Germany and, disastrously as it turned out, in Italy itself.[68]

Payments to Rome's barbarian neighbours took place on an important scale under Commodus.[69] Pertinax even succeeded in retrieving gold that Commodus had despatched to the barbarians, and was praised for being strong enough to have no need to make barbarian payments.[70] Dio shows Scottish tribes being bought off with a large sum in AD 197. He makes Macrinus claim that Caracalla increased payments to the barbarians to the point where they cost the treasury as much as army pay.[71] But within months,

---

[56] For client kingdoms, see Braund 1984.   [57] Cf. Gordon 1949, 60–2.
[58] For their further history in the Late Empire, see Hendy 1985, 261–3.
[59] *Hist.* 4.76; *Germania* 42; 15.3.
[60] Frontinus, *Strat.* 2.11.7. This recalls Caligula's refund of tribute to the kingdom of Commagene (Table 1.2, no. 7), but its scale was probably much lower.
[61] Dio 67.10.5.   [62] Pliny *Pan.* 12.2.   [63] *HA Hadr.* 6.8.
[64] Dio 69.9. *HA Hadr.* 17.10–11.   [65] *HA Hadr.* 6.8, 17.11, 21.13.   [66] *HA Hadr.* 17.11.
[67] Dio 71.19.1.   [68] Dio 71.11.4–5.
[69] For hoards outside the empire and government payments to tribes, see for example Mihailescu, 202–4.
[70] Dio 74.6.1, with Herodian 2.2.8; Herodian 1.6.9.   [71] Dio 75.5; 78.12.3.

Macrinus himself bought peace with Parthia for HS200 million.[72] Dio mentions that regular payments were already being made to the Armenians.[73]

The sources do not give figures for subsidies before the Severan period, when the cost had clearly become high. The first payments may have been relatively small in terms of the Empire's budget. The most significant escalation in cost may have taken place under Hadrian, whose doubling of expenditure on *congiaria*, like his building programmes, showed an exceptional willingness to spend heavily.

8. TOTAL INCOME AND EXPENDITURE

Three of the headings discussed have been left unquantified, the Emperor's household costs, the Emperor's gifts, and external subsidies. Here any estimate must be arbitrary. But a figure of HS50–100 million can be assigned to the three items combined, rising to HS100–50 million in the Severan period, when external subsidies evidently increased.[74] The numerical results can then be summarised (Table 3.7).[75]

These figures are partly notional, but a large part of the total is accounted

Table 3.7 *Schematic estimates of the Empire's annual budget*
(figures in millions of sesterces)

	c.150 AD		c.215 AD	
Category	Low figure	High figure	Low figure	High figure
1. Army	643	704	1,127	1,188
2. Civilian employees	75	75	75	75
3. Handouts	44	44	140	140
4. Building	20	60	20	60
5. Other items	50	100	100	150
Total	832	983	1,462	1,613

Note: The items in category 5 are the Emperor's household costs, the Emperor's gifts, and external subsidies. For details, see the preceding discussions.

for by army expenditure, where estimating is relatively detailed. On present estimates, army cost makes up approximately three-quarters of the Empire's budget in the mid second century (between 72% and 77%). The escalation in

---

[72] Dio 78.27.1.   [73] 78.27.4.
[74] But external payments were not always in cash: *HA Hadr.* 17.11.
[75] This broad computation does not attempt the even more difficult task of separating the Emperor's revenues from state revenues.

budget cost by the mid-Severan period, again largely accounted for by army spending, is shown as approximately 70% (between 64% and 75%). On minimum figures, state turnover appears to be roughly HS832 million in the mid-second century, having increased from about HS656 million in the early Flavian period.[76]

It seems clear that Vespasian achieved a significant increase in imperial revenues, perhaps by as much as 20%.[77] The revenues which he inherited presumably included the HS340 million that the empire had after Pompey's conquests; approximately HS300 million from Egypt and Gaul; and perhaps HS30 million from the more recent provinces of Pannonia, Cappadocia, Mauretania and Britain.[78] That would give a total of HS670 million, which when increased by 20% would become HS804 million.

Domitian's pay increase must have been carried out from revenue that was already there. Thus this assessment of tax-revenue is close to the estimated budget figure in Table 3.7 of HS832 million after Domitian's increase (it includes an allowance for funds belonging to the Emperor). This can be compared with the rough assessment of the volume of coin produced in chapter 11. In very rough terms, mint-output appears to match one-quarter of the budget.[79] The proportion of revenue raised in money was probably substantially higher, though a considerable part of Rome's taxes were paid in kind.[80]

[76] Army pay HS150 million less (Table 3.3), handouts HS26 million less (Table 3.6).
[77] Cf. p. 12.
[78] For Pompey, Egypt and Gaul, see Appendix 4 and Table 4.6.
[79] The estimate by Hopkins is considerably higher (HS824 million in the early first century; Hopkins 1980, 119). But its basis, coupling a notional population figure with notional subsistence costs, is *a priori*, not empirical. It is difficult to reconcile such estimates with the known changes in the Empire's income and expenditure.
[80] Duncan-Jones 1990, chapter 12.

4

TAX AND TAX-CYCLES

A. THE CASE OF EGYPT

1. INTRODUCTION

Egypt provides our one practical example of how Rome taxed her provinces.[1] The source is stray documentary survivals, which are cumulatively impressive, although they are concentrated in particular districts. The tax-system is apparently thorough and minute, with farm land surveyed and taxed almost to the last square foot. The tax assessments take into account irrigation status and to a lesser extent poor harvests. But tax-yield declines substantially over the long term, suggesting that the land was being taxed too heavily or over-exploited.[2]

Hyginus shows tax-rates of one-seventh and one-fifth in different provinces, and rates as low as one-tenth are also known.[3] But only Egypt provides enough evidence to show in detail how provincial taxation worked under the Empire. The position here was complicated by Egypt's unique dependence on the Nile flood. Nevertheless, Egypt remains the one province where extensive tax-details have survived, and since it was one of the most important provinces, the government's handling of this resource should provide some index of its financial policies as a whole.

2. THE AVERAGE TAX-RATE FOR GRAIN LAND

A primary aim of this discussion is to assess the scale of tax-revenue and how this changed. But that means some investigation of how taxes worked and how they were applied. Whether land was public or private made an enormous difference to how much tax it paid. The tax liabilities of public

[1] For a brief sketch which partly complements the account here, see Sartre 1991, 437–41. For the origins of the Roman tax-system in Egypt, and for comparability with other provinces, see now Rathbone 1993.
[2] See sections 6 and 9 below.
[3] Duncan-Jones 1990, chapter 12. In Asia, tax of $\frac{1}{10}$ on grain, wine and oil is cited in the recently discovered customs-law of the first century (Engelmann, Knibbe 1989, l.72 ff.). More explicit tax-regulations from eighth-century Syria, probably influenced by Roman practice, show taxes of $\frac{1}{5}$ on new refined metal, a basic land-tax of $\frac{1}{10}$ of crops, levied as $\frac{1}{5}$ on land owned by some non-Muslims. Poll taxes on non-Muslims were levied on adult males at three different rates according to wealth. Customs-dues were $\frac{1}{40}$ on goods above a certain value carried by Muslims, and $\frac{1}{20}$ and $\frac{1}{10}$ for other taxpayers. (Abou Yousouf Ya'koub 1921, 33–4, 79, 186, 187–8, 204–5).

land were so great that even finding tenants for it could be difficult. Sometimes it had to be assigned compulsorily, as with crown land under the procedure called *epibolē* or *epinemesis*.[4] Some crown land was also sold off to private owners.[5]

But substantial amounts of land remained in the public categories and carried a much heavier tax-burden. The tax-rates themselves can be roughly assessed by taking a cross-section of land-registers from our period. Table 4.1, based on nine such registers, shows the average rate for public land as 4.13 artabas per aroura, and the average for private land as 1.29. These figures represent gross average yield, dividing the area paying tax into total tax-revenue. This bypasses any variations in water-regime and land-quality.[6]

The ratio of public to private in terms of area is equally crucial. Although this varied from one district to another, a rough average can be found by taking a further cross-section, in this case based on land-registers in which land status is specified. Tables 4.2 and 4.3 show a median nome average for public land of 33.6%.[7]

The three co-ordinates provided by Tables 4.1–4.3 allow us to calculate a composite tax-rate for land in Egypt. The median percentage of public land is seen as 33.6%, and the average revenue of public land 4.098 artabas.[8] The median percentage of private land is 66.4% and its average revenue 1.29 artabas. Thus the notional composite tax-rate is $(0.336 \times 4.098) + (0.664 \times 1.292) = 2.23$ artabas per aroura.

2.1. SUPPLEMENTS TO THE BASIC LAND-TAX

There were standard additions to the basic tax-rates, including the *dichoenicion*, about 5%, and the *prosdiagraphomenon* of $6\frac{1}{4}$%. Money-taxes also imposed a banker's commission of $\frac{1}{60}$ on the taxpayer because they were assessed in old-style copper currency, but levied in silver.

A register of the late first century AD illustrates this.[9] A short entry reads: '6 arouras of privately owned land. Tax: $7\frac{1}{2}$ artabas of wheat. *Dichoenicion*: $\frac{1}{3}$ artaba. Supplementary charges: $1\frac{1}{24}$ artabas. Total: $8\frac{21}{24}$ artabas. *Naubion*: 900 copper drachmas with supplementary charges of 180 copper drachmas.'

The tax-charge here has no less than five different components, three in wheat and two in money. The total wheat-payment is 18.3% more than the basic tax. The money charge for *naubion* or dike-tax adds 6% more,

---

[4] Wallace 1938, 2–21; *PCair Isid* 11, p.102; Swiderek 1971, 39.
[5] *POxy* 721, AD 13/14, see also Johnson, 158.
[6] For these variations, see Appendix 3.
[7] The percentage of public land apparently tended to decline, but the latest figure from the Arsinoite nome remains substantial (Table 4.2). Using evidence from a longer period allows a wider cross-section of nomes than in the figures from the Principate alone.
[8] Ousiac land in Table 4.1 is excluded here.
[9] *PLond* 193 (Arsinoite); Johnson, 51–3. Money-charges are virtually the same, about 0.588 drachmas per aroura, in accounts from the Mendesian nome under Marcus Aurelius (Kambitsis 1985, 34: the total for *naubion, chōmatikon, allagē* and *prosdiagraphomenon*).

Table 4.1 *Overall tax-rates in nine lists*

Land-type	Gross tax-yield (artabas per aroura)	Area (arouras)	Source
All public	4.13	49,519	1–9
All private	1.29	7,163	1–9
Public			
Prosodikos	7.79	684	3
Ousiac	4.67	5,387	2, 3
Basilikos	4.30	38,488	1, 3, 4, 5, 6, 8, 9
Hieratic	1.76	4,960	4, 5
Private			
Cleruchic	1.71	2,084	5, 7
Royal let as private	1.40	672	4, 5
Catoecic	1.08	4,407	3, 4, 7, 9

Sources: 1. *BGU* 20, AD 141; 2. *BGU* 1636, AD 156/7 (Johnson no. 312); 3. *PBour* 42, AD 167 (Johnson no. 16); 4. *PFlor* 331, AD 117 (Johnson no. 13); 5. *PGiss.* 60, AD 119 (Johnson no. 14); 6. *PGron* 2, AD 219/20; 7. *PLond* 193, AD 50–100 (Johnson no. 12); 8. *POxy* 918, c.2 AD (Johnson no. 21); 9. *SB* 4325, c.2–3 AD (Johnson no. 23). A small percentage of payments were in barley, here translated into wheat at a ratio of 5:3, as in *PTeb* 1, p. 224.

Table 4.2 *The percentage of public land in seven Egyptian land-lists*

Percentage public	Land identifiable as public or private (arouras)	Place	Nome	Date (AD)
1. 68.5	8,701	Naboo	Apollonopolite Heptakomias	119
2. 59.1	5,284	Theadelphia	Arsinoite	158/9
3. 52.8	7,784	Hiera Nesos	Arsinoite	167
4. 33.6	11,253	Phernouphitou	Mendesian	297/308
5. 47.2	4,189	Karanis	Arsinoite	312
6. 27.6	4,423	(7 villages)	Hermopolite	(c.300)
7. 19.2	202,534	Oxyrhynchite	Oxyrhynchite	300–350

Note: Ousiac land is not included in this Table; see Appendix 3 section 1. For the main land categories, public and private, see Table 4.1 above.
Sources: 1. *PGiss* 60; 2. *PBerl Leihg.* 5; 3. *PBour* 42; 4. Swiderek 1971; 5. *PCair Isid* 11; 6. Bowman 1985, 148 (*SPP* 5.120; *PLandlisten*); 7. Bagnall, Worp 1980 (*PMich* inv. 335 verso)

Table 4.3 *The percentage of public land in local samples*

Nome	
Apollonopolite Heptakomias	68.5
Arsinoite	52.8
Mendesian	33.6
Hermopolite	27.6
Oxyrhynchite	19.2

Note: The figure for the Arsinoite is the median of the three figures for this nome shown in Table 4.4.
Source: Table 4.

producing a total tax-supplement of 24.3%.[10] But these supplements made much less difference on public land with its higher basic rates.

3. VINES AND OLIVES

Although their total area was very small, vines and olives were worth more than grain crops, and they were taxed at higher rates. Under the Principate, the median rate for vineland is four times the private rate calculated for wheat (Table 4.4).[11] In a sixth century document at Aphrodito, vines pay four times the money-rate for wheat, and at Antaeopolis they pay almost six times the rate.[12]

In a schedule from the Arsinoite, vineyard pays 20.33 drachmas per aroura, with a fixed rate supplement of $8\frac{1}{2}$ drachmas per holding of vineland. Olives and orchard-land (*paradeisos*) paid between 10.28 and 11.53 drachmas per aroura. In a list from Upper Egypt, private vineyard pays 40 drachmas in several cases, but hieratic vineyard pays 150 drachmas. In the Oxyrhynchite in AD 205/6 a plot of vineyard was paying 62.9 drachmas per aroura. This range of rates for vineland is shown in Table 4.4. The main differences seem to be regional.

Where figures are known, the proportion of cultivated area under vines is very small: $3\frac{1}{2}$% in the Phernouphitou toparchy in the Mendesian nome under Diocletian, and 4.99% in sixth-century Antaeopolis in the northern Thebaid.[13] If vines were about 4% of the cultivated area of Egypt overall, and brought in a median rate of 40 drachmas (Table 4.4), equivalent to 5 artabas per aroura,

[10] The conversion is at standard rates of 300 copper drachmas per silver drachma, and 8 silver drachmas per artaba. In Ottoman Egypt, supplements included a charge of 8–12% on tax-payments in grain, and a $2\frac{1}{2}$% charge on money taxes (Shaw 1962, 168–70).
[11] This converts 40 drachmas to 5 artabas at the conventional equivalence of 8 drachmas per artaba of wheat.
[12] *PLond* 1674, c.AD 570; Johnson, West 1949, 256–7.
[13] Swiderek 1971; *PCair Masp* 67057. Outside Egypt, the proportion of vineland in fourth-century registers from Asiana is higher (cf. Duncan-Jones 1990, 203, n.15). But cultivation-norms may well have differed from those in Egypt. Land-lists in papyri maintain a crucial distinction between land under vines and old vineland (whose area could be much larger).

Table 4.4 *Tree-crops: specimen tax-rates*

Rate (drachmas)	Place	Culture	Source
10.28–11.53	Arsinoite	Olives	*SB* 6951 = Johnson no. 320, c.2 AD
20.33	Arsinoite	Vines	*SB* 6951 = Johnson no. 320, c.2 AD
40	Upper Egypt	Vines	*PLond* 109 = Johnson no. 323, c.2 AD
62.9	Heptanomia	Vines	*POxy* 2129 = Johnson no. 324, AD 205/6

they would add about 9% in wheat-equivalent to the revenue paid in wheat $((\frac{5}{2.3}) \times 4 = 8.97)$. Olives were less profitable (Table 4.4), and they perhaps added no more than 3% to the revenue collected in wheat.

The calculation for vines is money-based, and the reckoning for olives adds one-third (or less) to their total. An estimate for tree-crops can then be calculated as: (median tax-rate per aroura × estimated area under vines) + $\frac{1}{3}$ = (40 × 316,600 arouras) + $\frac{1}{3}$ = 16.89 million drachmas.

4. OTHER TAXATION

4.1. POLL-TAX AND OCCUPATIONAL TAXES

The most widespread money-tax in Egypt was poll-tax. The rates in Table 5 show considerable variation. They are higher in the Arsinoite, and less in towns than in villages. A rough assessment of total yield can be made from known rates, in conjunction with population-estimates. A possible population figure is 3–4 million, starting from Diodorus's total of 3 million for Egypt excluding Alexandria at the end of the Ptolemaic period.[14] If there were $3\frac{1}{2}$ million citizens outside Alexandria in the mid-Principate, the number of poll-tax payers (adult males aged 14–65) should be about 1 million, from normal demographic ratios. Occupational taxes could be as high as 40 drachmas per head, but were usually much less. If the combined proceeds of poll tax (Table 4.5) and occupational taxes are reckoned as 20 drachmas per taxable male, the yield would thus be about 20 million drachmas.[15]

4.2. SALES TAX AND CUSTOMS DUES

The most prevalent rate of sales tax was 10%, levied on sales of land, houses and slaves.[16] Heavy tolls of 25% on goods imported and exported were

---

[14] 1.31.6–9; cf. Rathbone 1990, arguing that the scale of agricultural production may have imposed a ceiling of 5 million.

[15] For taxes on trades see Wallace 1938, 191–213, *POxy* 2412, and Rea 1982. The present estimate assumes a mean occupational tax of 12 drachmas, paid by one-third of free male adults (land-workers were excluded).   [16] Johnson, 558–9.

Table 4.5 *Poll-tax: specimen rates*

Rate (drachmas)	Place	Source	Notes
40–44	Arsinoite	Wallace 1938,122–4	Unprivileged
24.3	Heracleopolite	*POxy* 2412 (AD 28–9)	
10–24	Thebes	Wallace 1938, 131	
20	Arsinoe	*SP* IV pp. 62 ff.	Privileged
16–17	Elephantine	Wallace 1938, 128	
16	Mendesian nome	Kambitsis 1985, 36	Villages
16	Tentyra	*Archiv* 6, 127	
16	Oxyrhynchite nome	Wallace 1938, 126–7	Unprivileged
12	Oxyrhynchus	*POxy* 1452	Privileged
8	Hermopolis	*PRyl* 193	Privileged
8	Memphis	*PFlor* 12	Privileged
8	Mendesian nome	Kambitsis 1985, 36	Towns
8	Coptos	Wallace 1938, 133	

charged in Egypt.[17] A very large part of the luxury goods drawn in from the East by the demand in Rome and other large cities passed through Egypt, and paid dues twice in the process. As a result, Alexandria was said to be the greatest trade-centre (*emporion*) in the world.[18] While this trade was flourishing, its effect on Egypt's tax-revenues must have been great. The total produced by sales taxes depends on liquidity and velocity of circulation. But sales volume in a large province with a number of cities, one of them very large, must have been significant. The evidence for the importance of Alexandrian customs-dues suggests that, together with the sales taxes, they might have accounted for as much as 30% of Egypt's revenues. On the figures so far, that corresponds to about 77.4 million drachmas (Table 4.6).[19]

5.   TOTAL REVENUE FROM EGYPT

The yield from grain-tax at the composite rate of 2.23 artabas calculated above would be about $17\frac{1}{2}$ million artabas, if the area under grain in the Principate was roughly 90% of the irrigated area estimated for 1880 by

[17] Harrauer, Sijpestein 1985. Sijpestein 1987. For the important first-century customs-law of Asia discovered recently, see Engelmann, Knibbe 1989.

[18] Strabo 17.1.13.

[19] Here land-revenue provides 62% of the total; in Ottoman Egypt in the seventeenth century the corresponding figure was 64% (Shaw 1962, 182). The present estimate is inevitably very approximate, and depends on the typicality of the parts of Egypt that yield documents. If the Delta, which is largely unrepresented, produced more tax-revenue on average than the sample data, total revenue from land-tax would be greater than is shown.

Table 4.6 *Estimates of tax-revenue in Egypt under the Principate*

	Value in wheat (million artabas)	Value in money (million Egyptian drachmae/sesterces)	Percentage
Grain revenue	17.5	(140.0)	54.0
Money-taxes on land	(0.59)	4.7	1.8
Tree-crops	(2.11)	16.9	6.5
Poll-tax and occupational taxes	(2.5)	20.0	7.7
Other money-taxes	(9.7)	77.4	30.0
Total	32.4	259	

Note: Residual money-taxes on land are calculated at a rate of 0.6 drachmas per aroura (section 2.2 above).

Barois.[20] Strabo, as a recent visitor, was keenly interested in the revenues of Egypt. He implies that revenue had grown by Augustus's time, and indicates that the irrigation system was now more efficient.[21] But his only figure is the 12,500 talents (HS300 million) given in a speech of Cicero as Egypt's revenue under Ptolemy Auletes.[22] Unfortunately, Cicero's figure is a common conventional amount, and it merely suggests an order of magnitude.[23]

In the sixth and seventh centuries, there is explicit evidence for the money:wheat ratio in tax-revenue. In four papyri, wheat-revenue is close to half the total, on median average (49.6%).[24] This percentage for wheat-revenue approximates the figure for the Principate of 54% suggested in Table 4.6.

6. TAXATION AND PRODUCTIVITY

The tax-rate was affected by whether the land was classified as flooded or unflooded (Appendix 3). But the relationship between taxation and productivity was not always close. Grain-taxes were normally levied at fixed rates, a practice from earlier times which contrasts with the percentage taxes customary elsewhere in the empire, for example in Sicily. In other words, a plot liable to pay tax at 3 artabas would pay at this rate regardless of harvest-size unless its owner could have it rescheduled. Some Egyptian land did pay pro rata tax, but this is not seen as the dominant practice.[25]

In some cases, tax was constant whether land was planted with high-yielding

---

[20] 2.41 million hectares (Johnson, 7). 90% would mean 7,838,815 arouras of the traditional Egyptian size (100 cubits squared or 2,767 m²). A smaller aroura of 96 cubits squared, equivalent to the iugerum, was sometimes used in Egypt in the Roman period (Duncan-Jones 1982, 371).   [21] 17.1.13, 17.1.3.

[22] See n.21. For other ancient figures for Egypt's revenues, see Appendix 4.

[23] See pp. 16–17 above.

[24] *PCair Maspero* 67320 37.4% (for these totals see A. H. M. Jones *JHS* 71 (1951) 271–2); *POxy* 2196 46.7%; *POxy* 1907 59.3%; *POxy* 1909 52.5%.   [25] See e.g. *POxy* 2847, ll. 2–3.

or low-yielding crops. At Philadelphia in the Arsinoite in AD 156/7, 12 arouras of ousiac land paid wheat-tax at a gross rate of 4.82 artabas of wheat per aroura. Yet only half was planted with wheat, the remainder containing 2 arouras of barley, 1 of vegetable seed, and 3 arouras of grass. This was part of a large holding of some 700 arouras which paid taxes in grain at the high gross rate of 6.44 artabas per aroura: yet the seed figures for the following year show wheat as less than 40% of the total.[26]

Modifying tax-rates with the level of the flood allowed the abuse of using old flood-data to assess tax-liability, which is mentioned in the decree of Ti. Iulius Alexander.[27] Nevertheless, carried out fairly, the annual inspection, *episkepsis*, could bring substantial reductions in the area of unflooded private land liable to tax. In one document, the reduction was 64%, from 140 to $50\frac{1}{4}$ arouras in one case; and 30%, from 123 arouras to 86, in another.[28]

Some concessions were also made to the difficulties of exploiting disused or inferior land. Disused arable land was reckoned to take three years to become fully yielding. Thus in AD 13/14, 19 arouras of confiscated land bought from the state were allowed a 3-year tax-immunity.[29] And in AD 140 three years' immunity was given for land bought at Karanis.[30] The revision of royal land which is *aphoros* takes place every three years in an early third-century code of tax-practice.[31] And in a Byzantine lease of AD 616, 5 arouras of dry land, leased alongside $12\frac{1}{2}$ arouras of seeded land, only start to pay rental in the fourth year.[32] Vines and fruit-trees received longer exemption than arable, five years in a late Ptolemaic document, and a further three years at reduced tax-rates. There are echoes of this outside Egypt in the five-to-ten year concessions in Hadrian's legislation about uncultivated land in Africa, in Dio's Euboean Oration, and in Herodian's report of a land-law of Pertinax.[33]

As a whole, the evidence gives the impression that tax-revenues were maintained as far as possible, sometimes even if crop-yields were inferior, and even if crop-rotation meant shortfalls in production. But the law also allowed some realistic concessions to the initial difficulties of exploiting disused land, and to the limited productivity of land with insufficient water.

7. TAX AS A PROPORTION OF GRAIN PRODUCTION

The composite wheat tax-rate for the Principate of 2.23 artabas (section 5 of Part A of this chapter) can be related to wheat-yield figures. The productivity

[26] BGU 1636 = Johnson, no. 312.
[27] Châlon 1964.
[28] Land in divisions 8 and 9 in *PBrux* 1, analysed by Westermann 1921.
[29] *POxy* 721; Johnson, no.87, p.158.
[30] *BGU* 422, Johnson, 151.
[31] *POxy* 2847.
[32] *PLond* II 483, from Westermann 1922, 29.
[33] *PTeb* 1.5, 93–8; Westermann 1925, 167; cf. Flach 1978 for the parallel African evidence.

of Egyptian grain-growing land is often taken as tenfold.[34] Rents in wheat, and wheat and money, in the Oxyrhynchite and Hermopolite nomes show median levels of 5 artabas of wheat or wheat-equivalent per aroura.[35] Since *mezzadria*, where the crop was shared equally with the tenant, was certainly less prevalent and thus less popular with landlords, the fixed rents paid instead presumably took at least half the expected net crop. Otherwise *mezzadria* would have seemed preferable, since the landlord normally had to pay the land-tax.[36] The median production suggested is thus 9 artabas per aroura or less (gross rent = 5 artabas; net rent = 4 artabas; net rent = at least half of net production).

Related to a conventional sowing quantity of 1 artaba per aroura, the gross revenue taken by tax in grain is approximately 25% (2.23/9) or 28% allowing for supplements (p. 48).[37] This result places Egypt in or above the upper bracket of land-based provincial tax-rates as defined by Hyginus, 20% instead of 14%. A late source, Orosius, describes Egypt as paying one-fifth (20%) of its harvests in tax.[38]

In schematic terms, relating state revenue from all sources solely to the land-tax base, Egypt's tax-rate is about 41% (Table 4.6: 32.4 million artabas of wheat equivalent/8.8 million arouras = 3.68). But some activities such as the luxury trade naturally brought more income than agriculture. The propertied class faced additional taxes such as a 5% inheritance tax, a 5% tax on slave manumission, and a 4% tax on slave-sales.[39]

In Africa Proconsularis, another prime grain-producer, the tax-rate on imperial or estate land in domain inscriptions of the second century is 33% (one-third of the grain and one-third of the fruits, after an initial tax-holiday of five to ten years).[40] This allows possible comparisons with Egyptian rates on ousiac land (a composite rate of 4.67 artabas per aroura under cultivation is shown in Table 4.1). But in this case, as with *prosodikos* land in Table 4.1, agricultural productivity may have been higher than the mean figure calculated above, making it difficult to assess tax in percentage terms.

---

[34] Crawford 1971, followed by Rathbone 1991, 243. Specific rates for sown plots on the Heroninos estate show a gross figure of $11\frac{1}{2}$ artabas per aroura (ibid.), but no summary of land sown and unsown on this estate has survived. Egyptian figures from the Napoleonic period may suggest a gross yield of approximately 12-fold; but even in traditional societies, agricultural practices may change over periods of thousands of years.

[35] Unpublished work by the author, supplementing Hennig 1967.

[36] Pliny, who decided to try *mezzadria* as an experiment, did so in a part of the empire where there was no land-tax (*Ep.* 9.37).

[37] Related to net yield after subtracting seed, the corresponding figure implied by a composite tax of 2.23 artabas per aroura is 24.8%. But where percentage taxes were applied, tax-liability appears to have been normally based on gross yields. In Egypt, tax-rates on grain land were normally at fixed amounts, not based on a percentage, and where the land was cultivated by a tenant, the seed was returnable separately from any stipulated payment of rent or tax (see e.g. *PLond* 256e = Johnson, no. 291).

[38] 1.8.9.

[39] Cf. Duncan-Jones 1990, 195.

[40] Kehoe 1988 and sources cited there.

8. CHANGE IN TAX-LEVELS

8.1. CHANGE DURING THE PRINCIPATE

Clumping of data often makes it difficult to interpret the chronology of tax-evidence of the Principate. The basic rate for private or catoecic land was essentially stable (Table 4.7 below). But tax-rates on crown land from different places show some tendency to increase.[41] At least two changes emerge from individual documents. They both belong to periods of acute fiscal strain following civil war, and both refer to public land.

In AD 71/2 the priests of Socnebtunis at Tebtunis in the Arsinoite nome complained that 200 artabas of barley had just been added to what they had to pay on the 500 arouras of crown land which they had been assigned, apparently under Augustus.[42] Barley being about $\frac{3}{5}$ of the value of wheat, the increase would be about $\frac{1}{4}$ artaba of wheat per aroura.[43] This is $\frac{1}{16}$ of the rental of about 4 artabas that crown land was typically paying by the second century; but the priests probably paid less on land assigned to them as an asset. The episode is more significant for its date than for its scale. It falls early in the reign of an Emperor who increased taxes in the empire in general and in Egypt in particular.[44]

The second case shows extra levies on public lands of about 200 arouras cultivated by a lady from Oxyrhynchus. Her long petition claims that the new tax was completely ruining her. The tax imposed by Aemilius Saturninus, prefect in AD 197 was the crown tax levied at 8 drachmas per aroura.[45] In wheat terms, its amount would have been about $\frac{1}{2}-\frac{2}{3}$ of an artaba per aroura.[46] The extra amount seems to be about twice that seen previously. In this case the context is again the aftermath of civil war, and a new Emperor in urgent need of funds.[47]

These examples show that taxes could be increased, and they both belong to times of obvious fiscal pressure. Hadrian's tax-concessions can be seen as complementary evidence, whose importance lies not so much in showing that taxes could be reduced, as in suggesting that some charges may already have been self-defeatingly high. Documents at the start of his reign show Hadrian allowing lessees of crown land to move to a much lower rent at approximately the rate for private land.[48] And less than twenty years later, after years of low

---

[41] Johnson, 483–4 n.1 followed by Wallace 1938, 339.
[42] *PTeb* 302 (Johnson, no. 52).
[43] For relative wheat and barley values, see *PTeb* 1, p.224.
[44] P. 12.
[45] *POxy* 899, 916, 1441, cf. Katzoff 1972, 268–9.
[46] Wheat prices by this date were probably 12–18 drachmas per artaba, Duncan-Jones 1990, 147.
[47] P. 15.
[48] The very big concession here may even illustrate some of the processes behind the erosion of the percentage of public land. Johnson no. 35, p.108; *PGiss* 4–7, *PLips Inv* n.266; *PBremen* 34; *PRyl* 96. Westermann 1925 explained the tax-reduction by damage caused by the Jewish revolt at the end of Trajan's reign. Although his nine examples all come from a single nome, Apollonopolis Heptakomias, the theory is not convincing. Hadrian's similar activity outside

flood, Hadrian allowed postponement of Egyptian money taxes for periods ranging from three to five years.[49]

9. CHANGE BETWEEN PRINCIPATE AND DOMINATE

The composite rate of grain-tax for the Principate can be compared with three rates from the Late Empire (Table 4.7).[50] The table suggests that tax-yields tended to fall. In the early fourth century the two rates shown for public land are 47% and 16% below the composite public rate calculated for the Principate (line 1). The rates for private land are 16% and 12% below the earlier figure. And in the sixth century, all land at Antaeopolis is taxed at low 'private' rates, and none at higher 'public' rates.

Table 4.7 *Early and late tax-rates in grain (artabas per aroura)*

	Aggregate rate	Public rate	Private rate	Date (AD)
1. Principate	2.23	4.098	1.292	(50/250)
2. Late Arsinoite	—	2.19	1.09	312
3. Late Oxyrhynchite	1.59	3.43	1.14	300/350
4. Late Antaeopolis	1.29	1.29	—	mid-c6

Notes: Lines 1 and 3: Aggregate rate based on specified large-scale areas containing land taxed at differing rates. In line 1, public and private rates are also composite (see Table 4.1)
Line 2: Arsinoite barley-payment of 0.9 artabas on public and private land converted at 5:3 ratio (*PTeb* 520) and added to payment in wheat.
Line 4: based on 47,276 arouras of grainland, taxed at 1.25 and 1.5 artabas.
Sources: Line 1, Table 4.1 and section 5 above; line 2, *PCair Isid* 11; line 3, *PMich Inv* 335 verso with Bagnall, Worp (1980); line 4, *PCair Masp* 67057 with A. H. M. Jones *JHS* 71, 1951, 271–2.

There are also some figures for vineland. In the Principate, a typical figure was 40 drachmas per aroura (Table 4.4, from Upper Egypt). In the late sixth century, rates of 4 and 8 carats per aroura are known at Aphrodito in the Thebaid.[51] In wheat terms, these rates are about 5 artabas for the Principate, and 1.7–3.4 for the later evidence (converting at 8 drachmas, and 2.4 carats per artaba). A clear fall is implied.

In the sixth century, global comparisons with the Principate also become

Egypt (his enormous concession over tax-debt made at this time) was evidently not a response to the Jewish revolt (Table 4.8).
[49] Johnson, no. 319, p. 522; *SB* 6944. The discount depended on locality, the south being given longest to pay.
[50] For comparisons between tax in early and late Empire, see also Jones 1974, 82–9, 179; MacMullen 1987.
[51] *PLond* 1674; Johnson, West 1949, 256–7.

possible. An important document published recently, probably written in AD 533/9, shows that the assessment in wheat levied by area fell by 18% at Antaeopolis after a census survey in 524.[52] This suggests shrinkage in cultivable area.[53] Dramatic shrinkage of cultivated area had already taken place by the fourth century in parts of the Arsinoite, because of decay of the irrigation system on which land in this nome heavily depended.[54]

At Antaeopolis, wheat for the *annona civilis*, intended for Constantinople, took 201,842 modii (61,674 artabas). In terms of the figure for Egypt as a whole of 8 million (artabas) in AD 539, that would give Antaeopolis $\frac{1}{130}$ of Egypt's total.[55] Its tax-revenue was about 110,861 artabas in wheat terms.[56] Thus if the proportion of tax for the *annona civilis* was consistent across the province, Egypt's total bill for government taxes would be some 14.378 million artabas of wheat-equivalent, apart from tolls and customs. This is 63%, or about two-thirds of the figure estimated for tax-revenue from agriculture under the Principate. The overall figure for the Principate is broadly comparable with Ptolemaic figures for Egypt's revenue (Appendix 4, p. 253).

Thus a decline in tax-revenue is implied by global extrapolations, by tax-rates for grain and vines, and by the size of the implied taxable area. A trend of this kind suggested by separate indexes is very difficult to dismiss. The late evidence predominantly comes from the sixth century, but there already appear to be substantial falls in tax-rates by the fourth century (Table 4.7).

Substantial decline in tax-yield may well imply over-taxation.[57] Excessive demands by tax-collectors are a glaring feature of Roman Sicily as Cicero describes it in the *Verrines*. The same is true of Egypt as shown by the edict of Ti. Iulius Alexander, and by the cases of depopulated villages that occur even

---

[52] Gascou 1989. This crucial document, with its summaries of the taxes of Antaeopolis at three different points in the sixth century, supplements and in some respects supersedes the slightly later account in *PCair Masp* 67057. It shows incidentally that West and Johnson's view that money taxes were high at the date of *PCair Masp* 67057 for purely short-term reasons cannot be correct (rejected by A. H. M. Jones in *JHS* 71 (1951) 271–2, but since revived). The current totals for Antaeopolis in this document are (Gascou 1989, 288): wheat, 223,863.66 modii; meat, 106,179.25 pounds; wine, 212,358 xestai; barley, 40,819.75 modii; straw, 83,600.25 capita; money, 862.16 solidi. For two sets of corresponding totals earlier in the sixth century, see Gascou 1990, 99. The similar comparisons for Aphroditopolis by Rémondon involve disputed datings (Gascou 1990, 98).

[53] One effect of taxation on Egypt in the Ottoman period was shrinkage in the cultivated area, which the authorities attempted to meet by reducing units of land-measurement in order to preserve the tax-yield (Shaw 1962, 72).

[54] Bagnall 1985. In the Arsinoite, this was associated with progressive desiccation in an area which depended heavily on artificial irrigation.

[55] Converting tax modii to tax artabas at $3\frac{3}{11}$:1 (Gascou 1989, 288; the crucial document is *PCair Isid* 11 of AD 312: see Duncan-Jones 1976B, 56 and n.7). Justinian: *Edict* 13.8, AD 539.

[56] Converting modii to artabas as before, and converting barley at $\frac{2}{3}$ wheat, wine at 4 xestai per modius of wheat, meat at 4 pounds per modius of wheat, and straw at 4 capita per modius (Gascou 1989, 307). Money is converted at 10 artabas of wheat per solidus: *POxy* 1909.

[57] See Jones 1974, 82–9. For the phenomenon in general, compare the finding of the Napoleonic mission in Egypt that at least a quarter of tax-revenue went to those who collected it (Shaw 1962, 75).

in the first century.[58] From local knowledge, Philo describes a tax- collector in Egypt who impoverished and terrorised the taxpayers.[59] Cicero's dossiers suggest that under Verres Roman tithe-collectors even took more for themselves than they left for the state.[60] Roman governors notoriously enriched themselves in many cases in the late Republic, and they still had some tendency to do so under the Principate.[61]

B. TAX REVIEWS AND TAX-REMISSIONS

1. THE FIFTEEN-YEAR CYCLE

Impressive though a synopsis of the revenues of a large province may seem, in fact tax-collection was inefficient, and each tax-period brought arrears to be pursued or written off. From the very start of the Empire, Emperors granted tax-remissions, beginning in 31 BC with remission of tax-liabilities from before the battle of Actium.[62] Hadrian prided himself on writing off more tax-debt than any of his predecessors (Table 4.8).[63] Julian at one point suspended the practice, after discovering that it helped the rich, who could postpone payment, but not the poor, who had to pay up promptly.[64]

The timetable of tax-reviews was formalised and regular, more so than has been generally understood. The first century tax-changes after Augustus mostly fall on dates which correspond to the fifteen-year tax-cycle of the second century (Table 4.8). Co-ordinates from the two sources not only support each other, but they also agree with the numbered indiction-cycles that began in AD 312 (see Table 4.8).[65] All three sets of data show the same termini for the start of the cycle.[66] This means that the fifteen-year cycle went back

---

[58] Lewis 1983, 164, cf. 68, 108. Châlon 1964; MacMullen 1987, 740.

[59] de spec.leg. 3.159–62. Compare Plutarch's account of atrocities by tax-gatherers in Asia in the late Republic (Lucull. 120–2). [60] Jones 1974, 120–1.

[61] Jones 1974, 117–19; Brunt 1990, 53–95. For a case under Augustus, Velleius writing as a contemporary states that Quinctilius Varus found Syria a rich province, and left it a poor one (2.117.2).

[62] Dio 53.2.3: but tax-arrears secured on house-property were allowed to stand.

[63] MacMullen suggests that as the phrasing of Hadrian's inscription (ILS 309) refers to benefiting cives, the taxes concerned must have been special taxes paid only by citizens. But if that is true, the amount of HS900 million in the inscription is enormously high, almost certainly too high to support the interpretation (MacMullen 1987, 741n.). [64] Ammianus 16.5.15.

[65] This was 13 fifteen-year cycles after Hadrian's tax-remission in AD 118 (tax-year 117/18), eleven cycles after the remission of Antoninus Pius in AD 147 (tax-year 147/8), and nine cycles after the remission of Marcus Aurelius in AD 178 (tax-year 177/8; see Table 4.8). For a table of indiction-cycles and indiction years from 312, see Kubitschek 1928, 107.

[66] This allows for the fact that Roman years bridge two years of the Christian era. The starting point of the system is evidently early. The Chronicon Paschale, probably written in the early seventh century AD, makes the first year of Julius Caesar, 49 BC, the starting point both of the Antiochene era (Downey 1961, 157–8), and of the fifteen-year indiction-cycle (Chron. Pasch. Dindorff 355,4; see Stauffenberg 1931, 112 ff.). 48 BC would fit the known fifteen-year cycle; 49 BC is one year too early. The Chronicon date might be imprecise, or civil war after Caesar's death might have upset the sequence. Augustus's first two censuses, in 28 and 8 BC, belong to the lustral cycle visible later on, and thus they do not support the Chronicon date of 49 BC. The

Table 4.8 *The fifteen-year tax-cycle and tax-events, AD 41–180*

Cycle date	Date of tax-event	Nature of event	Source
1. [42/3]	42	Board of 3 praetors set up to pursue tax-arrears	Dio 60.10.4
2. [57/8]	57 and 58	Nero's tax-proposals, tax-reforms and remissions of indirect taxes	Tac. *Ann.* 13.31; 50–1
3. [72/3]	73–4	Census of Italy	*PIR*² 3, p. 182
4. [87/8]		?	
5. [102/3]		?	
6. 117/18	118	Tax-arrears of HS0.9 billion written off	*ILS* 309; Jerome, Helm p. 415 h; Dio 69.8.1; *HA Had.*7. 6
7. 132/3	133	(Tax-arrears written off)	Dio 71.32.2
8. 147/8	147	Tax-arrears written off	*Chron. Pasch.* (*Chron. Min. I,* p. 224)
9. 162/3		?	
10. 177/8	178	Remission of tax-debts 60 years after Hadrian's remission	Dio 71.32.2; *Chron.a.354* (*Chron. Min. I,* p. 147); Jerome (Helm p. 207); Helm p. 423, 207f

Notes AD **102** Trajan made a tax-remission, assigned however to AD **106** by Jerome (Helm); this event is shown in a famous relief in Rome, Torelli 1982, 89–118.
AD **118** Hadrian's remission was explicitly described in an inscription as the biggest made so far. AD 117/18 was the only year when the starting-dates of the fifteen-year cycle and the Egyptian fourteen-year tax-cycle coincided (for the Egyptian dates, see Hombert, Préaux 1952).
AD **132/3** The remission in 178 (line 10) was explicitly made for forty-five years, not including the fifteen of Hadrian (Dio), implying that another remission had taken place forty-five years earlier in 132/3.
AD **178** This date from Jerome and other chroniclers is confirmed by the sixty-Ayear interval indicated by Dio (see note on AD 132/3).

much further than Diocletian, and makes it a long-standing feature of imperial taxation, not an innovation of the Late Empire.[67]

2. THE FOURTEEN-YEAR CYCLE

In Egypt, the tax-cycle was slightly different, being based on an interval of fourteen years. This lasted at least until AD 257/8. The Egyptian poll tax started from age fourteen, and required a fresh scrutiny of the population every fourteen years.[68]

In Egypt as at Rome, the time for tax-initiatives was the beginning of the cycle. Thus in AD 89, the prefect of Egypt produced an edict requiring registration of property and loans at Oxyrhynchus within six months.[69] At the start of the next Egyptian cycle, in AD 103, the prefect ordered the record-office at Arsinoe to be relocated and rebuilt, acting on a report from the local procurator.[70] One cycle later, in AD 117/18, Hadrian made a major tax-concession to some holders of crown land in Egypt.[71] At this point the Egyptian and Roman cycle-dates happened to coincide, and Hadrian's response for the empire as a whole was an enormous remission of tax-debt (Table 4.8, line 6). The fifteen-year cycle probably had some repercussion in Egypt even when the cycles were out of phase. Thus in AD 72 (Table 4.8, line 3), an edict was issued at Oxyrhynchus requiring the registration of contracts.[72]

3. FIVE-YEAR CYCLES

A few further traces of tax-cycles can be seen. The five-year *lustrum* fitted exactly into the fifteen-year cycle, and Augustus's first two censuses in 28 and 8 BC, together with Claudius's census in AD 47/8 all fall on the dates of this cycle.[73] For the next lustral year, AD 52/3, Tacitus reports as many as five tax-concessions: Ilium, Rhodes and Cos gained tax-immunity, while Byzantium and Apamea received five-year remissions.[74] Similarly, AD 62 (lustral year 62/3) was the year when a commission of three consulars was appointed to review public revenues. One of their tasks was revising the customs-law of

---

first Augustan census in 28 BC took place one *lustrum* after a fifteen-year 'cycle-date' in 33/32 BC, and the second in 8 BC fell two *lustra* after a 'cycle-date' in 18/17 BC (RG 8).

[67] For long-term continuity in other features of taxation, see Duncan-Jones 1990, chapter 13.

[68] Hombert, Préaux 1952. The first census in the fourteen-year cycle belongs to AD 33/4, but for census declarations as early as AD 11/12 and 12/13, cf. Rathbone 1993, 89–90.

[69] *POxy* 237, Johnson, 268.   [70] *SB* 7378, Johnson, 638.   [71] Westermann 1925.

[72] *POxy* 238, Johnson, no.441, p.709. The tabulation of poll-tax payments for the previous 3 years recorded in the Heracleopolite nome in AD 28/9 falls 1 year after the start of a fifteen-year tax-cycle (*POxy* 2412).

[73] N.66 above; Tac. *Ann.* 11.25. The censorship was held for eighteen months, thus bridging two twelve-month periods.   [74] *Ann.* 12.58; 61; 62–3.

Asia, whose text has now been discovered.[75] The start of a tax-period was the obvious moment for redefining tax-obligations, since some taxes were still leased out for five-year periods. Another general abolition of tax-debt is reported in AD 218 (the corresponding lustral year is 217/18, eight *lustra* after Marcus Aurelius's remission).[76] Domitian early in his reign dispensed taxpayers from tax-debt if it went back to a previous *lustrum* ('ante quinquennium proximum').[77]

An inscription from Rome names the lessee of some granaries as the 'conductor lustri tertii'. This perhaps meant the third segment of a fifteen-year cycle.[78] The cycle-number is not specified, but this omission is echoed in most indiction-year dates from the Late Empire. Another Rome inscription which shows 'ministri lustri secundi' refers either to the tax-cycle, or to a collegiate calendar of some kind.[79] Finally, the record of a tax-farmer at Savaria in Pannonia in 'ann(o) XII' may refer to the twelfth year of a fifteen-year tax-cycle.[80]

Five-year tax-periods and a fourteen-year tax-cycle could not be kept in phase with each other, but the two co-existed in Egypt nevertheless.[81] The prefect who required the registration of property at Oxyrhynchus in AD 89, an Egyptian cycle-date which was out of phase with the *lustra* at Rome, nevertheless stipulated a revision of the lists every five years.[82] And in a second-century list of registration-fees for newly acquired land in the Arsinoite, one category paid a fee 'up to the second census-term of five years'.[83]

In Egypt, fourteen-year intervals had apparently been abandoned by AD 287, 30 years after the last Egyptian census known under the old system.[84] Five-year *lustra* now emerge more clearly in Egyptian practice, and the co-ordinates become those used in other parts of the empire. *Lustra* in Egypt are known to have run for four terms from 287/8 to 301/2.[85] The prefect of Egypt issued his edict about the revision of tax-liabilities in his province at the start of a fifteen-year cycle in AD 297, and he followed earlier practice in using

---

[75] Tac. *Ann.* 15.18; Engelmann, Knibbe 1989, ll.1-7, 144-9; cf. Heil 1991. For dates of other initiatives belonging to lustral years seen in this law, see Eck 1990, 140-1: the years include 72 BC, 17 BC, 12 BC, 2 BC, AD 19, AD 57 and AD 62.

[76] *Consularia Constantinopolitana, Chron. Min.* I 226. But AD 218, like AD 117, was an accession year, and as such a time for expansive gestures.

[77] Suet. *Dom.* 9.2.

[78] *CIL* VI 9471.

[79] *CIL* VI 30982.

[80] *AE* 1968, 423.

[81] For mismatch in the later Empire, note the co-existence of the fifteen-year indiction-cycle with a four-year cycle for the collection of *chrysargyron* (cf. Delmaire 1989, 358).

[82] *POxy* 237.

[83] *PIand* 137; Johnson, no.335, p.583.

[84] The new system is first attested exactly thirty years (six *lustra*) after the last extant glimpse of the old one, possibly suggesting that a quinquennial system may have begun after AD 257/8. Documentation in the period AD 260-85 is sparse (cf. Duncan-Jones 1990, 58 fig.14, 168 n.72).

[85] Thomas 1978.

the start of the cycle as the moment for tax-reviews.[86] At the beginning of the next cycle, in AD 312, the well-known system of yearly indictions explicitly numbered one to fifteen was introduced in the empire at large.[87] This system had certainly begun in Egypt by AD 314.

4. CONCLUSION

The Empire's tax-system can be seen as detailed and elaborate. There were regular reviews, with readjustments or reforms at the beginning, and reconciliation of accounts at the end. The level of taxation appears relatively high from the example of Egypt, perhaps partly because of its high proportion of public land with heavier rents. In practice, tax-receipts regularly fell below target, and unpaid taxes might be written off at the end of the tax-cycle. Even so, the amount extracted from the taxpayers probably exceeded the official target by a substantial margin in many cases. The system of collection was always open to abuse, even where tax collection was not farmed out, and many vivid examples show intermediaries taking too much from the taxpayer. The long-term drop in revenue in Egypt over a period of centuries may reflect the drain on the taxpayer of the way tax was collected, as well as the tendency for heavy taxes to drive marginal land out of cultivation.

[86] *PCair Isid.* 1. Something in the Diocletianic tax-changes in Egypt left Egyptians with grievances which were still being pursued in the courts almost seventy years later. Ammianus writes that in order to be rid of this litigation, Julian moved the adjudication to Chalcedon, and debarred ships from carrying Egyptians (22.6.1–4).

[87] *Chron Pasch.* cf. Bagnall, Worp 1978; in Egypt this was briefly preceded by a system using indictions numbered one to five, based on the lustral cycle (Thomas 1978).

PART II

THE COIN-EVIDENCE

5

COIN-HOARDS AND THEIR ORIGIN

'abite, inquit, laeti, abite locupletes'

('Go away happy, go away rich', the Emperor Caligula addressing his troops;
Suetonius, *Gaius* 46).

1. INTRODUCTION

Roman hoards have usually been seen as cross-sections of coin in ordinary
private ownership, either drawn from current circulation ('circulation' hoards)
or accumulated over an extended period ('savings' hoards). Although this
dual classification remains widespread, its validity has been questioned, and it
does not seem to fit the hundreds of precious-metal hoards from the
Principate.[1] Analysis of this evidence instead suggests a specialised and
artificial origin.

The present survey uses a very large sample of substantial precious-metal
hoards between 31 BC and AD 235.[2] They come from an enormous area, which

---

Note: The discussion of coin-evidence concentrates on coin-hoards, because relatively little
precious-metal coin from stray finds has been published. For some stray-find data, see Table 5.1
below, and Table 8.1. Bronze coin had too low a denominational value to contribute
substantially to the volume of money in circulation (p. 169). For bronze hoards, see n.2 below.

[1] Crawford 1969A, 76 n.1. See also Reece 1987A, 61. For a hoard to be safely classified as a savings
hoard, the identification needs to show: (1) that the contents differ substantially from those of
the typical circulation hoard; and (2) that the differences cannot be plausibly explained by
unevenness in the circulation pattern. Such demonstrations are difficult, and however
widespread buried private savings hoards may once have been, the overwhelming majority of
hoards surviving from this period do not seem to belong to this category (see below).

[2] The need for a full-scale collection of Roman hoards of the Principate with thorough analysis
and tabulation of material still remains pressing. The present sample, based on an extensive
search, is limited to gold and silver hoards from 31 BC–AD 235 dated by reign and above HS400 in
face-value. For hoards of eastern silver, see p. 74 below. Large bronze hoards are too few to
show any detailed chronology, but see pp. 132n and 186–90 below. The 230 precious-metal
hoards in the main sample are listed below in Appendix 10 and cited by number in the text. For
hoards cited by name, see Index p. 285. Appendix 10 serves the limited purpose of describing
economic data, and is not meant as a primary numismatic repertoire. The other material used
includes 66 coin-finds from Pompeii (section 3 below); 72 smaller hoards from different parts of
the empire (Appendix 6); 16 tetradrachm hoards from Egypt (pp. 90–2 below); and, as samples
of evidence from beyond the frontier, 28 denarius hoards from Moldavia and 18 from Little
Poland (pp. 92–4 below).

The main sample is based on regional hoard-lists; on the overviews provided by Bolin,
Mihailescu and Carradice; on material in coin-hoard journals; and on the computer database
edited by Michael Crawford, as well as on various scattered publications of individual hoards.

stretches from Hadrian's Wall to Upper Egypt, and from Portugal to eastern Syria (Table 5.2).[3] Roman hoards survive from an even bigger area, but hoards from beyond the frontier have been considered separately.[4] Any find of more than one or two coins can be called a hoard. But for most serious purposes, a sampling minimum is necessary, and the threshold of 100 denarii adopted here should eliminate some cases of incomplete survival.[5]

2. SIZE-CLUSTERS

Conclusions about hoard-size cannot always be pressed very far, because recovery may be incomplete, and some reported totals may be inexact.[6] Nevertheless, any large-scale sample is worth examining for signs of patterning. This reveals a number of size-clusters.

At the bottom of the scale, five gold hoards have a face value below HS1400. Four have the identical value of HS500. The smallest silver hoards show some tendency to cluster round values of 550, 600, 700 and 800 sesterces (fig. 5.1). In the hoards as a whole, there are noticeable clusters at 1,500, 1,600 and 1,800 sesterces (fig. 5.2). Higher up the scale, four hoards cluster at 13,000 ($\pm$ 1%). Near the top of the scale, the gold hoards between 20,000 and 35,000 concentrate around 20,000 and 30,000 sesterces (fig. 5.3). Finally, at the very top of the scale, the four largest hoards consist of two doublets, one of 1,200 aurei, and one of 1,600.[7] Further obvious stereotyping of hoard-size can be seen in regional averages (p. 75).

3. DENOMINATIONS

Nine out of ten hoards in the present sample contain only one denomination, either aurei or denarii.[8] This is a complete contrast to the pattern of coin in

---

[3] The aggregate value of the 230 hoards from inside the empire is almost HS2 million (HS1,991,444). The silver total (HS518,144, including silver in mixed hoards) is three times larger than the corresponding sample in Bolin's list, which omits Julio-Claudian hoards, but includes hoards from outside the empire, and hoards below 100 denarii, categories omitted here. A big gold hoard from Belgium, Appendix 10 no.59, is studied here from photographs and weight-lists provided by Dr A.M. Burnett. To his kind help I also owe advance knowledge of the definitive large-scale survey of Romano-British hoards by A.S. Robertson. Shortage of evidence means that reigns of less than three years are omitted from most analyses below (Galba, Otho, Vitellius, Titus, Nerva, Pertinax, Didius Julianus, Macrinus). The reign of Caligula, with no hoards in this sample, is also omitted.

[4] See chapter 6, section 3. External hoards sometimes show different chronological concentrations (and, in the hinterland of the empire, little gold coin in this period).

[5] Bolin's threshold is much lower, 20 denarii. Any threshold is arbitrary, but some hoards well below 100 denarii may be the product of incomplete survival, and a source of misleading information about size. For anomalous results thrown up by samples of very small hoards, compare Mihailescu, 109. As a control, some hoards below 100 denarii are also considered separately (see Appendix 6).

[6] Where there are several hundred coins, exact round figures for hoards not described in detail can be suspicious.   [7] Appendix 10 nos. 49, 51, 57, 61.

[8] 151 (65%) are silver, 61 (27%) gold, and 18 (8%) a mixture of the two (N = 230). The tiny amounts of bronze coin present in a few silver hoards are not enough to change this picture (e.g.

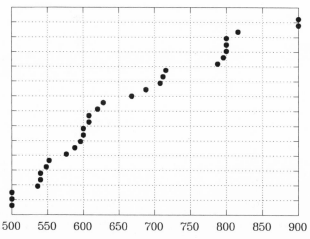

Figure 5.1 Concentrations of precious-metal hoards, HS500–900 (Appendix 10).

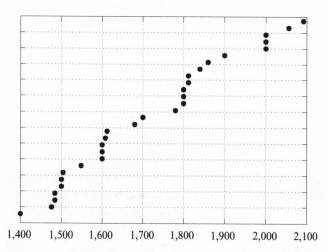

Figure 5.2 Concentrations of precious-metal hoards, HS1,450–2,000 (Appendix 10).

private possession. Pompeii has left many cross-sections of the money carried by inhabitants on 24 August AD 79 when Vesuvius erupted.[9] They typically had coin in two or three metals.[10] Evidently then as now, few people organised

1 sestertius and 1 as in the Bristol hoard of 1,478 denarii, Appendix 10 no.198; 2 asses in the Verona hoard of 2,804 denarii and 2 aurei, Appendix 10 no.72).

[9] For other monetary survivals from the Vesuvius eruption of AD 79, see also the important Boscoreale gold hoard (Canessa 1909).

[10] Out of 66 Pompeian coin-finds (almost all from Breglia 1950), 52 (82%) have a mixture of at least two metals (gold, silver and bronze 32%, silver and bronze 26%, gold and silver 24%). Coin-finds mostly accompany corpses at Pompeii, or come from houses and bars (see Bolin, 85–6). Pompeii is much the biggest source of samples of coin in current use, but other finds

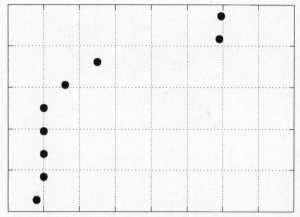

18,000 20,000 22,000 24,000 26,000 28,000 30,000 32,000 34,000

Figure 5.3 Concentrations of gold hoards, HS18,000–34,000 (Appendix 10).

their affairs to the point where all their cash was in one denomination.[11] Thus these patterns of private coin-ownership are different from the single-denomination hoards in the main sample.

The different types of hoard show clearly marked patterns. Gold hoards, making up less than 27% of the hoard total, contribute almost three-quarters of the total face value. Gold hoards become fewer as the period progresses. But by face value, the cumulated figure for gold rises from a low point under the Julio-Claudians to a running figure between 67% and 77% from the Flavians onwards (fig. 5.4). The quotient reached by the end of the period is 74%, including gold from mixed hoards.

The sampling threshold of 100 denarii might be a source of distortion in the hoard calculation. Below this threshold, denarii may outstrip aurei in value. But in practice very small hoards seem to account for too little coin to affect the gold:silver ratio significantly. As a trial, silver hoards below 100 denarii in Bolin's sample were added to the rest of his denarius sample for the period AD

show the use of coin in more than one denomination. Two small finds of money on corpses, apparently casualties of the battle of Lugdunum in AD 197, show a mixture of metals, suggesting that the coin in the hands of soldiers from day to day might be as mixed as that of civilians. *CTMAF* 5.1, p.63 (Lyon, first *arrondissement*; and St Didier au Mont d'Or). Personal money was also found near the corpses of Roman soldiers killed in the last assault on Dura after AD 256 (Bellinger 1949, 187: 82 coins found on corpses in the counter-mine by Tower 19). In a Greek parallel, the contents of Lysias's strong-box when suddenly impounded by the Thirty were again a mixture: the coin consisted of 3 (Athenian) talents, 400 cyzicenes, and 100 Persian darics (Lysias 12.11).

[11] Changing denominations could be expensive. In Cicero *Verr.* 4.181 Verres is criticised for having charged 'collybus' where only one denomination was in use; see also *OGIS* 484 (an imperial letter at Pergamum regulating the conversion-price between asses and denarii, presumably Hadrianic: see Macro 1976; Buttrey 1991). In Roman Egypt, *prosdiagraphomenon* was a standard charge levied on the taxpayer to take account of assessment in fictive Ptolemaic currency (Wallace 1938, s.v. *prosdiagraphomenon*; Gara 1976).

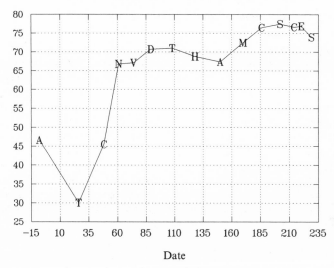

Figure 5.4 Cumulated percentage value of gold coin in precious-metal hoards from Augustus to Severus Alexander (Appendix 10). (Symbol: Emperor's initial.)

69–235.[12] This increased the face value by only 6.4%.[13] A corresponding adjustment applied to the figures above would reduce the overall gold percentage from 74 to 72.8%. But small gold finds would offset this difference. Thus there is little sign that including the smallest hoards would have a significant effect.[14]

The predominance of gold in the hoards in terms of face value is quite clear. It can be compared with other evidence. Returning to Pompeii, finds there show gold as 71.1% of face value for gold and silver (69% for all coin).[15] This is very close to the gold quotient in the main sample of gold and silver hoards.

Stray finds provide a third set of indications about the importance of gold. Some results are shown in Table 5.1. In three samples the quotient for gold approximates 70% in face value (lines 1, 3 and 5). Of the remaining two samples, one depends on the survival of as few as 8 gold coins (line 4). In SW Germany, pre-Severan coin in line 1 conforms to the main result, but the inclusion of Severan coin (line 2) reduces the gold quotient to 53%. Thus the two big samples investigated, the hoards and the Pompeii finds, and most of the scattered finds in Table 5.1 show a gold quotient of approximately 70% in terms of value.

---

[12] Bolin's sample starts in AD 69 and his threshold is 20 denarii.
[13] Of hoards of specified value, 72 totalled 100 denarii or more, and 57 99 denarii or less.
[14] Any practical adjustment would need to include gold hoards below the size threshold, of which there is no convenient list.
[15] Data from Breglia 1950, with Pozzi 1958–9. The total value appears to be HS79,425, with gold worth HS54,806, silver HS22,307 and bronze (under-represented in Breglia's listings, which exclude finds below a certain value) HS2,312.

Table 5.1 *The face-value of gold as a proportion of gold and silver in stray finds*
(amounts in sesterces)

Region	Date	Gold	Silver	Percentage gold
1. SW Germany	31 BC–AD 192	8,500	3,408	71.4
2. SW Germany	31 BC–AD 235	8,900	7,800	53.3
3. SE Alpine	31 BC–AD 192	2,900	1,360	68.1
4. Carnuntum	31 BC–AD 192	800	1,800	30.8
5. DDR	31 BC–AD 235	800	368	68.5

Sources: 1 and 2. Christ 1960; 3. Kos 1986 (Emona, Poetovio, Neviodunum and Slovenia); 4. *FMRÖ* 3.1, 1976; 5. Laser 1980.

4. CHRONOLOGY AND DATING

The hoard-sample shows some stereotyping by date as well as by size. For example, both hoards worth 300 aurei ($\pm 1\%$) belong to the reign of Marcus Aurelius.[16] The two gold hoards of between 360 and 380 aurei end in adjacent years, AD 165 and 166. Two of the four hoards of 5 aurei belong to adjacent years, AD 74 and 75, and come from the same province.[17] Two of the four gold hoards between 70 and 75 aurei belong to the reign of Domitian (73 and 75 aurei).[18] When added to the size-clusters already noted, these suggest a non-random pattern.

Similarly, the chronological variations within the sample are too great to suggest that they are the product of any obvious natural pattern (fig. 5.5). For example, the fourteen years of Nero's reign yield only two hoards, compared with the nine from the preceding thirteen-year reign.[19] Even more striking is the tripling of frequency under Marcus Aurelius.[20] The average declines after Marcus. But it remains very high under Commodus, and is still above mid-second century levels at the end of the period. In terms of value, the hoards increase under Marcus by as much as eightfold, rising even further under Commodus (fig. 5.6). A still higher peak is briefly generated under Elagabalus.

5. GEOGRAPHICAL DISTRIBUTION

A simple geographical pattern is obvious. In general, the heavily garrisoned regions produce more major hoards than other regions. Thus in the West,

[16] Appendix 10 nos. 41, 48.   [17] Appendix 10 nos. 38, 39; 14, 15 (both from Britain).
[18] Appendix 10 nos. 16, 17.   [19] Appendix 10 nos. 11, 63; 4–10, 92–3.
[20] Appendix 10 nos. 38-48; 71–6; 134–64.

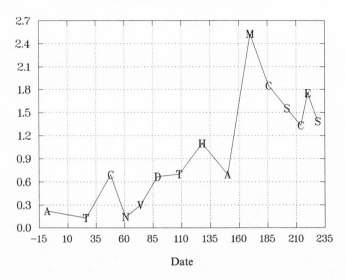

Figure 5.5 Average number of precious-metal hoards per reign-year, Augustus to Severus Alexander (Appendix 10). (Symbol: Emperor's initial.)

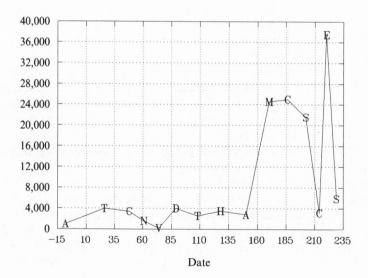

Figure 5.6 Average value in sesterces of precious-metal hoards per reign-year, Augustus to Severus Alexander (Appendix 10). (Symbol: Emperor's initial.)

Table 5.2 *Regional summary of hoard-sample*
(threshold value HS400)

	Britain	West Continent	Italy	Danube	East
Hoard total	41	75	14	83	17
Percentage	17.7	32.5	6.1	35.9	7.4
Sum (HS)	91,900	1,260,964	134,560	294,920	209,100
Percentage	4.6	63.3	6.8	14.8	10.5
Median value (HS)	1,186	4,492	7,064	1,900	3,132
Mean value (HS)	2,242	16,813	9,611	3,553	12,300

Note: The five-zone classification is an elaboration of Bolin's division into four zones. West Continent includes Gaul, Germany, Spain; Danube also includes Balkans (Roman areas of Austria, Hungary, Yugoslavia, Bulgaria, Romania); East includes all Greek-speaking provinces (the one very small hoard from Latin North Africa is also counted here).

frontier zones such as Britain and the Danube provinces typically show much hoard material; while inner regions of the empire such as Africa and Italy offer rather little, despite much greater urbanisation and plentiful archaeological survivals. Some regional differences can be seen in Table 5.2.

Linking hoards to other forms of bulk evidence again yields obvious contrasts. For example, in a province where non-military inscriptions number tens of thousands, as in Africa, reported hoards are very few.[21] But they are quite common in a province such as Britain, where civilian inscriptions are scarce.[22] In the East, overall patterns are less clear, because of the shortage of published evidence. But Egypt, where army detachments were relatively numerous, has left a significant number of hoards, possibly more than in the larger and more urban provinces of Asia.[23]

Size and denomination also show significant geographical contrasts (Tables 5.3 and 5.4). Significant regional differences in hoard-value are seen in Table 5.3. The West Continent and the Danube provide the biggest samples, making up over two-thirds of the evidence (N = 75 and 83). They show the median value of gold hoards as 7 or 4 times that of silver (7.1 and 4.1). The ratio in Italy is comparable (6.2), but it is much lower in Britain (1.8).

[21] Hoards are more numerous in North Africa in the fourth century: see Salama, Callu 1990.
[22] A total of 1,000 dated Romano-British hoards has been quoted (Robertson 1956, 262). Most of them end after AD 235, many are below the present size-threshold, and many depend on imprecise early reports.
[23] For Egypt, see Christiansen 1985 with Kunisz 1983, and chapter 6, section 2 below. In the rest of the eastern Mediterranean, reporting of hoard-finds seems to be more limited.

Table 5.3 *Analysis of hoards by region*
(amounts in sesterces)

Region (zone)	Gold	Silver	Mixed	Gold/Silver	All hoards
Britain (A)					
Median	2,100	1,144	2,232	1.8	1,186
Mean	5,175	1,847	2,417	—	2,242
Sum	20,700	59,116	12,084	—	91,900
Hoards	4	32	5	—	41
West Continent (B)					
Median	12,900	1,812	2,916	7.1	4,492
Mean	29,035	5,285	3,263	—	16,813
Sum	1,074,300	163,820	22,844	—	1,260,964
Hoards	37	31	7	—	75
Italy (C)					
Median	7,400	1,200	6,828	6.2	7,064
Mean	11,550	9,106	6,576	—	9,611
Sum	69,300	45,532	19,728	—	134,560
Hoards	6	5	3	—	14
Danube (D)					
Median	7,300	1,812	14,600	4.1	1,900
Mean	10,500	2,489	14,600	—	3,553
Sum	84,000	181,720	29,200	—	294,920
Hoards	8	73	2	—	83
East (E)					
Median	13,000	1,170	4,268	11.1	3,132
Mean	30,600	2,123	4,268	—	12,300
Sum	183,600	21,232	4,268	—	209,100
Hoards	6	10	1	—	17
Aggregate					
Median	10,000	1,480	3,588	6.8	2,310
Mean	23,474	3,104	4,896	—	8,658
Sum	1,431,900	471,420	88,124	—	1,991,444
Hoards	61	151	18	—	230

Table 5.4 shows two more striking contrasts. The first is a 'North/South' difference in the frequency of gold hoards. In Britain and the Danube, the main frontier regions, gold hoards are rare, about 1 in 10. But in Italy, the East and the West Continent, they are 1 in 3 or 1 in 2. In contrast to this, the gold percentage of face value in mixed hoards (N = 18) is high in frontier regions and low elsewhere: 56% in Britain and the Danube combined, compared with 11% in the West Continent and Italy combined, on median average.

Table 5.4 *The regional incidence of gold coin in hoards*

Region (Zone)	Gold hoards as percentage of hoard numbers	Gold coin in hoards (including mixed hoards) as a percentage of face value in present hoard sample
Britain (A)	10	28.5
West Continent (B)	49	85.4
Italy (C)	43	53.7
Danube (D)	10	37.5
East (E)	35	89.8

Stereotyping of hoard-size is also clearly seen here. Broadly speaking, the five zones show only three median values for gold hoards, and only two for silver. The median amounts for gold are 2,100 in Britain, 7,350 in Italy and the Danube ($\pm$ 1%), and 12,950 in the West Continent and the East ($\pm$ 0.5%). For silver, the levels are 1,170 in Britain, Italy and the East ($\pm$ 3%), and 1,812 in both the Danube area and the West Continent. Thus the size-stereotyping already noted also emerges quite definitely from the regional evidence (p. 68). It is suggested once more in the median averages for silver hoards by period: HS1,200 (31 BC–AD 96); HS1,204 (96–161); HS1,324 (161–92); HS2,000 (193–235).

A further striking feature is the relatively under-privileged position of Britain. Its gold hoards are few and small (Table 5.4). Elsewhere they are several times bigger: the multiples of the British median level are Italy and the Danube 3.5, and the West Continent and the East about 6.15. British silver hoards are at the bottom of the range, though the differences are smaller. For precious metal hoards as a whole, the hierarchy shows Britain as 1, the Danube as 1.6, the East as 2.6, the West Continent as 3.8, and Italy as 6.0 (indexing the median figures in Table 5.3).

Stray finds may also imply lack of gold coin in Britain. A recent survey shows some 150 aurei from Britain in this period, compared with over 1,000 from Gaul.[24] These features seem to suggest a relatively limited official input of gold into Britain. Access to gold through market exchange was not helped by Britain's geographical isolation.[25]

---

[24] 151 aurei of the period 31 BC–AD 235 in Britain, compared with 1,036 from Gallia Narbonensis, Aquitania, Lugdunensis, and Belgica (Callu, Loriot 1992, 26, giving further summaries for Spain, Raetia, Noricum, Venetia-Histria and the Agri Decumates). But this ratio is probably affected by fuller searching of French antiquarian sources. The period of deposit in Britain is also substantially shorter than in Gaul, only starting systematically with the Claudian invasion in AD 43. The Gallic finds are described in detail in Callu, Loriot 1990 (for Raetia, see Loriot 1988).

[25] These differences show themselves despite the fact that gold was being mined at Dolaucothi in Wales under the Empire (Frere 1987, 276).

6. EXISTING THEORIES

The findings so far can be summarised briefly.

1. The hoard-sample displays clear signs of patterning by size and by date (sections 2, 3 and 5).
2. The chronological series shows very marked peaks and troughs. Because the sample is spread over a very large part of the empire, trying to explain its overall contrasts by local events is generally unconvincing.
3. The hoards usually contain one denomination, in contrast to the spread of denominations in ordinary private coin-holdings (section 3).

Existing interpretations tend to assume that surviving Roman hoards represent either assets buried for casual reasons, or assets buried urgently at times of military upheaval.[26] But a steady-state process of casual accumulation hardly explains a dating pattern with substantial gaps (section 3), still less a pattern with stereotyped amounts and clusters at particular dates (sections 2 and 3).

The diagnosis based on warfare and unrest faces equal difficulties. It does not explain why hoards show stereotyping by size and denomination (sections 3 and 5).[27] And even if one cluster of hoard-burials near the Rhine and Danube frontiers broadly coincides with the Marcomannic invasions under Marcus Aurelius, the contemporary hoards in parts of the empire not exposed to the Marcomanni can hardly be explained in this way.[28] Interpreting hoards as a barometer of insecurity becomes even less convincing when its logic argues more insecurity under Claudius than under Nero or Vespasian, and more under Hadrian than under Trajan or Antoninus Pius (fig. 5.5).

7. A DIFFERENT INTERPRETATION

In Italy the hoard-pattern shows a prime contrast between Republic and Empire. The hoards of the later Republic are numerous enough for their listing to fill a well-known book.[29] A similar volume for Italy in the Empire would probably be very short, despite the much longer period represented (compare Table 5.2). It would be unrealistic to see the Augustan peace as a time when Italy was less monetised. Instead, the contrast in the number of

---

[26] For explanations that invoke warfare and unrest, see for example Mommsen 1875, 3.111n.; Blanchet (still useful for its long survey of hoard material); Blanchet 1936; Van Gansbeke 1955, 18, and Mocsy 1974, 102–4, 202. For associations between violence and unrest, and hoards in Italy under the Republic, see section 7 below.

[27] For the thesis, see Blanchet and Mocsy cited above. This line of argument is not helped by readiness to believe that hoards ending in the 130s AD could be connected with an invasion fully a generation later (Mocsy 1974, 102–4, reporting other work). For a valuable discussion of weaknesses in warfare explanations, and for cases where the hoard-pattern is seen to ignore important historical events, see Mihailescu, 68 ff. and 177 ff.

[28] See Appendix 10 nos. 38–40, 42, 74–6, 136–9, 142–51.

[29] Crawford 1969B.

hoards is probably linked to differences in levels of security between the Empire and the turbulent years of the late Republic.[30]

This striking difference suggests clues to the potential conditions under which hoards came to be buried and not retrieved. As already seen, hoards of the Principate are most plentiful in northern frontier provinces, even though some troops were stationed elsewhere. Conditions especially prevalent in these provinces, such as sudden redeployment of army units, high rates of crime and brigandage, and even sudden death of army personnel, probably added to the number of hoards not retrieved by their owners.

The special characteristics already seen in the hoard-sample do not seem compatible with the casual private accumulation of money. Instead, they argue a pattern of amounts and a pattern of events imposed on the empire as a whole, not merely on single regions. Finds of coin in a single denomination which suggest set monetary amounts and specific dates, concentrated especially in frontier regions, almost inevitably look like army payments.

Army payments took three main forms: pay (*stipendium*), retirement bonuses (*praemia*) and bonuses while in service (*donativa*). The first two types were more or less regular, in contrast to a hoard-series whose chronology is extremely uneven. That leaves the third type of payment, army donatives, as the potential origin of hoards. Donatives were intermittent, and their size varied when they reflected army rank.[31] The institution of army donatives is well known from the literary sources.[32] Since the sources show army donatives and handouts in Rome as companion events which celebrated the same occasions, this identification can be tested by comparing the chronology of the hoards with the chronology of handouts in Rome (section 9 below).[33] Groups of dated hoards can also be examined for potential links with individual donatives (chapter 6, section 1).

8. *CONGIARIA* AND COIN-HOARDS

Unlike army donatives, *congiaria* paid to the *plebs* of Rome were often commemorated on the coinage. The coin-legend LIBERALITAS, sometimes with

[30] For an illuminating discussion of the genesis of Republican hoards in Italy, see Crawford 1969A, noting correlations between the concentrations of dated hoards and known periods of warfare and civil disturbance in Italy.

[31] Retirement bonuses (*praemia*) cannot be entirely excluded. Dio 55.23.1 gives HS12,000 as the amount of the legionary *praemium* fixed by Augustus, and there seems to be some clustering at about this level (11 hoards out of 230 fall in the range between HS11,000 and HS13,000; most are silver). But the intermittent chronology of the hoard-sample as a whole means that *praemia* cannot be its primary origin. (For a possible link between *praemia* and short-term coin-output, see Duncan-Jones 1990, 73–6.)

[32] For a synopsis of the literary evidence from the Principate, see Bastien 1988, 7–16. For the link between donatives and handouts in Rome, see n.33 below. See also Kloft 1970, 104–10. Campbell 1984, 165–71, 182–98 provides stimulating discussion, but some uncertain reconstructions of amounts paid. For amounts per head known from literary sources, see Appendix 7: the payments specified tend to be abnormal, or belong to some special context.

[33] For *congiaria* and donatives as companion events, see Tac. *Ann.* 12.41, Suet. *Nero* 7.2; Pliny *Pan.* 25.2; *HA Had* 23.12–14, *Ael.* 6.1–4, *Pius* 10.2; Dio 76.1.1.

Table 5.5 *Summary of hoards and* congiaria *for fifteen major reigns* (hoard-minimum HS400)

Reign	Hoards	Hoard-sum (sesterces)	Congiaria
Augustus	10	45,644	5
Tiberius	3	91,704	4
Claudius	9	44,652	2
Nero	2	21,780	1
Vespasian	3	1,536	1
Domitian	10	60,272	3
Trajan	14	51,424	3
Hadrian	22	70,100	7
A.Pius	16	65,248	9
Marcus	47	465,780	7
Commodus	24	324,718	6
Severus	28	388,372	6
Caracalla	8	18,968	4
Elagabalus	7	149,896	4
S. Alexander	18	76,780	5

Note: Congiaria totals from Barbieri. Minor reigns are not shown.

a serial number, usually meant a *congiarium*.[34] Thanks to this source, together with literary references, and figures in the Chronicle of the year 354, the number of *congiaria* in each reign is reasonably well known.[35] Their size is less fully documented, although some norms are apparent, usually in figures representing multiples of an aureus (HS100). A frequent rate is 3 aurei (or 75 denarii), less often 4, and once or twice 6 or 8 aurei (Appendix 1 below).

Statistics for *congiaria* and for hoards are shown by reign in Table 5.5.[36] Correlation-tests show a series of associations between the two. First, there is a general broad correlation between the number of hoards and the number of *congiaria*. This can be resolved into two main patterns. Five main reigns from Claudius to Trajan show a close correlation (fig. 5.7; $r^2 = 0.892$; the equation reads: hoards = (*congiaria* × 4.75) − 1.900). The last six main reigns in the period, from Marcus Aurelius to Severus Alexander, show another strong correlation (fig. 5.8: hoard-numbers = (*congiaria* × 12.091) − 42.318; $r^2 = 0.930$).

Another potentially interesting relationship is suggested by hoard-value per *congiarium* (fig. 5.9).[37] This shows a steady decline for more than a century, from Tiberius to Antoninus Pius (with a brief deviation under Vespasian). The

[34] As so often in Roman terminology, the formulae were not rigid, and army donatives could be called 'liberalitates' in inscriptions (*ILS* 2445, 9099, 9100; *CIL* III 1378; Barbieri, 875).

[35] See Barbieri; for dates, see also Kienast.

[36] For *congiaria*-totals, see Barbieri, 874. Hoard-figures are based on the catalogue in Appendix 10. For secondary reigns which are omitted, see n.3 above.

[37] Though this comparison would be invalid if the size of *congiaria* was falling, in reality amounts tended to rise (see Barbieri).

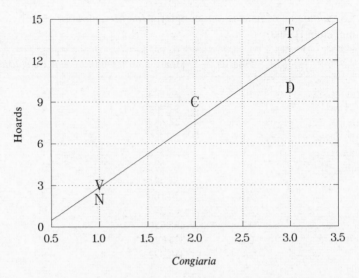

Figure 5.7 Correlation between number of precious-metal hoards and number of *congiaria* in Rome, AD 41–117 (Table 15.5). (Reigns (from left): Vespasian, Nero, Claudius, Trajan, Domitian.)

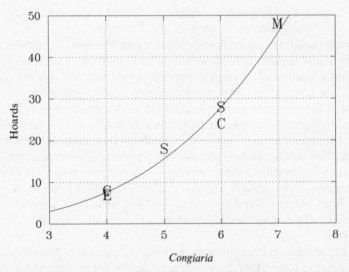

Figure 5.8 Correlation between number of precious-metal hoards and number of *congiaria* in Rome, AD 161–235 (Table 15.5). (Reigns (from left): Caracalla, Elagabalus, Severus Alexander, Septimius Severus, Commodus, Marcus Aurelius.)

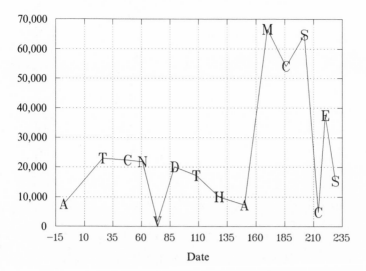

Figure 5.9 Aggregate value in sesterces of precious-metal hoards per *congiarium,* Augustus to Severus Alexander (Appendix 10).

frequency of *congiaria* tended to rise during this period (fig. 5.10). Thus, if the hoards were generated by army bonuses or by money for bonuses, possibly these failed to keep up with civilian handouts in the period up to Antoninus Pius. But with Marcus Aurelius the level leaps by a staggering amount, before falling away sharply under Caracalla (fig. 5.6).[38] By then, big increases in army pay had taken place.[39]

During the periods discussed, *congiaria* totals per reign are closely reflected in hoard-levels.[40] By themselves, correlations may not always prove that a relationship exists. But patterning by size, denomination and date already suggests that hoards represent payments, not random savings. Thus the close relationship of hoards with *congiaria* for most of the period argues a direct connection, rather than coincidence.[41] If there were no connection, these

[38] For Marcus's spending on handouts, including a first donative of prodigious size, see pp. 88–9.

[39] But donatives continued at this time nevertheless: see *ILS* 2445; *CIL* III 1378 with *AE* 1958,231 (Kloft 1970, 107). For literary references to donatives by Severus and Caracalla, see Bastien 1988, 12–14.

[40] Hoard-numbers and reign-length sometimes also correlate. But where the relationship is strong, hoards correlate more closely with *congiaria* than with reign-length. Some comparisons are as follows:

First correlation	r^2	Second correlation	r^2	Data
Hoards/*congiaria*	0.892	Hoards/reign-length	0.621	Fig.5.7
Hoards/*congiaria*	0.937	Hoards/reign-length	0.834	Fig.5.8
Hoard sum/*congiaria*	0.918	Hoard sum/reign-length	0.744	14–117

[41] And in a specific case, numerous hoards belong to AD 161–9, when there were 5 *congiaria* in Rome, but none to 170–4, when no handouts took place in Rome (p. 89 below). A further systematic effect is the high incidence of dated hoards seen at the junctions between reigns (chapter 6, p. 86 below).

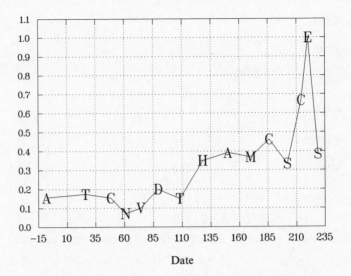

Figure 5.10 Number of *congiaria* in Rome per reign-year, Augustus to Severus Alexander. (Symbol: Emperor's initial.)

patterns would be extremely difficult to explain. They are discussed further in chapter 6.[42]

9. CONCLUSION

Most hoards seem to derive from the army donative, which gave cash to one segment of the provincial population on an impressive scale. The contents were normally in a single metal, either silver or gold.[43]

In the Roman Empire, almost anyone going on a journey, or living away from home, or living under communal conditions, as in army barracks, might bury coin temporarily for safe-keeping.[44] As a rule the owner would retrieve his deposit, leaving no later trace. Occasionally, some accident might intervene, with the result that coin remained in its hiding-place.[45] But the settled populations of major urban areas seem to have left relatively few

[42] Timelag effects (chapter 6, section 1.1) may mean that some hoards were generated by payments made in the following reign. But if so, additions at one end of each reign would compensate subtractions at the other, and the correlations remain visible despite any blurring from this effect.

[43] Major bronze hoards appear to be much rarer than precious-metal hoards for most of this period (cf. p. 186). Some silver hoards also contain a minute amount of non-denarius coin, such as Lycian drachmae, and even plated coins, though these were presumably part of the payment (see p. 175 n.10).

[44] *Dig.* 41.2.44.pr. Paulus (if a man buries money before going on a journey, and later cannot remember the hiding-place, is it still legally his?).

[45] For some indications of how little survives, see below, pp. 170–1.

hoards.[46] Presumably wherever there was family or communal knowledge of where money was kept, people were unlikely to lose track of it.[47]

Thus very large hoard categories in the Roman period have probably not survived to any significant extent: those buried in secure regions by civilian or soldier; those buried in insecure regions by people living there in family or household groupings; and hoards accumulated by way of trade. Hoards in these categories would typically contain a mixture of denominations, and would thus belong to the Pompeii model. As already seen, this is generally rare in what survives from our period, and it owes its widespread survival at Pompeii to the freak events of AD 79.[48]

Thus the present evidence provides little scope for contrasting circulation hoards with savings hoards. If savings hoards were common in what has survived here, the lack of premium coin would be puzzling in any case. In practice, second-century hoards usually reflect the early disappearance of such coin.[49] Most surviving hoards seem to owe their composition to army paymasters, who may occasionally have paid out in older worn coin for preference.[50] But silver hoards show considerable internal similarities, reign by reign, after allowing for the effects of wastage.[51] To all appearance, they were compiled from a common monetary stock, which was not usually manipulated significantly.

The fact that some hoards come from military sites, but others from locations with no known military connection could be seen as a weakness of the present interpretation. But hoards are certainly most abundant in heavily garrisoned provinces, and in major recruiting areas such as Gaul.[52] Defining any location as exclusively civilian is usually very difficult. Army units were often highly dispersed, and soldiers certainly did not spend all their time in

---

[46] There was probably a tendency for continuous occupation of Roman urban sites to remove coin buried there before our hoard-records begin.

[47] For a classic illustration of keeping track of hidden coin, see *Sel. Pap.* 278.

[48] For other examples, see n.10 above. The recently discovered late Roman hoard from Hoxne in Norfolk, with its profusion of gold coin, silver coin, and silver plate has all the signs of being a civilian deposit (unpublished at the time of writing).

[49] Coin rarely seen in hoards includes Domitian's denarii of AD 82–5, which were heavier and purer than any others after Nero, and the aurei struck by Domitian, Nerva and Trajan before AD 101 (heavier than any others after AD 64; see p. 217). The recently discovered Snettisham 'jeweller's' hoard, which also contains much unworked silver, is an interesting but rare exception (ASR. no.202; there is too little coin to bring it within the present survey). This mid-second century hoard concentrates quite disproportionately on coin of Domitian, with its high silver content. But even in this case, the owner did not manage to find more than one coin from Domitian's best period (coin-list from Dr A.M. Burnett).

[50] See chapter 16, section 3.

[51] Cf. Mihailescu, 109; Reece 1981.

[52] The Gallic hoards assembled here are chiefly from Tres Galliae. The Gallic *alae* were mainly replenished from sources in Gaul (Holder 1980, 115). More than a quarter of men of identified origin in the legions of Germany came from Narbonensis in the period up to Trajan, and more than a quarter from Tres Galliae in the period after Trajan (N 253 and 87). Legionaries of known origin are listed in Mann 1983, 73 ff.

camp.[53] They might furthermore visit or retire to home towns in civilian areas.[54]

It is highly relevant to compare this evidence with the numerous hoards found in England from the Civil War period in the seventeenth century. Their pattern is highly dispersed, and they do not usually come from the scene of battles. They suggest that 'soldiers concealed their money at home when they left for the campaigns, and these unrecovered hoards probably represent the property of casualties in the conflict'.[55]

No single diagnosis of chance survivals can claim to be entirely comprehensive. Some hoards may certainly have a different origin from the one suggested.[56] But the present interpretation is strongly supported both by the undoubted patterning of the data, and by the definite correlations with *congiaria*, which are considered further in chapter 6. Such correlations could hardly exist if the hoard evidence included many private savings hoards, whose chronology would have no reason to follow the pattern of handouts in Rome.

9.1. SUMMARY

Analysis of a very large sample reveals features of the hoard evidence which are historically crucial. The size of hoards is sometimes noticeably stereotyped, their contents are normally restricted to a single denomination, and their dates are clustered and intermittent. In combination, these features point to something different from random private savings. The irregular chronology does not correlate satisfactorily with outbreaks of warfare or unrest. But for most of the period, the finds correlate reign by reign with the civilian handouts in Rome known as *congiaria*. *Congiaria* were typically matched by donatives, or handouts to the armies of the Empire.[57] In the hoard-sample, evidence tends to be lacking at times when there were no handouts. But the civilian handout, paid in Rome to modest inhabitants of the city, would not show itself in deposits of coin all over a vast empire. Thus, the find-pattern only becomes intelligible if most hoards originate from the second type of handout, that is, from army donatives.

Clearly global patterning cannot define individual cases, and some hoards may have a different origin. But the definite correlations with the *congiaria* in Rome, and the stylised features of the hoards themselves, suggest that exceptions in the present sample must be few. If most hoards came from donatives, and follow the chronology of handouts in Rome, they cannot also show the chronology of hoarding tendencies in their own right. Nor can they show the incidence of warfare or unrest. Their likely historical implications

---

[53] Cf. *Rom. Mil. Rec.* 63, 47 ff.; Thomas, Davies 1977; Bowman, Thomas 1991. For army routines, see in detail Davies 1989, 33–68. Speidel's article on furlough is also highly revealing (Speidel 1985). For a horrific episode when soldiers returned late from leave, Sen. *de ira* 1.18.3–6.

[54] The findspots of auxiliary discharge-certificates (*diplomata*) indicate that veterans sometimes settled somewhere other than the bases where they had served (Roxan 1981).

[55] Casey 1986, 61.   [56] See n.49 above.

[57] For *congiaria* and donatives as companion events, see n.33 above.

are thus narrow but specific. The hoards appear to be more homogeneous than has been assumed, and in most cases they presumably reflect the contents of army pay-chests.[58]

Geographically, hoard-finds are heavily skewed towards frontier regions. To some extent this mirrors troop-concentrations. But it also implies that hoard burial, or non-retrieval of buried hoards, was more common in insecure regions. The undoubted military presence in the more peaceful regions such as Africa and Spain seems to have left few such traces.[59]

---

[58] It has been argued from coin-motifs that in the Late Empire coin was minted specially for use in donatives (Bastien 1988). But evidence from the Principate shows too much timelag to suggest any parallel or confirmation (p. 86).

[59] The search yielded only one dated African precious-metal hoard of sufficient size (Appendix 10 no.109; there are occasional African bronze hoards from outside this period, see e.g. p. 132 n.21). And it produced very little Iberian material from the main part of the period.

6

THE IMPLICATIONS OF COIN-HOARDS

1. CHRONOLOGY

1.1. INTRODUCTION

In the last chapter, it was argued from correlations by reign with civilian handouts in Rome that most coin-hoards in this period originated from the parallel handouts to the provincial armies. If correct, that identification must mean that particular handouts generated particular groups of hoards. The first part of this chapter explores this association chronologically.

Looked at in detail, most known handouts at Rome seem to have a potential echo in the hoards found in the empire at large. But hoard-dates and the dates of handouts are often slightly out of alignment. Taken by itself, that could call the present interpretation into question. But granted the strong correlations by reign between hoards and handouts at Rome, what it suggests is that in many cases the latest coin available for handouts in the provinces may have been several years old, because of slow circulation. The amount of timelag appears to vary, thus blurring arguments from detailed chronology which could otherwise contribute to the main diagnosis. The detailed implications of that diagnosis must still be examined. But it should be understood that the associations suggested below cannot be firm identifications in the absence of more specific evidence.

Army donatives of the Principate and civilian handouts in Rome figure as joint events in the sources.[1] Certain special occasions tended to trigger handouts. They included the accession of a new Emperor, the naming or coming of age of an heir, and the holding of a triumph. Another was the *decennalia* celebrating the tenth anniversary of an Emperor's accession.[2]

On present arguments, clusters of dated hoards are potentially associated with provincial donatives. The most obvious candidate is the cluster at the start of a new reign. Most changes of Emperor see hoards or hoard-clusters close to the moment of accession. Thus hoards end in AD 15; 41 and 41/2; 68/9 (two); 80/1; 96/8 (two); 98, 98/9; 114/17; 137/8; 159/60, 161, 161/2; 179, 180 (two); 193 (four); 211; and 222 (two).[3] This series is potentially linked to

---

[1] See chapter 5 n.33.
[2] Cf. Bastien 1988. For the dates of individual *decennalia* and *vicennalia*, see Kienast, who gives full citations of bibliography.
[3] Appendix 10 nos. 88; 4, 90; 12, 92; 96; 99, 100; 22–3; 107; 122; 36, 70, 133; 162, 75, 163; 55, 180–2; 60; 212–13.

accession donatives, which are implied as normal practice by Pliny. Pliny sees it as a virtue that Trajan gave only part of the expected army donative, while paying the people their *congiarium* in full.[4] Thus the Roman *plebs* and the soldiers both expected payments from a new Emperor, who in his turn would receive an accession-payment (*aurum coronarium*) from Italy and the provinces.[5]

1.2. REIGN-STUDIES

Under Augustus and Tiberius, lack of close dating makes it difficult to pursue connections between hoards and *congiaria*. But Claudius is known to have given a *congiarium* in AD 45, and a *congiarium* and donative in 51.[6] The present sample shows hoards ending in AD 44/5 (Italy), 46/7 (Greece), 48 (Italy) and 51 (Gaul) (all four are gold hoards).[7] Assuming that costly provincial donatives were no more frequent than *congiaria* in our period, the three later hoards may be associated with the *congiarium* in 51, which celebrated Nero's coming of age. No Claudian hoard here is dated after 51.

Another hoard-cluster close to a *congiarium* date is seen under Domitian. AD 89 was the year of his German triumph, and evidently of his second *congiarium*.[8] The dated hoards belong to 84/5 (Danube), 87 (Britain) and 88 (Italy).[9] The other dated hoard of the reign, a Danube gold hoard of AD 92/4, is close in date to Domitian's third *congiarium* in AD 93.[10]

Two hoards which end under Nerva, like hoards dated to 98 and 98/9, may belong to an accession donative paid by Trajan, coinciding with his first *congiarium* in 99.[11] Most Trajanic hoards are not closely dated, but the triumphs for which *congiaria* were paid in 103 and 107 presumably generated donatives as well.

The hoard from 114/17, one of the few denarius finds in Egypt, could reflect an accession donative by Hadrian, associated with his initial *congiaria* in

---

[4] *Pan.* 25.2. The life of Pertinax also spells out what was expected from even the most shortlived Emperor: 'Congiarium dedit populo denarios centenos. Praetorianis promisit duodenis milia nummum, sed dedit sena. Quod exercitibus promissum est, datum non est, quia mors eum praevenit'(*HA Pert.* 15.7).

[5] The element of exchange was only nominal, since the money for crown gold came from taxpayers who themselves received nothing. For *aurum coronarium*, see p. 7. For the limited size of the body which received *congiaria*, see n.16.

[6] For *congiaria* and their dates, see Barbieri, 874. For the donative of 51, Tac. *Ann.* 12.41 and Suet. *Nero* 7.2.

[7] Appendix 10 nos. 5, 7, 9, 10. Where hoard-dates bridge two years, the twelve months is normally the tribunician year of the Emperor (for dates, see Kienast under each Emperor). From Nerva onwards, full tribunician years start on 10 December and so almost coincide with Julian years (Kienast, 32–3).

[8] Kienast 115–17. Domitian's first *congiarium*, associated with his triumph over the Chatti, and his new title 'Germanicus', took place in AD 84, from the *Fasti Ostienses*. Army pay was increased in AD 83/4 (for the date, shown by a coin-legend, see Kraay 1960, contested unconvincingly by Campbell 1984, 185 n.26).   [9] Appendix 10 nos. 97, 64, 16.

[10] Appendix 10 no. 21; Kienast, 117.   [11] Appendix 10 nos. 99, 100, 22, 23.

117–18.[12] Under Hadrian, an important donative was also given in 136, together with a *congiarium*, to celebrate Hadrian's adoption of Aelius Caesar. Hoards ending in 128/34, 133/4 and 134/8 come from Italy, Germany, Austria, Palestine and Britain.[13] Aelius's early death deprived Hadrian's gift of its purpose, and the sources report a rueful remark by Hadrian, in which the amount spent is specified three times.

In one version, the *Historia Augusta* gives the expenditure as HS300 million on the soldiers, in another, HS300 million on soldiers and people, and in the third, HS400 million on soldiers and people. HS300 million may have been the cost of the donative, and HS400 the cost of donative and *congiarium* combined, as claimed by the better source.[14] That loosely fits contemporary *congiaria*, probably HS300 for a normal distribution, and HS600 on a special occasion such as this.[15] At the special rate, total expenditure would be HS90 or 100 million.[16] The donative would then have cost between HS200 and 310 million. If the late Hadrianic hoards belong to this event, the survival rate would be between 1 in 9,000 and 1 in 14,000.[17]

The sixteen hoards under Antoninus Pius are about two-thirds of the number from Hadrian's shorter reign. The marriage of Marcus and Faustina in AD 145 brought a *congiarium* of 100 denarii or 4 aurei.[18] A donative was given as well.[19] The gold hoard from Switzerland and the Dacian silver hoard which both end in 140/4 might reflect this.[20] The *decennalia* celebrated in 148 (LIBERALITAS 5) and the *vicennalia* in 158 (LIBERALITAS 8) were also obvious potential occasions for donatives. But the hoard-sample shows no echo in 148, which was also the year when Rome celebrated her 900th birthday.[21] The later event, in 158, may be echoed in hoards ending in 157 and 158 (from Egypt, Britain, Austria and Dacia).[22]

Hoards increase dramatically in size and number under Marcus Aurelius (N = 48). The reign began with an enormous and presumably extravagant donative, which gave the Praetorians HS20,000 each, and proportionate

---

[12] Appendix 10 no. 107. About one-tenth of this hoard from an eastern province is denominated in Greek drachmae (34 out of 300 coins). Kienast, 130.

[13] Appendix 10 nos. 67–8, 119–21.

[14] The higher figure comes from the life of Hadrian, the others from the life of Aelius. For the better sources underlying the main lives up to Caracalla in the *Historia Augusta*, see Barnes 1984, 4.30. *HA Had.* 23.12–15 (HS400 million to soldiers and people); *Ael.* 3.3 (HS300 million to the soldiers), 6.1–4 (HS300 million to soldiers and people). For the date, see Kienast, 129–30.

[15] Cf. Barbieri 845–6.

[16] Under Tiberius and Caligula, the citizens entitled to *congiaria* and imperial bequests numbered 150,000; they were still rather fewer than 200,000 under Septimius Severus (Van Berchem 1939, 144–6, 29). This privileged group, whose membership was controlled by *tesserae* carrying entitlement to corn and other privileges, was only one part of the total citizen population at Rome, cf. Duncan-Jones 1982, 346; the *congiarium* in AD 202, like the final *congiarium* of Augustus nearly two centuries earlier, explicitly went to the *plebs frumentaria* (Dio 76.1.1; *RG* 15.4).

[17] The survival-rates for precious metal coin suggested by entirely different evidence also fall within this range (Table 11.3). The hoard-aggregate is HS22,436.

[18] Barbieri, 847; *Fasti Ostienses.*   [19] *HA Pius* 10.2.

[20] Appendix 10 nos. 33, 132.   [21] Kienast, 134.   [22] Appendix 10 nos. 34, 128–30.

amounts to other troops.[23] A British gold hoard which ends with coin of 159/60, and a Syrian hoard which is mainly gold ending in 161 may reflect this event.[24] Further concentrations of dated hoards rapidly follow:

Year	Number
164	4
165	2
166	5
167	4
168	4

The six hoards from 164 and 165 seem to coincide with the *congiarium* paid in 165 for the marriage of Lucius Verus.[25] The five in 166 parallel the *congiarium* paid that year for the Parthian triumph.[26] The hoards in 167 echo the *congiarium* paid then for Verus's third consulship.[27] And the four in 168 probably parallel the fifth *congiarium* of the reign, paid in 169, the year of Verus's death.[28]

After the unprecedented spending on handouts for most of the 160s, *congiaria* now ceased altogether for six years, until 175. The dated hoard-sample, so abundant up to this point, likewise ceases for at least six years. This direct parallel is the plainest suggestion of a link between hoards and government spending, apart from the correlations already studied (chapter 5). In 175 Marcus gave a *congiarium* for the coming of age of Commodus. There are no matching hoards. But year-dated hoards resume more clearly with a cluster of five examples, one in 176, and four in 177, which may echo the *congiarium* paid in 177 for the first German triumph.[29]

A gold hoard from Egypt in 178, and a small silver hoard from Britain end Marcus's dated series.[30] As no further *congiaria* took place under Marcus, these examples, like two hoards ending in 180, might belong to an accession donative by Commodus in 180, coinciding with his *congiarium* for the triumph in that year.[31]

Under Commodus, an initial cluster of relatively small silver hoards, one in 181 and two in 182, may echo the third *congiarium* of his reign given in 182.[32] The next *congiarium* was in 186, and close to this there are hoards in 184, in

---

[23] *HA Marcus* 7.9, corroborated by Dio 74.8.4.
[24] Appendix 10 nos. 36, 70.   [25] Appendix 10 nos. 38, 134–7, 140.
[26] Appendix 10 nos. 39, 72, 141–3.   [27] Appendix 10 nos. 73, 144–6.
[28] Appendix 10 nos. 40, 74, 147–8. The fact that there are more hoards in even-numbered than in odd-numbered years may recall the coinage peaks in even-numbered years under Marcus already noted (Duncan-Jones 1990, 73–6).
[29] Appendix 10 nos. 45, 155–8.
[30] Appendix 10 nos. 48, 162. Kunisz suggests that the 299 aurei from Sakha may be part of a much larger hoard, from die-links with specimens in Berlin (Kunisz 1983, 162). But even in the abundant gold of Hadrian's reign, die-links are frequent enough for completely separate samples to have many dies in common (Table 10.10, p. 158). See also the die-links listed by Thirion.
[31] Appendix 10 nos. 75, 163; Kienast, 147, 149.
[32] Appendix 10 nos. 164–5, 50.

186 and two in 185.[33] There is a cluster of three silver hoards in 187 and 188. The *congiaria* resume in 190.[34]

The four hoards from 193 parallel the *congiarium* given by Severus in 193, suggesting an accession donative.[35] Severus's next *congiarium* was in 196, and there are five hoards from the two previous years.[36]

Severus's historic increase in legionary pay took place early in 202.[37] Later in the year, at Severus's *decennalia*, the Praetorians received as a donative 10 aurei, the amount also given to the *plebs frumentaria* as their *congiarium*.[38] The final *congiaria* of the reign took place in 205 and 208. The first may be echoed in hoards of 204 and 205.[39] The two last dated hoards of the reign, dated 208 and 209, are both from Britain, where Severus spent his last years on campaign.[40]

Under Caracalla, the hoards dated to 213 and 214 may echo the *congiarium* of 214 which honoured a triumph.[41] The seven hoards in Elagabalus's reign of less than four years, and his four *congiaria* may also be connected.[42] The two hoards that end in 222 might belong to an accession donative by Severus Alexander.[43] And the three hoards of 227, 228 and 229 may echo the *congiarium* of 229.[44] Similarly, silver hoards of 230 and 231 may reflect the next *congiarium* in 233.[45]

Thus where there are hoards dated by year, their dates loosely mirror *congiaria* dates in Rome. The lack of exact matching probably indicates that many hoards were fractionally later than their latest coin, because slow circulation often prevented new coin from reaching the provinces quickly. Nevertheless, the matching becomes relatively precise under Marcus Aurelius, when hoard evidence is most abundant. In the 160s, an unprecedented leap in the number of *congiaria* coincides with an unprecedented leap in the number of dated hoards. After this spectacular short-term peak, *congiaria* and hoards both suddenly cease for half a dozen years from 169.

2. HOARDS FROM EGYPT

Egypt was mainly a closed currency area, with a local coinage of silver alloy minted in Alexandria, which was used in army pay accounts.[46] The tetradrachm was tariffed at 1 denarius, making the drachma equal the sestertius.[47] Egyptian documents describe some military transactions in a mixture of denarii and

---

[33] Appendix 10 nos. 169–71, 173.   [34] Appendix 10 nos. 176–8; Kienast, 149.
[35] Appendix 10 nos. 55, 180–2; Kienast, 158.   [36] Appendix 10 nos. 184–8.
[37] P. 33.   [38] Dio 76.1.1.   [39] Appendix 10 nos. 59, 195.
[40] Appendix 10 nos. 198–9. A third hoard of this period published since the sample was compiled likewise comes from Britain (Much Hadham: 129 denarii and 36 sestertii ending in AD 210/11). For donatives to armies on campaign, see Table A.4 (Pannonian legions and army in Gaul).
[41] Appendix 10 nos. 202, 206.   [42] Appendix 10 nos. 61, 209–14; Kienast, 173.
[43] Appendix 10 nos. 212–13.   [44] Appendix 10 nos. 218, 226–7.
[45] Appendix 10 nos. 228, 230. The hoard material for Severus Alexander classified in detail by Carson in the introduction to *BMCRE* 6 suggests that little silver coin was produced after 230, which could increase timelag between hoards and the date of donatives.
[46] *Rom. Mil. Rec.* 68–9.   [47] West, Johnson, 1944, 72–3.

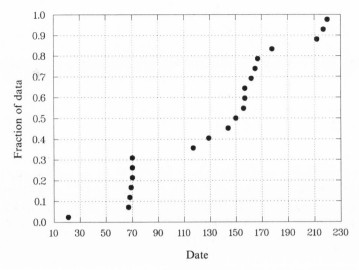

Figure 6.1 Dating concentrations of Egyptian coin-hoards, AD 15–225.

obols.[48] Like the survival of denarius and aureus hoards from Egypt, this indicates that currency also entered the province from outside, perhaps in significant amounts.[49]

At least sixteen dated tetradrachm hoards of our period are above the size-threshold.[50] The hoard evidence, including gold and denarius hoards, shows an obvious pattern of clusters and long gaps (see figure 6.1).[51] The clumping is so obvious that it would be difficult to see Egyptian hoards, even in isolation, as random private savings.

Some clusters parallel those outside Egypt. Vespasian's initial bid for the throne took place in Egypt, and there are three Egyptian hoards which end in AD 70.[52] Two hoards in the main sample end in AD 69.[53] After AD 70, the Egyptian sample ceases until a denarius hoard in 114/17, followed by a tetradrachm hoard in 129.[54] The next cluster does not occur until the pair of tetradrachm hoards in 156 and 157, which accompany a gold hoard of 157.[55] The *vicennalia* of Antoninus Pius in 157/8 were celebrated by a *congiarium*;

---

[48] Cf. e.g. *PCol* VIII 221 (AD 143); *Rom. Mil. Rec.* 70.
[49] For gold hoards in Egypt, see Kunisz 1983, arguing that gold was part of the circulating medium in Egypt during the Principate. For denarii, see Appendix 10 nos. 107, 203, Bolin 350, no.42 (cf. Christiansen 1985, A66).
[50] The threshold remains 100 denarii (here tetradrachms). Christiansen 1985, nos. A22, A25, A26, A27, A28, A29, A43, A45, A52, A58, A62, A78; Milne 1910, 333 (cf. Christiansen A14); Botti 1955, 245, cf. Christiansen A37); Metcalf 1976, 76 (cf. Christiansen A60); Dattari 1903, 285, n.1 (cf. Christiansen A80).
[51] The plot also includes two Egyptian denarius hoards, and three gold hoards (Appendix 10 nos. 107, 203, 34, 48, 61).   [52] Christiansen 1985, A27, A28, A29.
[53] Appendix 10 nos. 13, 92.   [54] Appendix 10 no. 107; Botti (n. 50 above).
[55] Christiansen 1985, A52, A54. Appendix 10 no.34.

outside Egypt there are denarius hoards of 157 and 158.[56] Hoards of 162, 165
and 167 recall the *congiaria* of 164, 165, 166 and 167.[57] The dated hoards then
show a gap until the middle Severi (212, 212/17, and 211/18).[58] If it refers to
handouts, the Egyptian hoard-series suggests serious gaps compared with the
series from the rest of the empire. But the sample is small, and its coverage is
too limited to suggest any firm conclusion about differences between Egypt
and the rest of the empire.

3. HOARDS BEYOND THE FRONTIER

Hoards from beyond the frontier show a different dating pattern from those
inside the empire.[59] Hoards from Romanian Moldavia collected by Mihailescu-
Birlibà provide a useful illustration. There are twenty-eight reign-dated silver
hoards above the threshold of HS400.[60] Their dating pattern can be compared
with the pattern for the Danube provinces (fig. 6.2).

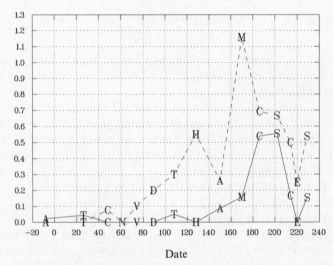

Date

Figure 6.2 Dating comparison of Moldavian hoards beyond the frontier with empire
hoards from the Danube region. (Symbol: Emperor's initial; straight line: Moldavia;
dotted line: Danube.)

---

[56] See p. 88 above.   [57] Christiansen 1985, A58, A62; Metcalf (n.50 above).
[58] Christiansen 1985, A78; Botti 1955; Appendix 10 no. 203.
[59] Publications which include hoard material from beyond the Roman frontier: Guey 1955–6;
Kromann 1989; Kropotkin 1961; Krzyzanowska 1976; Kubiak 1979; Kunisz 1973; Kunisz
1985; Lind 1981; Mihailescu-Birlibà 1977; Mihailescu; Mitkowa-Szubert 1989; Nohejlová-Pratová
1955–8; Ondrouch 1934; Ondrouch 1938; Sasianu 1980; Sey-Katalin 1986; Wolters 1990, 1991,
29–31. For a denarius hoard in Ireland, see Bateson 1973, and for finds in Scotland, see
Robertson, forthcoming. For further bibliography, see Grierson 1979, 87–8.
[60] Mihailescu, 251 ff., nos. 8, 11, 22, 30, 58, 64, 69, 74, 120, 130, 135, 141, 157, 159, 166, 172, 184,
208, 211, 215, 223, 230, 231 & 232, 254, 279, 285, 287.

The comparison shows that the external sample does not begin much before the mid-second century, whereas within the empire, hoard numbers are already significant in the first century. The external peak comes very sharply under Commodus and Septimius Severus, while empire hoards show their clear peak under Marcus (fig. 5.5). In a second external sample, from Little Poland, hoards are again heavily concentrated under Commodus and Septimius Severus (out of eighteen silver hoards, four belong to Commodus, and ten to Septimius Severus).[61]

Such an overwhelming peak in a short period does not suggest a pattern due to normal rhythms of commercial exchange, even if deposit may be later than the end-date in some cases.[62] Given such constricted dating, it is more likely that the hoards have an artificial origin.[63] But there are obvious problems about linking the denarius hoards to barbarian subsidies.[64] One is the fact that the subsidies tended to be paid in gold, whereas these hoards consist of silver coin.[65] Another difficulty is that the external hoards are widely dispersed, and mostly small, whereas subsidies must have been relatively few and would usually have been large lump sums.

Various other possibilities have been suggested to account for external finds of Roman coin.[66] These include:

1. Ransom for captives.
2. Diplomatic gifts.
3. Booty from raids across the frontier
4. Payment to those serving in Roman armies.

---

[61] Kunisz 1985; because of the restricted total available, the smallest hoard used here has 36 denarii, but eleven lie above the threshold of 100 denarii. Kunisz 1985 nos. 9, 27, 39, 110, 138, 160, 160 *bis*, 202, 209, 211, 225, 227, 230, 248, 267, 279, 305, 338.

[62] For example Mihailescu, 201–4. This discrimination is not made by Bursche 1989, who suggests extensive correlations between the dating of coin-populations found outside the empire and individual historical events. This is unconvincing because it depends on identity between the date a coin was struck and the date at which it left the empire. In reality, external hoards, like those inside the empire, contain a chronological spread of coin (see Drzewicz Nowy, La Puriceni and La Magura, Tables 16.8–16.9, pp. 245–7 below). Hoards consisting of new coin remain extremely rare: one case is the hoard found at Genas composed of denarii of one type of Clodius Albinus from AD 197, presumably funds belonging to the army of Albinus which Septimius Severus defeated that year nearby at Lugdunum (Appendix 10 no.190; for other monetary traces of this battle, see p. 70, n.10).

[63] In itself this argues nothing about levels of cross-frontier trade. Trading, whether monetised or not, did not necessarily leave a trail of coin-hoards behind it. For literary and archaeological evidence for trade with Moldavia, see Mihailescu, 222–34. For external coin-hoards interpreted as evidence of trade, see Wielowiejski 1980.

[64] This link is suggested by Lind 1988, 209 ff. for denarii found in Sweden. See p. 246 n.16 below.

[65] Dio 74.6.1 (gold), 77.14.3 (gold throughout Caracalla's reign), 78.27.4 (silver). A contemporary Chinese source writing about the Roman Empire states that 'When the embassies of neighbouring countries come to the frontier . . . on arrival in the capital they are presented with golden money' (Hirth 1885, 42). In the Late Empire, evidence for gold-payments beyond the frontier is clear; and the numerous external gold coin-hoards have been linked with literary evidence for barbarian subsidies: see Iluk 1985, with hoard inventory in Iluk 1988. For Moldavia in this period, see Mihailescu, 207 ff. For the Baltic regions, see Lind 1981, and Fagerlie 1967.

[66] See Bursche 1989, 284; Bateson 1973, 29. For literary references to subsidy, ransom, booty and barbarian mercenaries, see Mihailescu, 248. For subsidy, see also Gordon 1949, and Robertson 1982, 225; Todd 1985; Wolters 1991, 116–21.

Of these possibilities, ransom is unlikely in the widespread form implied by the external silver finds. Diplomatic gifts are a variant of the subsidies already considered, not strictly an alternative. Booty again is likely to have been only sporadic, and could be expected to produce jewelry and bullion, not simply money in a single denomination.

But payment to mercenaries or foreigners serving in the army is more difficult to discard. In aggregate, the external finds are surprisingly similar to hoards in the main sample, which appear to have been mainly military payments (chapter 5). Both are very largely monometallic. The mean hoard-size in the two external samples is relatively consistent, HS2,023 in Moldavia and HS2,425 in Little Poland (N = 30 and N = 11, using the threshold of HS400 as before). The mean figure in the 73 Empire silver hoards from the Danube, HS2,489, is very similar (Table 5.3). Thus similarity of size, the restriction to denarii, and geographical proximity make a common origin quite likely.

If so, the external hoards were probably army payments, to auxiliaries, or to members of tribal detachments.[67] Other chronology strongly supports this identification. The strong concentration of external hoards under Commodus and Septimius Severus directly coincides with the fact that large-scale army recruiting across the frontier started just before this date, late in the reign of Marcus Aurelius. Marcus acted under pressure of military and other disasters.[68] In Britain, as in Moldavia and Little Poland, the concentrations of hoards outside the Roman province begin under Commodus.[69] The findspots may indicate zones of recruitment, suggesting payments taken home at some point, which in these cases remained in their hiding-places.[70]

[67] Roman army units were sometimes present beyond the frontier, because of frequent patrols and even outpost forts set beyond the *limes* (Davies 1989, 58). For the secret service operating beyond the eastern frontier in the sixth century, see Procopius *Anec.* 30.12–14.

[68] Speidel 1987, 192; cf. Wolters 1991, 107–16. Note Marcus's immediate deployment as Roman troops of adversaries defeated in battle (8,000 cavalry of the Iazyges, 5,500 of whom were sent to Britain, Dio 71.16.1–2). For Marcus's settlement of tribesmen in Dacia, Pannonia, Moesia, Germany, and even in Italy, see Dio 71.11.4–5. For the grave crisis in army recruitment during the plague under Marcus, see Duncan-Jones 1990, 72.

[69] Marcus: County Antrim. Commodus: five hoards in Scotland beyond the Wall, and one in the Orkneys (ASR, nos. 311, 335, 345–9).

[70] Note also the concentration of substantial Swedish denarius-finds from this period in the island of Gotland (p. 246 n.16).

PART III

MONEY AND MONEY-SUPPLY

7

COINAGE AND CURRENCY: AN
OVERVIEW*

1. COINAGE AS SEEN BY CONTEMPORARIES

Ancient writers say notoriously little about currency.[1] The accounts of change under Nero, Commodus and Septimius Severus that might have been expected are not there in the narrative sources. And their fleeting allusions to changes by Trajan and Caracalla would be misleading by themselves. The most interesting coinage initiative of all, Domitian's revival of earlier standards, is also passed by in silence.[2] Dio's text says nothing of Trajan's change in silver fineness or in the weight of the aureus. Caracalla's new denomination Dio apparently ignores, although as a contemporary he presumably knew of its existence. And Dio's complaint about plated gold currency under Caracalla is not borne out by the coin evidence, which shows only a weight-reduction.[3] It is natural to infer from all this that there was little awareness of coinage change among the upper classes. The gold currency on which they mainly depended altered little before Caracalla, and once that had changed, some criticism of minting policy does emerge, even if not in a coherent form.

Another pointer is the failure to exploit the propaganda potential of the coinage to the full. The obverse of a coin from the central mint showed the Emperor, his consort, or another member of his family. But most coin reverses have motifs of a quite conventional kind, whether symbolic, religious, or mythological.[4] This use of iconography may be merely unimaginative. Or it

---

* This chapter outlines main themes. It is primarily intended to signpost the fuller discussions in the chapters that follow, but also acts as a short summary.
[1] A technical work such as Pliny's *Natural History* is of course an exception. But for limitations in Pliny's account of coinage, see p. 218 n.20.
[2] It would have conflicted in any case with the evil stereotype adopted by surviving sources such as Pliny's *Panegyric*. For the reforms, see Carradice.
[3] Dio 77.14.4. Dio's text is not preserved in full at these points, but positive inaccuracies are presumably his. In theory it is possible that Dio originally described Trajan's coinage reforms more fully, even if his handling of Severan changes makes that unlikely.
[4] Cf. Jones 1974, 63–4. Even so, by most modern standards, imperial coin-types were numerous and varied. Their numbers may indicate that coin-types were used as markers within the mint for quantities of coin produced (cf. Burnett 1977, 53: 'one of the functions of ancient coin-types was to enable a check to be kept on the different *officinae* in the mint'). Despite obvious variation in individual amounts, the average quantities of coin per type in really large samples are considerably more stable than they would be if types and coin-quantities were unrelated (see chapter 9, p. 136). At the start of the Empire types were fewer, and Rodewald may be right in questioning Frank's inferences from type-numbers under Tiberius about the amount of coin struck (Rodewald 1976, 10).

may show that the Emperors rarely took the initiative in deciding the details of coinage, and that the officials who took these decisions were conservative and unoriginal.

But the coinage shows obvious repercussions at the accession of Hadrian, who, to an almost unique extent, saw himself as a ruler with important commitments to the empire as a whole. Most notable are his Adventus series of coins, reflecting his travels round the empire, the Exercitus series honouring provincial armies, and the Restitutor series portraying Hadrian as the saviour of stricken provinces. But even in these cases, the design was not executed fully, and the gaps suggest delegation of the Emperor's plans to a somewhat inefficient bureaucracy.[5]

The historical writers seem to view coin under the heading of morality or self-advertisement, but not in economic or financial terms.[6] Under the Empire, coin was a political affirmation of the individual normally reserved for the ruler. Almost every new claimant to the throne immediately issued his own coin. Coin struck for private individuals was a sign of overweening ambition.[7] Its connection with the potency of the individual meant that coin of the unjust ruler, or coin of a political rival, could be seen as obvious targets for destruction, regardless of any economic considerations.[8] Thus the Senate's decision to melt down bronze coin of Caligula after his assassination for once included coinage in the inevitable destruction of statues and inscriptions.[9] It was held that Vitellius might have wished for similar reasons to destroy coin of Nero, Galba and Otho, and that he was magnanimous in not doing so. Caracalla's melting down coin of Geta showed this hostility to a rival in practice.[10] The tradition similarly sees Trajan's benign removal of worn coin, and Caracalla's alleged issue of plated coin as examples of moral behaviour, rather than as economic devices.[11]

Historical writers very rarely show interest in coin-motifs, but Suetonius mentions a Capricorn-type of Augustus, and a coin-type of Nero on which the Emperor played the lyre.[12] Not until the later Empire do we have narratives of

---

[5] Gaps: *BMCRE* 3, cxliii, clxxiii–clxxv. The survival of many thousands of Hadrian's coins should provide a relatively comprehensive view.

[6] The archetype of the money-changer who distinguishes good coin from bad tends to be subordinate to general discussions of morality (cf. Epictetus 2.3).

[7] Coin was allegedly struck for Perennis, Praetorian Prefect under Commodus (Herodian 1.9.7); coin or medals with his own likeness struck privately for the senator Valerius Paetus were taken as a sign of treason (Dio 80.4.7).

[8] Other echoes of *damnatio* on the coinage occasionally included the erasure of coin-portraits of the disgraced ruler. Some countermarks on coin of such rulers may indicate re-validation of their coin (Howgego 1985, 5–6).

[9] But in a reversal of the usual transformation of statues into coin (p. 10), Messalina used the metal to make statues of her lover Mnester (Dio 60.22.3). Burnett suggests that under Claudius, Caligula's gold and silver coin was also withdrawn, but that is difficult to establish without some contemporary index of the scale on which it was produced (Burnett 1977, 55).

[10] Dio 65.6.1, 77.12.6.

[11] Dio 68.15.3, 77.14.4.

[12] *Aug.* 94.12; *Nero* 25.2.

currency crises described in economic terms.[13] In the sixth century, Malalas shows sudden coin-debasement causing popular riots, as a result of which Justinian had to bring back the earlier standard.[14] Coin was just as much an economic medium under the Principate as under the Late Empire. But the facts of Roman commercial life and the realities of monetary exchange could not penetrate the upper-class indifference shown by the historical sources in our period.

2. CHRONOLOGY

Under the Republic, Rome had depended on an abundant silver coinage, with few issues of gold.[15] In the 40s BC, Caesar began to mint gold coin on a large scale, presumably using the enormous proceeds in gold from his conquest of Gaul, as well as other booty and spoils.[16] Heavy gold minting continued under Augustus, now helped by spectacular supplies of treasure from Egypt.[17] By the mid-first century AD, Rome's gold supplies were being sustained by important gold-mining in Spain and Dalmatia.[18] Under the early Empire, Republican issues still made up most of the silver coin in circulation in Italy, and it was not until decisive moves by Nero and Trajan that Republican coin largely disappeared.

In terms of minting, Augustus's extraordinarily long reign was a time of experiment, during which the main coinage was produced in different places at different times. The mints included Emerita in Spain, Lugdunum and Rome.[19] There is no narrative of minting decisions to explain this, and the internal numismatic indications are partly uncertain. But it seems that Augustus was experimenting with minting close to the main sources of precious metal, and that this must explain the location of mints in Spain and Gaul. Presumably that allowed some state payments to be made direct to armies on the Rhine and Danube without moving metal south to Rome and then north again. Possibly dispersal of mints presented security problems. By the end of Augustus's reign, minting seems to have been concentrated at Lugdunum. This arrangement was maintained for a further half-century, until Nero's changes in AD 64 brought a transfer of the main mint from Lugdunum to Rome.[20]

---

[13] Cicero and Pliny fleetingly mention a monetary disturbance in the early first century BC: see Crawford 1974, 620 and Lo Cascio 1979.

[14] 18.117 (AD 553).

[15] Republican minting provides evidence about the mechanics of Roman coin-production which is more explicit than anything from the Principate (pp. 149–50 below).

[16] Suet. *Iul.* 54. For Caesar's relentless extraction of funds from all sources, see Frank *ESAR* 1.336–7.

[17] Suet. *Aug.* 41.1. P.9. During the first century AD, gold grew as a proportion of the precious-metal coin in circulation: see fig. 5.4.

[18] P. 103.

[19] *RIC* 1² 38–9 gives suggested dates; Crawford 1985, 256 ff. For the first few years of the reign, while there was still booty to consume, minting was at Rome (*RIC* 1² 39).

[20] P. 121.

Minting of precious-metal coin seems to have been low for most of Tiberius's reign. But it increased at about the time of the credit crisis of AD 33 (pp. 250–1). Tiberius's coin did not circulate for very long: the Alexandrian tetradrachms disappeared in the 60s (p. 233), while the denarii mainly disappeared in the 90s, and the aurei under Trajan (pp. 195, 117). Under Claudius the amount of minting was relatively low (cf. p. 221). But one development was a substantial reduction in the fineness of Alexandrian tetradrachms, by about 30% (p. 234).[21]

Nero's reign is an important focus of monetary change, with a metal-reduction in AD 64 whose effects proved to be far-reaching. Gold, silver, orichalcum and provincial silver all received reductions in their prime-metal content, or reductions in weight. The main reductions ranged from about 17% for Alexandrian tetradrachms to 4.5% for aurei. But Nero reduced zinc in the sestertius by over 20%, also lowering its weight from $11\frac{1}{2}$ to 12 coins per pound.[22] Nero evidently also moved the mint from Lugdunum to Rome, in the aftermath of the great fire at Rome. The move, passed over in silence by the sources, potentially increased the Emperor's control over minting processes.[23] The new lower standards meant more coin from a given amount of precious metal. Nero's reductions led within a few decades to the disappearance from circulation of almost all earlier coin, and most hoards of the Principate contain almost nothing from before these wholesale changes.

Heavy minting continued under Nero's three short-lived successors, and coin output remained high under the Flavians, with particularly heavy production of gold and silver by Vespasian. This run of accelerated production suggests a continuing wish to profit from the new lower weight standards, using earlier coin as well as new precious metal. Under Vespasian, silver fineness declined slightly, recovering under Titus. Domitian, in a remarkable experiment, attempted to restore pre-Neronian standards.[24] But after only three years he had to resume Nero's silver fineness, while retaining higher denarius-weight. The net precious-metal content for both silver and gold remained high throughout his reign. As a result, much of this coin soon disappeared, making the scale of Domitian's minting difficult to assess from hoard-survivals.

In his brief reign Nerva seems to have maintained Domitian's coinage standards almost unchanged. But Trajan returned to Nero's weight for the

---

[21] For other provincial coinages, see Burnett, Amandry, Ripolles 1992.

[22] Table 15.11 and text. The Emperor's involvement in technical minting decisions is uncertain, and the convention of ascribing change to him is followed here purely for convenience. For distorted views of Nero's monetary reforms, see p. 221 n.35 below.

[23] For the slowness of long-distance communication, see Duncan-Jones 1990, chapter 1. Greater control may have been the operative reason for the move. But Gaul, a major source of wealth under Caligula and Claudius, is heard of less in the Flavian period, when the main gold sources seem to be Spain and Dalmatia (pp. 108 n.61,103).

[24] While still Caesar, Domitian had published a book which Pliny cites as one of his sources for the section that deals with coinage (kindly pointed out by Professor Lo Cascio; Pliny NH 1 33).

aureus, and in the middle of his reign brought silver-content of the denarius down below the Neronian level. Trajan's reminting was acknowledged by issues of 'restored' earlier coin, as in some earlier reigns.[25] This reminting offered a profit, and in at least one case where there was no profit, older issues were allowed to go on circulating.

Under Hadrian there were no major currency changes. The sestertius and dupondius started to lose weight slightly (Tables 13.3 and 13.10), and also lost some of their remaining zinc content (Table 15.11). This deterioration in the orichalcum coinage continued under Antoninus Pius. But more important, silver fineness fell by a sizeable amount in the later part of his reign.

Under Marcus Aurelius, silver fineness was again reduced. Under Commodus, the volume of central coin production seems to have fallen substantially, with little gold and modest amounts of silver being struck (Tables 8.2 and 8.7). But even this low output was accompanied by substantial reductions in the weight of the denarius, amounting to a cut of 20% in silver content by the later years of the reign. Moreover, the sestertius was reduced by about 30% in weight (p. 189) and its zinc content approximately halved (Table 15.11). These were the biggest single changes in coinage standards up to that time, and considerably more than the reductions by Nero. Weight-reduction, although technically easier, was much more conspicuous than debasement. This use of an option which would tend to undermine confidence in the currency suggests ineffective or short-sighted management. As so often, the historians show no awareness of the coinage initiatives.

Septimius Severus at first returned to Commodus's early denarius-weight, before restoring the full Neronian weight. But he pushed debasement much further, with the result that denarii of his main period contained less silver than those of Commodus, a drop of about 12% (Tables 15.5 and 15.6). Gold minting continued relatively unchanged, but some of it may have depended for raw material on older coin (Table 15.2).[26] Under Caracalla, reduced weight and fineness created a further 11% drop in the silver in the denarius. In 215 a new coin (the radiate or 'Antoninianus') was issued, with a net reduction in silver content of 33% compared with the denarii of Severus, after allowing for its higher face-value (Table 15.3 and p. 222). Caracalla's other main innovation was a 10% reduction in aureus-weight, the largest single reduction up to that point (Table 15.2). Under Elagabalus further falls in weight and fineness reduced silver-content of the denarius by a further 16%, and the rate of silver minting apparently reached new heights (Table 15.5). But at Antioch, somewhat surprisingly, gold minting at the heavier standard brought back by Macrinus was allowed to continue.[27] Under Severus Alexander the denarius

---

[25] The issues of restored coin were struck from very few dies, and were evidently tiny compared with the amounts reminted at this time (p. 151). For other restored coin, see pp. 117, 195–7.

[26] Shortage of new metal is suggested by the low volume of minting under Commodus. Dispossessions gave Septimius access to great quantities of private wealth, which if not already in the form of bullion could be readily sold off for cash (cf. p. 10 above).

[27] West 1941, Table AA.

remained steady, but aureus-weight began to vary, falling by as much as 14% in some cases (Tables 15.2 and 15.5).

3. AWARENESS OF CURRENCY DIFFERENCES

Awareness of coinage differences could exist at two levels. One was the government's knowledge of metallic anomalies in the coinage; that might or might not be accompanied by a similar awareness among coin users. In classical economic theory, Gresham's Law, that bad money drives out good, should be triggered by quite small differences in quality. In practice during the first two centuries of the Empire, coins with differing metallic content seem to have gone on circulating on more or less equal terms, unless there was a state initiative to remove the better coin.[28] State withdrawals in this period seem to have been typically motivated by profit, rather than by any wish to modernise the coinage for its own sake. Most coinage withdrawals can be recognised as relatively sudden events caused by state initiatives, not long processes of attrition.

The early Domitianic denarii struck to higher weight and higher fineness were allowed only the briefest lifetime, being withdrawn (presumably in 107) long before they can have shown significant signs of wear. But many later Domitianic denarii which were merely overweight were not withdrawn, and went on circulating freely for many decades.

Nevertheless, weight-reductions were likely to alert the consumer to the fact that manipulation was taking place. A $7\frac{1}{2}\%$ weight loss in the denarius under Nero may not have triggered this reaction, but the further 15% weight-reduction under Commodus may well have done so.[29] Unfortunately, the reactions of the market remain unchronicled by extant sources, and they are difficult to reconstruct from physical survivals.

If serious monetary dislocation drove some coin out of circulation, this might be indicated by shorter timespans in surviving hoards. In an entirely static monetary system, hoards should go back the full natural lifetime of the coinage, and span several centuries. At the opposite extreme, rapid debasement or weight-reduction should make Gresham's Law operate fully, shrinking the contents of circulation hoards to a few decades of coin-issue at most. A version of the second pattern is suggested by hoards from the middle and late third century.[30] But in practice the sequence is difficult to verify even at that date, because under extreme conditions a fast-deteriorating coinage may feed on itself, with recent coin providing the raw material for new inferior issues. Thus short timespans within hoards may sometimes imply subtraction and reminting of older coin, and not merely the operation of Gresham's Law.

---

[28] See p. 198 n.20.

[29] The weight of Roman silver coin was so variable that it took quite large reductions to make it obvious from individual specimens that the standard had changed (cf. p. 198 n.20).

[30] Duncan-Jones 1982, 375, using data from Callu 1969.

4. MINTING AND METAL SUPPLY

Using physical changes in the coinage to deduce monetary policy faces serious ambiguities, in the absence of other explicit evidence. There are various possibilities. Thus by itself, debasement of the silver currency could be consistent with:

1. Increases in government spending, and a constant supply of silver.
2. Efforts to maintain government spending, and a falling silver supply.
3. Efforts to maintain government spending, and a falling supply of gold.
4. Or increased spending, despite falling metal supplies.

None of this can be clear without direct indications about the supply of precious metal. The few indications of mine-output at this date refer only to gold.[31] Pliny gives a figure of 20,000 pounds of gold per year for the rent of gold mines in Asturia, Callaecia and Lusitania, presumably based on his first-hand knowledge as a procurator in Spain. If credible, this amount is enough by itself to account for most of the annual gold coin production tentatively estimated under Hadrian.[32] Pliny also indicates that a gold-strike in Dalmatia under Nero yielded 50 pounds of gold per day. The annual equivalent would be more than 15,000 pounds, but the mine was presumably short-lived.[33] The quest for new metal can also be seen in Caligula's attempts to extract gold from orpiment, Nero's hunt for African buried treasure, and probably in the Neronian expedition to Nubia, one of the prime gold-producing areas of early times, and the main source of Egypt's gold.[34]

To be set against production of new metal is the loss of bullion through external trade. From Pliny's well known remarks, Rome's eastern balance of payments was unfavourable, to the extent of HS50 or 100 million per year. The outflow was mainly of gold coin, to judge from finds in India.[35] Pliny's figures

---

[31] For recent work, see Domergue 1990, 367–74; Andreau 1989–90. For the Late Empire, see Depeyrot 1991, 207–9.

[32] NH 33.78. Translated into post-Neronian aurei, the equivalent is 880,000 coins, compared with an annual production under Hadrian tentatively estimated at 1,100,000; Table 11.1.

[33] NH 33.67. The fact that all mines had a finite lifetime (Paus. 1.1 for example mentions the Athenian silver mines at Laurium as a thing of the past) is a reason for not taking Republican silver-mining figures as relevant here. Spain and Dalmatia similarly figure as gold-sources in Statius's eulogy of an a rationibus (Silv. 3.3.89–90). The mine-output figure of HS600 million in Macmullen 1987, 745 is based on a misreading of the figures for copper mines in Frank ESAR 5.51.

[34] Pliny NH 33.79; Tac. Ann. 16.2; Pliny NH 12.18–19. For Nubia, cf. Bovill 1968. Under Claudius, a provincial governor employed legionaries to mine for silver in the land of the Mattiaci (Tac. Ann. 11.20).

[35] Pliny gives HS100 million a year as the cost in bullion outflow of Rome's eastern trade including trade with China, and HS50 million as the cost of trade with India (12.84 and 6.101; bullion outflow certainly continued on the grand scale in East–West trade in the Renaissance period, Cipolla 1981, 230–2). Significant amounts of Roman coin are found in India, but not in China. See Turner 1989, with Berghaus 1989. For China, see Hirth 1885 and Ferguson 1976. For eastern trade in general, see Jones 1974, chapter 7, Raschke 1978 and Casson 1989. For trade and currency, see Crawford 1980. Pliny's statements about bullion loss are rejected by Veyne 1979.

appear very high, and are evidently more indicative than exact.[36] Nevertheless, loss of precious metal through trade was real, and it was increased by loss through external subsidies, which were again typically paid in gold.[37]

The fact that there was never any retreat from debasement after the first century AD may in itself imply that silver mining was not keeping pace, and was perhaps even in decline.[38] There are potential signs of metal shortage under Commodus, which may be associated with the serious check under Marcus Aurelius, partly due to plague.[39] And there are unmistakable signs of increased spending, with the army pay increases under the first Severan Emperors. New gold coin is apparently rarer under the Severi than under the Antonines.[40]

Thus a working diagnosis of monetary events between 180 and 220 must contain elements of explanations (1) and (4) above. At a time when metal supplies were apparently falling, government spending was increased.[41] Greater debasement of the silver coinage was the inescapable result. This effect was probably accelerated by parallel shortages of gold bullion, which could not be stretched because of the continued taboo on debasing gold coin. For much of the Severan period, denarius-production was apparently much higher than under the Antonines. But in terms of the silver used, the increase was probably slight.[42]

Debasement tended to be accompanied by increased mint-activity, whose biggest peaks evidently took place when precious-metal content had just been reduced. Thus the intensive minting of gold by Nero and Vespasian followed Nero's reductions in metal content, as did Nero's frenetic silver minting in Alexandria, and Vespasian's heavy silver minting at Rome. Later peaks under Septimius Severus and Elagabalus followed the spectacular reduction in silver content by Commodus, and the substantial reduction by Septimius himself.[43]

In cases like these, reminting existing coin offered obvious monetary gains, and allowed the government to spend more than it otherwise could have done. Minting under Nero and Vespasian clearly rolled up earlier Julio-Claudian coin, and issues under the Severi partly depended on Antonine coin. The minting after Trajan's debasement liquidated almost all Republican silver coin still in circulation, and Republican types figure on Trajanic restored

---

[36] See pp. 111–12 below.   [37] See p. 93 n.65 above and pp. 111–12 below.
[38] Earlier, Pliny mentions the Livian copper mine in Gaul being worked out, and the Salutariensian copper mine in Baetica being abandoned before it was re-let at a higher rent (*NH* 34.3; 165).
[39] Interruption to mining activity resulting from the plague under Marcus Aurelius has sometimes been suggested. A serious break at this point is certainly seen in other evidence (Duncan-Jones 1990, 71–5). Records of catastrophic falls in the number of taxpayers in villages of the Mendesian nome in Egypt by the late 160s cite plague amongst other causes (Kambitsis 1985, 104, 70, 76, 77, 99, 116). Further vivid evidence comes from the marble quarry on Teos, suddenly abandoned in the mid-160s. The dates on 26 inscribed blocks left in the quarry and never used are all between 163 and 166 (Fant 1989B, 213 n.44; 215).
[40] See p. 206.
[41] For signs of metal shortage in the silver currency in the middle and late third century, see Depeyrot, Hollard 1987.   [42] Table 8.7.   [43] See Tables 11.1 and 11.2.

issues. The finest Domitianic coin, although still very recent, apparently also disappeared then. But much of the coin which offered little minting profit, the older issue of Antony, was allowed to go on circulating.

Important though reminting became, it was of course not the only source of raw material. The amount of denarius-coin in circulation was apparently stable or even grew, despite the steady wastage that took place within a vast monetary system.[44] Since wastage losses in this period were almost certainly greater than gains in volume due to debasement, minting was bound to use new metal as well as old coin.[45]

5. COINAGE MANIPULATION

Debasements and weight-reductions tend to occur at times of financial stringency, as has just been seen. But it is not clear that before the Severi coinage manipulation was a primary tool of fiscal policy. Some rulers who faced very serious fiscal shortages, such as Caligula, seem to have minted relatively little. And some currency manipulation apparently did not have the aim of producing more coin. Thus the hoard evidence strongly suggests that the substantial gold minting under Marcus and Verus depleted the stock of Trajanic and Hadrianic aurei in circulation.[46] Reminting such recent coin brought no financial profit, since weight and fineness remained unchanged. The one gain, and the evident motive here, was the propaganda advantage of portraying the living Emperor. Propaganda pressure is shown also by the temporary drop in silver fineness in some accession issues of denarii. Here the need for more coin of the new ruler meant that metal supplies were deliberately stretched.[47]

In another case, Nero reduced silver content substantially, but minted too few denarii to profit from it significantly. However, aurei and Egyptian tetradrachms were produced on the largest scale.[48] As in the Renaissance period, rapid reminting on a large scale almost certainly required a recall of coinage.[49] The Neronian evidence probably suggests recall of existing aurei and tetradrachms, but not of denarii.

Similarly, Commodus faced serious deficits, and instigated or allowed the boldest attack on silver standards up to that date.[50] But the volume of his minting appears to have been too slight to produce any large-scale gain.

---

[44] See pp. 193–4.   [45] For wastage, see pp. 205–6; for debasement, pp. 223–31.
[46] See p. 206.   [47] See pp. 238–9.   [48] See pp. 31,120.
[49] In seventeenth-century Spain, the government enforced recall by demonetising the coin in question, making it worthless to the owner after a certain date (in 1603: see Hamilton 1934, 76). Procedures under Trajan resulted in a very sharp drop in amounts on the Continent, which was less in Britain and perhaps other outlying areas (pp. 197–8 below).
[50] Contemporary sources suggest that for many purposes Rome was run by powerful Prefects during much of Commodus's reign (cf. n.8 above; Grosso 1964). Deterioration of coin in Commodus's name apparently starts in the 170s (p. 241).

Apparently his silver debasement was a response to the need to produce more coin, but without serious effort to obtain large amounts of existing coin for reminting.[51]

Sudden eclipse overtakes certain blocs of coin in the hoards. This is true of Julio-Claudian denarii in hoards from the 90s AD onwards. Under Trajan several more coin-groups virtually disappear, including Republican denarii, fine silver of Domitian, and the heavy aurei of AD 81–100.[52] We can choose to think that these coins were merely culled from a stream of recycled tax-payments that was continually passing through the treasury. But the speed with which coin-issues disappear argues that this mechanism could not possibly have been enough. Almost certainly a specific recall of coin was needed, and that is presumably what Dio's passing mention of Trajan's coinage initiative may reflect.

6. MONETARY CIRCULATION

The rate at which coin was diffused from the mint was apparently slow. Also, its circulation velocity as measured by loss of coin-weight was much less than in comparable modern currencies, implying that there were fewer physical transactions per coin.[53]

Coin was disseminated from the mint by public spending. That had two primary elements, army pay, spent mainly in the provinces, and spending by the Emperor, mainly in Rome and Italy. Civilian salaries were a smaller component. State spending was enough to distribute coin very widely, mainly because army posts were spread over most of the empire.[54] In Britain, coin-finds show essentially the same chronology in aggregate whether they come from military or civilian sites (fig.7.1).[55]

But some large and prosperous areas had small garrisons. Where this was true in the East, notably in some of the Asian provinces, local minting in silver was allowed to continue.[56] That could be seen as a recognition of the need for monetary exchange, which was independent of the primary need to make state

---

[51] In Egypt, however, he minted heavily (see p. 31).

[52] See pp. 102, 196, 83 n.49.   [53] Chapters 6, 13, and 14, section 4.

[54] For the size of the main troop concentrations, see Birley 1981B, Table 5. There were also bureaux of civilian tax-employees in the provinces (cf. *ILS* 1359, 1421, 1492–5, 1498, 1506–8, 1510–1, 1514–5, 1555).

[55] The aggregates use data assembled and classified by Reece 1991. The components are 11 groups of finds classified as civilian (N = 8,022; Verulamium nos. 6, 7 and 8, Colchester 34 and 37; Cirencester 39 and 43; Wroxeter 24; London 31; Silchester; Aldborough), and 3 groups classified as military (N = 2,111; Richborough; Chester 122; Ribchester). The two chronological profiles are essentially the same; the weighting towards earlier coin for the military sites merely implies that the period of deposition began earlier there (the figures are percentages).

[56] But the widespread local minting in the East also took in garrisoned regions (Sartre 1991, 91–103). For troop strength in Asia, see Speidel 1984 with Birley 1981B. The main concentrations were in Cappadocia, with an estimated garrison in the mid-second century of about 22,000, including two legions (Birley 1981B, Table 5).

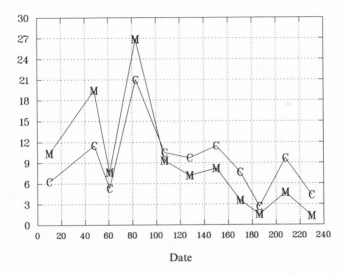

Figure 7.1 Percentage profiles of coin-finds from military and civilian sites in Britain (M: military; C: civilian).

payments.[57] In the West, no such compensations were allowed, and local coinage soon disappeared under the Empire.[58] Where gaps existed in the system of supplying coin through government mechanisms, long-distance trade may have produced some compensating effects.[59] But discontinuities in the circulation pattern show such compensations failing to operate, or doing so only on a small scale. And whether Roman trading mechanisms led to many long-distance monetary transfers is still a matter of debate.[60]

[57] Where it contributed to local self-glorification (cf. Sartre 1991, 96), the continuation of civic minting could be seen as part of the pressure for special treatment successfully exerted by eastern cities (cf. Duncan-Jones 1990, 171 and n.85; for the mass of local mints, more than 300 under Septimius Severus, cf. Sartre 1991, 96). Dio makes Maecenas advise Augustus against allowing cities to have their own coin or weights and measures, apparently from his dislike of local autonomy (52.30.9). Recent work directly associates much of the production of eastern civic mints with the needs of Roman administration (Burnett, Amandry, Ripolles, 1992, 8). For some suggested correlations between eastern mint output and military expeditions, see Sartre 1991, 92 n.9. For state payments as the basis for coinage, see Crawford 1970, and for the Greek and Hellenistic worlds, see Hackens 1987, 155–60. For other suggested reasons for minting, see Howgego 1990, drawing attention to late fourth-century evidence, *de rebus bellicis* 1.6 and 1.9.

[58] Most of it had gone by the death of Tiberius, and the remainder went by the death of Claudius. Crawford 1985, 271–2; Burnett, Amandry, Ripolles, 1992, 18.

[59] 'The raising and spending of the imperial revenue effected a certain redistribution of wealth between the provinces. The bulk of the revenue was raised in the richer provinces . . . but the greater part of it was spent on the army, mostly stationed in poorer and underdeveloped areas' (Jones 1974, 127). This insight was given wider currency by Hopkins 1980, proposing a model for its monetary consequences. The effectiveness of the monetary model is questioned in Duncan-Jones 1990, chapter 2 (see chapter 12 below).

[60] For an illustration of long-distance monetised trading without long-distance movement of coin, see Duncan-Jones 1990, 42.

The most obvious discontinuity in monetary circulation is the impact of mint location under the Julio-Claudians. Until AD 64, the central mint was located outside Italy, at Lugdunum, and this seems to have starved Italy of current coin. In the first century, much less Julio-Claudian gold and silver is found in Italian hoards than in hoards from western provinces, despite the fact that state spending in the capital obviously continued.[61] Regional circulation differences are also seen in the bronze coinage, where types of Nero struck in Lugdunum are numerous in northern provinces, while those struck in Rome are numerous only in Italy.[62]

Inertia in the circulation of bronze coin is seen again at the end of the second century. From the start of the Severan dynasty, the bronze coin that was still being minted in Rome ceases to be found in northern provinces such as Gaul and Britain, although abundant there up to that point.[63] Where change is so clear cut, the reason is clearly the ending of government supply. It implies that northern army camps were no longer being furnished with bronze coin under the Severi, and that market movement of bronze coin was too slight to compensate for this.

The evidence for discontinuities in the distribution of precious metal coinage is usually less explicit after the Julio-Claudian period. But tests show significant unevenness in the later circulation pattern, again arguing that the market's ability to compensate by trade-flows was limited.[64] Specific gaps in the exchange system are sometimes also reflected in the scale on which counterfeit coin was produced.[65] The capacity of markets to operate without money cannot be ignored, and barter may always have predominated in some areas.[66] But elsewhere, monetary shortages, both local and regional, are clearly implied, and the production of counterfeit coin indicates a clear need for coin in its own right.

7. COIN PRODUCTION

7.1. LAYOUT AND DEMARCATION WITHIN THE MINT

Evaluation of the enormous Rome coinage of the Principate is made difficult by scattered and incomplete survivals. But detailed analysis of immense

---

[61] Caligula's choice of Gaul for activities which included auctioning palace furniture fetched with great difficulty from Rome, and proscribing Gallic nobles for their wealth, might also suggest higher monetary levels in the province where the mint was located (Suet. *Gaius* 38.4–39; Dio 59.22.4). Its original location in that province could be a reflection of high precious-metal stocks. The most expensive statue known to Pliny was one commissioned by the Arverni under the early Empire (*NH* 34.45); the most costly wine he knew came from Vienne, another Gallic town (*NH* 14.57); and the bigger of the two golden crowns offered to Claudius for his British triumph came from Gallia Comata (*NH* 33.54; it weighed 9,000 pounds). For Gallic wealth, see also Duncan-Jones 1980.

[62] See p. 121.   [63] See p. 22.   [64] See pp. 172–6.   [65] See p. 22.

[66] See chapter 2, pp. 20–1. For the extent of rural monetisation, see de Ligt 1990, 33–43.

hoards is almost bound to reveal features of its organisation. At present, the one available resource of this kind is the published Reka Devnia hoard of denarii and radiates, with more than 80,000 coins. Its contents for major reigns have been analysed here using a computer database.

The scale of production under the Principate was so large that internal subdivisions may easily have existed in the mint at all times.[67] But demarcations have not so far emerged clearly during the reigns when coin-output was mainly in the Emperor's name. Production on a substantial scale for more than one individual meant by definition some demarcation within the production process. The lines of demarcation were systematised in obvious ways, to judge from Reka Devnia evidence. Thus under Septimius Severus, the ratios between Severus, Caracalla and Geta in terms of quantity of coin are very close to 6:3:2 in the main part of his reign. When Marcus Aurelius was striking in parallel with Lucius Verus, the denarius ratio between them is seen as 2:1, as it is later in the reign between Marcus and Commodus.[68]

Coin-data also suggest different production norms for some blocs of coin minted for different individuals within the imperial family, presumably implying some separation between minting authorities. These variations, usually small in themselves but big enough to be perceptible and sometimes systematic, appear under Vespasian, Antoninus Pius and Marcus Aurelius. The evidence again comes from the abundant silver coinage.[69]

7.2. PRODUCTION LEVELS

The Reka Devnia evidence suggests further regularities under Septimius Severus. In the five periods of his reign, the average number of coins per type struck for the Emperor approximates ratios of 1:4:6. The corresponding figure for Caracalla in this reign is about 3 in each of the three periods examined. For Julia Domna and Plautilla the levels are about 7 and 6, because coin-types for female members of the 'Domus Divina' changed less frequently.[70]

At the 'microscopic' level, dies for a given reverse coin-type were evidently produced in set amounts, or up to a set target figure. Typical totals for gold dies of 25 or 50 per reverse type emerge from the detailed studies described below.[71] With substantial types, the overall amount of coin to be produced

[67] A Rome inscription from AD 115 shows five 'conductores flaturae argentar. monetae Caesaris'. This five-part division of silver smelting recurs in an undated inscription showing a 'manceps officinarum aerariarum quinque item flaturae argentariae' (*CIL* VI 791; VI 8455 = *ILS* 1470, whose formulae suggest a second-century date). Alföldi 1958–9, 44 n.47; Hirschfeld 1905, 184–6. Three inscriptions from the Rome mint, also of AD 115, give lists of mint employees by name, which show 90 staff including a manager. They are divided into *officinatores, signatores, suppostores* and *malleatores*: *CIL* VI 42–4. Fifty-one were freedmen, and the rest slaves. The lists are apparently complete for the categories shown. Cf. Carson 1956, 233–5.

[68] Pp. 140–1. Reka Devnia samples for the Flavians, though still large by any other standard, are much smaller than those for the Antonines and Severi, and have not been used in this context.

[69] Pp.240–2.   [70] P. 136.   [71] Pp. 159–60.

was evidently also set in advance.[72] But die-utilisation often appears to be very skewed, with some dies being used far more heavily than others.[73] Obverse and reverse coin-dies usually existed in approximately equal amounts in coinage of this period.[74]

Coin-types could be struck in parallel from gold and silver on apparently equal terms. But gold dies, of higher quality, and presumably more long-lived, might occasionally be used to strike silver, whereas transferred use of silver dies is not seen in the evidence studied. Coin-types could also be divided unequally between the precious metals. Thus, the types of Aelius examined show production of silver coin in very small amounts from mainly gold types, and production of gold coin in very small amounts from mainly silver types.[75]

7.3. STABILITY AND FLUCTUATION

Over the medium to long term, production of precious-metal coin appears to be relatively stable for much of the period.[76] But estimates from coin-survivals of relative output per reign-year seem to differ considerably between the later first century and the second century. In AD 54–81, the percentage coefficient of variation for gold reign by reign is as high as 90, whereas in AD 98–180 it falls to 10. The corresponding figure for silver in this later period is 16.[77]

In the shorter term, within reigns of substantial length divided into periods of several years, the percentage coefficient of variation is appreciable. Thus under Vespasian, Trajan and Hadrian, figures of 36, 54 and 24 are seen for gold, and 14, 27 and 40 for silver. Bronze figures for Trajan and Hadrian are 87 and 31.[78]

At the year-to-year level, variation is more difficult to study because of shortage of year-dated coinage. But a trial study of the years 148–61 from the evidence of large hoards showed substantial oscillations in coin-production for all three metals: the percentage coefficient of variation is 63 for gold, 50 for silver and 64 for bronze.[79] Year-to-year movement is again considerable in silver figures from the reign of Severus Alexander.[80]

As a whole, these figures suggest a hierarchy in which rapid short-term fluctuation in coin-production co-existed with smaller fluctuation in the medium term, and relative stability over the long term. This could suggest that for much of the time stable targets were maintained over the longer term, but that in implementing them, short-term stability was affected by interruptions

---

[72] P. 162, from Hadrianic evidence. Stability in production targets per type is also implicit in the stable figures for the number of coins per type (pp. 136,140).

[73] P. 162.

[74] Pp. 154–5.   [75] Pp. 152,160.

[76] Lack of coin-evidence makes the position before AD 64 more difficult to assess. For the small quantities of denarii struck between 37 and 64, note Burnett, Amandry, Ripolles 1992, 7.

[77] Chapter 8.

[78] From data in Tables 9.2–9.5. 'Bronze' refers to sestertii.

[79] Pp.131–3.   [80] P. 127.

in the metal supply.[81] Nevertheless, some long-term change clearly also took place, with certain reigns showing marked deviations from normal levels of coin-output.[82]

7.4. VOLUME OF COIN

Some progress can be made towards working out how much coin was produced.[83] The number of coin-dies can be estimated from a calculation with three elements.

1. Establishing actual die-numbers and ratios of dies to coins, type by type for a range of coin-types, after collecting coins or coin-illustrations in large numbers.
2. Using this information to estimate original die-totals for these coin-types after modelling large type- and die-samples statistically, by means of discrete distributions.
3. Using the resulting die-estimates to extrapolate die-totals for entire populations of types, from the representation of these types in the largest available hoards.

The results for the reign of Hadrian imply a population of roughly 40,000 silver reverse dies. Gold proves to be more complex. For gold coin, dies were evidently used at one of two levels of productivity, a high-output category and a low-output category, whose ratio was approximately 2:1. Hadrianic gold coin was produced from a mixture of low- and high-output dies. The estimated total for gold under Hadrian is the equivalent of roughly 530 high-output dies or 1,030 low-output dies. The average yearly equivalents for Hadrian's twenty-year reign are about 2,000 silver reverse-dies and 25–50 gold reverse-dies.

The number of coins produced is much more uncertain and will probably remain so. Judging from parallels and from the fact that in large samples of coin-finds, gold accounts for about 70% of precious-metal coin by face value, a possible order of magnitude for production from the central mint under Hadrian is 16 million denarii and 1.1 million aurei per year.[84] At that rate, precious-metal coin-output would be worth roughly HS170 million per year. The output of eastern silver and of base-metal coin might have increased this by about one-fifth, making approximately HS200 million per year.[85]

This can be no more than a rough order of magnitude, but it suggests certain comparisons. It makes Pliny's HS100 million for the annual drain of bullion

---

[81] But there are also what appear to be short-term systemic effects (p. 126).
[82] Tables 8.7 and 8.8.
[83] See chapters 10–11.
[84] See chapter 11, p. 167. The modern assumption has been that silver was the dominant currency of the Empire (see e.g. Jones 1974, 194, 201). But coin-finds from our period analysed in large amounts show substantially more gold than silver in terms of monetary value (p. 71).
[85] Pp. 169–70.

eastwards difficult to accept literally.[86] It is unlikely that an empire with large
armies to pay could have afforded such a high net loss. And since the minting
estimate is only a fraction of the Empire's estimated budget (p. 45), it suggests
that, year by year, government expenditure must have depended more on tax
revenue than on its ability to produce new coin.[87]

[86] P. 103 above.   [87] For the budget, see pp. 45–6.

8

THE CHRONOLOGY OF MINT-OUTPUT

1. COIN-HOARDS AND MINT-OUTPUT

Roman coin-hoards of a given date tend to show chronological similarities, which can be extremely close.[1] No records of Roman mint-output survive. But in a later case where a large hoard can be compared with year-by-year mint records, the two chronological profiles are very similar.[2] Even without this specific example, close resemblances between the chronology of Roman hoards would be very difficult to explain if the hoards did not reflect mint-output.[3]

These similarities are illustrated in figs. 8.1–8.4. The best test is year-by-year analysis based on large samples. The first diagram compares year-totals for the period AD 41–71 in the two largest hoards of Egyptian tetradrachms listed by Milne. Hoard 3 ends in AD 165, and Hoard 6 in 191. Milne's totals of dated coins are 4,344 and 2,243 coins; 3,548 and 1,700 belong to the period shown here.[4] Figure 8.1 shows that the annual percentages are extremely close ($r^2 = 0.983$). Both hoards clearly illustrate the enormous surge in tetradrachm output in the last years of Nero.

The second diagram comes from the reign of Trajan. Trajan's coinage, like most of the central coinage of our period, is not dated by year, but is divided into six chronological segments.[5] The hoards are the gigantic Reka Devnia hoard from Moesia ending in AD 251/3, and the via Braccianese hoard from outside Rome which ends in 230. The reported coin-samples for the reign of Trajan are 5,216 and 1,051. Figure 8.2 again reveals extremely close agreement: $r^2 = 0.992$.

The third example again uses the Reka Devnia hoard, this time matching it

---

[1] Hopkins 1980, fig.4 gives an impressionistic account. However, this assimilates hoards and stray finds, which raises problems of method (see below, p. 115 and Duncan-Jones 1990, 38–9).
[2] A hoard of 18,000 Swedish silver coins deposited in the mid-eighteenth century can be checked against surviving mint records, Thordeman 1948. Volk's percentage comparison shows close similarity between the profiles for hoard- and mint-output for 1, 2 and 4 mark pieces (Volk 1987, figs. 1a and 1b). His diagrams clearly show the effect of wastage, with the latest clump of coin over-represented in percentage terms, and the earliest clump under-represented.
[3] For use of Republican denarius hoards to estimate the number of dies used per issue, see Crawford 1974, 2,642–74 (recently discussed in Volk 1987).
[4] The hoards are A60 and A69 in Christiansen 1985.
[5] The Braccianese hoard has not been published as a whole. Figures for Trajan are summarised year by year in Lo Cascio 1978, 98, using Hill's dating. They have been regrouped here into the longer periods where dating is secure. For specific problems in Hill's results, see Walker, 3.152–3.

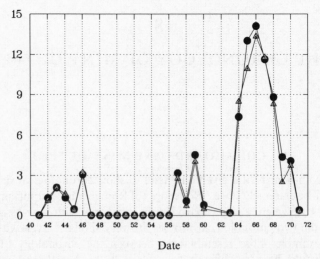

Figure 8.1 Percentages of coin per year in two large tetradrachm hoards, AD 41–71 (Milne nos. 3 and 6). (Circle: hoard 3; triangle: hoard 6.)

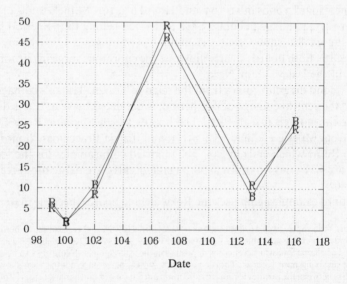

Figure 8.2 Percentages of Trajanic denarii in Reka Devnia and via Braccianese hoards. (R: Reka Devnia; B: via Braccianese.)

against coins from the hoard from Elveden in Britain, which ends under Philip II. The comparison is based on denarii of the reign of Severus Alexander, 7,573 year-dated coins at Reka Devnia in Carson's analysis, and 395 at Elveden.[6] The annual percentages are shown in fig. 8.3. Overall agreement is once more very close ($r^2 = 0.951$).

A final example comes from the short reign of Claudius II in 268–70. This reign is too brief to allow useful analysis by year, but the coins are divided between twelve numbered *officinae*, which can be used for comparison in place of year-dating. The Normanby hoard which ends in AD 286/93 has 1,483 radiates of Claudius's issue II(a) identified by *officina*, while an aggregate of 22 other hoards, partly Continental, has 7,552 such coins.[7] The overall similarity in fig. 8.4 is again obvious ($r^2 = 0.978$).

2. GOLD OUTPUT BY REIGN

A recent discussion suggests that hoards and stray coin-finds show the same chronological patterns.[8] But that should not logically be so, and where it seems to be the case, there is a possibility that coin seen as stray finds may owe its origin to hoards.[9] Hoards normally represent cross-sections of coin in circulation at a particular date. Because of wastage, the older the coin in the hoard, the less of it there will be. By contrast, coin in stray finds may have been deposited at any date within its circulation-lifetime.[10] Stray finds thus give fullest representation to early coin, because the later the coin, the shorter the possible period of deposit.[11] By contrast, circulation hoards must emphasise later coin, which has had least wastage.[12]

For gold, three main sources were considered, a group of five gold hoards ending between AD 166 and 205; assemblages of stray finds of gold coin from Gaul and Germany divided into three regional samples; and a large gold hoard ending in AD 79. The totals in the hoards were adjusted for wastage using the wastage rate of $\frac{1}{360}$ per year.[13] The circulation-period is taken as the period up to the date of the final coin in the hoard. The figures in the stray finds were adjusted in two ways:

---

[6] *BMCRE* 6, 42–45.   [7] Bland, Burnett 1988, 130, Table 14.   [8] Hopkins 1980, 114–15.
[9] In theory, genuine similarities could arise in regions where monetisation was late, if much of what came in was older coin. But this is rarely what the finds suggest.
[10] Defining when a circulation-period ended may sometimes be difficult, but in gold currency of this period, sudden weight-reductions could bring the circulating lifetime of existing coin to an end.
[11] On the assumption, which certainly applies here, that the coin did not go on circulating indefinitely, but reached the end of its circulation period at a particular point (cf. p. 117).
[12] Silver hoards whose chronology runs counter to the wastage effect (such as the Rome hoard from via Braccianese) tend to belong to the Severan period, when premium older coin may have been deliberately chosen for some payments (see p. 184 n.17 on Viuz).
[13] See pp. 206–10. Wastage of course applies to the original population, not to the part that remains visible after wastage has taken place. Hence the formula to compensate for it is $X/(1 - \text{wastage-factor})$, where X is the quotient for coins remaining. Here the wastage-factor equals (circulation-period in years)/360. For this rate of gold wastage, see p. 210.

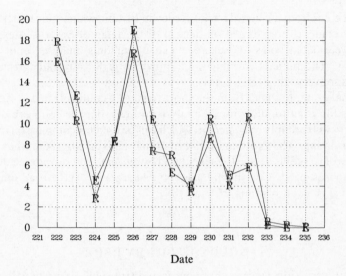

Figure 8.3 Annual percentages of denarii of Severus Alexander in Reka Devnia and Elveden hoards. (R: Reka Devnia; E: Elveden.)

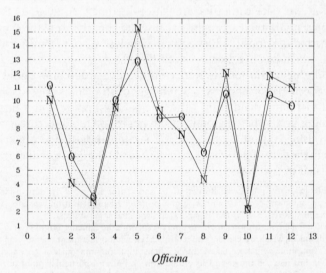

Figure 8.4 Percentages of coin of different numbered *officinae* in the Normanby hoard and in twenty-two other hoards (Claudius II, issue II (a)). (N: Normanby; O: other hoards.)

Table 8.1 *Stray finds of gold coin from France as percentages*

Period	Narbonensis/ Aquitania (N)	Lugdunensis (N)	Belgica/ Germanies (N)
Augustus	14.41 (33)	8.43 (22)	5.96 (28)
Tiberius	10.92 (25)	13.79 (36)	10.43 (49)
Claudius	9.17 (21)	5.75 (15)	4.89 (46)
Nero	20.52 (47)	12.64 (33)	25.96 (122)
Flavians	14.41 (33)	17.62 (46)	19.36 (91)
Trajan	9.17 (21)	9.58 (25)	7.23 (34)
Hadrian	6.99 (16)	8.81 (23)	8.09 (38)
Antoninus Pius	6.55 (15)	10.34 (27)	9.36 (44)
Marcus Aurelius	3.06 (7)	8.43 (22)	5.11 (24)
Commodus	1.75 (4)	0.38 (1)	0.21 (1)
Severus/Caracalla	0.87 (2)	2.30 (6)	2.13 (10)
Elagabalus/S.Alexander	2.18 (5)	1.92 (5)	1.28 (6)
TOTAL for reigns shown	100 (229)	100 (261)	100 (493)

Source: Callu, Loriot 1990, 82, and index entries for individual reigns for pairs of reigns conflated in their summary.

(1) By calculating the amount of coin deposited per year, allowing for its circulation-period. The termini assumed are AD 86 for aurei minted up to AD 64, and AD 220 for aurei minted from that date onwards.[14]

(2) By including in this calculation an allowance for wastage during the period of circulation. Gold wastage is reckoned as $\frac{1}{360}$ per year. But to obtain a mean figure, the calculation assumes wastage over half the circulation-period (in other words, a rate of $\frac{1}{720}$ per year for the whole period).[15]

The stray finds form the longest series (Table 8.1; Vespasian and Titus have to be combined here because some find-records conflate the two).[16] Their

---

[14] AD 86 was chosen because it is half-way between AD 64 and AD 107. Reminting at lower weight began on a serious scale in AD 64. It evidently continued in the heavy gold production of Vespasian ('restored' aurei of Augustus were struck at this time, *BMCRE* 2, 68). What was presumably the final liquidation of Julio-Claudian gold took place in AD 107 (Julius Caesar, Augustus, Tiberius and Claudius all received 'restored' issues of gold, *BMCRE* 3, lxxxix and 142–3). Caracalla's 10% weight-reduction in AD 215 probably drove out earlier coin quite soon. Even the oldest gold coin then circulating (that of Nero) would have had a premium over Caracalla's new aurei, since its weight-loss by then would have been about 5% (see p.191).

[15] Half the period because during its active lifetime the mean coin-population is half-way between its size at the start of the circulation period and its size at the end of that period, assuming linear wastage. The formula for restoring stray-find amounts is thus: (percentage observed/circulation-period in years) × 1/(1 − (circulation-period/720)). For the first entry in Table 8.2 column 2, Augustus, the circulation-period is estimated as 31 BC–AD 86, or 117 years, taking AD 86 as the mean terminal date (see n.14). This means $(8.43/117) \times 1/(1 - (117/720)) = .086$, or as an integer, 8.60. For the third entry, Claudius, the circulation-period is 45 (AD 41–86), and the calculation reads $(5.75/45) \times 1/(1 - (45/720)) = 0.136$, or as an integer, 13.6.

[16] The coin of Domitian struck to higher weights had a very short lifetime in circulation and

Table 8.2 *French stray-gold finds compensated for wastage and circulation-period*

Period	Median percentage compensated for wastage	Median percentage uncompensated
1. Augustus	8.60	8.43
2. Tiberius	16.80	10.92
3. Claudius	13.60	5.75
4. Nero	16.10	20.52
5. Vespasian and Titus	14.40	17.24
6. Trajan	9.05	9.17
7. Hadrian	9.17	8.09
8. Antoninus Pius	12.90	9.36
9. Marcus Aurelius	9.43	5.11
10. Commodus	1.01	0.38
11. Severus and Caracalla	8.85	2.30

Notes: Source: Table 8.1. Circulation-period ending AD 107 (lines 1–3); AD 220 (lines 4–11); see p. 117. Wastage-rate $\frac{1}{720}$ per year (see n.15). The compensated amounts are shown as integers.

median averages provide the starting point for a series of compensated figures, (Table 8.2). Similarly, the five gold hoards provide quotients which then yield compensated figures (Table 8.3). The two sets of results are compared in Table 8.4. The stray-find results are indexed to a total of 100, and the hoard-quotients are then recalculated to the same base, taking as the starting point the four periods from Vespasian to Antoninus Pius. The chronological differences between the raw figures produced by hoard and stray-find evidence are substantial. But both sources reflect the same monetary reality, and the compensated amounts from Vespasian to Antoninus Pius in fact agree quite closely (Table 8.4). The correlation between them is very high ($r^2 = 0.923$).

The results for the other two reigns in the hoard series are more divergent. The hoard quotient for Nero is 20% below the stray-find figure (12.82/16.1). And for Marcus Aurelius the hoard-quotient is as much as 45% below (5.23/9.43). But both discrepancies have an obvious explanation. Nero's gold production between AD 54 and 64 is entirely missing from these second-century hoards, but in the nature of things, not from the stray finds, which must include coin deposited before 64. And the hoards must under-represent the reign of Marcus Aurelius, since four out of five end before Marcus's death.

hardly affects the totals, although the few explicitly Domitianic coins have been excluded. Apart from the contents of the Zemun hoard, most gold coin in Domitian's name seen in hoards was struck under Vespasian or Titus.

Table 8.3 *Gold hoards compensated for wastage*

Period	Quotient compensated for wastage
Nero 64–8	26.7
Vespasian and Titus	31.6
Trajan	19.9
Hadrian	18.8
Antoninus Pius	24.7
Marcus Aurelius	10.9

Note: Source: median percentages from Belgium, Braga, Rome, Liberchies, Diarbekir hoards. Wastage-rate $\frac{1}{360}$ per year to end-date of the hoard. The reigns of Vespasian and Titus are combined to allow comparability with stray-find data where the two cannot be fully separated.

Table 8.4 *Hoard and stray-gold profiles compared*

Period	Compensated stray-find quotients	Hoard-quotients equalised to stray-find index using column 1 total for periods 5–8 as the base
1. Augustus	8.60	—
2. Tiberius	16.80	—
3. Claudius	13.60	—
4. Nero	16.10	12.82
5. Vespasian and Titus	14.50	15.17
6. Trajan	9.05	9.56
7. Hadrian	9.17	9.03
8. Antoninus Pius	12.90	11.86
9. Marcus Aurelius	9.43	5.23

Source: Tables 8.2 & 8.3.

Slow input of new coin, from the much fuller evidence of silver hoards, could easily mean that representation did not reach full strength until years or decades after an Emperor's death.[17]

The hoards with their larger samples still offer slightly better evidence, other things being equal. In the working matrix of gold output (Table 8.5), the hoard quotients are accepted for Vespasian, Titus, Trajan and Hadrian (here Titus is separated from Vespasian, using the ratio of 1:9 between the two reigns found in an aggregate of six gold hoards).[18] The remaining figures are based on the

[17] See p. 205.
[18] The hoards are Belgium, Liberchies, Rome, Diarbekir, Braga and Corbridge. Coins of Titus are too few to justify individual ratios hoard by hoard.

Table 8.5 *A matrix of gold output*

Period	Output quotient	Annual quotient per reign-year (× 100)
Nero 54–64	3.28	30
Nero 64–8	12.82	291
Vespasian	13.65	131
Titus	1.52	63
Trajan	9.56	44
Hadrian	9.03	40
Antoninus Pius	12.90	51
Marcus Aurelius	9.43	45

Note: See Table 8.4 and text above, pp. 117–19.

Table 8.6 *Comparisons of pre-Neronian gold output*

Reign	Boscoreale hoard compensated for wastage	Boscoreale result indexed (Nero = 100)	Compensated Gallic stray finds indexed (Nero = 100)
Augustus	59.3	8.6	53.5
Tiberius	118.4	17.3	104.9
Claudius	119.6	17.5	84.8
Nero	684	100	100

stray find matrix as shown in Table 8.4. But the reign of Nero is divided into two production-periods (54–64 and 64–68), taking the hoard-quotient, which contains nothing from the period 1, as the source for period 2, and taking the stray-find quotient as indicating the value for periods 1 and 2 combined.[19]

2.1. OUTPUT BEFORE NERO: REGIONAL PROBLEMS

Table 8.2 shows impressive totals for Julio-Claudian gold output before Nero. But the different circulation-periods mean completely different compensation factors for gold struck before and after Nero's weight-reduction in AD 64. More serious are the regional differences in the figures for gold output under Nero's predecessors. Compensated figures from the big Boscoreale hoard make output in the three previous major reigns 44% of the total for Nero. But in the Gallic

[19] The ratio between periods is 1:3.90, compared with 1:5.64 (99/558) in the Boscoreale hoard (Boscoreale appears to under-represent all gold produced before AD 64; see below). Because of the different circulation-times of the two segments of Nero's gold coin, the true ratio between them cannot be reconstructed from the undated stray find evidence.

stray-find index the figure is 240%. The contrast is enormous. In the Boscoreale figures earlier Julio-Claudian gold is relatively insignificant, whereas in the Gallic evidence it is more important than minting under Nero (Table 8.6).

The vivid contrast between Italy and the provinces in coin of this period is also seen in silver. In eight Pompeian denarius finds of coin up to AD 79, the four reigns before Nero provide only 2.3% of the coin on median average.[20] In contemporary provincial hoards the median is 15.9%.[21] These figures make pre-Neronian gold more than five times as important in the provinces as in Italy; and pre-Neronian silver nearly seven times as important. In further Flavian evidence pre-Neronian coin is 26% of a provincial gold hoard, but 3% and 1% of gold hoards from Pompeii.[22] And in a pair of Flavian silver hoards of similar size, the earlier Julio-Claudians account for 22% of the provincial hoard, Aubenton, but less than 1% of the hoard from Rome.[23]

These violent geographical contrasts suggest two main possibilities. Either a recall of existing coinage starting under Nero drained Italy but not the provinces of earlier precious-metal coin. Or the pattern of coin-supply before AD 64 was such that the provinces received relatively more precious-metal coin than Italy.

The first explanation is difficult to accept: a government under Nero determined to remint coin, and able to mint very heavily as far away as Egypt, would hardly ignore the western provinces in its search for metal.[24] The second explanation is much more likely in itself. Strong regional effects produced by mint-location are certainly shown by Nero's bronze coinage: types with 'Globe' obverses predominate in the provinces, whereas in Italy, and only in Italy, 'non-Globe' types predominate. The Globe-types were struck at Lugdunum, the non-Globe at Rome.[25] The gold and silver mint, certainly at Lugdunum when Strabo wrote under Tiberius, seems to have remained there until AD 64, the year of Nero's changes.[26]

The pattern of coin-finds thus argues a severe constriction before AD 64 in the flow of precious-metal coin to Italy as compared with the western provinces.[27] Most provinces benefited from shipments of army pay. Italy

---

[20] See p. 201 n.35.   [21] Six hoards of AD 69–79, see p. 201 n.35.

[22] Utrecht; Pompeii 1812; Pompeii 1957.

[23] Bolin, 336–8 (Aubenton ends in 80/1, N = 371; Rome ends in 80, N = 294).

[24] Even if the historians, who are quite graphic, left any scope for envisaging restraint in Nero's fiscal policies late in his reign (chapter 1, n.94). For Egypt, see fig. 8.1 above.

[25] MacDowall 1979, 30. For the as denomination, the percentage of Globe-types is: Britain 99% of all Neronian asses, Lower Germany 97%, Upper Germany 92%, Belgica 87%, Lugdunensis 87%, Aquitania 84%, Narbonensis 73%, Raetia 75%, and Italy 3% (from finds listed in MacDowall 1979, 18 ff.; other regions listed usually contribute only a few coins).

[26] Metcalf notes that the gold and silver coinage from AD 14 to 64 shows 'overwhelming stylistic continuity' (Metcalf 1989, 69–70). Cf. Burnett 1987, 30. For recent advocacy of Rome as the mint for precious-metal coin under Claudius, see von Kaenel 1986, with comments by A.M. Burnett, NCircular 95 (1987) 77.

[27] The available Italian evidence is mainly Campanian, but Campania was certainly not a backwater. The Rome hoard of AD 80 with 84 Flavian denarii likewise shows virtually no Julio-Claudian coin (Bolin, 338).

contained few troops, although some of Italy could have received fresh coin if this was used for the *congiaria* in Rome. However surprisingly, the present evidence implies that fresh Julio-Claudian coin was in short supply there before AD 64. The similarities between Italy and the provinces which begin after AD 64 probably suggest new mechanisms for disseminating current coin within Italy from that date.

If the diffusion of Julio-Claudian precious-metal coin was seriously uneven, basing output estimates on one set of regional finds must be uncertain. This is made worse by the fact that the fullest series of finds comes from the zone in which the mint lay. The regional distribution of bronze types from the two main western mints operating under Nero shows some Rome output in regions nearer to Rome, such as Narbonensis, but almost none in regions far away, such as Britain (n.25 above).[28] Thus gold coin struck while the mint was at Lugdunum will probably register more strongly in Gallic finds than gold coin struck after minting had moved to Rome, causing the Gallic stray finds to over-represent production volume before AD 64, just as Italian finds probably under-represent it. The reality of how much coin was produced evidently lies between these two extremes.

3. SILVER OUTPUT BY REIGN

Output of silver coin can be assessed in relative terms from the many large silver hoards. The main hoard-series starts from Nero's reduction in the silver content of the denarius in AD 64. This change, and the reminting which continued up to 107, drove previous denarii out of circulation within a few decades, unfortunately before the large hoards which survive from the 130s onwards.

Relative silver output was analysed by two techniques. These were:

1. Finding the median ratio of reign A to reign B in hoards which end in reign C, where A, B, and C are successive major reigns.
2. Smoothing the resulting reign-index figures by a linear regression of index against date within individual large hoards.[29]

The results shown in Table 8.7 later received unexpected support from another source. There proved to be a strong inverse correlation between the output index and the values of negative binomial k for individual reigns (fig. 8.5).[30] The values of the output index are shown in Table 8.7.

[28] But bronze is not an exact analogue for gold, and high-value coin, worth taking on a journey, was probably more mobile over long distances.
[29] Despite the relatively simple results in the denarius index in Table 8.7, these estimates are the product of many successive stages of calculation, making their workings too lengthy to reproduce here. In the case of Vespasian, the estimates are based on the ratio with coin of Trajan, hoard-samples of coin of Domitian being generally truncated (see below).
[30] This statistic was generated by Program 1 in Appendix 8 from totals for coins and types in the

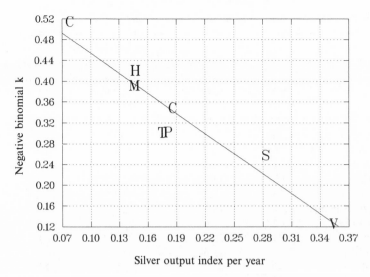

Figure 8.5. Denarius coin correlation between negative binomial k, and annual out-put ratios per reign. (Symbol: Emperor's initial. Reigns (from left): Commodus, Hadrian, Marcus Aurelius, Trajan, A. Pius, Caracalla, Severus, Vespasian.)

4.   GOLD AND SILVER FLUCTUATIONS COMPARED

For part of the period, gold and silver output seem to show the same broad profile. The index-figures for Trajan, Hadrian and Antoninus Pius in Table 8.8 correlate closely (r^2 is 0.953).[31] This of course says nothing about any equivalence in terms of volume, since the indices only reflect the internal chronology of each category. But it implies that long-term fluctuations in gold output were mirrored by long-term fluctuation in silver output. This pattern is more or less maintained under Marcus Aurelius. After AD 180, quantitative assessment of gold output becomes more difficult, though for both metals the indices for Commodus are low, while those for Severus are high (Tables 8.2 and 8.7).

There is more discrepancy at the beginning of the period. For Nero relative silver output is only a small fraction of the figure for gold, gold being exceptionally high, and the silver exceptionally low. It is easier to see what the comparisons imply when they are tentatively translated into absolute amounts (see Table 10.13).

enormous Reka Devnia silver hoard, related to reign-totals in the RIC–Cohen type-matrix (see pp. 147 n.12). Eight of the 9 major reigns between AD 69 and 217 produced the strong inverse correlation shown in fig. 8.5 (r^2 = 0.908; Domitian, whose coinage is seriously under-represented in the main silver hoards including Reka Devnia, was omitted).

[31] The calculations for silver were carried out in the early 1980s; those for gold in 1991, using important hoard and stray find material made available in 1989–90. The workings for gold and silver remain completely independent of each other.

Table 8.7 *Index of silver output for major reigns*

Reign	Denarius index	Denarius index per reign-year (× 100)	Denarius index compensated for base-metal content of the denarius	Compensated denarius index per reign year (× 100)
Nero 64–8	0.30	7.5	0.30	7.5
Vespasian	3.36	35.3	3.28	34.5
Trajan	3.41	17.5	3.38	17.3
Hadrian	3.00	14.7	2.89	14.1
Antoninus Pius	4.16	18.1	3.92	17.0
Marcus Aurelius	2.77	14.6	2.33	12.3
Commodus	1.00	7.8	0.79	6.2
Severus	5.00	28.3	2.97	16.8
Caracalla	1.15	18.6	0.63	10.2
Elagabalus	1.85	48.7	0.90	23.7
Severus Alexander	2.67	20.5	1.29	9.9

Note: Scaling: Commodus = 1. Column 3 uses Table 8.3, p. 119 (here the fineness in 64–8 of 93.5% equals par). Domitian omitted because of skewed coin-survival.

Table 8.8 *Percentage chronology of gold and silver, AD 64–180*

Period	Gold	Silver	Gold per reign-year (× 100)	Silver per reign-year (× 100)
Nero 64–8	19.1	1.8	478	45
Vespasian	20.2	19.8	212	208
Trajan	14.2	20.0	73	102
Hadrian	13.4	17.6	66	86
Antoninus Pius	19.1	24.5	83	107
Marcus Aurelius	14.0	16.3	74	86
TOTAL	100%	100%		

Note: Major reigns are shown. Domitian is omitted because of lack of evidence.

5. CONCLUSION

Coin-hoards show similar profiles year by year where the evidence of large year-dated samples is available. Their similarities argue that variations within hoard-series reflect variations in mint-output. After allowing for wastage, hoards can be used to estimate changes in gold and silver output from one reign to another. For gold, the careful recent collections of stray-find evidence are also useful. The output readings that they give after compensation are similar to those from gold hoards.

Output indexes by reign are constructed for gold running from AD 54 to 180 and for silver running from AD 64 to 235. Reign by reign, the gold and silver profiles between AD 69 and 180 do not differ greatly. Serious regional distortions affect the estimates for gold under the Julio-Claudians that would otherwise be possible. Nevertheless, these regional effects are interesting in themselves for what they reveal about patterns of monetary supply and circulation under the early Empire.

9

REIGN-STUDIES: THE CHRONOLOGY AND STRUCTURE OF COIN-OUTPUT

1. INTRODUCTION

To study mint-output year by year, we need big hoards and coinage which is dated by year. This evidence can reveal big fluctuations. Thus annual differences in the Egyptian hoards illustrated in fig. 8.1 show a coefficient of variation of 245% (hoard 3) and 230% (hoard 6). This is primarily due to the enormous production surge in the mid-60s AD. In denarii of Severus Alexander (fig. 8.3), the coefficient is still high, 80% overall at Reka Devnia and 81% at Elveden. At Reka Devnia between 148 and 161, the variation in year-dated coin of Antoninus Pius struck for the Emperor is 55% (n = 4,081). Emperor coin under Commodus at Reka Devnia shows variation of 42% (n = 2,364).[1]

These results undermine any assumption that annual output was constant. Usually there seems to be movement within the year-to-year figures, a movement which at times becomes regular and even systematic.[2] Nevertheless, precious metal output from the Rome mint appears to have been broadly continuous in the main period studied. This contrasted with mints for provincial coinage, which were sometimes closed for years on end.[3] But usually lack of year-dating means that the Rome evidence has to be conflated into blocs of several years.[4] The longer blocs still show some fluctuation. Gold and silver indices run in parallel reign by reign for part of the period (Table 8.8). But over shorter periods they do not do so consistently. In a trial analysis for a thirteen-year period year by year, the annual amounts of gold, silver and bronze prove to be closely aligned for the first five years, before diverging quite widely (Section 3.4 below).

---

[1] Based on coin struck for the Emperor dated by year. A further 62 coins belong to 186–9, and 112 to 191–2. Coins of Crispina (N = 596) appear to have been struck over a large part of the reign, though a few may belong to the last years of Marcus. For Crispina's survival as Empress at least until 187 (contrary to prevailing belief), see *CIL* III 12487 and Grosso 1964, 661–4.

[2] For a regular pattern which coincides with the cycle of legionary discharges under Marcus Aurelius, see Duncan-Jones 1990, 73–6.

[3] For Egypt, compare the production profiles implied by the hoards summarised in Milne 1933 Table. Chapter 14, p. 211.

[4] But there is much year-dated evidence from Antoninus Pius onwards, coupled with blocs of coin for Empresses and princesses which are not closely dated. For Marcus Aurelius, see Duncan-Jones 1990, 73–6, and for Septimius Severus and Caracalla, see sections 4–5 below.

Table 9.1 *Early silver minting by Severus Alexander shown by year*

Year (AD)	Coin at Reka Devnia
222	1,353 (8–9 months' production)
223	778 (full year)
224	215 (full year)
Reign year average	541

Source: BMCRE 6, 43–5.

2. SHORT-TERM EFFECTS

Most short-term output-fluctuation appears random as far as we can tell, presumably reflecting fluctuations in metal supply. But a few effects are evidently systematic.[5] For propaganda reasons, a new reign urgently demanded new coinage, which could if necessary be recycled from existing coin. Silver fineness tended to fall at this point, showing that the metal supply was being stretched (see Table 16.1). In long reigns, increased mint-activity at the start of a new reign often creates obvious peaks in output. And in very short reigns, the same effect makes short-lived Emperors appear to mint more heavily. One of the clearest illustrations of heavy minting at accession, from the reign of Severus Alexander, is shown in Table 9.1.

3. INTERNAL FLUCTUATION: PRE-SEVERAN REIGNS

3.1. VESPASIAN

Coin produced under Vespasian, Trajan and Hadrian can be assigned to periods within each reign, and compared period by period. Gold and silver can both be studied in this way.

The results for Vespasian from a sample of seven silver hoards and four gold hoards are shown in Table 9.2.[6] The silver figures are relatively stable. Gold varies much more than silver. Gold-production is very high at the outset, as in the last years of Nero (Table 8.5). It then falls by half, recovering only slightly in the final years. For gold the initial output and the reign-aggregate (Table 8.5) are both exceptionally high. The coefficient of variation is 36%.

[5] See n.2.

[6] The analysis takes the median hoard-percentage for each fraction of the reign, re-indexing the reign-total to 100 if the resulting aggregate of median figures is below 99 or above 101. The result is then divided by the number of years in the period to give a percentage per year. The hoards used are: (silver) Londonthorpe, Vyskovce, Erla, La Magura, Sotin, Stockstadt and Bristol; (gold) Liberchies, Rome, Diarbekir and Corbridge.

Table 9.2 *Vespasian: median annual percentages for gold and silver*

Period (AD)	Percentage per year (gold)	Percentage per year (silver)
69–71	14.6	8.3
72–74	7.5	11.0
75–79	9.1	10.2

Mean annual percentage: 10.5

Table 9.3 *Trajan: median annual percentages for gold and silver*

Period (AD)	Percentage per year (silver)	Percentage per year (gold)
98–100	2.9	2.8
101–2	4.9	5.4
103–11	5.6	3.4
112–17	5.7	8.9

Mean annual percentage for the reign = 5.1

3.2. TRAJAN

A similar analysis can be made for Trajan.[7] This reign is divided into four main periods (Table 9.3). As far as these crude divisions show, the Trajanic figures again give a predominant impression of stability.[8] Initial output is little more than half the mean figure, but it is virtually the same in percentage terms for both metals. This modest start is unusual and provides a vivid contrast with other major reigns (compare Table 16.1). Higher precious-metal content means that early Trajanic coin may be under-represented in later hoards. But this effect in the case of silver seems to be of the order of 30% or less, and thus

---

[7] The same hoards are used for gold; for silver, Egypt (Delta), La Magura, Tell Kalak, Stockstadt, Londonthorpe and Bristol.

[8] A surge in output with the reminting of AD 107 is likely, but at present coin of 107 cannot be differentiated clearly from other coin of AD 103–11 (see chapter 8, n.5). In the eastern silver coinages, a considerable increase in minting certainly took place after the debasement of c.108 (Walker 2.104; and Butcher, forthcoming).

Table 9.4 *Trajan: bronze, silver and gold*

Period (AD)	Percentage per year (bronze)	Percentage per year (silver)	Percentage per year (gold)
98–100	1.2	2.9	2.8
101–2	12.2	4.9	5.4
103–11	6.3	5.6	3.4
112–17	2.7	5.7	8.9

Mean annual percentage for the reign = 5.1

Note: Bronze source: Garonne. For silver and gold, see Table 9.3.

is not enough to account for the lower quotients.[9] The silver hoards show high output immediately before Trajan's accession, under Nerva.[10]

For the rest of the reign, the silver figures analysed in these long units appear very stable, apparently suggesting a steady state in denarius-output in the main part of the reign. The gold figure is close to the mean in period 2. In period 3 it falls noticeably, but then rises very sharply in period 4, with the large-scale mobilisation and war with Parthia. If this affected coin-output, it is interesting that gold production should increase substantially, but not apparently output of silver.[11]

For bronze currency, there are few large published hoards covering this period. The fullest coherent source is the Garonne hoard of nearly 4,000 sestertii beginning under Nero, and ending late in the 150s, which is used below. Its dated samples for Trajan and Hadrian are 857 and 1,077 coins.[12] Wastage of bronze, though not easily quantifiable from the data available, was, like its rate of wear, faster than for gold or silver, perhaps $\frac{1}{100}$ or $\frac{1}{150}$ per year.[13] This would certainly affect the hoard-quotients within a single 20-year reign, and it could create artificial ascending gradients.

Comparing Trajan's sestertius-output with precious-metal output leads to contrasts which are shown in Table 9.4. Bronze output is extremely low in period 1, when gold and silver minting are both fairly low. Bronze reaches its

---

[9] From chronological analysis of a sample of large second-century denarius hoards.

[10] Calculated on the same basis as the figures in Table 8.7, the output quotient for Nerva's silver is 0.379, or an annual index figure of 28.

[11] For the view that increased production at this point reflected the use of new metal from Dacian treasure, see Depeyrot 1987B, 709, n.9 (accepting Carcopino's interpretation of late figures from Malalas for the amount of Dacian treasure). Walker's die-count for a sample of 314 aurei of Trajan implies annual percentages of 4.9, 5.0, 5.1 and 6.3 for obverse dies in the four main periods of the reign (Walker, 3.151). The increase in the final period is less than that shown by coin-numbers in the hoards (Table 9.3), thus seeming to suggest that die-productivity may have been increased in the final period. But a sample of 314 aurei for the whole of Trajan's reign is clearly too small for these purposes (the sample assembled below for a single gold type of Trajan is 94 coins, Table 10.13) and much more material is required.

[12] A few of the coins cannot be read.

[13] For wastage-rates of gold and silver, see pp. 205 and 210.

Table 9.5 *Hadrian: bronze, silver and gold*

Period (AD)	Percentage per year (bronze)	Percentage per year (silver)	Percentage per year (gold)
117–18	3.6	8.5	6.6
119–28	3.7	5.1	5.4
128–38	6.0	4.0	4.0
Mean annual percentage for the reign = 4.9			

peak of more than twice the mean average in period 2, at a time when gold and silver output are low or close to average. Bronze output is fairly close to silver in percentage terms in period 3; but its drop in the final period deviates sharply from the gold and silver patterns. Thus here bronze seems to follow a different pattern from gold and silver.

3.3. HADRIAN

The main dated evidence for Hadrian's reign falls into three periods, the first extremely short.[14] The remaining periods each run for virtually 10 years (Table 9.5). From these very sparse indications, Hadrian's minting consists of a period of initial high output, followed by two periods of stable but slowly declining output. High output at the start of a reign is seen also in the case of Vespasian's gold currency (Table 9.2), and even more clearly in the reign of Severus Alexander (Table 9.1). The most noticeable Hadrianic feature is the way that gold and silver follow similar overall patterns, which become almost identical in periods 2 and 3. But the periods are long and must contain more fluctuation than is seen.

The bronze figures show a roughly inverse relationship with precious metal: when precious metal striking is above average in period 1, bronze is below average. When precious-metal striking is roughly average in period 2, bronze is still below average. When precious-metal striking is below average in period 3, bronze is well above average.

Taken overall, the evidence for Trajan and Hadrian suggests that production of bronze and of precious-metal coin tended to run inversely. In the nature of things, large-scale minting in one metal might easily limit the amount of minting in another metal, if capacity was in any way limited. When precious-metal output was high, base-metal output tended to be low (Tables 9.4 and 9.5). When precious-metal output was low, this tended to be made up

---

[14] The same hoards are used for gold as in the previous reigns; for silver, La Magura, Stockstadt, Bristol, Viuz-Faverges, Londonthorpe and La Salasuri.

by output in base metal where possible. European mints at a much later date show a similar pattern.[15] Thus the fact that production peaks in the three metals are rarely synchronised may reflect inherent limits in the capacity of the Rome mint.

There is an analogy under Tiberius, when heavy accession minting takes place entirely in one precious metal, gold eclipsing silver (Appendix 2). And a somewhat similar effect is seen under Domitian. When Domitian raised denarius fineness to pristine levels and restored pre-Neronian aureus-weight, from AD 82 to early 85, output of sestertii very largely ceased. This is suggested both by the Garonne figures, and by stray finds from the northern Continent: neither sample contains any sestertii from 83 or 84. In 83 dupondii and asses are also deficient, although they are found from 84.[16]

3.4. ANTONINUS PIUS

The mint began producing coin for the Empress in appreciable quantities in the second half of Hadrian's reign, as well as for the Emperor's heirs at the end of his reign.[17] Antoninus Pius carried this much further, with large amounts of coin for Faustina I, most of it struck after her death, as well as substantial amounts for the senior heir, Marcus Aurelius and his wife, Faustina II. 'Female' coin cannot be dated closely, but the coin of the Emperor and his heir is clearly dated by year from AD 148 onwards. 'Male' production accounts for most of the coin: Emperor and heir have 63% of the denarii of the reign at Reka Devnia (n = 13,565), and 72% of the aurei in a sample of 226 coins from five gold hoards.[18]

For the year-by-year analysis, five large silver hoards were investigated.[19] Seven gold hoards offer 175 year-dated aurei of Pius in this period.[20] In this evidence, gold and silver for Pius match closely for the first five years (r^2 = 0.848). But from 153 to 160 the match is much weaker (r^2 = 0.394). Thus gold and silver run parallel for five years, then often diverge (see fig. 9.1).

Bronze output in these years can be studied also. A sample of 410 year-dated sestertii struck for Pius was assembled from three French hoards, a British hoard, two sets of British underwater finds, and a large North African

---

[15] In Milan mintings from 1581 to 1610, base-metal output reaches its peak when precious-metal minting is at its lowest point. This is also true of French minting from 1560 to 1600. See minting data in Cipolla 1952, 90 ff.; and Spooner 1956, 522 ff.

[16] Carradice, Table S, 132. N = 153 sestertii, 169 dupondii, 557 asses. The Garonne sample of clearly dateable Domitianic sestertii used here contains 175 coins.

[17] For the varying proportion of coin of Sabina in different denarius hoards, see Duncan-Jones 1990, Appendix 1 and p.40.

[18] Liberchies, Rome, Diarbekir, Braga, Le Cannet.

[19] Reka Devnia, La Magura, Stockstadt, Tell Kalak and Drzewicz Nowy. The index used is the mean percentage per year, based on the year-dated samples for Pius from 148–61. Denarii of Marcus Aurelius are excluded, because his denarii and those of Pius do not correlate closely by year in a combined sample of more than 5,000 coins of this period at Reka Devnia.

[20] Belgium, Liberchies, Rome, Diarbekir, Braga, Corbridge, Le Cannet. Because these reign samples are very small, the gold percentages are based on a simple aggregate of coins.

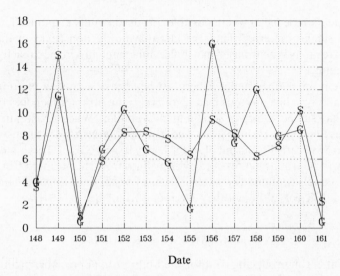

Date

Figure 9.1 Percentages of denarii from silver hoards and aurei from gold hoards, AD
148–61. Coin of the Emperor, AD 148–61. (G: gold; S: silver.)

hoard.[21] The index used for bronze is based on the mean percentage for these
seven samples.[22] When production for Pius in the three metals for the period
148–61 is compared, bronze correlates closely with the precious metals for the
first five years, but much less thereafter. For bronze/gold the correlation (r^2) is
0.974 at first, then 0.147. For bronze/silver, it is 0.876, then 0.102 (see fig. 9.2).
Thus these samples provide definite evidence for continuous production at
parallel rates in all three metals for part of the period.[23]

The bronze dossier also reveals quite striking circulation-differences.
Representation of coin of Marcus Aurelius as heir is very uneven, with 30% of
the French sample, 17% in North Africa and a mere 7% in Britain. Three
western sources had no year-dated coin of Marcus from this period (the hoard
from Gare in Cornwall, the Bath series, and Vannes in Brittany). The
sestertius coin struck for the Emperor consists of an assemblage from Gaul
(n = 193), one from Britain (n = 122) and one from Africa (n = 95).[24] Gallic

[21] France: Arnouville-lès-Gonesses (end Postumus), Puy-Dieu (end 244/9), Vannes (end
Postumus). Britain: Gare (end Postumus), Bath (sacred spring), Coventina (sacred spring).
North Africa: Guelma (end c.258). The hoards seem to belong to a time and place in which
precious-metal currency was in short supply. The important Garonne hoard ends in 159/60,
and its year-dated series ends in 156/7, making it unusable for the present test.
[22] The Guelma hoard may define the pattern of coin entering North Africa, thus implying a
circulation difference between Africa and the North-west.
[23] Further year-by-year comparisons between the three metals are desirable. But lack of
continuous year-dating rules out almost all earlier periods, and published gold evidence starts
to falter in the 160s.
[24] In the two regional samples from more than one source, the comparisons use the mean
percentage per year.

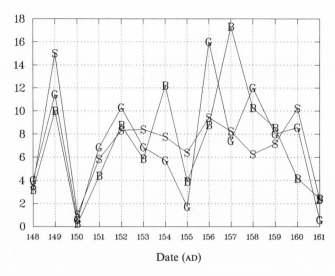

Figure 9.2 Percentages of denarii from silver hoards, aurei from gold hoards, and sestertii from hoards and finds. Coin of the Emperor, AD 148–61. (G: gold; S: silver; B: bronze.)

and British data correlate moderately well year by year (r^2 = 0.530), whereas the African data show a weak relationship with Gaul (r^2 = 0.139) and an even weaker one with Britain (r^2 = 0.086).[25]

4. INTERNAL FLUCTUATION: THE REIGN OF SEPTIMIUS SEVERUS

4.1. CHRONOLOGY

In the conservative dating-classification of *RIC*, the denarius-output of the reigns of Septimius Severus and Caracalla can be divided into four or five main periods. The Reka Devnia sample for the first reign, more than 15,000 coins, is so large that it should provide something like a directory of central silver coin-output.[26] The main pattern for dated coin is shown in Table 9.6.[27]

The output of Severus is seen as below average in period 1, during which he was disputing the throne with two other contenders who also minted coin.

---

[25] The non-parametric Spearman correlations show a similar hierarchy (0.701, 0.355 and 0.154).
[26] Although Reka Devnia ratios need not reflect the configuration of silver coin output fully, they are almost certainly closer than any other available source. Some of what emerges appears systematic, not random. For specific similarities between Reka Devnia and western hoards, see figs. 8.2 and 8.3, and p. 135 and 138 below. Further very large hoards exist (cf. p.145 n. 5), and it is very desirable that they be made available for study.
[27] This is based on the coinage of Severus and Caracalla, which makes up about $\frac{2}{3}$ of the reign-sample: the smaller coinage of Geta cannot be exactly reconciled by date, and coinage for Julia Domna and Plautilla is mostly not dated by year.

Table 9.6 *Reka Devnia: denarii struck for Severus and Caracalla (n = 10,508)*

Period (AD)	Percentage per year
1 (193/5)	3.8
2–3 (195/8)	8.9
4 (199/201)	5.9
5 (202–10)	4.7

Mean annual percentage for the reign = 5.7

Table 9.7 *Reka Devnia: denarii struck for Severus (n = 7,228)*

Period (AD)	Percentage per year
1 (193/5)	5.5
2 (195/7)	8.6
3 (197/8)	12.1
4 (199/201)	5.9
5 (202–10)	3.9

Mean annual percentage for the reign = 5.7

Output then rises to an early peak, which can be isolated more closely by looking at coin of Severus alone (Table 9.7). A clear burst of mint-activity, more than double the reign-average, takes place in 197/8 when Severus became sole ruler, after the most difficult struggle for the throne since the start of the Empire. This flourish at the start of his period of undisputed rule is Severus's equivalent of the heavy minting that other rulers carried out at their accession (Table 9.1 above and text).

4.2. CHANGE IN TYPE-PRODUCTIVITY

The Reka Devnia hoard also provides so far unique evidence about the relative abundance of coin-types.[28] For the reign of Severus the mean number of coins per type shows notable stability at different dates, but it also contains obvious contrasts. Table 9.8 shows the number of coin-types per year.

The number of types per year produced for Severus at Rome remains

[28] It is generally a much better guide to quantity than the scarcity ratings for individual types given in successive editions of *RIC*; where checked, these ratings, even in the new edition, often depart wildly from what the hoards imply. But in later volumes of *BMCRE*, Mattingly made a point of citing Reka Devnia figures when discussing types.

Table 9.8 *Septimius Severus:*
denarius-types per year at Reka Devnia

Period (AD)	Rome mint
Coin of Severus	
1. 193–5	17.5
2. 195–7	15.0
3. 197–8	14.0
4. 199–201	9.3
5. 202–10	7.4
Coin of Caracalla	
2–3. 195–8	5.7
4. 199–201	6.0
5. 202–10	6.7

Note: Eastern denarii omitted (see below).

roughly stable for the first three periods.[29] In period 4 there is a sharp fall, which continues to the end of the reign. This presumably reflected the impact of the additional types now being struck for Caracalla and Geta. The types of Caracalla appear as approximately six per year from the Reka Devnia evidence, while those of Geta (omitted from Table 9.8 because of divergent dating-periods) are just under four per year overall.

Eastern mints (not shown in Table 9.8) contribute 5.3% of all Severan denarii at Reka Devnia. As this hoard comes from the eastern end of the northern frontier, heavier representation of eastern mints might perhaps be expected. But limited comparisons suggest no obvious regional difference. In the samples for this reign in two major western silver hoards, eastern mints contribute 3.7% at Viuz-Faverges (n = 486) and 7.5% at Colchester (n = 1,266). The number of coins per type for eastern mints is always much lower at Reka Devnia than in its figures for Rome. But the individual mint-identities for eastern material of this reign cannot be pursued further here.[30]

The number of coins per type shows a fourfold jump in period 2, and a 50% increase in period 3, in the Rome figures (Table 9.9). But the number of types per year slightly declines (Table 9.8; in period 1 Rome contributed less than half of Severan denarii, but thereafter well over 90%, Table 9.13). Thus the leaps in output in periods 2 and 3 were achieved without increasing the number of types. The need for more coin was evidently met here by cutting more dies, or striking more coins from existing dies, without taxing ingenuity by creating extra coin-types.

[29] The Reka Devnia sample of denarii of Clodius Albinus struck up to 197 shows 23 coins per Cohen-type (N = 184).
[30] Dr Kevin Butcher kindly pointed out the defects of the schema for identifying individual eastern mints in the *RIC* and *BMCRE* classification.

Table 9.9 *Severus: coins per type at Reka Devnia*

Period (AD)	Rome mint
1. 193–5	9.9
2. 195–7	40.9
3. 197–8	59.8
4. 199–201	42.9
5. 202–10	37.5

Note: Eastern denarii omitted (see p. 135).

Table 9.10 *Severus for Caracalla: coins per type at Reka Devnia*

Period (AD)	Rome mint
2–3. 195–8	32.1
4. 199–201	31.5
5. 202–10	32.1

Note: Eastern denarii omitted (see p. 135).

In Table 9.9, three of the four periods in the main part of Severus's reign show a mean of about 40 coins per type at Reka Devnia. Even greater stability, at a slightly lower level, is seen in the evidence for Caracalla (Table 9.10). In the Rome issues, the variation between periods is almost negligible. Caracalla's midpoint is approximately 80% of the level for Severus.

The remaining Rome evidence from Severus's reign is summarised in Table 9.11. Geta's quotient of 37.6 is close to Caracalla's level of approximately 32 (Table 9.10). The female levels are much higher, Julia Domna showing almost double Geta's quotient, and Plautilla almost double the quotient for Caracalla. This contrast suggests a shortage of types, perhaps reflecting the relative poverty of female motifs in imperial propaganda, but more immediately indicating slower rotation of types. This evidence again suggests that mean coin output per type was relatively stable.

Consistency in mean numbers in such large samples, at different 'male' and 'female' levels, implies a stable relationship between the output target and the number of types struck. Nevertheless, productivity type by type remained extremely variable.[31]

[31] The coefficient of variation for the coin-abundance of all types of Severus at Reka Devnia is as high as 155%, while the figure for Julia Domna in his reign is 126%. On the other hand, the Reka Devnia evidence shows many repeated amounts. Thus for example, in issues of Commodus struck in AD 191, 4 of the 7 Reka Devnia types have 33–5 coins each.

Table 9.11 *Severus for Geta, Domna and Plautilla: coins per type at Reka Devnia*

Individual	Rome mint
Geta	37.6
Domna	69.6
Plautilla	61.25

Note: Eastern denarii omitted (see p. 135).

Table 9.12 *Reign of Severus: 'male' coin of periods 2–5 at Reka Devnia*

	Observed total	6:3:2 ratio	Percentage difference
Severus	6,437	6,481	+0.7%
Caracalla	3,280	3,240	−1.2%
Geta	2,164	2,160	−0.2%
Aggregate	11,881	11,881	

4.3. STRUCTURE OF THE COINAGE

Although part of the Severan coinage cannot be dated, other important outlines can be seen from the Reka Devnia evidence. Coin was struck for five members of the imperial family, the Emperor, his wife Julia Domna, his two sons Caracalla and Geta and, more briefly, for Caracalla's wife Plautilla.[32] Coinage for the sons did not begin until period 2. The figures for the three male members of the dynasty in periods 2–5 at Reka Devnia are: Severus 6,437, Caracalla 3,280 and Geta 2,164. These are close to ratios of 6:3:2 (Table 9.12).

By contrast, the female totals at Reka Devnia under Severus follow no obvious schema. Minting for Domna was about two-fifths the size of that for Severus (39%). Coin of Faustina I under Antoninus Pius at Reka Devnia, though mainly posthumous, is 38% the size of the total for Pius. The minting for Plautilla reached 26% of Caracalla's level in the period 202–10, but belongs to a limited period of less than three years.

The earlier denarii of the reign were partly struck at eastern mints, though the eastern contribution was important only in the earliest period (Table 9.13 shows the pattern for coin of Severus and Caracalla). From 196 onwards, denarius-production was very largely concentrated at Rome. Eastern denarii

---

[32] For the *officina* system as such, see below, pp. 142–3.

Table 9.13 *Reign of Severus: provenance of Reka Devnia coins of Severus and Caracalla*

Period (AD)	Rome	Eastern mints	N
1. 193–5	44.0%	56.0%	791
2–3. 195–8	95.9%	4.1%	3255
4. 199–201	95.4%	4.6%	1854

Sources: Coin of Severus (periods 1–4) and Caracalla (periods 2–4). Later coin of the reign was struck at Rome.

were also struck on a small scale for Geta (4.3% of his output at Reka Devnia), Plautilla (3.4%) and Julia Domna (2.5%).

5. THE REIGN OF CARACALLA

The denarii Caracalla struck in his own name after his accession are almost all dated by year. His silver output as Emperor can thus be examined in greater detail (the same would be true for gold if any large gold hoards of the period had been published). The best known features of his monetary policy were the introduction of the radiate or antoninianus in AD 215, and his reduction in aureus-weight by 10% in the same year. The radiate, heavier than the denarius, but not twice its weight, was evidently tariffed at 2 denarii.[33] In view of its reduced silver-content, the circulation of the radiate may well been unstable, and there are extreme contrasts between later hoards which are rich in radiates and others that are starved of radiates.[34] The radiate seems to have been originally produced on a limited scale. Its percentage importance as a proportion of Caracalla's silver coin is almost the same at Reka Devnia (11.5%; n = 2,425) as at Colchester (12.2%; n = 441).

The outline at Reka Devnia of Caracalla's silver production is shown in Table 9.14. Denarius output at the start of the reign was exceptionally low. As joint Emperor, Caracalla had already become a familiar face on the coinage, and this presumably reduced the propaganda need for heavy minting at his accession (Table 9.10). Commodus, likewise well established on the coinage before his accession, also minted less than average in his first year, from the Reka Devnia evidence.

Caracalla's first output-peak is in 213 and at Reka Devnia accounts for almost 40% by value of the silver coin struck in his reign. Output falls sharply in 214, perhaps in reaction. The arrival of the radiate in 215 coincides with a

[33] See p. 222 n.39.
[34] Thus in the hoards summarised in Appendix 10, radiates reach 75% of hoard-coin in one case (Lay), but of 23 other silver hoards between 216 and 235, most have no radiates, and only two show radiates as more than 1%.

Table 9.14 *Caracalla: silver coin at Reka Devnia struck in the Emperor's name*

Period (AD)	Denarii	Radiates	Percentage of silver coins struck as radiates
1. 211–12	251	—	—
2. 213	928	—	—
3. 214	276	—	—
4. 215	369	102	22%
5. 216	171	39	19%
6. 217: Jan–April	59	25	(30%)
7. Not dated by year	93	112	55%

doubled output figure. In 216 output falls again to a figure which is below average.

Some radiates are not dated by year, although they must belong to the period from 215 onwards (Table 9.14, period 7). That slightly increases the combined output figure for the years 215–17, but the output-peak for the reign was clearly reached before the introduction of the radiate. Granted Caracalla's troubled finances, its purpose was evidently fiscal, not cosmetic, and the new denomination was presumably introduced in order to increase government spending power. But the reign ended so soon that Caracalla's minting plans may well have been seriously curtailed.

The proportion of silver coins struck as radiates after 214 is about 30% at Reka Devnia.[35] This would imply that in face value, the radiate accounted for almost half of Caracalla's silver after 214.[36] A comparable calculation for Julia Domna is not possible, but radiates are less important in her coinage of this reign, 8.2% at Reka Devnia compared with 11.5% for Caracalla.

Under Caracalla, the number of coins per denarius-type is at first very close to his figure under Severus (Table 9.15). But the pattern starts to break up, with strong deviations in 214 and 216. These may reflect the impact of the larger changes now taking place in the coinage.

The denarii struck for Domna under Caracalla total 549 at Reka Devnia, that is 25.6% of the number for Caracalla himself (2,147). Thus the output ratio between Domna and Caracalla is shown as virtually 1:4. Under Severus, the overall ratio between Domna and the three male members of the dynasty was 1:4½ at Reka Devnia (2,812:12,672 = 1:4.51).

---

[35] 28.7% if the undated denarii all belong to 215–17, 31.7% if all the undated denarii fall before 215.
[36] 30 radiates for 70 denarii means a face-value ratio of 60:70. $\frac{60}{130} = 46\%$.

Table 9.15 *Reka Devnia: coins per type from the Rome mint, AD 199–216*

Period (AD)	Severus	Caracalla	
	Denarii	Denarii	Radiates
199–201	42.9	31.5	—
202–10	37.5	32.1	—
211–12	—	35.9	—
213	—	35.7	—
214	—	46.0	—
215	—	33.5	11.3
216	—	24.4	9.8

Table 9.16 *Empress and Emperor at Reka Devnia: denarii per type*

Empress	Coins per type	Emperor coins per type	Empress/Emperor	Reign
Sabina	28.3	18.6	1.52	Hadrian
Faustina I	70.5	29.0	2.43	Antoninus Pius
Faustina II	59.3	27.1	2.19	Marcus
Crispina	54.2	16.2	3.35	Commodus

Note: Most of the coin for Faustina I was struck posthumously by Antoninus Pius.

6. THE INTERNAL STRUCTURE OF SILVER COIN-OUTPUT

The enormous Reka Devnia samples allow us to examine ratios within the output of silver coin, although no similar exercise is possible at present for gold or bronze. Most obvious is the fact that the number of coins per type in 'Empress' issues is much higher than for 'Emperor' issues. The amounts are usually double or even higher (Table 9.16). It seems clear that, whatever the individual variations, types taken in aggregate were a marker related to volume of output, and that the production-runs allowed for Empress types were on average two or three times as long as those for Emperor-types.[37]

The Reka Devnia evidence also suggests specific ratios between coin struck for different individuals. A ratio of approximately 6:3:2 between coin of Severus and that of his two sons during his reign was seen above (Table 9.12). Coin of Empress-Dowagers was roughly one-quarter of that of Emperors in volume (Table 9.17). Other strong schematic differences are seen under Marcus Aurelius (Table 9.18).[38]

[37] Presumably Empress-types used correspondingly more dies.
[38] The complex ratios under Antoninus Pius proved difficult to disentangle from the Reka Devnia evidence.

Table 9.17 *Coin of Empress-Dowagers as a fraction of Emperor coin (Reka Devnia)*

Individual	Reign	Ratio of Empress-Dowager to Emperor coin
Julia Domna	Caracalla	1:3.94
Julia Maesa	Elagabalus	1:3.51
Julia Mammaea	Severus Alexander	1:4.50

Note: Based on radiates and denarii.

Table 9.18 *Production-ratios under Marcus Aurelius (Reka Devnia)*

Individual	Coin	Emperor coin	Percentage	Presumed ratio
1. Lucius Verus, 161–8	1,253	2,564	48.9%	1:2
2. Faustina II, 161–75	3,015	5,933	50.8%	1:2
3. Commodus, 176–80	381	753	50.6%	1:2

Note: Line 1 separates Lucius Verus from the senior Emperor, Marcus Aurelius. Line 2 combines the two. Before Verus's death, the target ratios appear to have been: Marcus 4, Faustina 3, Lucius Verus 2; and after his death, Marcus 6, Faustina 3. Line 3 compares coin of Commodus with contemporary coin of Marcus Aurelius.

7. CONCLUSION

The detailed denarius evidence suggests that output varied significantly year by year, but that it was more stable over periods of several years. At the year-to-year level, target figures may have been affected by random variations in metal supply. Gold and silver may behave differently within reigns, their output varying inversely under Vespasian. Under Trajan gold-production appears to vary more than silver. Bronze varies most and tends to be out of phase with precious-metal output. Under Hadrian precious-metal output seems more stable, but bronze and precious metal still behave inversely.

Year-by-year evidence starts under Antoninus Pius and shows considerable fluctuation. But for a five-year period, AD 148–52, the patterns for gold, silver and bronze are very close. The profiles of annual denarius-production for Emperor and heir do not match at all closely in this reign. Denarius-production under Marcus as Emperor shows alternate high and low years for most of the reign. The high years coincide with years of legionary discharge.[39]

[39] N.2 above.

Denarius-production under Septimius Severus shows a strong peak in AD 197/8 at the end of the Civil Wars. The average number of coins per type is relatively stable in the very large Reka Devnia sample, but it increases sharply in 197–8 without a corresponding increase in the number of types. The evidence at Reka Devnia also suggests output ratios between Severus, Caracalla and Geta. The Reka Devnia evidence for Caracalla makes his output peak 213, before the introduction of the new radiate silver coin, which once introduced accounts for about 50% of Caracalla's silver by value.

Silver output is sometimes divided between contemporary individuals in simple ratios such as 2:1 or 4:1 (Tables 9.17 and 9.18). The emergence of these ratios in evidence for whole reigns must argue for simultaneous production of different streams of coin in parallel, and against serial production. This is because serial production of one stream at a time would typically create uneven ratios when the Emperor's death brought the reign's minting to a sudden halt. Thus coin-production in the central mint was clearly segmented, even before the date when evidence for separate *officinae* becomes explicit.[40] Streaming is also suggested by the different standards of weight and fineness within contemporary silver output (pp. 240–2).

But the segments seen here are unequal, whereas those assumed in modern reconstructions of *officinae* should ideally have uniform output.[41] Theory can then only be reconciled with practice by assigning more than one *officina* to the larger segments. Thus Mattingly proposed to allot three *officinae* to Severus, one to Caracalla, and one to Julia Domna and Geta in 198–201, and then two to Severus, two to Caracalla (and Plautilla), and one to Julia and Geta in 202–9.[42]

But reconstructions like these represent an effort to subdivide output totals into tidy fractions, whereas the segmentation seen from Reka Devnia is unequal, and later explicit evidence suggests considerable inconsistency between the amounts produced at different *officinae*.[43] If the amount of coin a given *officina* produced was elastic, using relative volume to reconstruct the number of *officinae* becomes practically impossible.[44] The streaming seen above makes mint subdivisions clear beyond doubt. But in this period, looking for standardised production-units, and translating any visible dividing-lines into *officinae* on the assumption that such standardised units

---

[40] See p. 115; cf. 109 n.65 above.

[41] MacDowall 1979, 115: 'The whole object of an *officina* scheme must have been to divide the output of the mint into blocks of manageable, and no doubt, generally equal proportions.' But there is very little support for this in the ratios between the types assigned to different *officinae* in MacDowall's summaries of precious-metal hoards (10–11, Tables 2–3). And the production pattern of *officinae* directly attested at a later date proves to be very uneven (see fig. 8.4).

[42] *BMCRE* 5, xxv–xxvi. The combination of male and female output in one *officina* also seems unlikely in view of the differences noted in Table 9.16.

[43] See fig. 8.4.

[44] For criticism of attempts to translate differentiation by reverse types into differentiation by *officinae*, see Metcalf 1993.

existed seems unconvincing.[45] Nevertheless, the ratios indicated by the impressive totals at Reka Devnia probably offer some indication of the minting subdivisions that existed in reality.

[45] The hunt for *officinae* can also lead to surprising fluctuations: for example MacDowall (1979, 117) finds 'traces first of two *officinae* ... then of an expansion to six ... and eventually a return to the earlier pattern of two', all within the space of one of Nero's four issues between AD 64 and 68.

IO

THE SIZE OF DIE-POPULATIONS

1. METHODS OF EXTRAPOLATION

1.1. INTRODUCTION

With large ancient coinages, so much is missing that a simple die-count is usually not enough to show how many dies were there originally. Thus in the Crepusius die-set with explicit numbering, the die-series remains seriously incomplete, despite the very large samples that have been collected.[1] And with the larger coin-populations of the Principate, even a three-quarter sample of dies is usually far out of reach.[2] The need to extrapolate is widely recognised, but there is much less agreement about how to do this.

Existing methods of extrapolation cannot be discussed individually here. But most are too simple to be capable of modelling the frequencies of Roman coin-types or dies. These frequency-patterns are usually highly skewed, although their skewness varies. Modelling them requires the use of two parameters, which reflect the degree of dispersal as well as the ratio of dies to coins.[3] But most methods applied to coin-evidence rely on the second parameter alone.[4]

The present discussion uses general statistical theory in preference to any of the formulae specially devised for coin-evidence. Roman numismatic data are

[1] At a later count, 1,800 Crepusius denarii had yielded less than 400 obverse dies, from information kindly communicated by Professor Buttrey. For the issue and its problems, see Buttrey 1976. The reverse die-numbering runs to 519 (see n.19 below). In the survey published in Carter 1981A–B, reverse and obverse die-totals were very close (358 and 347).
[2] This anticipates conclusions reached below: see chapter 11, section 4.
[3] For frequency-patterns, see n.22; cf. n.18.
[4] A partial exception, based on a form of the negative binomial, is described in Müller 1981. Using the published version of this test depends on readings from a small diagram. The Carter formula, despite using only one parameter, is effective with the Republican Crepusius denarii for which it was devised (Table 10.3 below). But it is derived from computer modelling of co-ordinates which here include the original die-totals. Carter's formula is divided into three sub-formulae, and so emulates a more complex distribution. There is no sign that it can be extended to the larger coin-populations from the Rome mint of the Principate, where negative binomial k is typically much lower.

    Published tests of some other methods using Crepusius data make those methods appear relatively efficient (Carter 1981B). But if the dies already known are removed from the reckoning, the efficiency of these tests in reconstructing the missing population proves to be much lower. For extrapolation techniques, cf. also Gruel 1981; Preston 1983; Esty 1986; Hackens 1987, 152–3; Helly 1991, 851.

in fact highly amenable to modelling by a well-known statistical distribution, and modelling by this distribution is considerably more efficient than by most other techniques. The distribution happens to be laborious to calculate, and it is applied here by means of computer programs.

1.2. EXTRAPOLATION: METHOD A

The present study deliberately began with the Reka Devnia silver hoard of more than 80,000 coins. The hoard is about twenty times bigger than its largest rival in print from our period, and it provides a unique resource, relatively free from size-limitations.[5] A joint evaluation of the Reka Devnia type-frequencies led R.A. Kempton, the writer's statistical collaborator, to identify their pattern as negative binomial.[6] This observation provided the essential starting point for the estimates below.

The negative binomial distribution is described in standard textbooks. Fitting it to data means finding the mean and variance of the dataset, then calculating a fitted value by a relatively complex formula, which is repeated for every cell in the dataset.[7] The result depends on negative binomial k, and the whole test has to be repeated a number of times with different trial-values of k until the closest fit between fitted and observed values is found.[8]

These involved calculations can be performed rapidly using MLP, a powerful computer program by G.J.S. Ross, based on maximum likelihood estimation (section 2 below).[9] An example from statistical literature uses the negative binomial to model concentrations of mites on the leaves of apple trees. The close fit between data and model is shown in Table 10.1, section A.

In this case, all relevant data are provided, including the number of leaves with no mites. But even if the number of leaves which were mite-free had not

---

[5] Other hoards of great size have been discovered without being published: another Bulgarian denarius hoard of the first half of the third century (Nis/Naissus, Gerasimov 1938). A gold hoard of more than 80,000 coins ending in 38 BC was discovered at Brescello in the eighteenth century and soon dispersed (Calzolari 1987). For a published hoard of comparable size whose contents largely fall outside the present period, see Besly, Bland 1983.

[6] The 2,700 Reka Devnia type-frequencies divided by reign were first entered in a computer database. For the results of the tests first carried out by Kempton, see Table 10.2. For an independent but partly similar observation by Müller, based on other data, see n.4 above.

[7] 'The Negative Binomial distribution depends on two parameters, m and k, and the probability of observing r is

$$p_r = \binom{r+k-1}{k-1}(m/(m+k))^r(1+m/k)^{-k}$$

The mean is m and the variance is $m + m^2/k$' (G.J.S. Ross, *MLP: Maximum Likelihood Program*, Oxford 1987 [Version 3.08], 6.4).

[8] For a full technical account of the distribution, see Johnson, Kotz 1969, chapter 5. For an arithmetical example worked out in detail, see Pollard 1977, 115–17. Practical examples are given by Bliss 1971, using biological data.

[9] G.J.S. Ross (n.7 above). The writer began with the mainframe version, before using a later version for personal computer. For a useful description and explanation of how to use MLP for negative binomial work, see Ross, Preece 1985.

Table 10.1 *Concentrations of the European red mite on apple trees in Connecticut*

Number of leaves with X mites per leaf		Number fitted by the negative binomial
A. Using all observations		
F0	70	69.7
F1	38	37.2
F2–3	27	30.6
F4–7	15	11.4
F8+	0	1.0
B. Using all observations except the zero cell		
F0	*	60.0
F1	38	36.3
F2–3	27	31.3
F4-7	15	11.5
F8+	0	0.9

Source: Ross, Preece 1985, 328, showing MLP results based on grouped data.

been recorded, their total could still be estimated using the negative binomial (called the 'truncated' negative binomial where the zero cell is missing). Table 10.1, section B shows a result for the zero cell which is within 15% of the observed figure.

This methodology can be applied to numismatic evidence where there are large data-sets. Because of missing data, the negative binomial must normally be fitted in truncated form. Table 10.2 below shows examples from Reka Devnia, where the negative binomial predictions approximate the numbers expected from the known matrix of basic coin-types. Table 10.4 shows a further example based on the Crepusius die-set.

1.3. EXTRAPOLATION: METHOD B

A second method of extrapolation using the negative binomial (Method B) employs a formula which defines the relationship between k and population-size.[10] Here coin-types, whose frequencies are built up from die-frequencies, are taken as a proxy for dies.[11] For a given reign, the original matrix of coin-types, from existing catalogues, is used as a third co-ordinate, in conjunction with the number of types and coins of that reign in a given

[10] Formula kindly contributed by R.A. Kempton.
[11] This substitution is made necessary by the lack of explicit information about die-numbers in coin populations of the Principate.

Table 10.2 *Reka Devnia: type-totals and type-predictions for ten major reigns using Method A*

Reign	RIC–Cohen type-total	Number missing at Reka Devnia	NB estimate	Percentage error	PLN estimate	Percentage error
Vespasian	241	137	122	−11	23	−83
Trajan	221	58	58	0	13	−78
Hadrian	444	101	157	+55	42	−58
A. Pius	406	62	55	−11	16	−74
M. Aurelius	424	82	64	−22	17	−79
Commodus	232	36	17	−53	6	−83
Severus	693	214	411	+92	83	−61
Caracalla	161	36	35	−3	10	−72
Elagabalus	201	79	54	−32	11	−86
S. Alexander	208	62	16	−74	4	−94
Total		867	989		225	

Note: NB = negative binomial; PLN = Poisson lognormal. The estimates were produced using MLP (see n.9). The present Reka Devnia coin-samples run to several thousand for almost every major reign, the smallest being Vespasian with 1,985 coins.

hoard-sample.[12] Negative binomial k is then derived from the three co-ordinates by the following formula. For a given value of k

$$p/c = P/c(1 - \exp(-k \times \ln(1 + 1/k/P/c)))$$

where p = dies or types observed, c = coins observed, and P = total population of dies or types. The formula is efficient, but cannot be inverted to give direct values for k or for P. For convenient use, a short computer program was written which gives direct values of k (Program 1, Appendix 8).[13]

In themselves, calculations from types do not define die-populations. But types and dies represent the same population partitioned in different ways. Tests show that they emulate each other statistically, and that both can be fitted effectively by the negative binomial distribution (Tables 10.2 and 10.4).[14] Consequently, the value of k found by Method B can be transferred to calculations based on dies. When k has been calculated, the size of the total

[12] The Reka Devnia hoard furnishes a few types not in the Cohen repertoire in every major reign. But more than 99% of its coin comes from Cohen-types nevertheless, and only one statistically important type is not in that list (Vespasian *RIC* 10, with 202 coins). For Cohen as a source, cf. Mattingly *BMCRE* 5, xxvii–xxviii. Although Cohen included occasional coins which have not been authenticated, the Cohen material endorsed by *RIC*[1] must represent a basic matrix of coin-types.

[13] The alternative would be to print out a comprehensive and immensely long table of values for different co-ordinates.

[14] Thus the values of k obtained from the silver types at Reka Devnia by Method B correlate closely with the denarius output-index (n.15). Differences in that index measure differences in the total coin population, and thus reflect the totality of types and dies.

population is given by a second computer program which uses this formula (Program 2, Appendix 8)

Frequency-fitting (Method A) proved effective with the plentiful data from Reka Devnia and the Crepusius die-series (Table 10.2 and 10.4). Elsewhere it was less useful, because of shortage of large datasets. Furthermore, it was found that Method B values of k correlated more closely than Method A values with the independent index of denarius production (calculating k from Reka Devnia evidence in both cases).[15] For these reasons, Method B was adopted as the source of the readings for k in the die estimates in section 4.[16]

2. MODELLING COIN-FREQUENCIES

The type-frequencies at Reka Devnia were first analysed by method A, using MLP. As a further test, a number of other discrete distributions were also applied. But only the negative binomial gave an efficient estimate of missing types. Results for the Poisson lognormal distribution are also shown in Table 10.2.[17]

Table 10.2 shows the negative binomial distribution as relatively efficient in estimating missing types.[18] Its mean error is -6% of the expected figure. The Poisson lognormal distribution, though it provides the next best result, gives a

[15] See fig. 8.5. For eight major reigns from Vespasian to Caracalla (omitting Domitian for lack of evidence), the inverse correlations between Reka Devnia values of k and the silver output-index per year (p. 124 Table 8.7) are: Method A, $r^2 = 0.712$; Method B, $r^2 = 0.908$. The equations are (Method A) k = 0.583 − (output-index per year × 1.287); and (Method B) k = 0.728 − (output-index per year × 1.948). The percentage differences ($\pm$) between actual and fitted values are as follows:

Reign	Method A	Method B
Vespasian	254.1	1.1
Trajan	18.9	15.6
Hadrian	34.3	6.9
A.Pius	4.6	13.4
Marcus	8.9	0.8
Commodus	33.8	6.7
Septimius	21.9	17.9
Caracalla	6.9	1.6
Median percentage difference ($\pm$)	20.4	6.8
Mean percentage difference ($\pm$)	47.9	8.0

[16] Extensive tests of the die-frequencies underlying Tables 10.5 and 10.10 by Method A indicated that the existing samples were individually too small to produce consistent readings of k by frequency-fitting.

[17] Of the other distributions tested using MLP, applied to Trajanic evidence at Reka Devnia, the geometric distribution predicted 5 missing types instead of 58; the Poisson and logarithmic series were unable to predict the missing cell; and Neyman Type A and Polya-Aeppli models could not be fitted because the variance was too great.

[18] As an illustration, the type-frequencies for Trajan, with the negative binomial fit modelled by MLP in brackets, are: F_1 18 (17.7) F_2 + 24 (20.3) F_4 + 21 (23.3) F_8 + 21 (26.3) F_{16} + 28 (27.8) F_{32} + 28 (25.4) F_{64} + 20 (17.3) F_{128} + 5 (6.8) F_{256} + 1 (1.0). Negative binomial k here is 0.315 and its standard error 0.03.

mean error of -77%. Where coin was struck for different parties (Emperor, Empress, prince, princess), as in reigns from Antoninus Pius onwards, negative binomial estimating can be made more efficient if each segment of Reka Devnia coin is modelled separately.

3. APPLYING THE NEGATIVE BINOMIAL TO A KNOWN DIE-POPULATION

The late Republican denarius issues with serially numbered dies provide a valuable tool for testing die-estimates. A big sample for the Crepusius issue of 82 BC has been collected and analysed by Buttrey and Carter.[19] Carter summarised statistical evidence for Crepusius die-frequencies, which showed reverse die-numbers spanning a range from 1 to 519 (possibly terminating at 525). 358 reverse dies were reported, representing about 70% of the original series. The execution was not flawless: in at least five known cases, two different reverse dies received the same serial number.

By applying computer optimisation to all the co-ordinates, Carter produced effective simple formulae for reconstituting the original die-totals from surviving Crepusius samples.[20] If the sample is divided into five segments, applying Carter's formula produces the results shown in Table 10.3.[21]

Table 10.3 *Carter estimates of missing Crepusius reverse dies*

Die-numbering	Dies	Coins	Numbered dies missing	Carter prediction	Percentage error
1. 1–100	77	220	23	23	0
2. 101–200	74	216	26	21	−19
3. 201–300	66	155	34	29	−15
4. 301–400	73	146	27	46	+70
5. 401–519	68	128	51	50	−2
Aggregate	358	865	161	169	

Mean error per sector $+7\%$.

The estimates for each sector of the reverse die-numbering using the Carter formula are within 20% of the expected values in four sectors out of five. In the

[19] Die-frequency figures were published by Carter 1981A for a sample of 865 coins.
[20] His three interlocking formulae (shown in Carter 1983, 202) are as follows:
  A. if d/c (dies observed / coins observed) exceeds 0.5, then D (total dies) $=$ d $\times$ c / (1.214c $-$ 1.197d).
  B. if d/c lies between 0.5 and 0.333, then D $=$ d $\times$ c / (1.124c $-$ 1.016d).
  C. if d/c lies below 0.333. then D $=$ d $\times$ c / (1.069c $-$ 0.843d).
Virtually the same results can be obtained from Program 2 in Appendix 8, using a value for k of 1.92.
[21] Carter's 1981 tests of the reverse dies were based on sets of 25 serial numbers (Carter 1981B, Table III).

Table 10.4 *Negative binomial estimates of missing Crepusius reverse dies*

Die-numbering	Numbered dies missing	Negative binomial prediction (Method A)	Percentage error	Negative binomial prediction (Method B)	Percentage error
1–100	23	25	+9	23	0
101–200	26	26	0	21	−19
201–300	34	22	−35	21	−38
301–400	27	48	+78	46	+70
401–519	51	39	−24	50	−2
Aggregate	161	160		161	

Mean error per sector +6% (Method A) +2% (Method B).

Note: The Method A estimate fitted frequencies using MLP. The Method B estimate used Program 2 in Appendix 8, with a value of k approximating the figure inherent in Carter's formula (k = 1.92); k could alternatively have been found from the aggregate Crepusius figures in Table 10.3, by using Program 1 in Appendix 8.

remaining sector, numbers 301–400, the error is 70%. But the data at this point evidently contain an abnormality which also affects the negative binomial extrapolations in Table 10.4.

The negative binomial distribution can also fit the Crepusius data. It is able to do so without any of the special optimisation used in constructing the Carter formula, which was specifically devised for this coin-issue. The negative binomial estimates are comparable with the Carter results, whether Method A or Method B is used. Both negative binomial estimates give a lower mean error than the estimate using the Carter formula (Tables 10.3 and 10.4).[22]

Tables 10.3 and 10.4 show that Carter's estimate and the two negative binomial estimates are all relatively efficient. But the negative binomial is a flexible general-purpose distribution with an enormously wide range of applications, whereas the Carter formula is specifically limited to data with the same value of negative binomial k as the Crepusius coin-issue.[23]

4. DIE-STUDIES

The published die-studies for major reigns of the Principate up to the Severi seem to be limited to the cistophoroi of Augustus, the coinage of Claudius, the

---

[22] As a further illustration of Method A, the frequencies for the first line in Table 10.3, with the negative binomial fit modelled by MLP in brackets, are: F1 28 (24.4) F2 10 (18.4) F3 15 (12.6) F4 12 (8.3) F5 5 (5.2) F6 2 (3.2) F7 2 (2.6) F8+ 3 (2.6) F12+ 0 (0.3).

[23] The values implicit in the Carter formula range between k = 1.85 and k = 2.0, where (dies/coins) lies between 0.16 and 0.84.

coinage of Domitian, and the restored coin of Trajan.[24] As part of a provincial coinage, the cistophoroi are excluded by definition from the main coin-hoards, as is almost all Julio-Claudian coin before Nero, for other reasons. High precious-metal content drove parts of Domitian's coinage out of circulation, making its representation in surviving hoards extremely uneven. And Trajan's restored coinage, struck from a tiny die-population, is much too rare to use for extrapolation.

An extensive search for new material was therefore carried out, and this focussed on more than a dozen gold types, and six denarius types.[25] As a measure of their scale, if extrapolated to whole reigns the resulting samples imply totals of about 2,500 aurei of Vespasian, 1,200 aurei of Trajan, 1,950 aurei of Hadrian, and 22,000 denarii of Hadrian.[26] All these figures are much higher than the largest sample in any known hoard.[27]

4.1. SILVER DIES

Denarii of Nerva, Trajan, Aelius, Sabina and Crispina were collected and examined for reverse die-links.[28] The only cases which provided die-links in significant quantities were types of Aelius and Crispina, Aelius being the more useful.[29] Two Aelius silver types were used, the Concordia and Pietas types of TR POT COS II. Both these types also yield a little gold coin of their own, despite the separate existence of substantive gold issues with the same motifs and almost the same legend, TRIB POT COS II (Tables 10.5–10.6). As a second potential source of confusion, the gold types in their turn also provide a little silver (Table 10.12).

---

[24] Sutherland, Olcay Merrington 1970; Von Kaenel 1986; Carradice, 78–92; Mattingly 1926 and BMCRE 2. For die-study of Galba's bronze, see p. 169 below.

[25] This involved very prolonged work. The writer examined virtually all relevant series in the library of auction catalogues in the British Museum Coin Department. The dossiers also use the British Museum photofile, the photofile of the Vienna Kunsthistorisches Museum, and the specimens in the British Museum, the Museo Nazionale in Rome, the Paris Cabinet des Médailles, the American Numismatic Society, the Ashmolean Museum, the Fitzwilliam Museum and the Hunterian Museum in Glasgow, as well as illustrated hoard publications where these exist.

The die-dossiers, gold and silver, were almost all examined by patient numismatic colleagues who are thanked in the Preface. This usually affected the die-identifications relatively little, but repeats of gold coins known from cast-photos were eliminated in significant numbers.

[26] Multiplying the coin-samples shown in Tables 10.5, 10.6, 10.10 and 10.13 by the quotients for hoard-representation indicated below. Thus 61 aurei of a Vespasianic type making up 2.44% of his aurei on median hoard-average (Table 10.13) presuppose an aureus sample for the reign of 2,500 coins (61/0.0244 = 2,500).

[27] Fully illustrated publications of the largest hoards, such as Reka Devnia, would obviously be a prime resource for die-study. But no such publications exist for silver, and access to the Reka Devnia hoard was not available at the time of writing. In the case of gold, the published illustrations of the Liberchies hoard have been included in the present dossiers.

[28] No estimates for bronze were attempted, major bronze hoards from this period being relatively few. The published details of the Garonne hoard show that die-populations of sestertii were large.

[29] A die-study was carried out for Crispina's DIS GENITALIBUS type from a sample of 60 specimens struck from 37 reverse dies (RIC 281). But diffusion of the type in the hoards proved to be so uneven that its importance remains difficult to establish.

Table 10.5 *Aelius TR POT COS II CONCORD denarii and aurei*

Design (all with CONCORD exergue)	Reverse dies	Coins	*RIC* no.
1. Seated figure with cornucopia	59	122	436
2. On high-backed throne	16	22	(436)
3. Without cornucopia	3	3	437
Silver aggregate	78	147	
Gold (design 1)	3	10	

Table 10.6 *Aelius TR POT COS II PIETAS denarii and aurei*

	Reverse dies	Coins
Silver	31	62
Gold	3	11

Note: One gold die and one silver die are identical.

Table 10.7 *Aelius die-totals projected by negative binomial*

Concordia silver (1) & (3)	189
Concordia silver (2)	95
Concordia gold	6
Pietas silver	95
Pietas gold	6
Silver aggregate	379
Gold aggregate	12

Note: The value of k for Hadrianic denarii is given by Program 1 as 0.421, using the Hadrianic type/coin ratio at Reka Devnia in conjunction with the total of *RIC*-Cohen denarius types for the reign. Program 2 was then used to calculate these die-projections from the co-ordinates in Tables 10.5 and 10.6. For gold, see note on Table 10.11. For Progams 1 and 2, see Appendix 8.

1. Concordia, denarius of Aelius Caesar (*RIC* 436)

Three variants of Aelius's TR POT CONCORDIA reverse are found in the sample of 147 denarii summarised in Table 10.5 (Pl. 1). This evidence suggests that the type without cornucopia, although assigned a number in *RIC*, is statistically insignificant. By contrast, the high-backed throne type, missing from RIC and *BMCRE*, is found in appreciable numbers.[30]

The hoards suggest that the Concordia type made up approximately 0.69% of Hadrianic denarius output.[31] Thus the total for Hadrian projected by the Concord type is about 41,000 reverse dies in all (284/0.0069 = 41,159). The Pietas type (Pl. 2) is lacking from most large hoards, making a separate calculation difficult.

Nevertheless, it seems from Reka Devnia that Concordia and Pietas together made up about half the denarii of Aelius ($\frac{72}{149}$, or 48%). In that case, their combined projection of 379 dies can be related to the figure for Aelius as a fraction of Hadrianic denarii. Aelius denarii as a whole were roughly 1.99% of Hadrianic output.[32] The resulting projection is 39,678 dies for Hadrian ((379/0.48)/0.0199). This is within 4% of the 41,159 dies in the calculation for the Concordia type.

[30] Die-frequencies in precious-metal coin of this period usually show extreme variations, both in silver and gold (n.46 below). The silver variations are greater than those suggested by Republican evidence (Carter 1981A–B). Even in the nineteenth century individual variation seems to have been wide. One die-pair used for English florins produced four times the mean amount of coin. Identical dies at Brussels struck 20,000 coins in one case and 123,000 in another. And in British experiments, four steam-forged dies produced totals ranging from 42,060 to 119,170 coins, while the output from three dies forged by hand varied from 18,927 to 69,399 (Grierson 1968).

[31] This is the median figure in a sample of 16 large hoards where the type is represented (Stockstadt, Cologne, Bristol, Falkirk, Nietulisko Male I, La Salasuri, Sotin, Oboroceni, Tolna Megye, Osijek, Szombathely, Hemse, Puriceni, Tell Kalak, La Magura, Reka Devnia). Using hoards for extrapolation in this way (see also Crawford 1974) raises the question of how far regional skewing in the survival pattern may affect the results (cf. Reece 1987B). Clearly allowing for different patterning in what has not survived is impossible. But whereas the representation of individual types can certainly vary (see chapter 12), quantities in different hoards show strong similarity year by year (chapter 8, pp. 113–16 with figs. 8.1–3). Using the median, which defines the mid-point, also minimises any specific regional distortions.

[32] From the median of ten hoards (Salasuri, Lawrence Weston, Bristol, Falkirk, Nietulisko Male I, Nietulisko Male II, La Magura, Stockstadt, Tell Kalak, Reka Devnia).

Table 10.8 *Aelius denarii: obverse dies*

Design	Coins	Dies	Projected die-total
1. Undraped rt	217	148	746
2. Undraped lt	35	10	20
3. Draped rt	19	10	33
Total	271	168	799

Note: For the value of k, see Table 10.7.

2. Pietas, denarius of Aelius Caesar (*RIC* 438)

A third calculation of the Hadrianic die-total can be made from the obverse dies whose details are given in Table 10.8. The busts of Aelius fall into three categories, two of them relatively rare. The total die-projection here is 799 dies for Aelius's coins as a whole. This can be related to the median hoard fraction for denarii of Aelius as a fraction of Hadrianic denarii, which is 1.99% (see n.32 above). This again gives an estimate of about 40,000 dies of Hadrian (799/0.0199 = 40,151). Thus this projection from a spread of hoard samples closely supports the other two, if obverse and reverse dies were used in the same amounts.

Their ratio can be studied from Aelius's Concordia and Pietas types (Table 10.9).[33] This limited selection from Aelius's reverse types actually shows more obverse than reverse dies for a given reverse type. But obverse dies may span more than one reverse type, and the largest sample in Table 9 shows the lowest ratio of obverse to reverse, about 11:10. This trend suggests that a full study, including all the remaining reverse types, might show something like parity between obverse and reverse dies.

Similarly, totals for obverse and reverse are extremely close in the biggest published sample for a Republican silver-issue (347 obverse dies and 358

---

[33] Further specimens were added to the samples in Tables 10.5–10.6 after the analyses in Table 10.9 had been made.

Table 10.9 *Obverse and reverse dies in Aelius's denarii: Aelius rt undraped obverse (Table 10.8, line 1)*

Reverse type	Coins	Reverse dies	Obverse dies	Obverse/ reverse
Concordia	95	59	72	1.22
Pietas	44	25	28	1.12
Concordia and Pietas	139	84	92	1.10

reverse from a sample of 865 Crepusius denarii).[34] This is also true of one of Sutherland's two samples of early Augustan denarii, and of the largest Domitianic denarius-issue studied by Carradice.[35] Thus the big imbalance that could be expected if obverses with their longer potential lifetime were used to breaking point is not seen here, and production-runs were evidently kept within the capacity of the shorter-lived reverse dies.

Similar numbers for obverse and reverse strikings are again implied by the frequent die-pairings (pairs of coins which share obverse and reverse dies) that detailed studies show. In the Aelius denarii, the repeated reverse dies include 7 double die-pairs, 1 treble repeat, 1 quadruple, and 1 ninefold repeat (Table 10.9). Gold coin also shows frequent double die-pairs, from the detailed publication of the Liberchies hoard.[36]

4.2. GOLD DIES

4.2.1. HADRIAN

As the main gold sample, nine gold-types of Hadrian's reign were examined. Two are types of Aelius, the gold 'twins' of the two silver types already studied, and the rest types of Hadrian (Pls. 3–9). Their details are shown in

[34] Carter 1981A. A comparable result is cited by Crawford for denarius-issues of 44 BC, with 379 obverses and 414 reverses (Crawford 1974, 672). The Roman evidence contrasts with Greek practice, where substantially more reverse than obverse dies can often be seen. For example, 4 obverse and 22 reverse dies were observed in Athenian gold coinage of c.407–404 BC (Robinson 1960, 12–13); 7 obverse and 12 reverse dies in 26 Amphictionic staters of the fourth century BC (Kinns 1983, 2); 77 obverse and 432 reverse dies in Babylon tetradrachms of Alexander (Waggoner 1979, 274). Ratios in the cistophoroi of Augustus range from 25:32 to 27:50 (Sutherland, Olcay, Merrington 1970, 40 ff., types VIIa and VIIc).

[35] 216 obverse and 227 reverse dies in the Imp Caesar issue from 402 coins; but 124 obverse and 151 reverse in the Caesar divi f. issue from 286 coins (*RIC*² 1, 30). 140 obverse and 142 reverse dies from 155 coins in Domitian's issue 92.1 (Carradice, 84). In small samples of gold of Tiberius, obverse dies outnumber reverse (17 obverse and 13 reverse dies from 37 coins of Divus Augustus-type; 11 obverse and 9 reverse dies from 14 coins of Trib. Pot. 17; Giard 1983, 114 ff.).

[36] Full catalogue in Thirion, including many references to other specimens from the same dies. Similar patterns are shown by the unpublished Belgian gold hoard.

3. Concordia, aureus of Aelius Caesar (*RIC* 443)

4. Pietas, aureus of Aelius Caesar (*RIC* 444)

5. Hadrian on horseback, aureus (*RIC* 186)

6. Hadrian galloping, aureus (*RIC* 187)

7. Jupiter standing, aureus of Hadrian (*RIC* 63)

8. Jupiter seated, aureus of Hadrian (*RIC* 64)

Table 10.10 *Hadrianic gold dies*

Type	Reverse dies observed	Coins	Date (AD)	*RIC* no.
1. Aelius Concordia TRIB POT	9	108	137	443
2. Aelius Pietas TRIB POT	6	48	137	444
3. Hadrian riding	26	96	125–8	186
4. Hadrian riding (obv. PP)	10	52	132–4	348
5. Hadrian galloping	14	71	125–8	187
6. Jupiter standing	23	74	119–22	63
7. Jupiter seated	19	47	119–22	64
8. Wolf left	16	102	125–8	193
9. Wolf right	11	40	125–8	192
Total	134	638		

9. Wolf and twins right, aureus of Hadrian (*RIC* 192)

Table 10.10. The resulting die-projections are shown in Table 10.11.[37] The gold projections differ more from type to type than the projections for silver. But the much smaller gold hoards inevitably expose the hoard extrapolations for individual gold types to the random variation inherent in very small samples. By using gross figures instead of figures for individual types when calculating reign output for gold, this source of distortion is largely avoided.

The gross figures in Table 10.11 show a remarkable contrast, revealing the existence of separate categories of 'high-output' and 'low-output' types. In

[37] The die-projections are calculated as in Table 10.7. The aggregated type-frequencies from the seven largest hoard-samples of Hadrianic gold, set against figures for gold-types from *RIC*–Cohen, imply a value for k of 0.393. This is extremely close to the value of 0.421 for Hadrianic denarii based on the much larger Reka Devnia sample (Table 10.7).

Table 10.11 *Die-projections for Hadrianic gold*

Type	Projected die-total	Type as a percentage of Hadrianic coin (hoard median)	Die-total for Hadrian projected by hoard-extrapolation	Reference (Table 10.10)
A. High-output types				
Hadrian riding (obv. PP)	18	3.85	468	4
Aelius Concordia	13	2.5	520	1
Wolf left	26	4.40	591	8
High-output gross	57	10.75	530	
B. Low-output types				
Jupiter standing	50	5.94	842	6
Wolf right	23	2.60	885	9
Hadrian galloping	25	2.57	973	5
Hadrian riding	53	4.48	1,183	3
Jupiter seated	50	3.88	1,289	7
Low-output gross	201	19.47	1,032	

Note: The two gross die-projections in column 3 come from an independent calculation using the aggregates in columns 1 and 2. Program 1 gives the Hadrianic value of k for gold as 0.393, virtually the same as for silver (0.421, Table 10.7) (taking the median figure for seven gold hoards, related to the *RIC* type-total for gold: Belgium, Rome, Liberchies, Diarbekir, Erla, Vidy, Corbridge). Program 2 then gives the projections shown here. Figures in column 2 are based on the four largest gold hoard-samples for Hadrian (Belgium 113 coins, Rome 78, Liberchies 76, Corbridge 40). (The Aelius Pietas type in Table 10.10 line 2 is omitted because it has too little hoard evidence: the projected die-total is 9.)

aggregate, the types from high-output dies project a die-total for the reign of approximately 500 (530), whereas the low output versions project about 1,000 dies (1,032). That argues a variation in the mean production-life of a die by a factor of 2, depending on the category of type.

Thus part of the Hadrianic die-set for aurei (X) was used at a high mean productivity per die, and the remainder (Y) at a low rate. X high-output dies plus Y low-output dies added up to a total of Z dies. The actual die-total Z evidently lay between the high-output extrapolation of 530 and the low-output extrapolation of 1,032 dies.

The die-populations projected for individual gold-types, based on samples containing many die-repeats, are not affected by hoard-sizes. They are generally coherent, and suggest some consistency of practice. The six largest projections from Hadrianic material show the following die-totals: 23, 25, 26, and 50, 50, 53 (Table 10.11). This suggests obvious targets of 25 and 50 dies. Both Jupiter-types belong to the 50 module, and both Wolf-types (literally shown as 23 and 26) probably belong to the 25 module. The Vespasianic gold-type

Table 10.12 *Silver from Aelius gold-types: reverse dies*

Die-number and type	Silver coin-frequency	Gold coin-frequency
1. Concordia TRIB POT	6	2
2. Concordia TRIB POT	1	44
3. Concordia TRIB POT	1	—
1. Pietas TRIB POT	1	—
2. Pietas TRIB POT	1	—

10. Vespasian crowned by Victory, aureus (*RIC* 105)

studied below provides another example of the 25 module (Table 10.13).

The Aelius gold-types also generated small amounts of silver. That certainly meant some die-sharing, from the few specimens that survive, and possibly all of this marginal output was generated in that way (Table 10.12).

4.2.2. GOLD IN OTHER REIGNS

Die-studies were also carried out for gold-types of Trajan and Vespasian.[38] The type of Trajan is Hercules with club and lion-skin, which also existed as a silver type (*RIC* 49–50; Pl. 11). The words COS IIII date it to AD 101–2. The gold-type of Vespasian, which was apparently not struck in silver, is Vespasian crowned by Victory (*RIC* 105, COS VIII, AD 77–8; Pl. 10). The results are shown in Table 10.13.

The four largest hoard-samples show the Trajanic type, with a projected die-total of 81, as 7.86% of Trajanic gold coin, on median average.[39] The extrapolated die-total for the reign is thus 1,031 gold dies (81/0.0786).

[38] Die-studies were also made for selected types of Antoninus Pius and Faustina I, but smaller hoard-samples at this point in the published evidence make extrapolation more difficult.

[39] The Trajanic samples are Belgium 98, Rome 86, Liberchies 66, Corbridge 48.

Table 10.13 *Gold-types of Vespasian and Trajan*

Type	Dies observed	Coins	Projected die-total	Date (AD)	*RIC* no.
1. Vespasian crowned by Victory	13	61	25	77–8	105
2. Hercules standing (Trajan)	36	94	81	101–2	49–50

Note: The median values of k for gold-types of these reigns are (1) 0.346 (2) 0.477; for the method, see Table 10.11 Note.

11. Hercules with club, aureus of Trajan (*RIC* 49–50)

Although this is based on a single type, it is virtually the same as the more broadly based Hadrianic result of 1,032 dies for low-output types (Table 10.11). The two output quotients for gold calculated from other evidence, for these reigns of similar length are within 6% of each other (Trajan 9.56, Hadrian 9.03, see Table 8.5). Thus output-index and die-estimates agree to within 6% here, assuming that Trajanic gold dies used the low-output module identified under Hadrian.

For the gold-type of Vespasian, the projected total of 25 dies closely recalls the Hadrianic types with projections of 23, 25 and 26 dies (Table 10.11). The four largest hoard-samples in which the type occurs show it as 2.44% of Vespasianic gold coin, on median average.[40] That would make the extrapolated die-total for the reign 1,025. But this figure seems to be out of alignment with the output-index (Table 8.5). As few specimens of the type are seen in the available hoards, further evidence is probably needed before the die-population of this important reign can be assessed.[41]

---

[40] Belgium 141, Rome 88, Liberchies 82, Diarbekir 41.
[41] The gold output-index shows respective values for Vespasian and Hadrian of 13.65 and 9.03 (Table 8.5).

5. CONCLUSION

The rate of die-utilisation under Hadrian appears to be about 2,000 dies per year for silver, and 25–50 per year for gold.[42] The rate implied for Trajanic gold dies by the one type of Trajan studied in detail is again about 50 per year.[43] The modular die-totals such as 50 and 25 for individual types (Tables 10.11 and 10.13) imply that the die-set was determined in advance, and that the system was not based on producing new dies opportunistically when the old ones broke.[44] Die-utilisation respected the limitations of reverse dies, and did not usually exploit the higher capacity of obverse dies.[45] Gross output per type was evidently also set in advance, in view of the ratio of approximately 2:1 between high-output and low-output types seen in the Hadrianic evidence (Table 10.11). Coin-survivals suggest that there were big differences between the productivity of individual dies.[46] But these seem to reflect the inherent variability of poorly tempered metal under stress. Willingness to go on using dies which proved to be long-lived may suggest that die-utilisation in the mint was not always efficiently supervised.[47]

[42] Hadrian's reign lasted for 20.45 years, and an exact calculation from approximate die co-ordinates would thus give figures of 1,956 and 24–50.

[43] 53 per year, taking the estimate literally.

[44] Carter suggested that the lower productivity of dies late in the numbered Crepusius series could be due to recycling of metal from old dies. This must assume that the die-set was not produced all at once, and presumably envisages opportunistic production of new dies when old ones broke (Carter 1981A, 203). But numerical symmetries within the Crepusius issue probably make it more likely that the size of the die-set was predetermined, and that the falling-off in productivity had some reason such as the exhaustion of available silver. The number of coins known per 100 die-numbers declines progressively (Table 10.3), as does the percentage of reverse dies known from more than one coin: die-numbers 1–100 64%, 101–200 65%, 201–300 61%, 301–400 53%, 401–519 49% (Carter 1981A).

[45] Pp. 154–5.

[46] In these samples, the largest observed number of coins per die, 17 for denarii (Table 10.5 (1)) and 44 for aurei (Table 10.10 (1)), are respectively 5.9 and 2.1 standard deviations above the mean.

[47] For the widely varying lifetime of dies even under industrial conditions, see Grierson 1968. Despite the limitations of pre-industrial technology, dies could be copied or partly copied by the process of 'hubbing', potentially resulting in duplicate images from different dies. But if hubbing was common in the Roman mint in this period, little progress has yet been made in detecting it, and its incidence remains largely uncertain. For the process, see *RIC* I², 12 with citations.

I I

THE SIZE OF COIN-POPULATIONS

1. DIE PRODUCTIVITY

This chapter considers the implications of the die-estimates for the volume of coin minted. For Rome coin of Hadrian, the die-estimates in chapter 10 show a projected population of about 40,000 dies for silver and for gold, alternative levels of about 1,032 and 530 dies. But no Roman evidence directly shows how many coins a given number of dies produced.[1] Other figures for pre-industrial die-productivity nevertheless suggest broad orders of magnitude. In practice, the relatively stable ratio between gold and silver in large Roman coin samples narrows the range of possibilities.

In an important study of the Amphictionic coinage struck at Delphi in the late fourth century BC, Kinns combined die-study with analysis of the inscription recording the amount minted. He concluded that output was between 11,053 and 27,563 coins per reverse die.[2] These coins were silver staters, larger than Roman denarii. Modern experiments in striking large-diameter coins based on ancient Greek coinage suggested quantities in the range 10,000 to 16,000 for hot striking (Roman mints used hot striking).[3] Moving to the Middle Ages, detailed thirteenth-century evidence about mint-operations from England and France agrees in suggesting a production target per reverse die of between 16,500 and 17,000 coins (Appendix 9). This normally referred to cold striking of silver coins with low relief, using steel or

---

[1] Crawford's pioneering estimate, in which Republican die-counts are combined with figures for military spending from literary sources, seems to depend on somewhat uncertain data; the proposed figure of 30,000 denarii per obverse die was thought to be high in itself (Crawford 1974, 694; cf. H.B. Mattingly, *NC* 137 (1977) 199 ff., and B.W. Frier, *Phoenix* 30 (1976) 379). Moreover, the fact that surviving die-evidence is seriously incomplete as a rule (chapter 10, p. 144, and section 4 below) means that any figure for die-productivity which interprets a fixed sum of money in terms of a raw die-count must be scaled down substantially to allow for missing dies. That applies equally to Mattingly's alternative of 15,000 per obverse die, which still uses a raw die-count (Mattingly *NC* 137 (1977), 206–8). Buttrey conjectured an average output of between 4,500 and 11,500 coins per die, arguing a maximum number of anvils from detailed analysis of the reverse and obverse numeration of the Crepusius issues, on specific assumptions about the rate of daily production (Buttrey 1976, 101–3).

[2] Kinns 1983, 18–19. Although the sample is too small to allow effective modelling, the total of reverses may easily have been higher than the 19 assumed from a base of 12 dies found in 26 coins. The maximum output per reverse die would then be less than 27,563.

[3] Sellwood 1963. For hot striking, see Tylecote 1986, 116, and Cope 1972, 30: 'Roman silver coinage is now very much harder and more wear-resistant than when it was made.'

iron dies.[4] Experiments carried out in the nineteenth century with three dies forged by hand produced totals per die of 18,927, 22,432 and 69,399 coins.[5]

There are strong indications of the ratio of gold to silver coin in circulation in our period. By face value, gold makes up 71% of precious-metal coin in the finds at Pompeii from AD 79, 74% in precious-metal coin-hoards from the rest of the empire (Appendix 10), and 68% on median average in some samples of small-scale stray finds.[6] These figures are enough to suggest that in the underlying production pattern, gold made up about 70% of the face value of precious-metal coin. By value, the ratio of gold to silver coin would thus be 7:3.[7] Coin for coin, that means a ratio of 1:10.7 between aurei and denarii.[8]

Die-studies show silver dies outnumbering gold dies by much more than 10.7 to 1. The find-ratio therefore implies that gold dies produced more coins than silver dies. The estimate for Hadrianic silver is 40,000 dies, and for low-output gold 1,032 dies, a ratio of 1:39 (chapter 10). This could be interpreted using the 7:3 ratio. But that general figure need not apply exactly to a particular reign. A closer estimate can be made from the scales for gold and silver production. Taking the indices for six major periods of production from AD 64 to 180, the Hadrianic quotient is 13.398% for gold and 17.647% for silver.[9] Thus a specific gold:silver ratio for Hadrian can be calculated as $(7 \times 13.398):(3 \times 17.647)$ or 93.79:52.94. In percentage terms, this ratio is virtually 64:36.

Turning to specific figures, if for example 1,032 gold dies struck 22,000 coins on average, the monetary value would be HS2,270.4 million.[10] The corresponding silver value would be HS1277.1 million, at a ratio of 64:36.[11] This would result in 7,982 coins per silver die.[12] The mean output per gold die from the alternative Hadrianic estimate of 530 high-output dies would be 42,838 coins per die $(22,000 \times 1,032/530)$.[13]

---

[4] Cf. Johnson 1956, 88–9.

[5] Grierson 1968, 299, citing a Report from the Royal Mint of 1879. For other estimates for Rome, see n.1 above. A figure of 10,000 is used by medievalists (Metcalf 1986, 141; Jonsson 1987, 16 and 118).   [6] See pp. 70–2 above.

[7] It could be argued that the denarius being a low denomination coin which circulated faster and wasted faster than the aureus, silver would need to be replaced more often, and that it would therefore be under-represented by the ratio between it and gold in any cross-section of the coin in circulation. But this cannot be an important source of error, as the respective wastage-rates were of the order of $\frac{1}{250}$ and $\frac{1}{360}$ per year (p. 210), whereas the median age of the precious-metal coin in circulation in this period was usually a few decades. The median of the three gold:silver ratios quoted is 71:29, whereas the general ratio adopted is 7:3. This actually biases the result in favour of silver by about 5%, and thus offsets any under-representation of silver in the find-pattern.

[8] 7:3 by value means 7 aurei for 75 denarii; $\frac{75}{7} = 10.7$.

[9] Tables 8.5 and 8.7.

[10] Die-total × mean die-production × aureus-value: $1,032 \times 22,000 \times 100$.

[11] 2,270.4 million × 36/64.

[12] Estimated value/(total silver dies × denarius-value) = 1277.1 million/$(40,000 \times 4)$ = 7,982.

[13] The Hadrianic ratios between the die-productivity of silver, low-output gold and high-output gold would thus be roughly 2:5.52:10.74 (7,982:22,000:42,838). The ratios, which would remain the same in this calculation even with different productivity levels, are close to the more obvious archetype of 2:5:10.

Any such projections are obviously elastic. But the figures proposed are not purely arbitrary. The possible range of variation is limited, unless the known figures for pre-industrial die-productivity cited above have no relevance to Roman practice. Because the die-population estimates and the gold:silver ratio in the coin-finds both appear stable, varying these estimates to any substantial degree tends to push die-productivity outside the known limits. For example, if silver is set as high as 15,000 coins per die, that gives high-output gold a mean figure of 80,500 coins per die, almost certainly well above anything plausible from limited parallel evidence. Conversely, a much lower ceiling for gold of, say, 30,000 reduces silver to 5,600 coins per die, which is well below parallel figures.

Consequently, suggested figures that incorporate an upper mean level for gold of about 43,000 (relatively high) and a corresponding figure for silver of about 8,000 (relatively low) should give a plausible order of magnitude.[14] Most gold in the present results was struck at the lower level of productivity, with a mean on these projections of roughly 22,000 (Tables 10.11 and 10.12).[15]

2. DIE-PRODUCTIVITY: FURTHER PERSPECTIVES

Two points of note in these estimates are the relatively small calculating base for denarii, and the big differential in die-productivity between gold and silver. Both are worth considering further.

2.1. Despite a base sample of well over 200 coins, the silver estimates are extrapolated from approximately $\frac{1}{50}$ of the denarius-output of Hadrian's reign. All three calculations from different cross-sections of this sample nevertheless give virtually the same die-total for Hadrianic denarii (40,330 ± 2%). Assembling an adequate working sample even for this calculation required a very prolonged search.

A fuller evaluation of the denarius evidence as a whole would require efficient estimates for a larger segment of the total coin-issue. Ideally the samples should be big enough to show repeats for at least half the dies studied and should utilise central coin-issues. That would inevitably involve very large die-sets, and it might therefore require collection of material by a research team, possibly using mechanised scanning techniques for the die-analysis.

2.2. The estimates of relative gold and silver die-productivity are based on the co-ordinates set out above. They argue much higher productivity for gold

---

[14] None of the parallel figures quoted refers to striking of gold.

[15] Die-productivity for marginal issues was evidently much lower than for the mainstream gold issues. Gold of the main silver types of Aelius, Concordia and Pietas, was produced on a small scale (Tables 10.5 and 10.6). The projected die-populations are 6 in each case (for method of calculation, see Table 10.7). To judge from how much survives, coin from these gold dies was struck in much smaller amounts than coin of the main Aelius gold-types. The number of coins per die projected is 7.1 for the gold-types and 1.75 for gold from the silver types, a ratio of 4:1 ($\frac{156}{22}$ and $\frac{21}{12}$; Tables 10.5–10.7, 10.10–10.11; the die-projection for the Pietas gold-type is 9).

dies, although there are few obvious signs that these dies received greater wear. Various points should be taken into account.

2.2.1.   In the examples studied here, gold and silver die-populations are essentially distinct.[16] There are cases of denarii struck from gold dies, although these seem to be very marginal. But where any gold was produced from what were mainly silver types, this used dies not attested for silver. When the same type exists in major silver and gold versions, as with Trajan *RIC* 49, the gold and silver die-populations appear to be distinct. Thus it seems that gold and silver in the evidence examined were essentially struck from different dies.

2.2.2.   Potentially that means that different alloying techniques and a greater degree of metallurgical care could have been used in making gold dies.[17] Gold coins show more consistent image-quality than silver, whose best results are comparable with gold, but whose worst examples can be poor. On present calculations, the gold die-population for Hadrian was a tiny fraction of the silver die-population, between $\frac{1}{40}$ and $\frac{1}{80}$. Thus dies for gold coin, like the coins themselves, were a kind of elite.

2.2.3.   These considerations apart, longer average lifetimes are likely for dies striking gold, the softer metal.

2.2.4.   A result of the present estimates is that the survival-rate of gold coin and that of silver are shown as being approximately the same (Table 11.3 below).

2.2.5.   Analysis of gold production clearly suggests set die-totals, and different levels of mean productivity per die (p. 162 above). Thus the production-run from a given die-set was apparently defined by a pre-determined amount of coin, not by the point at which all dies wore out. Ensuring that the die-set could always produce that predetermined amount despite unforeseeable breakages would mean engraving more rather than fewer dies. The need to produce coin rapidly, using more operatives, may also have made die-sets larger than they would otherwise have been.

All of that argues that in general production targets probably fell well within the technical limits of what Roman dies could achieve. The excessive die-wear which is visible in coin from some silver dies probably indicates inefficient rotation of dies rather than high mean levels of productivity per die.[18]

2.2.6.   A wide discrepancy between the productivity of gold and silver dies might also suggest the possibility of hubbing.[19] If some gold dies were duplicated in this way, so that they struck identical images, that would disrupt any calculation of differences between the productivity of gold and silver dies from surviving coin-evidence. But in practice, coins of a given gold-type usually show many renderings of the same motif. This means that hubbing

---

[16] Tables 10.5, 10.6 and 10.12.

[17] For surviving dies, see Vermeule 1953–4.

[18] The large-scale published Crepusius evidence showed dies with a productivity as high as 13 surviving coins, whereas other dies in the numbered set had yet to yield a single coin in the 1981 survey (Carter 1981B).

[19] See p. 162 n. 47.

cannot have dominated die-production, and any lesser use of this technique by the central mint remains largely conjectural.

3. VOLUME OF PRODUCTION

3.1. AMOUNTS BY REIGN AND BY YEAR

The present rough estimates make output of gold under Hadrian HS2,270 million. That can be used to assess coin production by reign, from the general 7:3 ratio for gold:silver, when applied to the two output-indices already calculated. Table 11.1 shows the results for gold and silver up to Marcus Aurelius. Estimation for silver can be continued further, because of better hoard coverage, and Table 11.2 shows figures for major reigns extending to the end of the period. Second-century gold-output seems to be of the order of 1.1 to 1.4 million aurei per year.[20]

Table 11.1 *Estimates of gold and silver coin by reign: AD 64–180*

Reign	Aurei (millions)	Per year	Denarii (millions)	Per year	Combined value in sesterces (millions)	Per year	Gold:silver ratio (by aggregate weight)
Nero, 64–8	32.26	8.07	31.9	8.0	3,353	838	1:0.45
Vespasian	34.33	3.61	357.6	37.6	4,864	512	1:4.8
Trajan	24.03	1.23	362.9	18.6	3,855	197	1:6.9
Hadrian	22.70	1.11	319.3	15.6	3,548	173	1:5.4
A. Pius	32.42	1.41	442.7	19.2	5,013	218	1:6.3
M. Aurelius	23.70	1.24	294.8	15.5	3,549	187	1:5.7

Note: All estimates are very approximate, and depend on the output figures per die in the text. Exact figures are shown in order to avoid unnecessary rounding error, using the ratios from Tables 8.5 and 8.7. Major reigns are shown, Domitian being omitted because of insufficient evidence.

For a comparison with other pre-modern figures, gold-production at the Venice mint in the fourteenth and early fifteenth centuries has been estimated at 600,000–1,200,000 ducats per year. The ducat weighed 3.56 grams, just under half an aureus.[21] Compared with estimates of 1 to 1.4 million aurei per year in the first half of the second century (Table 11.1), this makes Venetian gold coin production between a quarter and a half of the projected Roman figures.

[20] Recent output estimates for Domitian's silver give an annual figure of about 15 million denarii. The die-totals extrapolated using a conventional formula are extremely low, implying values for negative binomial k as high as 13,100 and 305,000 for the two largest coin samples. This yields die-totals of 214 and 741, where a more plausible approximation for k at this date such as 0.4 would give 626 and 2,497 (Program 2, Appendix 8). Low bias here is offset by a high productivity figure of 30,000 coins per die (Carradice, 83–6, cf. p.155n above).
[21] Lane, Müller 1985, 199–201; 175.

Table 11.2 *Estimates of silver coin by reign: AD 64–235*

Reign	Denarii (millions)	Per year
Nero, 64–8	31.9	8.0
Vespasian	357.6	37.6
Trajan	362.9	18.6
Hadrian	319.3	15.6
Antoninus Pius	442.7	19.2
Marcus Aurelius	294.8	15.5
Commodus	106.4	8.3
Septimius Severus	532.1	30.1
Caracalla	122.3	19.8
Elagabalus	196.8	51.6
Severus Alexander	284.1	21.8

Note: See note on Table 11.1.

3.2.   TOTAL COIN IN CIRCULATION

The output estimates for Hadrian can also be used to extrapolate the total volume of precious metal in circulation, reflecting coin surviving after allowing for wastage. The fraction of output still circulating, as shown by individual hoards, can be estimated hoard by hoard and then averaged (for the method, see p. 193 below). The usable gold hoards cluster round the 160s AD.[22] They give a median cumulated index-value for gold of 42.87 (for the index see Table 8.5), This reflects coin surviving after allowance for wastage (see chapter 14, p. 210). The gold output index gives a figure for Hadrian's reign of 9.03. Compensated for wastage by the 160s, this is about 8.1.[23] Hadrian's gold-production is estimated at HS2,270 million (p. 164). This makes gold worth HS280.2 million per index point (Table 8.5).[24] The cumulated index-value for gold then works out at HS12,012 million.[25] At the schematic gold:silver ratio of 7:3 (p. 71), that makes silver from the central mint worth HS5,148 million. The gross value for precious-metal coin from Rome is then HS17,160 million.[26]

As before, this result can indicate a likely order of magnitude, but little more. It gives a view of the rough size of the main circulating medium

---

[22] Liberchies and Rome end in 166 and 165, Corbridge in 159/60. The Belgium hoard ends in 205, but contains little coin after the 160s (its coin after Marcus Aurelius is excluded from the calculation). The median is the average of the values from Rome and Liberchies.

[23] On average, Hadrianic coin had received approximately thirty-seven years of wastage by the mid-160s. The wastage-rate for gold is taken as $\frac{1}{360}$: p. 210.

[24] $\frac{2,270}{7.4}$.   [25] 306.8 million × 38.93.

[26] For estimates of total coin circulating under Augustus as HS4 billion in gold and HS3 billion in silver, see Goldsmith 1987, 41.

stemming from the central mint, as reflected in provincial samples of the 160s.

The value of the base metal coinage, and of silver currency struck in the East probably lies beyond the reach of any systematic estimate at present. But seemingly the total cannot be very high. By face value, bronze makes up 2.9% of finds in a summary from Pompeii whose bronze listing is apparently incomplete.[27] Direct die-estimation for bronze is difficult, because of large die-populations and very high wear-factors (many coins in sestertius hoards are almost too worn to be identified). The large Garonne hoard, published in admirable detail, contains too few die-repeats to allow effective statistical modelling.[28] Another resource is Kraay's die-study for bronze of Galba.[29] But even if there were companion die-studies of Galba's gold and silver, evidence from such a brief reign might under-represent bronze output, because of the pressures of accession minting in gold and silver.

Simple guesswork suggests that by value, bronze might have made up between 5% and 10% of the coin in circulation, possibly nearer the upper figure, about 8%.[30] This figure still implies a very large coin-population. Ratios between the bronze denominations are not known, but the total given below is enough to allow for example 800 million sestertii, 400 million dupondii, 1,600 million asses, and 2,700 million quadrantes. There are very strong signs in the find-pattern that small change was in short supply in northern provinces.[31]

For eastern precious metal currencies, the case studied most is Egypt. But even there, the available die-observations for individual types seem too few to allow efficient estimation of die-populations.[32] A silver currency which circulated in only one province was by definition much smaller than the silver issue from Rome. In Egypt, the most remarkable feature is the fact that more than half the coin circulating for the next hundred years was minted in a single four-year period under Nero (AD 64–8). Presumably mint operations at Alexandria were enormously expanded at that time.[33]

Silver minted in the East apparently circulated little outside its region of production.[34] And it was used alongside Roman denarii, whose presence in the market-place of Pergamum is known from a famous inscription. Despite restricted publication of eastern finds, notable denarius hoards are known

---

[27] See p.71 n.15.
[28] The die-repeats are all illustrated, and could form the nucleus for further studies.
[29] Kraay 1956.
[30] For purely arbitrary comparison, the value of minting in precious metal in the state of Milan between 1581 and 1700 was more than 95% of the total (Cipolla 1952, 13–14). Some figures from medieval Florence show ratios by face-value of: gold 58%, silver c.40%, billon 2%; and gold 50%, silver 49%, billon 1% (sums invested by a small banker in 1315–23; and payments of church tithe in 1296); de la Roncière 1973, 32, 34.   [31] Cf. Boon 1988.
[32] For some die-observations, see Christiansen 1988. The resulting estimates are not always supported by the hoard-quotients: the ratio between the tetradrachm output of Nero years 10–14 and that of Trajan is given as 80:1, whereas Milne's two biggest hoards show this ratio as 31.5:1 and 41.3:1 (Christiansen 1988, 1.96; 1.240. Milne 1933, hoards 3 and 6). Wastage over a few decades could not account for a twofold difference. For other difficulties, Bruun 1991, 71; W.E. Metcalf, JRA 3 (1990) 466.   [33] See pp. 31, and 211.   [34] Butcher 1988, 27.

from Turkey, Syria, Egypt and Cyprus.[35] After the large issues of cistophoroi by Antony and Augustus, die-populations for individual issues appear to be generally small; but there are a great many local issues at different times.[36]

It seems unlikely that eastern silver represented more than a fraction of the equivalent silver population minted centrally, perhaps not more than one-third.[37] On that basis, the increment for eastern silver would be 1,716 million (5,148/3), giving all silver coin a value of HS6,864 million, and making gold and silver combined 18,876. A bronze increment of 8% of total face value would then increase the overall total to HS20,517 million. These calculations again are very approximate. But they suggest that the total circulating medium might have amounted to roughly HS20 billion in the mid-second century.[38]

As bullion, the calculations for the 160s make gold weigh 880 metric tonnes.[39] Reckoned as denarius-equivalent, the estimated silver total of HS6,864 million contributes 5,766 tonnes.[40] The gold:silver ratio in terms of bullion is nominally 1:6.55, but debasement of silver would make a true figure somewhat lower.[41]

4. THE SURVIVAL-RATE OF COIN

Estimates of the number of coins produced can be related to the number discovered, showing something about the processes of loss and survival. The true limits of what has survived are inevitably imprecise. As an illustration, an impressively large sample of 865 Crepusius denarii, struck at the Rome mint during a single year, was summarised in work by Buttrey and Carter in 1981. But their further searches had more than doubled this total by a later date.[42] For relatively common types like those studied here, many further examples must exist in private hands, in trade, and in a host of further museums.[43] These specimens would presumably add substantially to the present totals.

Nevertheless, this inherent limitation does not seem to undermine the linearity of the available samples, since their results are reasonably stable.[44]

---

[35] *OGIS* 484 = *ESAR* 4.892–5, almost certainly Hadrianic (Macro 1976; Buttrey 1991). Larnaka, Tell Kalak, Turkey 1 and 2, Egypt 1 and 2.

[36] Cf. Burnett, Amandry, Ripolles 1992, 6.

[37] For substantial increases in the number of cities striking coin and in the die-populations from which eastern coins were struck, see Johnston 1984, Fig.A, p.246 and Fig.B, p.254.

[38] Thus the manuscript figure of HS40 billion for the deficit at Vespasian's accession, which is accepted by some, does not seem remotely plausible (Suet. *Vesp.* 16.3).

[39] 120.12 million aurei estimated; 1 million aurei = 7.33 tonnes. Estimates by Depeyrot of the amount of gold coin circulating in the later Empire appear low (59 tonnes in AD 310, rising to 200 tonnes by 370, then falling back to 95 by 490); Depeyrot 1991, 212.

[40] 1,716 million denarii; 1 million denarii = 3.36 tonnes.

[41] The silver figure suggested for the Roman Empire in AD 150 in broad assessments by Patterson is 10,000 tonnes, of which half or 5,000 tonnes would be in coin (Patterson 1972, 216).

[42] Carter 1981A–B. Information kindly communicated by Professor Buttrey.

[43] For the scope of the present searches, see chapter 10 n.25.

[44] For another result from this period which is similar to those in Table 11.3, see p. 88 above. For a higher survival-rate in coinage from recent centuries, see Appendix 9, section 1.A below.

Table 11.3 *Coin-survival: the ratio between samples and projected numbers*

Types	Sample (N)	Projected coins	Ratio	Metal
1. Aelius Concordia and Pietas	214	3,025,178	1:14,136	Silver
2. Hadrian low output (nos. 3, 5, 6, 7, 9)	328	4,422,000	1:13,482	Gold
3. Hadrian high output (nos. 4, 8)	154	1,884,872	1:12,239	Gold
4. Vespasian with Victory	61	825,000	1:13,524	Gold
5. Trajan Hercules standing	94	1,782,000	1:18,957	Gold

Note: For line 1, see Tables 10.5–10.7. The numbers in lines 2–3 refer to Table 10.10. The coin-projections are calculated from the die-totals estimated in Tables 10.7, 10.11 and 10.13, together with the projections of die-productivity in section 1 of this chapter.

The quotient for silver and the median quotient for gold are within 5% of each other (1/14,136 and 1/13,503: see Table 11.3). Four of the five quotients lie between 1/12,200 and 1/14,200.[45]

5. THE PROPORTION OF DIES REPRESENTED

The negative binomial distribution used here as the main statistical tool can also show how large a coin sample it would take to reveal a given proportion of dies.[46] Thus in the case of silver, with a Hadrianic value for k of 0.421 (Table 10.7), a 50% sample of the Concordia dies (projected total die-population 284) would need 486 coins, and a 75% sample 3,012. For a gold type, Hadrian's Jupiter standing (projected die-population 50, and projected k 0.393, Table 10.11), a 50% sample would need 94 specimens, and a 75% sample 666. The higher targets are certainly far out of reach.

This means that extrapolation is essential, and that die-counting by itself is not enough to produce meaningful results. But the present extrapolation tool is powerful. Its effectiveness in compensating for incompleteness in the coin data can be judged from its application to Crepusius and Reka Devnia material, as well as from the coherent patterns shown by the projected die-totals for gold (Tables 10.2, 10.4, 10.11 and 10.13).

[45] The Aelius data cannot be fully assessed, because of the lack of hoard-representation of the Pietas-type (Table 10.11 note).

[46] This uses the programs in Appendix 8 and assumes linear cross-sections. Naturally, no small sample is a perfect cross-section except by accident. But consistent skewing would be needed to change these predictions significantly.

12

MOBILITY AND IMMOBILITY OF COIN

1. INTRODUCTION

Once a system of regional mints is established at the end of the third century, mint-marks immediately show that coin tended to remain where it was produced.[1] In general the coin commonest in Italy was minted in Italy, the coin commonest in Egypt was minted in Egypt, and so on.[2] In important regions without mints, such as Spain, coin predominantly came from the closest neighbouring areas.[3] There was also supplementation from neighbouring mints if production was insufficient for local needs, as it probably was in Britain and Africa.[4] In small amounts, coin could certainly travel from one end of the empire to the other. But the dominant circulation pattern in this explicit evidence is highly localised.

Evidence before the Late Empire is inexplicit, since there are no local mint-marks on the main coinage. It has even been assumed that under the Principate money-flows were homogeneous and free from localised patterns.[5] But that is dangerously close to an argument from silence, and it has to suppose that radical change in circulation patterns took place between early and Late Empire. In the earlier period, regional patterning is naturally more difficult to study, and co-ordinated attempts to do so are rare. But material for analysis exists even here, and what it suggests about natural patterns of circulation is as localised as in the later period. Thus the case for significant long-term change in the motor patterns of Roman coin-circulation under the Empire remains uncertain.

---

[1] For analyses of coin-finds of the Late Empire by mint of origin, see J.P.C. Kent, *RIC* 8 (1981), 74–7, 96–115; Fulford 1978; Callu 1969, 390 ff.; 454–5. Private information from the owner of a large collection of solidi of Constantine indicates that specimens acquired in the Near East came from eastern mints and from one western mint (Arles); solidi from western mints in general could be obtained only from sources in Europe. In a gold hoard of the reign of Anthemius found at Rome in 1897, about 90% of the solidi were struck in Rome (354 out of 397 coins; Ungaro 1985, 48). For exceptions to localised patterns in the Late Empire, see Ermatinger 1990, 108–9, 112–14.

[2] For Italy, cf. Callu 1969 and Kent (n.1), 110, no.335; for Egypt, cf. Metcalf 1976 and Kent, 108.

[3] For Spain, cf. Fulford 1978, 105; Kent (n.1), 103 and 110.

[4] For Britain, cf. Fulford 1978, 91–6; for Africa, cf. Callu 1969, 454–5.

[5] This of course refers to the main currency, not to eastern issues minted for local circulation.

2. REGIONAL PATTERNS OF DIFFERENCE

Table 12.1 *Main components of three gold hoards*

	Rome		Liberchies		Diarbekir	
Ruler	Coins	*RIC* types	Coins	*RIC* types	Coins	*RIC* types
Nero	69	13	68	11	67	9
Vespasian	87	46	82	36	42	28
Trajan	86	41	66	39	40	28
Hadrian	78	44	76	43	39	24

Table 12.2 *A coefficient of divergence applied to gold hoards*

Ruler	Diarbekir–Rome	Diarbekir–Liberchies
Nero	$0.4 \left(\frac{4}{9}\right)$	$0.9 \left(\frac{6}{7}\right)$
Vespasian	$1.7 \left(\frac{34}{20}\right)$	$2.0 \left(\frac{32}{16}\right)$
Trajan	$1.7 \left(\frac{31}{19}\right)$	$3.2 \left(\frac{41}{13}\right)$
Hadrian	$2.3 \left(\frac{36}{16}\right)$	$2.5 \left(\frac{37}{15}\right)$

Note: The fractions show the number of types found only in one hoard, divided by the number of types that the two hoards have in common.

Three gold hoards from the reign of Marcus Aurelius of approximately equal size have been published. The writer analysed these hoards using *RIC* classifications.[6] They come from completely different regions: the city of Rome, Liberchies in Gallia Belgica, and Diarbekir in Turkey, on the border of Roman Syria.[7] Their figures for four major reigns are shown in Table 12.1.

From Vespasian onwards the Table 12.1 totals differ too much to allow the hoards to be compared on equal terms. Taking either of the larger samples as the starting point produces purely artificial differences because of the reduced coverage in the third case. Comparisons were therefore based on Diarbekir, the smallest sample. A coefficient of divergence was constructed by pairing hoards, and expressing the types found in only one of the two hoards as a

[6] The lack of a single inventory of coin-types remains a serious obstacle to studies of this kind. More aids like the concordance between Cohen[2] and *RIC*[1] are needed (Chantraine, Alföldi 1978). Some hoards are classified by other typologies: *BMCRE* (the fullest listing, although strictly an inventory of specimens, not of types; references are given there to Cohen[2], but not to *RIC*); Strack; and Cohen[1]. For the essential concordance between *RIC* I[2] and *RIC* I[1] (unaccountably missing from *RIC* I[2]), see Schmidt-Dick 1987.

[7] Cesano 1929; Thirion; Regling.

multiple of the types common to both. The results in Table 12.2 show that the divergences between Diarbekir and Liberchies are greater than those between Diarbekir and Rome.

These comparisons are based on the amount of 'non-overlap'. The proportion of data in common can also be compared. These data are not always normally distributed, which makes a non-parametric test the most appropriate. The results of the Spearman correlation test are shown in Table 12.3. For three reigns out of four, the Diarbekir correlation with Rome is higher than the one with Liberchies. Both analyses thus show systematically that the range of types at Diarbekir is closer to those at Rome than to those at Liberchies. The three locations are very far apart, but similarity is greatest between the two hoards from the Mediterranean basin.[8]

Table 12.3 *Spearman correlations between types in common*

| Ruler | Diarbekir–Rome | | | Diarbekir–Liberchies | | |
	Correlation	N (type-pairs)	Probability	Correlation	N (type-pairs)	Probability
Nero	.829	9	>20%	.494	7	<20%
Vespasian	.515	20	>5%	.368	16	>20%
Trajan	.307	19	>20%	−.128	13	—
Hadrian	−.231	16	—	−.170	15	—

3. DISTRIBUTION EFFECTS AND REGIONAL ANOMALIES IN THE REPRESENTATION OF COIN-TYPES

In the explicit evidence from the fourth century, where a coin-set is found is closely related to where it was minted. Finds of Nero's bronze coinage also show the effect of distance. As already seen, Globe-types minted at Lugdunum predominate in the provinces, whereas the non-Globe-types minted in Rome predominate in Italy. Some non-Globe coin reached the provinces, but its frequency diminishes with distance from Rome.[9] Precious-metal coin minted at Lugdunum before AD 64 also seems to be more heavily represented in the provinces than in Italy.[10]

---

[8] The progressive deterioration in the correlations may be affected by increases in the number of coin-types per reign.

[9] See chapter 8 above, p.121 n.25. As further evidence for the relative immobility of bronze coin, the bronze series found in provinces north of the Alps virtually ends with the Antonines, although in the Mediterranean the series clearly continues under the Severi (Buttrey 1972; Walker 1988, 300–1). Evidently army shipments of bronze coin to Britain and Gaul after the 190s were rare, and any natural movement of bronze coin northward was too slight to compensate for this.

[10] See pp. 120–2. There are also remarkable cases of transferred production which do not directly illustrate circulation patterns. These include production at Rome of eastern types used in Syria,

But there are regional differences in the circulation-pattern which are not a simple function of distance from the mint.[11] They are difficult to explain unless individual streams of newly minted coin were somehow channelled to particular zones. Some examples can be summarised briefly.[12]

3.1. In eighteen out of twenty hoards in a broadly based assemblage with a minimum of 100 coins of Hadrian's reign, the number of denarii of the Empress Sabina is 5–8% of the number of denarii of Hadrian. But in three large hoards from a separate area, the Black Sea, the fraction rises sharply to 11–18%.

3.2. The number of denarii struck for 'divus Marcus' is 8–12% of the number that were struck for Commodus himself in five large hoards from the East and Danube regions. But in large hoards from Britain and Gaul, the fraction is only 1% or less.

3.3. For denarii of Marciana and Matidia, a sample of over 600 Trajanic denarii from four hoards in north-west Europe shows a complete blank. And only one such coin is found in a much bigger Italian sample of over 1,900 Trajanic denarii from three hoards. But the issues do occur in hoards from the Black Sea, and in hoards from Syria and Egypt. This shows a contrast between East and West.[13]

3.4. Large hoards of sestertii show great unevenness in the regional representation of Marcus Aurelius as heir under Antoninus Pius. Coin of Marcus accounts for 30% of coin of 148–61 in French hoards, 17% in a big North African hoard, and a mere 7% in Britain. The coin was completely missing from three western assemblages, two of them British.[14]

3.5. A factor analysis of Trajanic coin in large denarius hoards based on common coin types produced two regional clusters consisting of the two British hoards and the two Danubian hoards. This suggests similarity when coin samples come from a given region and dissimilarity when they come from more than one region. Hoards from the Rhineland and Syria formed the third cluster.[15]

Egypt and Cyprus, and production at Alexandria of types used in Syria: Walker, 3.159; Burnett, Craddock 1983; Carradice, Cowell 1987; Burnett 1987, 30–1.

Eastern coins resembling the denarius such as the Lycian drachm are sometimes found in denarius hoards from other areas, although only in tiny amounts typically well below 1%. See Cesano 1925, 71–2: of nine western hoards with one or two Lycian drachms, seven show drachms of Trajan, and single hoards show drachms of Domitian and Nerva. For Britain, where these eastern coins are again mainly Trajanic, see Robertson 1993.

[11] Centrally produced coin-dies may potentially have been used outside the central mint, though it would take much more evidence to show that this was a regular practice (cf. Mattingly *BMCRE* 2, xii; 4, xviii; Grant 1955, 52–4). Individual coin-dies have been found at St Albans, and in Gaul at locations well removed from the official mint at Lugdunum (*BMCRE* 3, xx–xxi; Sutherland *RIC* I[2] 25, 88, 102–3). For other die-finds, see Vermeule 1953–4.

[12] Fuller discussions are cited in notes 13 and 15.

[13] Duncan-Jones 1990, 40–1; 211–12.

[14] See chapter 9, p. 132.

[15] Duncan-Jones 1989, 131–2 (diagram 1). For further striking evidence of regional patterning, see Duncan-Jones 1994.

4. IMPLICATIONS OF THE EVIDENCE

The fact that the same basic output of coin from Rome is found all over very large areas of the empire is not in dispute. But the results in sections 2–3 show noticeable regional and even local differences between cross-sections of types. Geographical distribution of precious metal and sestertius coin thus seems to have been significantly uneven.

Such unevenness has two main implications. First, that at a time when prosperity was arguably at its height, trade and long-distance exchange were still not enough to make the coin-population homogeneous throughout the empire. It is worth recalling Gaius' remark that in his world not only the prices of grain, wine and oil, but also interest-rates varied very widely from place to place.[16] As far as it goes, that suggests an economy divided into small local cells, rather than something large and unified.

The fact that local samples of coin sent out from Rome retained individual characteristics also means that they had not been sufficiently randomised by previous circulation to make their type-content consistent. This must argue that the coin sent to the provinces was, to a significant extent, new or recent in origin. In fact, clusters of unrandomised coin are sometimes seen in provincial hoards, which contain many specimens of the same type or even of the same die.[17]

It is sometimes envisaged that taxes paid in coin found their way back from the provinces to Rome, and were sent out again to pay the troops in the provinces. If this cycle were a prime determinant of the coin found in the provinces, it should have had a smoothing effect, which would tend to obliterate local characteristics in provincial coin-populations. Yet as we have seen, local characteristics remain clearly visible.

That second-century armies received cash payment in a precious-metal currency is not in serious doubt. Although it has been suggested that the bronze *as* was used for payment, the amount of metal potentially needed to pay a single legion in this denomination for one year would weigh 300 tonnes. No government has access to a limitless supply of bullion, and in the case of Rome, reductions in the precious-metal content of the coinage suggest strain on the bullion-supply.[18] Since army pay was the biggest running expense of the Empire, the government's dependence on recycled cash to meet the expense was inevitable, and recycling must have taken place.

---

[16] *Dig.* 13.4.3.

[17] In an Egyptian hoard of 60 aurei of Antoninus Pius, 26 coins belong to the same type, Strack, no.316 (Strack 3, p. 18). In the large denarius hoard from La Salasuri in Romania which ends in AD 158, the number of coins from the year 155 is out of all proportion, about 28% of the coins of the reign (424 out of 1,498). The two most frequent types, Strack nos.279 and 282, account for 148 and 145 of the coins respectively, each about 10% of the coins of the reign. By comparison, in the Reka Devnia reign sample, some ten times larger, the two most frequent types make up only 3.6% and 2.8%. The hoard of 72 aurei found under the floor of a house at Vidy in Switzerland contains 4 coins struck from the same die, which belong to a rare Hadrianic type not generally found in published gold hoards (*RIC* 444). The sizeable Genas hoard of AD 197 was entirely composed of denarii of a single type of Clodius Albinus.

[18] See chapter 15.

The present results show that, whatever processes took place, they did not include enough long-distance monetary exchange to create a homogeneous coin-population. That finding is straightforward. But the actual differences between provincial coin-populations are difficult to reconcile with the smoothing effect that tax-recycling should have had.

Three hypotheses can be considered. The first is that there was a 'streaming' of coin-populations such that money collected as tax in one region was sent back to that region and to no other. The second hypothesis is that coin collected in tax was reminted before being re-spent in the form of provincial army pay. The third is that coin mainly stayed in the province to which it was first sent; and that (trade-flows apart) coin journeyed thereafter only to the extent that local tax-revenues exceeded or fell short of local government expenditure. On this model, new coin would still be needed everywhere, but mainly as a replacement for what was lost through wastage and hoarding.

The first hypothesis assumes a rigid partitioning of the treasury at Rome on regional lines, which would have been very difficult to maintain, and lacked any obvious rationale.[19] The second hypothesis, involving reminting, may be partly correct, since reminting sometimes emerges as an important feature of government policy.[20] But the relatively long circulation-life of coin minted between Nero and Severus shows that reminting cannot have been enough to equal the yearly tax-turnover.[21] Consequently the third hypothesis, that the localisation of coin-types reflects the relative immobility of coin, remains the most likely. When adjustments to the coin-stock did involve central recycling, re-exported coin may have been reminted first.

In essence, this finding supports Jones's explanation of how coin stocks were organised.

Naturally, both for the sake of economy and to avoid loss in transit, as little coin as possible was shipped from Rome to the provinces and vice versa . . . Only surpluses of local revenue over local expenditure would be transmitted to Rome, and only when the expenses of a province exceeded its income would money be sent from the aerarium to a province.[22]

5. REASONS FOR REGIONAL DIFFERENTIATION

These discontinuities between type-populations presumably had a random origin. Most coin-types had no regional significance, and no propaganda meaning.[23] The potent message of the coinage was provided by the Emperor's

---

[19] The two provinces for which there were special *fisci* at Rome did not use the central currency to more than a limited extent (n.22, known from a series of inscriptions in each case).

[20] See chapter 14, p. 212.

[21] In any case, projections of the scale of mint-output make it considerably smaller than public revenue (pp. 111–12).

[22] Jones 1960, 102–3, 106, 107. The *fiscus Asiaticus* and *fiscus Alexandrinus* were bureaux at Rome which evidently handled revenue from the major provinces of Asia and Egypt, and a *fiscus frumentarius* handled expenditure for the corn-supply (ibid., nn.49, 52–3, suggesting innovation by Vespasian). The separate *fisci* for these two eastern provinces may be connected with the fact that the provinces used their own currency.

face, and, for the more literate, by his name and titles. Shipping coin whose reverse celebrated, say, Felicitas or Pietas to one region and not to another probably meant little in itself. Yet contrasts like these are implied by the finds.

The new coin which reached the provinces may have been sent out in rotation. The mean production-lifetime of individual silver types was of the order of one month or less, to judge from the number of types per reign. If one month's production mainly went to one group of provinces, and the next to another group, the types sent would usually differ.[24] Any rotation on these lines was bound to produce some regional differences in the coin-pattern.

6. SUMMARY

Finds argue that the type-content of the precious-metal coin distributed from Rome to the various parts of the empire was to some extent differentiated. The very fact that such differentiations remain visible today despite subsequent circulation of the coin in question implies that this circulation was mainly local. The constant need for tax-revenue for army pay meant that coin had to be recycled. Recycling existing provincial coin-populations through a central exchequer would tend to smooth out the find-pattern, thus erasing such regional differences. Thus the existence of regional differences suggests that recycling was provincial rather than national. But some recycling from the centre may have taken place, using reminted coin.

The pattern of finds provides little basis for arguing that coin of the Principate circulated about the empire through trade-flows.[25] This need not show an absence of all monetised trade-flows, but the main dynamic behind the long-distance transmission of coin seems to have been the state's need to pay the armies of the empire. Archaeological discoveries of coin cannot distinguish government-controlled movement of coin from natural movement due to trade, even if in frontier regions the places where coin is found tend to be army sites.[26] But the ceaseless pressure behind the need to pay the troops, and the very large scale of the payments involved are both quite clear, whereas the volume of long-distance trade remains inherently obscure. The distinctive regional configurations of coin-types undermine the hypothesis of heavy inter-regional trade based on transfer of coin.

Returning to the original comparison with the Late Empire, the relative

---

[23] Of the types with some regional content, one of the most important groups, Hadrian's Adventus series, seems to have been produced for general consumption, and distributed without any effort to concentrate coin in the province it referred to (cf. *BMCRE* 3, cxliii, clxxi–clxxii). The Britannia asses of Hadrian and Antoninus Pius found especially in Britain are a small exception, but have few parallels (Walker 1988, 290–1, 294–8). For the limitations of the content of coin-types, see Jones 1974, 63–4 and de Sainte Croix 1981, 392–4.

[24] Some types were produced in parallel with each other (p. 142), but that hardly affects this argument.

[25] For coin-finds within the empire interpreted as evidence of trade, cf. Hopkins 1980, 112–16, discussed more fully in Duncan-Jones 1990, chapter 2.

[26] Cf. for example Robertson 1978, 189, and Nash 1978, 23–4.

immobility of coin seen in the explicit later evidence seems to be anticipated in circulation patterns of the Principate. This may argue that the monetary unification of the empire, so striking in terms of the uniform denominations found throughout an enormous land-area, was always more a matter of form than of substance.

13

WEIGHT-LOSS AND CIRCULATION-SPEED

1. INTRODUCTION

Loss of weight through circulation is an important constant of coin behaviour.[1] In coin of the late twentieth century, wear tends to be masked by the use of hard alloys, and by frequent replacement with new coin. But the effects of wear were still very obvious in the Victorian pennies circulating in Britain a few decades ago. Roman coin was not deliberately hardened by alloy, and it was often allowed to go on circulating for very long periods.[2] As a result, surviving coin often shows obvious effects of wear, and large coin-hoards reveal different stages in this process.

Coin-hoards offer samples whose approximate date of deposit is normally indicated by the date of the latest coin.[3] A hoard will generally represent a sample of the coin circulating at a particular date in antiquity.[4] By contrast, museum or dealers' collections, however large, offer no scope for analysing wear, because they do not represent single samples of known date.[5]

Few large hoards of the period have so far been published in detail.[6] But the position has recently improved, and the biggest samples available provide enough detail to show patterns of coin-wear.[7] From these hoards we can

---

[1] For an illuminating general discussion of coin-wear, see Grierson 1965. A new monograph on coin wear was announced after this book had gone to press (Delamare 1993). The phrases 'circulation-speed' and 'velocity of circulation' are used here to refer to the physical movement of coin, as a result of which wear takes place. But in modern economic usage, 'velocity of circulation' can describe the relationship between the value of money in circulation and gross national product (cf. Goldsmith 1987, 41).

[2] For metallurgical reasons, the hardness of surviving Roman silver coin is substantially greater than its original hardness (Cope 1972, 30).

[3] For the relationship between the end-date of hoards and their date of deposit, see p. 86.

[4] For the nature of coin-hoards from the Principate, see chapter 5.

[5] The frequency table is often invoked as a means of calculating target weight from large samples irrespective of their origin. But it has no special properties, and it is quite ineffective in determining original weights from samples of coin whose circulation period is unknown (see p. 219 n.28).

[6] Ideally, a hoard publication should include coin-weights, and list and illustrate any internal die-links. Few published silver hoards of the Principate meet all of these criteria. For gold and bronze, two important exceptions are Thirion's publication of the Liberchies hoard in 1972, and the publication of the Garonne bronze hoard by Etienne and his colleagues in 1984, both of which report dies as well as weights, and include illustrations. Die-populations for imperial silver are dauntingly large; but Buttrey's excellent publication of the big Republican hoard from Cosa which shows die-links gives some indication of what should be possible (Buttrey 1980).

[7] Since the preliminary discussion in Duncan-Jones 1987, important new material has become

examine the rate of weight-loss over the extended periods for which weight-standards remained approximately the same. In big samples, the results suggest that the rate of wear was approximately linear, as in modern evidence (n.33). These results can be compared with the much fuller modern data.[8]

2. WEIGHT-LOSS IN GOLD HOARDS

Three gold hoards were studied, a hoard of 812 aurei from Belgium ending in AD 205, a hoard of 368 coins from Liberchies, also in Belgium, ending in 166, and a hoard of 160 coins from Corbridge in Britain ending in 159/60.[9] As expected, the biggest hoard, more than twice the size of the others, provides the most coherent pattern.

In this hoard (Table 13.1), a linear regression of median weight against median date for six major reigns between Nero and Marcus Aurelius provides extremely high correlations whether based on all coin or only on coin struck for the Emperor ($r^2 = 0.982$ and 0.968).[10] For all coin, the rate of weight-loss is 0.00226 grams per year, or $\frac{1}{3,246}$.[11] The date on which the regression reaches the full aureus-weight of 7.336 grams is projected as AD 222 for all coin and 208 for Emperor coin. Emperor coin thus gives the closer fit with the hoard end-date of 205. This makes the 'Emperor' loss rate the better measure (0.00249 grams per year, or $\frac{1}{2,946}$). In this hoard ending in 205, Neronian aurei struck in 64–8 weigh 6.97 on median average. This shows a loss of 0.366 grams (or 5%) in approximately 139 years, at an annual rate of 0.00263 grams per year, or $\frac{1}{2,789}$ per year.[12]

available. The much bigger Belgian gold hoard now takes the place of the hoard from Portugal (Braga), whose published weights are imprecise, and Little Brickhill is added to the denarius hoards. The new sestertius hoard from Puy-Dieu has been added also.

[8] Short-term deviations can also illustrate variations in the weight-standard (see pp. 187–90). Corrosion of coin does not normally appear to be serious enough to affect these readings significantly (for corrosion, cf. Clay 1988, 348–52).

[9] The findspot of the bigger Belgian hoard, which is not yet published, remains ill-defined, but it is not Liberchies, the source of the other important Belgian hoard of this period (information from Dr J. Van Heesch). The coin-types were identified for present purposes by the writer from photographs kindly provided by Dr Burnett, who also supplied a weight-list. The main contents are summarised in Table 13.1. The hoard also contains 8 coins of Galba, 5 of Otho, 6 of Vitellius, 3 of Domitian as Emperor, 5 of Commodus as Emperor, 2 of Pertinax, 5 of Julianus and 15 from the reign of Septimius Severus. As in almost all post-Trajanic gold hoards, Nerva's coin is missing, together with the higher-weight aurei of Domitian and Trajan.

[10] In each case the date is taken as the mid-point in the reign, except with Marcus Aurelius, most of whose coin in this hoard is early, meaning that AD 164, the date of the median coin, is used instead.

[11] It should be emphasised that the amount of metal lost annually is a constant for practical purposes, despite the steady reduction in the amount remaining. The fraction shown for annual weight-loss is therefore based on the coin *at full weight*, not on the lower weights reached year by year. The present equations read: median weight = 6.834 + (date × .00226) for all coin; and weight = 6.818 + (date × .00249) for Emperor coin.

[12] For weight-loss of 0.038–0.044% per year suggested for gold solidi of the Late Empire, see Depeyrot 1988. For the Roman pound as 322.8 grams, see p. 214.

Table 13.1 *Weights (in grams) in the Belgian gold hoard*

Reign	Median	Mean	% coefficient of variation	N
A. All coin				
Nero	6.97	6.95	2.6	125
Vespasian	7.01	6.99	2.6	140
Titus	6.96	6.97	1.7	14
Trajan	7.08	7.07	1.7	98
Hadrian	7.12	7.08	2.6	113
A. Pius	7.19	7.16	2.6	199
M. Aurelius	7.205	7.155	2.8	74
B. Emperor coin (reigns with segmented output)				
Vespasian	7.02	7.01	2.3	80
Hadrian	7.13	7.09	2.3	103
A. Pius	7.205	7.16	2.9	110
M. Aurelius	7.21	7.15	3.1	58

Note: All coin of Nero postdates the weight-reduction in AD 64. Both totals for Marcus Aurelius include coin struck for his co-ruler Lucius Verus.

Table 13.2 *Median weights (in grams) in two gold hoards*

	Corbridge (AD 159/60)		Liberchies (AD 166)	
	weight	N	weight	N
Nero	7.155	10	7.02	67
Vespasian	7.19	25	7.06	82
Trajan	7.195	48	7.095	66
Hadrian	7.22	40	7.14	76
A. Pius	7.20	24	7.16	44
M. Aurelius	—	—	7.20	7

The two smaller gold hoards both show less weight-loss (see Table 13.2 and figure 13.1). Their regressions give rates of 0.00158 grams per year or 0.022% at Liberchies and 0.000816 grams per year or 0.011% at Corbridge.[13] Found on the northern frontier, the Corbridge hoard could well belong to an area of very slow circulation. The Liberchies rate, although twice as fast, is still well below the figure for the 'Belgian' hoard from the same area.

[13] The equations are: weight = 6.9288 + (date × 0.00158), $r^2 = 0.961$ (Liberchies); weight = 7.1133 + (date × 0.000816), $r^2 = 0.786$ (Corbridge). Marcus Aurelius is here omitted because of the tiny sample, and the Corbridge figure for Antoninus Pius is omitted because it is inconsistent with the rest of the data (see fig. 13.1).

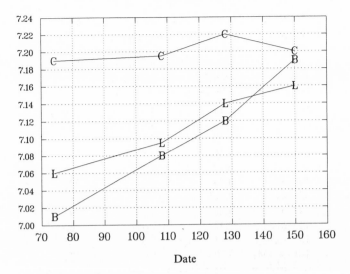

Figure 13.1 Median weights (in grams) for four reigns in three gold hoards. (Symbol: B Belgium; L Liberchies; C Corbridge.)

More surprisingly, both regressions project end-dates long after the latest coin in the hoard. The projection for full weight of 7.336 grams at Liberchies is AD 258, and at Corbridge AD 273, 92 and 113 years after the last coin. But it remains unlikely that hoards whose earliest coin is significantly heavier than that in the Severan hoard from Belgium still circulated for decades longer than that hoard. This problem may suggest an artificiality in hoard-composition, perhaps recalling the anomaly of underweight denarius hoards.[14]

In view of this difficulty, the Belgian gold hoard, which is also more than twice the size of the other two, remains the preferable guide to the wear-rate of gold.

3. WEIGHT-LOSS IN SILVER HOARDS

Four silver hoards were used, the largest with 2,830 coins, and the smallest with 420. The biggest is the La Magura hoard ending in AD 196, from Moldavia, north of the Dacian frontier.[15] Its weight-configuration is shown in Table 13.3, based on coin struck for the Emperor. The loss-rate indicated is $\frac{1}{1,576}$ or 0.063% per year.[16] The pattern is shown in fig. 13.2.

The remaining silver hoards are summarised in Table 13.4. Their annual loss-rates are $\frac{1}{1,644}$ or 0.061% (Viuz), $\frac{1}{1,673}$ or 0.060% (Londonthorpe), and

[14] See pp. 245–7.
[15] For hoards outside the Empire, see pp. 92–4.
[16] The equation based on Table 13.3 reads: weight = 2.949 + (date × 0.002132), r^2 = 0.965. The date co-ordinates are the mid-points in the periods shown in Table 13.3.

Table 13.3 *Median weight (in grams) at La Magura of coin struck for the Emperor (AD 196)*

Period (AD)	Weight	% coefficient of variation	N
69–79	3.11	4.3	260
100–2	3.15	4.9	90
103–11	3.19	5.1	292
112–17	3.20	5.8	203
117–28	3.19	5.4	305
128–38	3.24	5.0	222
138–44	3.245	5.7	80
147–55	3.265	6.0	96
155–61	3.30	7.6	66
161–9 (V)	3.31	6.1	33
161–80 (M)	3.30	5.6	134

Note: Coin struck at higher weight between AD 79 and 100 is omitted, as is coin struck at lower weight after AD 180 (see Table 15.5). Coin struck for Lucius Verus is shown in 161–9, and coin for Marcus Aurelius in 161–80.

Table 13.4 *Median weights (in grams) of pre-Severan coin struck for the Emperor in three silver hoards*

	Viuz-Faverges (251/3)		Londonthorpe (153/4)		Little Brickhill (187)	
	weight	N	weight	N	weight	N
Vespasian	3.085	24	3.14	41	3.05	69
Trajan	3.215	62	3.20	121	3.11	130
Hadrian	3.21	93	3.25	98	3.15	125
A. Pius	3.25	118	(3.21)	15	3.19	116
M. Aurelius	3.30	107	—	—	(3.265)	26

Note See note on Table 13.4.

$\frac{1}{1,816}$ or 0.055% (Little Brickhill).[17] Three of the four results for denarii are closely grouped round a median of $\frac{1}{1,644}$ or 0.061% at Viuz, while the figure at Little Brickhill is about 10% lower.[18] Fig. 13.3 shows La Magura compared with Londonthorpe and Little Brickhill.

[17] The totals are: Viuz-Faverges (French Alps, Département of Annecy) 2,306 denarii (of which 794 denarii are pre-Severan), Little Brickhill 627, and Londonthorpe 420. Pre-Severan coin in the Viuz hoard shows a coherent picture of wear up to the 190s, but not after that date (see Table 13.5).

[18] The equations are: Viuz, weight = 2.9545 + (date × 0.00204), r^2 = 0.914; Londonthorpe, weight = 2.9892 + (date × 0.00201), r^2 = 0.991; Little Brickhill, weight = 2.9122 + (date × 0.00185), r^2 = 0.999.

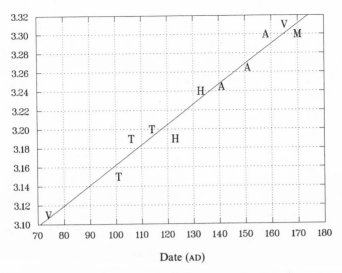

Figure 13.2 Median weights (in grams) of eleven samples from five reigns in La Magura denarius hoard. (Symbol: Emperor's initial.)

Table 13.5 *Projected end-date and latest coin in denarius hoards*

Hoards	Projected end-date (AD)	Latest coin (AD)
La Magura	193	196
Viuz	198	251/3
Londonthorpe	185	153/4
Little Brickhill	242	187

The end-dates at which full weight of 3.36 grams is attained are shown in Table 13.5. La Magura, with much the biggest sample of pre-Severan coin, shows a gap between the latest coin and the projected end-date of only three years. Viuz, whose weight-configuration is that of a second-century hoard superimposed without further circulation on a third-century hoard, likewise projects a date in the 190s. The projected date for Londonthorpe is thirty-two years after the latest coin; but the sample is too small to be pressed hard. The Little Brickhill figure, from a larger sample, shows an overshoot by more than half a century. But its regression is virtually a straight line (fig. 13.3). The weights are also significantly lighter than those at La Magura, which ends a decade later. Thus this hoard seems to be appreciably later than its latest coin.[19]

[19] The smaller hoard ending in AD 183 from approximately the same site, recently conjectured to be part of this recent Little Brickhill find, shows median weights 2% higher for the later Antonines, and is therefore presumably a separate deposit (published in Crawford 1969A; weights kindly made available by the Buckinghamshire County Museum).

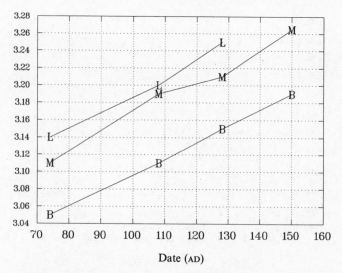

Figure 13.3 Median weights (in grams) of reign samples in three denarius hoards. (Symbol: M La Magura; L Londonthorpe; B Little Brickhill.)

4. WEIGHT-LOSS IN BRONZE HOARDS

Despite copious survival of bronze coin, few large bronze hoards have been fully published.[20] The most important from this period is the Garonne hoard, mainly of sestertii, dated to AD 159/61 (3,663 sestertii).[21] Another recently published hoard is Puy-Dieu, which ends in 244/9, but is largely second century (N = 778; Table 13.9).

The totals in the Garonne hoard are large enough to allow sampling by shorter periods than full-length reigns. Taking four short periods each with 80–100 sestertii struck for the Emperor, the pattern shown is highly linear, producing a virtually straight-line correlation between weight and date up to Trajan (fig. 13.4). These textbook results suggest extreme stability of target weight in sestertius-production from Vespasian to Trajan. The weight projected at the end-date of the hoard contents (AD 159/61) is 26.794–26.886 grams. As $\frac{1}{12}$ of a pound is 26.9 grams, this argues that the sestertius was being correctly struck at $\frac{1}{12}$ during this period. That was evidently a reduced weight standard set by Nero, who also changed the standards for gold and silver.[22]

[20] For a summary of sestertius-weights in four big museum collections, but with noticeable variation between samples due to wear, see Bastien 1967, 36–7.

[21] Etienne 1984. Also of note are the Guelma bronze hoard with 7,486 sestertii (Turcan 1963), and Arnouville-lès-Gonesses with 2,358 (Turckheim-Pey 1981), for which weights have not been published.

[22] Sestertii of Claudius weighed more, about $11\frac{1}{2}$ to the pound or 28.07 grams. For the change under Nero, see MacDowall 1979, 146 and 152, with MacDowall 1966. A change at this point is also implicit in the absence of pre-Neronian sestertii from second century hoards: thus the earliest coin in the 3,663 sestertii in the Garonne hoard of AD 159–60 is a single coin of Nero.

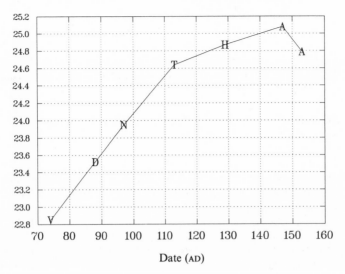

Figure 13.4 Median weights (in grams) of seven samples from six reigns in sestertii from the Garonne hoard. (Symbol: Emperor's initial.)

But the later part of the Garonne hoard shows that weight standards changed soon afterwards. Applied to later parts of the hoard, the regression based on Table 13.6 shows a widening gap between actual and expected weights. The change can be seen by reckoning the number of sestertii per pound for the striking-weights implied in Table 13.7 (multiplying 26.9 grams ($\frac{322.8}{12}$) by the fraction in column 4, and dividing the result into 322.8). The results are shown in Table 13.8. From Vespasian to Trajan, stability is almost perfect. Then a fall to $12\frac{1}{4}$ sestertii to the pound is seen by the middle of Hadrian's reign, and another fall in the first decade of Antoninus Pius, probably to $12\frac{1}{2}$. By the last decade of Pius's reign, the weight had fallen still further, probably to $12\frac{3}{4}$ or 13 to the pound.[23]

Some later developments can be seen from the Puy-Dieu hoard summarised in Table 13.9 and Figure 13.5. The median averages for the first three reigns show a highly linear pattern, and their regression would reach full weight of 12 coins per pound in AD 187, although the hoard ends in 244/9.[24] As with the Viuz-Faverges denarius hoard, this suggests very limited circulation of

The Mafumet hoard of little-worn and heavily die-linked sestertii of Claudius shows median weights of 27.75 (*RIC*[1] 67, N = 107) and 27.68 (*RIC*[1] 60, 61, 64, 78, 79, N = 140) (Campo, Richard, and Von Kaenel 1981).

[23] At this point the sample is too small to allow any precision, but the result would be consistent with a fall to 13 to the pound soon after AD 148. The editors of the hoard suggest a possible fall to 13 to the pound under Antoninus Pius (Etienne, 358–9).

[24] Weight = 16.994 + (date × 0.05294); r^2 = 0.997. This treats the reign of Hadrian as having a full-weight sestertius of 12 to the pound, despite the small drop which cannot be exactly dated by year (Table 13.8).

Table 13.6 *Garonne hoard: sestertii struck for the Emperor*

	1	2 Observed median weight	3 Fitted weight	4 Col.2/ col.3	5 % coefficient of variation	6
Emperor	Dates (AD)					N
Vespasian	69–79	22.85	22.88	0.99869	5.80	93
Domitian	85–91	23.52	23.52	1.0	8.73	98
Nerva	96–97	23.95	23.94	1.0004	9.80	84
Trajan	112–14	24.64	24.67	0.99878	8.19	85

Note: Intercept 19.46399; slope 0.0461025; r^2 = 0.9984. (Regression-dates: AD 74, 88, 97, 113.)

Table 13.7 *Regression applied to later Garonne samples of sestertii struck for the Emperor*

	1	2 Observed median weight	3 Fitted weight	4 Col.2/ col.3	5 % coefficient of variation	6
Emperor	Dates (AD)					N
Hadrian	128–9	24.865	25.365	0.97951	8.42	90
A. Pius	145–8	25.08	26.19	0.95762	9.97	79
A. Pius	149–56	24.785	26.47	0.93634	11.05	48

Table 13.8 *Number of sestertii struck to the pound*

	Date (AD)	Total	Presumed target
Vespasian	69–79	12.02	12
Domitian	85–91	12.00	12
Nerva	96–97	12.00	12
Trajan	112–14	12.01	12
Hadrian	128–9	12.25	$12\frac{1}{4}$
A. Pius	145–8	12.53	$12\frac{1}{2}$
A. Pius	149–56	12.82	$12\frac{3}{4}$

Source: Tables 13.6 and 13.7.

Table 13.9 *Median weight (in grams) in the Puy-Dieu sestertius hoard (AD 244/9)*

Reign	Median weight	% coefficient of variation	N
Domitian	21.725	10.9	24
Trajan	22.775	8.7	96
Hadrian	23.74	8.7	178
A. Pius	23.25	10.6	166
M. Aurelius	23.26	14.5	171
Commodus	18.68	17.9	77

Note: Insufficient data after AD 192.

Table 13.10 *Dupondius-weight (in grams) in the Garonne hoard*

Reign	Median	CVar	Sample	Fitted weight for sestertii	Actual dupondius-weight as percentage of fitted sestertius-weight
Domitian	11.21	11.8	37	23.567	47.57
Trajan, 98–116	12.01	12.6	62	24.397	49.23
Trajan, 116	8.11	14.3	38	24.812	32.69
Hadrian, 117–23	12.12	12.7	52	24.996	48.49
Hadrian, 123–8	11.89	9.1	26	25.273	47.05

Note: CVar = percentage coefficient of variation.

pre-Severan material in the third century, despite the mid-third-century date of both hoards. The expected weights for later reigns if standards remained the same are given by the regression as: Antoninus Pius 24.935, Marcus Aurelius 24.994, and Commodus 26.841. The difference between these figures and the actual weights in Table 13.9 yield the following estimates of changes in striking weight: Antoninus Pius 12.81 per pound, Marcus Aurelius 13.31, and Commodus 17.26. Thus under the late Antonines, decline in the denarius is evidently paralleled by an increasing decline in the sestertius.[25]

The dupondius or half-sestertius can also be studied from the Garonne hoard (see Table 13.10).[26] The coin is relatively stable at about half the weight

[25] For the denarius, see p. 225. These substantial hoards make the pattern of decline starting under Hadrian quite clear. The attempt by A.S. Hemmy in *BMCRE* 4, xv to claim stability for sestertius weight throughout the Antonine period should be disregarded. For decline under Commodus, cf. Turckheim-Pey 1981, 20.

[26] The large samples of dupondii in the Garonne hoard, as much as 11% of the coin of Vespasian and Domitian, mark it out from other big sestertius hoards. The fact that the hoard comes from a river shipwreck indicates coin in free circulation, presumably funds belonging to someone on board. In contrast to most hoards, it is clearly not a deliberate deposit.

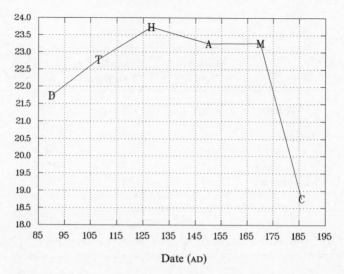

Figure 13.5 Median weights (in grams) from six reigns in the Puy-Dieu sestertius
hoard. (Symbol: Emperor's initial.)

of the sestertius for most of the period from Domitian to Hadrian. But for a
brief period of intensive output in AD 116, lasting less than twelve months, its
weight drops by one-third, reducing striking-weight from 24 to the pound to
36 to the pound.[27] The dupondius recovers again under Hadrian, but
deteriorates slightly before the reign ends.

In Table 13.10, the median dupondius-weights are fitted by the equation in
Table 13.6 based on weight-loss of the sestertius. Exact correspondence
between the two would give the dupondius a fitted weight of 50%. This is not
quite achieved in any of the figures, evidently because the smaller coin of lower
denomination circulated faster and wore faster than the sestertius. The second
Hadrianic figure in Table 13.10 suggests a decline in the dupondius which
corresponds to the contemporary reduction of 2% in sestertius-weight (Table
13.8).

The Puy-Dieu hoard shows weight-loss of $\frac{1}{508}$ per year, compared with $\frac{1}{583}$
in the Garonne sample.[28] These figures are reasonably close, and both very
much higher than those for gold and silver. The weight-accuracy of the
sestertius (Tables 13.6, 13.7 and 13.9) is significantly worse than in the
corresponding figures for silver or gold (Tables 15.2 and 15.5). This cannot be
primarily due to differences in wear, since in the bronze figures the coefficient
of variation increases over time, despite the lower wear factor for later coin.[29]

[27] In the figures in the final column of Table 13.10, the ratio between the median for this period
and the one for the previous period is 1:1.506. For mean averages by reign, see Etienne 1984, 346.
[28] The editors of the Garonne hoard obtain a slightly different result, equivalent to $\frac{1}{568}$ (ibid., 358,
based on a wider chronological spread, but excluding part of the sample, the coins found in
1965 (ibid., 30)).
[29] For weight-accuracy, see also Duncan-Jones 1987, 248, Table 13.

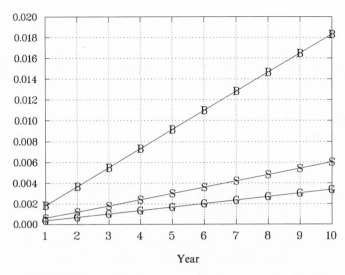

Figure 13.6 Percentage weight-loss per year for sestertii, denarii and aurei
(Table 13.11). (B bronze; S silver; G gold.)

5. SUMMARY: GOLD, SILVER AND BRONZE

The figures in Table 13.11 show the expected hierarchy, low-value coin losing weight faster than high-value coin. This reflects the higher circulation-speed of small change, which is equally obvious in modern experience (section 6 below). The wear-rates in Table 13.11 are compared in fig. 13.6. But precise comparisons in terms of circulation-speed remain difficult because of metallic differences. Complex technical adjustment would still be needed to compensate for the varying hardness of the three metals, the weight hierarchy between the coins, and the big differences in surface area.[30]

Table 13.11 *Summary of Roman rates of weight-loss as fractions of full coin-weight*

Denomination	Annual rate		Source
Aureus	0.00249 grams	(1/2,946; 0.034%)	Belgian gold hoard
Denarius	0.002025 grams	(1/1,659; 0.06%)	Median of 4 silver hoards
Sestertius	0.0493 grams	(1/546; 0.18%)	Average of 2 sestertius hoards

[30] Gold loses most face value per year. At the rates shown in Table 13.11, gold loses weight equivalent to 1 as every 7 years, the denarius does so every 104 years, and the sestertius every 137 years.

6. COMPARISONS BETWEEN WEIGHT-LOSS IN ROMAN AND MODERN COIN

The wear-rate for Roman gold coin can be compared with more recent figures. The weight of the English sovereign, 7.99 grams, made it comparable to the Roman aureus. The figures in Table 13.12 show a relatively stable wear-rate. The median of 0.037% is only slightly higher than the figure of 0.034% from the Belgian hoard. But it is well above the rates of 0.022% and 0.011% at Liberchies and Corbridge. The English sovereign at this date was alloyed for hardness, and thus for a given weight-loss it should have circulated more than the aureus.[31]

Table 13.12 *Weight-loss in the English Sovereign*

Years to:	1833	1869	1881
Annual weight-loss	$\frac{1}{2,632}$ (0.038%)	$\frac{1}{2,703}$ (0.037%)	$\frac{1}{2,875}$ (0.035%)

Source: Grierson 1965, x.

But in the case of silver, recent circulation-rates are very much higher than the Roman figures. In another nineteenth-century example, the French franc of 5.00 grams lost weight at 0.22% in the years to 1884/8. This is nearly four times the median rate for the Roman denarius (Table 13.11). The loss for the English shilling (5.23 grams) was higher still (0.26%) in the years to 1906/9.[32] The Dutch 25-cent piece, weighing 3.575 grams, lost weight at 0.15% per year between 1890 and 1935.[33]

As multiples of the median figure for the denarius, these modern rates are 4.3 (English shilling), 3.7 (French franc), and 2.5 (Dutch 25-cent piece). The implied difference in circulation-velocity is probably even greater, because of the alloying of modern precious-metal coin to make it harder and more wear-resistant.

Thus the modern comparisons show Roman wear-rates as very much less for silver, and somewhat less for gold than those in the industrialised world.[34] Roman coin-circulation is likely to have been correspondingly slower than in recent times, even without allowing for the fact that lack of alloy should have made it wear out faster.

[31] Grierson 1965, xi.   [32] Grierson 1965, xi.
[33] See Duncan-Jones 1987, 243, Table 8, using figures from Van Hengel 1982. As in the Roman evidence, the metallic loss-rate is effectively constant, and the percentage weight-loss is a percentage of the coin at full weight.
[34] Howgego 1992, 12 suggests that wear-rates are misleading as an index of circulation-speed. But it is not clear that this is so.

14

WASTAGE AND REMINTING OF COIN

The aim of this chapter is to look at the broad lines of coin-output, and then to show how coin disappeared from circulation through wastage and re-minting. Separate discussions are devoted to denarii, aurei and Egyptian tetradrachms.

1. CHANGES IN THE AMOUNT OF DENARIUS COIN IN CIRCULATION

It is possible to assess the amount of coin in circulation as a proportion of the coin produced. This involves a simple test based on the output-index for denarii in chapter 8 (Table 8.7). Comparisons between the output-index and the contents of individual hoards normally imply that in a given hoard one reign is better represented than the others. Almost all hoards show contrasting gradients, which are produced by progressive wastage of earlier coin, and by slow input of recent coin from the centre. The peak is the reign where the two gradients meet.[1]

The peak can be identified by dividing the coin for each major reign by the index figure for that reign. The peak is the reign with most coin per index-point, and this reign is taken as being represented at full strength. The number of coins in all major reigns, divided by the number of coins per index-point in the peak reign, then gives the representation quotient for the hoard as a whole.

As an illustration, in the Londonthorpe hoard of 420 denarii (AD 153/4), the peak reign proves to be Hadrian, after dividing the various reign-totals by the index figures in Table 8.7. The hoard has 108 coins of Hadrian, and 362 coins of all major reigns from AD 69. The index-value for Hadrian in Table 8.7 is 3.00. Thus the representation index is $362/(108/3) = 10.06$.

The figures for larger hoards calculated in this way produce a relatively stable picture (fig. 14.1). Those before AD 160 have an index figure of 8–10. In the 160s, a higher index figure of 12–13 begins a new plateau, which continues for the rest of the Antonine period and under the Severi. The median averages are 8.8 before 160, 12.3 in 160–92, and 12.0 in 193–235.

The index thus suggests that liquidity in terms of the silver currency

---

[1] A few hoards, such as La Salasuri ending in AD 158, show only the first gradient, because the latest reign in the hoard provides the peak. This has little effect on the resulting index of representation.

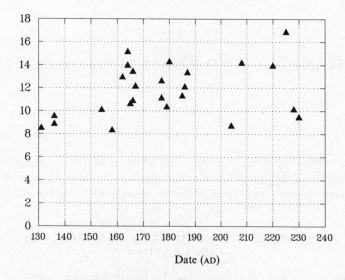

Figure 14.1 Output-index values for 25 denarius hoards plotted by date.

increased somewhat in the 160s, but remained relatively stable at the new level, despite the considerable currency changes under the Severi.[2] The index is based on simple procedures, but its results are reasonably coherent.

Potentially, such stability in evidence from different parts of the empire could show that the circulation pool was much the same from one region to another.[3] But in fact the relative degree of monetisation from region to region must have varied significantly. The stability of the index in itself only shows that the various local pools of silver currency, which all depended on the same central source, contained certain similarities. Nevertheless, because the regional samples are constituents of the aggregate coin-population of the empire, in combination they must show something of what that population looked like.[4]

2. SPECIAL EVENTS IN THE EROSION OF THE DENARIUS

Once a stock of coin is in circulation, it starts to diminish through hoarding, casual loss and inertia in the exchange system.[5] But this process of wastage

[2] The coin-material used in the calculation comes only from the major reigns included in the output-index (Table 8.7).

[3] The hoards used are Adamclisi, Alba Iulia, Allerton, Barway, via Braccianese (Rome), Bristol, Castagnaro, Castle Bromwich, Colchester, Larnaka, Edwinstowe, Eleutheropolis, Erla, Little Brickhill, Londonthorpe, Mocsolad, Osijek, La Salasuri, Sotin, Stockstadt, Szombathely, Tell Kalak, Tolna Megye, Verona and Baden Baden.

[4] The wide dispersal of coin-populations almost certainly meant that no contemporary was in a position to measure the aggregate position.

[5] For these purposes hoarding means the widespread private ownership of money and small change that exists in almost any monetised economy; it need not imply any deliberate removal of coin from circulation.

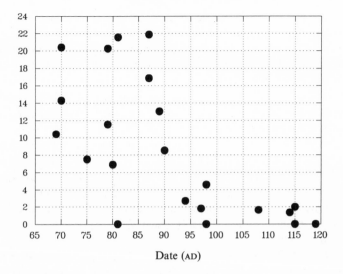

Figure 14.2 Percentage of Julio-Claudian coin before Nero in denarius hoards, AD 65–120.

may be accelerated by the deliberate removal of older coin. That is true *par excellence* of the Roman silver currency. The hoards show that some Roman silver-issues disappeared so suddenly that they must have been withdrawn.[6] These artificial events are almost as important as the phenomenon of natural wastage.

First to disappear was the coin of the first four Julio-Claudians, Augustus, Tiberius, Caligula and Claudius (with it went the pre-reform coinage of Nero). Fig. 14.2 shows that the maximum representation of this Julio-Claudian silver in hoards remains above 20% in the years AD 80–7. The level seems to be falling fast at the end of the 80s, with values of 13% in 89 and less than 9% in 90. In hoards ending after 90, the maximum drops to less than 5%. Hoards are missing from the start of the 90s, but the first hoard showing a figure below 5% ends in 93/4. This recall was presumably instigated by Domitian, whose reign continued to September 96.[7] The Julio-Claudians before Nero were commemorated on bronze coin by Titus and Domitian.[8] The initiative probably

[6] Some numismatists assume that the market was so sensitive to monetary anomaly that Gresham's Law would operate the moment any discrepancy occurred. But the Roman evidence shows that anomalies not eliminated by the government could persist over long periods (see n.20 below).

[7] For timelag in hoard dates, see pp. 30–1, 86, 205.

[8] *BMCRE* 2, 284–91, 414–17. The flurry of 'restored' Republican coin-issues under Trajan, who is known to have reminted heavily at the moment when extant Republican coinage disappears shows that restored coin was a specific recognition of old issues which were being withdrawn (Mattingly 1926). It may also show 'the natural conservatism of a people that loved tradition, and the conscious conservatism of a government seeking to link itself to an honoured past' (*BMCRE* 2, xxi). But clearly that was not its main *raison d'être*.

continued under Nerva, whose coin-types include denarii and sestertii commemorating Augustus.[9]

Next to disappear or go into steep decline was the Republican coin minted before Augustus.[10] Trajan's 'restored' coinage with Republican types and Dio's reference to reminting of worn coin in AD 107 both show that a withdrawal of Republican coin took place then. But here the hoards do not show such rapid eclipse of the old coin.[11] On the Continent, two Trajanic hoards still have relatively high percentages, but hoards under Hadrian show virtually no Republican coin.[12] This remains the position in later Continental hoards.

In Britain the picture is different. British evidence suggests liquidation of Republican coin under Hadrian, not under Trajan. British hoards ending between 110 and 125 still show a median percentage of Republican coin above 20%. But Republican coin is virtually absent from the hoards of the 130s, late in Hadrian's reign (fig. 14.3).[13]

If this were all, it would suggest that withdrawal was merely later in frontier areas than at the centre of the empire. But even from the limited Bolin sample, it can be seen that Republican coin tends to re-emerge in later hoards in Britain and the Danube, although it had vanished from hoards in other parts of the empire (Table 14.1). In both these frontier regions there is a gap in mid-century, under Hadrian on the Danube, and under Antoninus Pius in Britain. Then in both cases representation resumes in later hoards. Possibly for a short time the oldest and most worn denarii were deliberately excluded from army payments in these areas.[14]

Last of the major blocs of pre-Neronian denarii to disappear was the coinage of Mark Antony. Representation of Antony's issues tends to be very uneven. The highest quotients are found in the Danube zone. At Pompeii, finds of AD 79 show a median level for Antony of 20.6%.[15] In seven British hoards before AD 100, the median representation is 13%. For the period 100–30 (N = 9), the British median falls to 3%. By 150–79 it has fallen to 1.7% (N = 7). But substantial British hoards of 187 and 208 still show percentages of 2.8 and 4.0%.[16] Bolin's eleven early Severan denarius hoards from outside Britain show only one containing any coin of Antony. But his sample of five British hoards from the same period shows an aggregate for Antony's coin of

---

[9] Burnett 1987, 89. *BMCRE* 3, Nerva nos. 78 and 149–61. Tiberius similarly reappears on Trajan's coin.
[10] Coin of Antony is discussed separately below, not included under Republican coin.
[11] Data in Bolin, 340–3.
[12] Republican coin is abundant in some Danubian hoards in the 160s AD, notably at Gradistea and Tibodu, where the percentages of Republican coin are 43.7 and 26.5 respectively.
[13] For the persistence of Republican coin in British hoards of Hadrian, see also Reece 1974, 84–5.
[14] Cf. chapters 5–6.
[15] From analysis of 8 finds in Lo Cascio 1980, Table 2.
[16] Little Brickhill and Bristol (Appendix 10 nos.176, 198).

Table 14.1 *Denarii of the Republic (including Antony) as a percentage in hoards of different dates*

Zone	Hoard end-date (AD)				
	117/38	138/61	161/92	193/217	217–
Britain	13.6	—	1.4	3.6	2.1
Danube	0.5	3.3	7.8	2.6	—
Other regions	—	—	—	—	0.2

Source: Hoard-totals in Bolin.

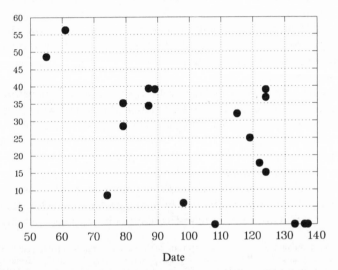

Figure 14.3 Percentage of Republican denarii in British hoards, AD 55–138, plotted by end-date.

3.6%.[17] Some of Antony's legionary denarii had been recalled under Marcus Aurelius, as a coin-type records.[18]

3. THE RATIONALE OF COIN RECALLS

Clearly the major withdrawals of silver coin were carried out by the government. The speed with which the older blocs of silver coin disappear once they start to decline makes this conclusion inescapable. Did the free market play a role nevertheless, despite the penalties for tampering with the currency?

[17] Bolin, 351–2.
[18] *BMCRE* 4, Marcus Aurelius nos. 500–1 (ANTONIVS AVGVR IIIVIR R P C/ANTONINVS ET VERVS AVG REST LEG VI).

Because surviving silver hoards of this period were not normally 'savings' hoards, they cannot be invoked as evidence for private withdrawal of coin, whether or not that was frequent.[19] But traces of counterfeiting, fairly numerous in Britain under the Principate, show that the integrity of the currency was not always respected.[20] Where there is steady erosion (fig. 14.9 below), some of it could potentially be due to private intervention of some kind. But the typical product of counterfeiters seems to have been largely base metal, and need not have depended much on authentic existing coin.[21]

The disappearance of older currency has sometimes been associated with Nero's reduction in the weight and fineness of the denarius in AD 64. Granted his massive production of lighter gold coins, Nero's significant reduction in the silver in the denarius looks like a declaration of intent. But he cannot have liquidated much of his predecessors' silver coinage.[22] Had he done so, his own denarii would be more abundant in the hoard record (see below). In theory, Nero's large-scale minting of gold might have hindered the production of silver on an equally grand scale. But the uneven chronology of his gold output hardly supports this.[23]

As we have already seen, the main withdrawals of silver coin before AD 193 evidently took place under Domitian, Trajan and Hadrian, with some further action under Marcus Aurelius. Why did the state act in this way? Was old coin melted down because it was too worn, or because it was too fine? Why did Julio-Claudian coin vanish before Republican coin, and why was coin of Antony allowed to circulate for so long?

Although any government may decide to withdraw coin because it is worn, that would not explain the withdrawal of Julio-Claudian coin before Republican coin (fig. 14.4). On average, Julio-Claudian coin perhaps contained more

[19] See pp. 82–3 above. Lo Cascio's interpretation of the survival of pre-Neronian silver after Nero depends on the hoards with older coin being interpreted as savings hoards (Lo Cascio 1980, 457).

[20] See Boon 1988 and Sutherland 1937, with Grierson 1956. Giard 1985, 232 concludes that the government tolerated the imitation bronze circulating under Claudius. But the fact that the anomalies eliminated by Domitian, Nerva and Trajan persisted for as long as they did, with little modification to the volumes of coin in question, suggests that 'private sector' ability to monitor or alter the currency was slight. For the difficulty of determining silver-content by eye, see Kolendo 1980, 170. Coin-weight was quite easily established, but even here, the persistence of 'overweight' denarii of Domitian and Antoninus Pius in hoards drawn from the circulation pool generations later suggests that there was relatively little awareness of monetary anomaly (cf. Duncan-Jones 1987, 247, Table XII).

[21] For plated coin as forged coin, see Crawford 1968 and MacDowall 1979, 14.

[22] The suggestion that the lower Neronian standards may not have been low enough to make it inherently worthwhile to melt down all older coin at this point (Lo Cascio 1980, 455) is not borne out by the reduction in silver weight of more than 11% in AD 64 (see Table 15.6; and n.24 below for the weight of worn Republican and Tiberian denarii).

[23] In the hoards about 85% of the gold and 70% of the silver struck at Rome after Nero's reform belongs to AD 64/6. For chronology and hoard-totals, see MacDowall 1979, 10, 159–60. At Alexandria, about 54% of the tetradrachms struck after Nero's reform belong to the equivalent years 11 and 12 (from hoard-totals in Christiansen 1988, 2.100–1). Sutherland's recent synopsis in RIC 1² strangely omits the last two of Nero's 12 'reformed' gold-types, both listed by MacDowall and RIC¹ (MacDowall 160 nos.32–3; RIC 1¹ nos.47, 54). Cf. Sutherland 1985, 241: 'coins of 67–8 seem to include no gold'.

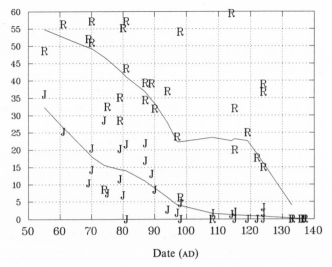

Figure 14.4 Percentages of Republican coin and of Julio-Claudian coin before Nero in denarius hoards, plotted by end-date. (R: Republican; J: Julio-Claudian.)

silver than Republican coin, after allowing for differing coin wear. But any difference was probably slight.[24] More important was the fact that both the older coinages, worn though they were, contained more silver than current denarii.[25]

Domitian's denarii of 85–96 contained about 3.28 grams of silver (Table 15.5). Those of Nerva, probably struck at 93 to the pound (3.47 grams) were about 93.25% fine, leading to a silver weight of 3.24 grams.[26] Denarii of Tiberius were struck at perhaps 86 to the pound, or 3.75 grams.[27] Their fineness was evidently the early Julio-Claudian standard of 98.0%. This implies an original silver weight of 3.674 grams. At a wear-rate of $\frac{1}{1,600}$ per year, this would fall to 3.53 grams in the 64 years between mid-Tiberius and AD 90. The excess over Domitian's denarii is 8%, and over denarii of Nerva about 9%. Thus the silver in the existing Tiberian denarii, if reminted in the 90s, would still have produced more coins than before.[28]

---

[24] Denarii of Tiberius, with a mean fineness of 98.0% (Walker) can be compared with Republican silver with a gross mean fineness of 96.8% (Walker 1980; see n.30 below). The median silver weights that this implies in two British hoards ending in AD 61 are Tiberius 3.60 grams, Republic 3.51 (Eriswell; N = 11 and 37) and Tiberius 3.59, Republic 3.48 (Scole; N = 15 and 15); the excess amounts are 2.6% and 3.2%.

[25] In an empire where hatred of past regimes was so strong, the choice of Julio-Claudian coin for early destruction may even have had a propaganda purpose (cf. Sen. *Apoc.*; Pliny *Pan.*; Julian *Caesares*).   [26] For Nervan striking-weight, see p. 225.

[27] Median weights of 3.67 and 3.66 grams in the Eriswell and Scole hoards ending in AD 55 and 61 roughly support this, after allowing for a wear factor of about $\frac{1}{1,600}$ per year (see chapter 13, p. 184).

[28] Calculations for the other Julio-Claudians are hampered by the different weight-standards under Augustus, and by lack of data for Claudius and Caligula. But results similar to those for Tiberius are likely.

Trajan's denarii, mainly struck at 96 to the pound, were about 91.5% fine overall, giving them a silver weight of 3.07 grams. Samples of Republican coin in British hoards ending in the half-century before Trajan weigh 3.63, 3.59 and 3.505 grams on average.[29] These figures from hoards ending in AD 61, 61 and 80 imply silver weights of about 3.51, 3.47 and 3.39 grams.[30] Allowing for wear at the rate of 0.00246 grams per year, the corresponding estimated amounts of silver under Trajan in AD 107 are 3.40, 3.36 and 3.33 grams, still well above Trajan's 3.07.[31] The respective differences are 11%, 9% and 8%.

Thus, reminting Julio-Claudian and Republican coin meant a profit, and this, rather than concern about worn coin, was what primarily inspired it. Some coin of Antony also disappeared then, and the part which was left probably offered little potential minting profit.[32] Analyses show the fineness of all Antony's silver as 94.6%, and that of the legionary denarii as 92.2%.[33] In six British hoards the weight of the legionary denarii falls steadily between AD 61 and 187 (r^2 = 0.969). This regression makes the projected weight for AD 107 3.32 grams (fig. 14.5). Legionary denarii with a mean fineness of 92.2% would thus contain 3.06 grams of silver at this point. Trajan's denarii, as already seen, contained about 3.07 grams of silver. Consequently, Antony's legionary denarii were not worth melting down for their silver at this point, although the decision to let them go on circulating undermines any claim that Trajan was concerned to eliminate worn coin.

4. EROSION OF THE DENARIUS

Four major reigns are worth looking at individually. Tests showed that collections of hoard-material without regional limits tend to give very dispersed results, whose implications are often unclear. The discussion

[29] Median averages at Eriswell, with 37 Republican coins, Scole with 15, and Beck Row with 78. The Flavian hoard from Howe is omitted because its exceptionally low averages suggest manipulation (as do low averages in the Woodham Mortimer hoard ending under Caligula); see chapter 16, pp. 245-7.

[30] At the gross mean silver fineness of 96.78% for the main samples of Republican denarii shown by Walker 1980, based on issues of 169-100, 97-81 and 78-41 BC. At certain times the fineness varied, though never dipping as low as the levels seen quite early in the Principate, and any gross figure is an approximation.

[31] The annual rate of metal loss is calculated as (322.8/82)/1,600. For 82 denarii to the pound, see p. 219. The calculation for Hadrian, under whom Republican denarii were largely withdrawn in Britain, would be similar, extra coin-wear being more than offset by the lower silver weight of Hadrianic denarii, struck at 90.0% fine.

[32] It is assumed that the maintenance of the mint with its permanent staff, which represented one of the standing costs of the Empire, was not recouped by or costed into minting operations. For another view, which is however very widely disputed, see Bolin, 127. It should be noted that the cost of unworked gold and the cost of gold coin in Diocletian's Price Edict are the same. For a list of mint employees, see p. 109, n.67.

[33] The gross average fineness, aggregating all Walker's data based on samples of 2 or more coins (Walker 1980). Walker's results do not support Sutherland's claim that Antony's legionary denarii 'were not equalled (in baseness) for the first two centuries of the Empire' (Sutherland 1937, 7). Antony's denarii were heavier than post-Neronian issues, and Trajan's mean fineness was already lower (91.5%) than in the legionary denarii (92.2%, Walker 1980 and 1976).

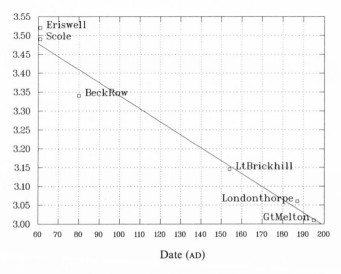

Figure 14.5 Median weight (in grams) of denarii of Antony in six British hoards, plotted by end-date.

therefore mainly concentrates on one set of data. This comes from Britain, chosen because it offers the largest provincial sample readily available.

Denarii struck for Nero before his weight-reduction in AD 64 are rare in most hoards. But Nero's 'reformed' denarii, though few compared with the blocs of pre-Neronian coin just considered, were slow to disappear.[34] On median average, Nero's denarii are 1.9% of all denarii in finds at Pompeii, which record coin ownership at a Campanian town in AD 79.[35] A large sample of British hoards shows a trend line for Nero's denarii which falls from 2.3% in AD 75 to 0.4% in 235 (fig. 14.6). The trend line makes British representation of Nero's coin lose 0.52% of its initial value each year. At this rate it would take almost 200 years to disappear entirely.[36] Coin of Nero is rarely missing from British hoards. Evidently it was not singled out for extinction at a particular moment, and went on circulating freely.

The coin of some of Nero's successors declined more rapidly. The most

[34] The hoards clearly imply that Nero's three short-lived successors struck more denarii in fifteen months than Nero had done between AD 64 and 68, probably at least 50% more (compare the percentages in Bolin, 336–57).
[35] Five of eight finds in Lo Cascio 1980, Table 2 include denarii of Nero. The representation of Nero's Julio-Claudian predecessors in these Pompeian samples is remarkably low, 2.3% for the four reigns combined, on median average. Outside Italy the corresponding figure in six hoards of AD 69–80 is 15.9% (Rheingonheim, Stein, York, Sapte, Budge Row, Beck Row). Since Flavian coin is quite plentiful at Pompeii, the low Julio-Claudian figures there do not seem to result from personal preference for Republican coin (for which, see Lo Cascio 1980, 452 ff.). For the reasons, see pp. 120–2 above.
[36] $r^2 = 0.380$; Neronian percentage = $3.192 - (date \times 0.0119)$.

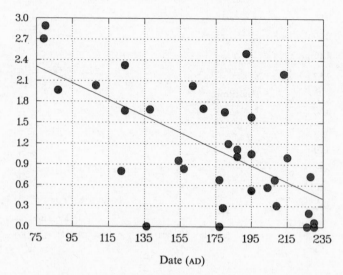

Figure 14.6 Percentage of coin of Nero in British denarius hoards, plotted by end-date.

obvious case is Domitian, whose coin has been discussed in detail in a valuable study by Carradice.[37] The British samples show representation of Trajan's coin enjoying an initial period of stability, before going into a rapid fall ending in the late Severan period (fig. 14.7). The first four decades after Trajan's death in 117 show no signs of decline. But from the 160s, there is a relatively rapid fall to a zero point in the 220s. The rate is surprisingly consistent. The later evidence (see fig. 14.8) shows a very high correlation between the percentage of Trajanic coin and date.[38]

Thus, representation of Trajanic coin appears relatively stable for the first four decades after the end of the reign. A similar pattern is suggested for Hadrian. The two clumps of data before AD 180 show little decline (fig. 14.9). The main fall occurs after 180, when Hadrianic representation, like that of Trajan, declines rapidly to a zero point under Severus Alexander. Here too the rate is relatively constant.[39]

The equation for Hadrian reaches zero by AD 230, close to the zero point of 227 for Trajan. In the Hadrianic case, the rate of decline is $\frac{1}{50}$ per year, and for Trajan, about $\frac{1}{67}$ per year. The fact that the two series end at about the same date is evidently a result of the much lower silver-content of Severan denarii. This gave early second century silver coin a premium value, which drove virtually all of it out of circulation relatively early.

[37] Carradice 1983.
[38] $r^2 = 0.927$; percentage $= 83.392 - (date \times 0.367)$.
[39] $r^2 = 0.853$; Hadrianic percentage $= 85.864 - (date \times 0.373)$.

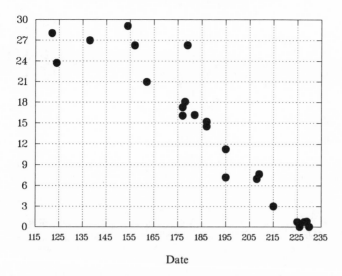

Figure 14.7 Percentage of coin of Trajan in British denarius hoards, AD 115–230, plotted by end-date.

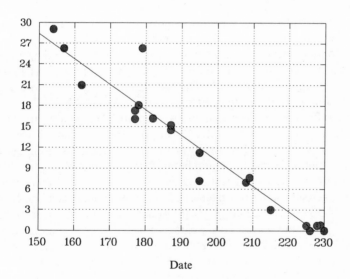

Figure 14.8 Percentage of coin of Trajan in British denarius hoards, AD 155–230, plotted by end-date.

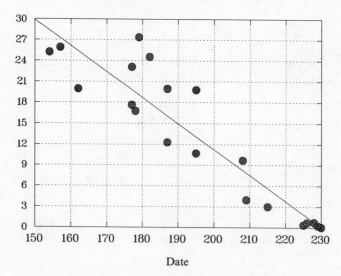

Figure 14.9 Percentage of coin of Hadrian in British denarius hoards,
AD 155–230, plotted by end-date.

These artificial wastage-rates are comparable with, or even higher than figures from modern Britain. For example, a post-war survey up to 1967 showed annual wastage of $\frac{1}{48}$ for the sixpence, $\frac{1}{83}$ for the two-shilling piece, and $\frac{1}{111}$ for the half-crown.[40] Early this century, the British penny was wasting at rates of between $\frac{1}{149}$ and $\frac{1}{103}$.[41] The two Roman rates are more rapid if anything. But the well-attested patterns of weight-loss show that Roman coin, although softer than modern coin, lost weight much less rapidly, implying less wear and tear, and less circulation.[42] Thus its circulation-speed seems to be much lower, whereas higher wastage-rates may suggest faster circulation.

The reason for this contradiction lies in changes in the silver-content of the denarius. By the late second century, this was in progressive decline. Walker's survey suggests median silver fineness of 91.5% for Trajan, 90% for Hadrian, 88% for Antoninus Pius, and 78.5% for Marcus Aurelius. A further decline to 74% under Commodus preceded a cataclysmic fall to 55.5% under Septimius Severus.[43] These changes made it increasingly worthwhile for the government to remint older denarii, as Domitian and Trajan had already done. The rapid decline of early second-century denarii in the Severan period strongly implies

[40] De Glanville cited in Volk 1987, 150. Annual wastage rates of $\frac{1}{200}$ and $\frac{1}{800}$ are claimed for silver and gold in mid-nineteenth-century Lombardy by Cattaneo (see Corbier 1986, 502). For contrasting figures, note $\frac{1}{100}$ for gold and $\frac{1}{13}$ for silver estimated for the nineteenth century (Spooner 1972, 304). Braudel states that 'it is normally agreed that the ratio between the annual coinage issued by the mint and the amount of money in circulation was 1 to 20' (Braudel 1984, 122 n.138). Depeyrot suggests that 6.5% of solidi were reminted annually in the Late Empire: Depeyrot 1991, 210.
[41] Cole cited in Volk 1987, 151.   [42] See chapter 13.   [43] See chapter 15.

further reminting at that date. But the same was probably already happening in the period between Trajan and the Severi, to judge from the steady shrinkage in the stock of Trajanic denarii in the second half of the second century. Reminting emerges explicitly in a coin-type under Marcus Aurelius and Lucius Verus.[44]

The dates at which Trajanic and Hadrianic denarii start their main decline are inconsistent, soon after AD 160 in one case, and soon after 180 in the other. If erosion of coin with higher silver-content lay behind the percentage decline, it is not obvious why one desirable coinage should have remained intact for two decades longer than another. In both cases the main decline starts forty to forty-five years after the end of the reign.

The conditions outlined do not explain a forty-year period of stability in themselves. But the input of new coin to a distant province was probably slow and protracted. Presumably in both cases enough additional coin of the issue concerned was reaching Britain for the first few decades to balance out losses due to wastage and erosion. This compensating effect then ceased, and the effects of wastage now became clearly visible. Whatever masking effects of this kind there may have been, it remains likely that significant wastage was always taking place.

5. WASTAGE AS A GENERAL MECHANISM

The results so far show cases in which the rate of natural wastage cannot safely be inferred from individual coin-issues. Artificial effects were at work, closely connected with fall in the silver-content of the latest coin. These effects accelerated natural wastage. Few of the coin-issues studied so far seem to have been immune to artificial erosion.

But in one case, legionary denarii of Antony were still circulating in the early third century, 240 or 250 years after they had entered circulation. This provides some indication of how long silver coin could go on circulating under natural conditions if allowed to survive. The wastage rate implied is approximately $\frac{1}{250}$ per year. Like the Roman rates of weight-loss, this wastage-rate is well below comparable modern figures.[45]

The overall rate at which denarii disappeared was much faster, thanks to deliberate withdrawals. It is difficult to quantify this. But the increase in the volume of denarii in circulation was relatively slow (fig. 14.1). That implies that the rate of minting was not much higher than the rate of wastage from all causes. On present projections, the total volume of denarii in circulation in the mid-second century was less than 100 times the typical yearly mint-output.[46]

---

[44] For reminted legionary denarii of Marcus and Verus, see n.18 above.

[45] See p. 204 above. For weight-loss, see pp. 191–2. Reminting under the Severi makes it difficult to see what would have happened beyond this period, and consequently a terminus at this point is assumed.

[46] Taking denarius volume as HS5.1 billion, and the rate of minting as about HS62 million (pp. 168–70).

Thus if volume of coin was rising only slowly, that would suggest a *de facto* wastage-rate from all sources of little less than 1% per year, in contrast to a natural rate of about 0.4% ($\frac{1}{250}$) from the calculations for Antony.

Hence wastage of the denarius owed much of its speed to recycling of old coin. Yet natural wastage was of course always present, as with all currencies in circulation. Consequently, maintaining the circulation pool at a given level always depended on there being some input of new metal. The increasing reliance on base metal for that purpose suggests that silver was in short supply.

6. WASTAGE OF GOLD

Published gold hoards are too few to allow an analysis of changes in the volume of gold coin in circulation. But gold wastage being less than that of silver, there should have been more tendency for the gold coin in circulation to build up.[47] As a result, gold could probably parallel the slow increase suggested for the volume of silver coin in circulation. Nevertheless, an apparent decline in gold minting from the 160s AD, and the recycling suggested at that time, may point to a decline in the volume of gold in circulation in the later stages of the period.

Some noticeable patterns are seen in a sample of gold hoards with 100 or more coins.[48] In Trajan's case, percentage representation falls steeply in the 160s (fig. 14.10). The rapid change which took place at this time seems to be flanked by relative stability before 160, when the percentage is relatively high, and after 170, when it is relatively low. The evidence for Hadrian (fig. 14.11) again shows a rapid fall in the 160s, with little major variation thereafter up to 211.[49]

These contrasts would suggest either that total volume of gold coin dramatically increased in the 160s, forcing down the percentage representation of all earlier reigns; or else that sudden erosion of existing issues, perhaps involving reminting, took place at this time. Surviving evidence about the volume of gold coin from samples of scattered finds suggests that gold minting in the 160s was sizeable, but probably no more than this.[50] Consequently, reminting at this time is more likely than the suggested increase in volume.

Nero's gold output from AD 64, patently much more important than his output of silver in the same period, is heavily represented in hoards, although

---

[47] The drain of coin eastwards outside the empire mainly affected gold (see p. 103 above), to judge from find evidence in India, and this would slightly offset the lower inherent wastage-rate for gold.

[48] The hoards used (see Appendix 10 below) are: Zirkovci, Erla, Corbridge, Rome 1, Liberchies, Braga, Vienna 1, Diarbekir, Troyes, Villach, Paris 2, Brigetio, Belgium, and Le Cannet. Erla and Villach include some silver.

[49] Gold hoards now become very rare, but the very big Karnak hoard of Elagabalus would provide important information if its contents were known.

[50] Callu, Loriot 1990, with evidence from other provinces in Callu, Loriot 1992, 26.

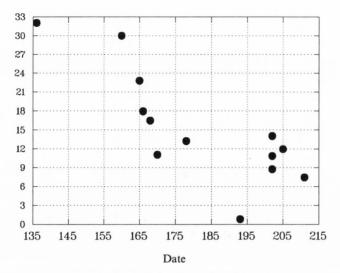

Figure 14.10 Percentage of coin of Trajan in gold hoards, AD 135–215, plotted by end-date.

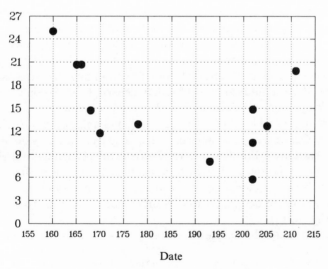

Figure 14.11 Percentage of coin of Hadrian in gold hoards, AD 160–215, plotted by end-date.

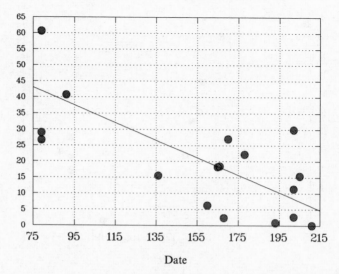

Figure 14.12 Percentage of coin of Nero in gold hoards, AD 75–215, plotted by
end-date.

as with his silver, there is wide variation (fig. 14.12).[51] Neronian gold does not
seem to have been eroded especially fast in the 160s. Thus this older segment of
the coin stock seems to show greater staying power, although it was
undoubtedly more worn than coin of Trajan and Hadrian. That suggests
another anomaly in the choice of coin for reminting, like the fact that
Republican denarii outlived Julio-Claudian denarii. It is clear that reminting
did not always mean singling out the oldest bloc of coin.

To explore the gold patterns further, a second analysis was carried out,
cumulating the average percentage of coin of a given reign. This smooths out
dispersed patterns.[52] For Trajan and Hadrian, the percentage still shows a
steep descent in the 160s, followed by a much gentler gradient after 170 (fig.
14.13). For Nero, the cumulated percentage shows a relatively flat and gentle
progression, with, as before, no decisive difference between the 160s and later
decades (fig. 14.14).

Cumulated values thus suggest essentially the same conclusions as the raw

---

[51] The Neronian component in Campanian gold hoards dating from AD 79 is as high as 61%
(Canessa 1909; Pozzi 1958–9); and represents 70% of the Utrecht hoard of AD 69. Production
on this enormous scale, most of it at lower weight, evidently depended on reminting existing
coin. The view that it could have been sustained by new mineral discoveries is hardly
convincing (Lo Cascio 1980, 459, 467 n.64; cf. also Perelli 1975, 730). Sutherland seems to
make Nero's later gold coin come from 'stocks economically conserved in the 50s' (RIC I², 135).

[52] The first percentage is based on the earliest hoard, the second on the mean percentage of the
first two hoards, the third on the mean percentage of the first three hoards, and so on. For
hoards ending in adjacent or identical years, a single value is entered, based on the mean of the
hoards in question. Two Severan hoards not dated by year (Paris and Brigetio) are assigned to
the mid-point in the reign, AD 202.

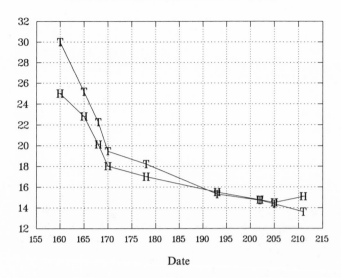

Figure 14.13 Cumulative percentages of Trajanic and Hadrianic coin in gold hoards, AD 160–215, plotted by end-date. (T: Trajan; H: Hadrian.)

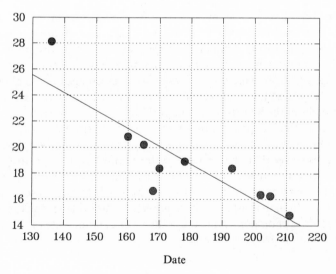

Figure 14.14 Cumulative percentage of coin of Nero in gold hoards, AD 130–215, plotted by end-date.

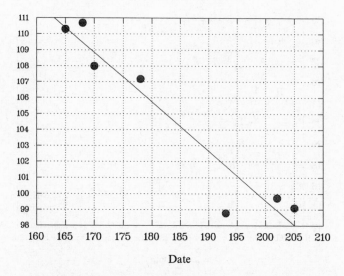

Figure 14.15 Cumulative percentage of Trajanic coin as a function of the cumulative percentage of Hadrianic coin in gold hoards, AD 160–210, plotted by end-date.

evidence. But they also allow a more effective calculation of the inherent wastage-rate for gold coin. The profiles for Trajan and Hadrian now become very similar (fig. 14.13). Coin of the earlier reign naturally disappears before coin of the later reign, diminishing it in relation to the later coin. This can be seen in fig. 14.15, showing gold of Trajan as a percentage of gold of Hadrian. From AD 165 to 205, the ratio forms a compact series, closely correlated with the end-dates of the hoards ($r^2 = 0.923$).[53] Modelled as a linear regression, the series would reach extinction in AD 522, 362 years from AD 160.[54]

The wastage-rate for gold that this implies is about $\frac{1}{360}$ per year. That is significantly lower than the figure of $\frac{1}{250}$ for natural wastage of silver inferred from the legionary denarii of Antony. This maintains the hierarchy between gold and silver seen in the figures for weight-loss.[55] In both cases, wastage is much slower than in most modern examples.[56] This evidence thus agrees with the weight-loss findings in indicating a slower circulation-rate for Roman coin than that seen in modern currency.

---

[53] Trajanic %/Hadrianic % = 161.471 − (date × 0.3096).
[54] The function could not be linear over its full extent, but its gradient in the early stages should reflect the inherent rate of wastage.
[55] Differences in hardness between gold and silver slightly complicate this issue, but do not change the hierarchy. Although gold coin undoubtedly suffers weight-loss in circulation, some of the impact of circulation may have been absorbed by metallic deformation rather than weight-loss. For weight-loss, see p. 191.   [56] See p. 192 above.

7. WASTAGE OF PROVINCIAL CURRENCY: EGYPTIAN EVIDENCE

In the provinces, Egypt has the one local currency which offers a useful set of published hoards. The output levels implied by hoards show a pattern which varies dramatically. Production under Nero, mainly in the last four years of his reign, accounts for more than half the tetradrachm output in Table 14.2. This contrasts very forcibly with Nero's output of denarii in AD 64–8, which is normally 1–2% of the contents of second-century hoards.[57] But published Egyptian hoard-material is too little to allow an output-index for this currency to be constructed.[58] Independent measures which potentially reflect coin erosion, such as changes in the ratio between two reigns in successive hoards, fail to show any sustained trend in Milne's hoard-evidence. That suggests a wastage-rate in the main Egyptian currency which is inherently very low.

Table 14.2 *Median representation of six reigns in tetradrachm hoards*

Ruler	Percentage
Claudius	8.1
Nero	60.0
Vespasian	4.3
Trajan	1.5
Hadrian	18.4
A. Pius	7.5

Note: Based on the six largest hoards dated between AD 128 and 212 in Milne 1933, Table of Hoards. Later reigns are omitted because of insufficient data.

The one clear trend occurs in the single Severan hoard in Milne's survey. For what it is worth, this hoard shows a relative decline in the representation of three first-century reigns, and a rise in the representation of the first three Antonine reigns.[59] Such a difference would suggest that by AD 212, a significant proportion of older coin had been withdrawn from circulation

---

[57] See pp. 201–2. This enormous discrepancy implies that any extra coinage produced by reminting money of Tiberius and the Ptolemies at a lower standard must have been struck in Alexandria. Christiansen nevertheless suggests that thousands of tons of silver from this source went off to Rome under Nero to be minted there (Christiansen 1988, 1.106, 308).

[58] Silver minting in Alexandria was certainly discontinuous, with periods of shutdown interspersed with periods of considerable activity (see Table 14.2 and fig. 8.1). The coin record may also contain artificial gaps. Domitian's reign is a blank in Milne's hoard-tabulation, save for one coin. This coin and the few specimens in coin-collections do however show that tetradrachms were being struck. If over-fine, like Domitian's early denarii, they may have disappeared from circulation very rapidly.   [59] The hoard is Milne no.7.

because of its higher silver-content.[60] The mechanism is familiar both at Rome from the denarius coinage, and in Egypt itself from the fate of Tiberius's tetradrachms.[61] If authentic, the present indications probably suggest that no Egyptian silver coin of the period remained untampered with for long enough to show much natural wastage. What are visible are artificial effects produced by the liquidation of older coin with higher silver-content. But natural wastage of the tetradrachm was probably lower than for the denarius, where an annual figure of $\frac{1}{250}$ has been suggested (see above).[62] Thus if natural wastage had been the only variable, Neronian coin in Egypt could probably have survived into the fourth century.

8. CONCLUSION

The Roman evidence shows slower rates of natural wastage than those found in modern currencies. Like the comparative figures for weight-loss, that plainly argues slower circulation-speeds.

But erosion was accelerated in each of the currencies studied by the deliberate removal of earlier coinage from circulation. This was in part routine substitution of fresh coin for worn coin. But some coin withdrawn was too recent to need replacement for any cosmetic reason. Other constraints were probably more pressing. One was the propaganda need to publicise the reigning Emperor on the coinage. Another was the profit yielded by reminting coin at a lower standard. Profit was probably the prime reason for melting down Julio-Claudian and Republican silver coin between AD 90 and 130. But in gold coin, the only rationale for the sharp fall in the representation of early second-century coin in hoards of the 160s seems to be reminting for propaganda reasons.

[60] Decline in the percentage of Neronian coin continues in the figures for mid-third-century hoards reported by Christiansen (1988, 2.93).

[61] See chapter 15 and n.55.

[62] See n.45 above. Christiansen suggests that because Egypt was a closed circulation area of limited size, its coin stock would have circulated faster than coin in other provinces (Christiansen 1988, 1.309). It is not clear that this is plausible. Limited mobility is also characteristic of coin from the Rome mint, despite the much larger circulation area available (see pp. 172-9).

15

CHANGE AND DETERIORATION

1. THE ROMAN POUND

The key to the calibration of the coinage is the Roman pound. The mint struck coins at so many to the pound. Thus Pliny gives the weight of the denarius as 84 to the pound in the time of Antony, and makes the aureus originally 40 to the pound, while metrological writers show the post-Neronian denarius as 96 to the pound.[1] The evidence is even clearer in the Late Empire, with coin-legends specifying modules of 60, 70, 72 and 96 to the pound.[2]

According to Boeckh's much-repeated view, the Roman pound weighed 327.45 grams. But this result dating from 1838 was based on relatively little evidence, although it won the support of Hultsch and Mommsen. Naville nevertheless made a more firmly based assessment in 1922. He calculated a weight of 322.56 grams from a sample of 500 gold solidi in mint condition.[3]

For almost all purposes, Naville's figure is accurate enough as it stands.[4] But it has won only limited acceptance, and is little used for example in the English-speaking world.[5] This makes it worth extending Naville's finding with material from the Principate.

[1] *NH* 33.132, 47. *MSR* 1.125. This chapter discusses gold (section 2), denarii (sections 3–4), Egyptian tetradrachms (section 5) and sestertii (section 6).

[2] *RIC* 6, 93, 99; 5, Diocletian 316–20; 7, Antioch 98–104; 8, Antioch 3–8. Although their message is clear, the coin-legends are sometimes misleading. For argentei of Diocletian marked XCVI or 96 to the pound, little-worn specimens in the large Sisak hoard show median weights of 3.075 grams for the Siscia mint, 3.172 grams for Rome, and 3.134 grams for Ticinum (N = 429, 420 and 259). Instead of $\frac{1}{96}$, the fractions of the pound are about $\frac{1}{105}$, $\frac{1}{102}$, and $\frac{1}{103}$ (Jelocnik 1961, 32–3, 66–9, suggesting even larger distortions based on the Boeckh pound; Rome and Ticinum are transposed in Table 2, p. 33). For problems of underweight coin in the Late Empire, see *CTh.*12.7.2 and Depeyrot 1987A, 117–18.

[3] Boeckh 1838, 165; Naville 1920–2 (see Duncan-Jones 1987, 250 n.1). For accounts of other versions of the pound, see discussions by Grierson 1964, and Crawford 1974, 2,590–1; more recently, Guey, Carcassonne 1978, 74–7; Suchodolski 1981; and Lopreato 1984, 71. The difference of 1% may seem trivial. But it is important for assessing striking targets and for studying rates of coin wear.   [4] See Duncan-Jones 1987, 249–56.

[5] Cf. Mattingly *BMCRE* 1, l–li: 'M. Naville's suggestion . . . is quite impossible.' The weight summaries in *BMCRE* are sometimes incomplete or otherwise erratic (see also Duncan-Jones 1987, 252 n.1, and n.28 below). Thus the Rome aurei of Elagabalus are summarised as 6, with a mean weight of 6.36 grams (*BMCRE* 5, xx), whereas the catalogue lists 17 weights, with a mean of 6.40 grams (a further coin weighing 7.24 grams might belong to Antioch, where Elagabalus struck at higher weight: *BMCRE* Elagabalus 39; 5, xx, cf. West 1941, 129).

Table 15.1 *Projections of the Roman pound from Naples weights in the main zone of concentration (310–27 grams)*

Minimum weight (pounds)	Median projection (grams)	Coefficient of variation (percentage)	Sample
3	322.8	0.6	39
5	322.8	0.6	31
10	322.85	0.6	20

Source: *CIL* x 8067.

The fullest indications come from the substantial sample of large stone weights from Pompeii and Herculaneum in the Naples Museum. Official specimens of weights and measures were distributed to secondary towns.[6] Small weights often have erratic calibration. But even after eliminating all weights below 3 pounds for this reason, the material at Naples still offers a sample of 39 weights with projections in the range between 310 and 327 grams.[7] Within this range the weight projections are entirely concentrated between 317 and 325 grams, flanked by gaps at 310–16 and 326–7 grams (Boeckh's module of 327 grams is thus conspicuous by its absence).

Median average weights for the whole sample and for two subdivisions are shown in Table 15.1. The stable results clearly imply that the Roman pound was about 322.8 grams. Percentage weight-loss due to wear is less with larger specimens, and the marginally higher quotient for the sample with the highest weights might potentially reflect that. But it is unlikely that Roman weighing technology could distinguish one part in 6,450 (0.05/322.8).

Naville was able to use a large sample of late gold coins in mint condition, gold being the only metal struck with sufficient accuracy.[8] Even so, because coin naturally circulates, some degree of wear is always possible. Naville's finding is fractionally below the module implied by the stone weights, and some larger gold coins, which because heavier lose a smaller proportion of

[6] *ILS* 8638 and note. Also *ILS* 8627, 8629. The material from Pompeii also provides evidence for a weight-standard some 5% higher, which was presumably local (the 6 weights of P. Stallius Felix show a median projected pound of 342.5 grams; *CIL* x 8067, 14).

[7] M. Le Roy used this material in a brief note, but without eliminating the smaller weights (Le Roy 1971). He suggests that wear is potentially a serious problem even in this evidence, but if that were the case, the results in Table 15.1 should differ according to size of specimen, since smaller specimens lose more of their weight through wear.

[8] In evidence from the Principate gold coin has a much lower coefficient of variation than silver (Duncan-Jones 1987, 248, Table XIII). Outliers for denarii may be as much as 25% above target (ibid., 247–8). Upper outliers for gold rarely reach 5% before the Severi, to judge from West's crude figures (a coin weighing 121 grains under Trajan, between 7.81 and 7.87 grams, is presumably at least 6% overweight; West 1941, 89, Table R).

their weight through wear, point to the same module of 322.8 grams as in the weights at Naples.[9]

The Boeckh and Naville modules are both unrealistic in claiming five-figure accuracy. But the choice between them is straightforward. Comparisons in terms of gold, silver and bronze coin clearly show that Naville's module gives a better fit with surviving evidence.[10] His module is also supported by the stone weights (Table 15.1).

2. WEIGHT-STANDARDS IN GOLD

2.1. CHANGES IN GOLD WEIGHT

Reconstructing the weight of the aureus is hampered by the small size of most gold hoards.[11] As a result, museum holdings have to be used in many cases. Nevertheless, gold was struck at greater accuracy, and small samples have a better chance of indicating a typical average than they would with silver or bronze. Gold also circulated more slowly, and was less subject to wear.[12]

A tentative reconstruction of target-weight is provided in Table 15.2.[13] The data before AD 64 come from samples of little-worn aurei collected by Bahrfeldt 1923, here allowing a maximum of 0.5% for wear.[14] Figures for Nero's reformed coinage are based on the Pompeii and Utrecht hoards from

---

[9] Nine triple solidi of Magnentius have a median weight of 13.45 grams. Triple solidi being struck at 24 to the pound, the implied pound module without allowing for wear is 322.8 grams (Jelocnik 1967, 231). For other weights showing modules of about 323 grams, see Duncan-Jones 1982, 370.   [10] See Duncan-Jones 1987, 249–56.

[11] Gold coin was normally not debased in this period, and its changes were changes in weight. Analyses of 40 aurei of successive dates in the period AD 63–235 show a gold content of 99.3% or more for all 38 coins struck at Rome, with deviations only in the 2 coins struck at Laodicea in AD 198–201 (93.3% and 91.6%); Morrisson 1985, 82–3.

[12] The main objection to using museum samples for weight analysis is that their contents normally come from different sources, and show differing degrees of coin–wear (see Duncan-Jones 1987, 256, n.1). Some coins may also have been deliberately selected for quality and weight.

[13] The reigns shown are ones in which new weight-levels came into force. The British Museum Caracalla sample is small, and yields a median weight of 6.475. But other samples gave lower weights, suggesting that some specimens were more worn (for example, a median weight of approximately 6.42 grams in West's sample of 21 aurei, specified in grains; West 1941, Table V). Some secondary variation also took place, for example between Vespasian and Titus: the median for Titus as a fraction of Vespasian is $\frac{6.96}{7.02}$ in the Belgian gold hoard of AD 205 (N = 14 and 80); and in the less worn British Museum samples for the Rome mint cited by Mattingly, the mean fraction is $\frac{7.23}{7.27}$ (N = 25 and 86; BMCRE 2, xiv).

[14] Duncan-Jones 1987, 253, Table XV (the wear-factors shown there have to be increased slightly to take account of a pound set at 322.8 grams, but are still smaller than those posited in Table XVI, p.254). At these weight-levels, weight-loss of 0.5% is about 15 years' wear at the rate implied in the big Belgian gold hoard.

Table 15.2 *Change in the target weight of aurei from the Rome mint*

Ruler	Coins per pound (target)	Target weight (grams)	CVar	Coins	Sample source
1. Caesar, 46 BC	40	8.07	—	155	1987,252–3
2. Augustus, 11 BC–AD 1	41	7.87	—	129	1987, 253
3. Tiberius, AD 13–15	41.5	7.78	1.0	46	1987, 253
4. Nero, 60–4	42	7.69	1.0	32	1987, 253
5. Nero, 64–8	44	7.34	0.6	62	1987, 249–52
6. Domitian, 82–5	41.5	7.78	—	60	Zemun
7. Domitian, 85–96	42.25	7.64	—	125	Zemun
8. Trajan, 100–17	44	7.34	1.8	97	Belgium
9. Commodus	44.5	7.25	1.1	47	*BMCRE*
10. Caracalla, 215–17	50	6.46	1.7	12	*BMCRE*
11. S. Alexander ('high')	50	6.46	4.3	50	*BMCRE*
12. S. Alexander ('low')	58	5.57	2.6	5	*BMCRE*

Note: The target figures are based on median weights of the samples in the last column, after allowances for coin-wear. For lines 1–5, see Duncan-Jones 1987. The data for Domitian in lines 6–7 come from the Zemun hoard of AD 98/9 summarised by Carradice 1983, 49–50, using the median of his mean averages (no figure for coefficient of variation is available here). The observed median weights are: (1) 8.03 (2) 7.84 (3) 7.75 (4) 7.645 (5) 7.31 (6) 7.745 (7) 7.59 (8) 7.08 (9) 7.22 (10) 6.40 (11) 6.46 (12) 5.54.[15]
CVar = percentage coefficient of variation.

the late 60s and 70s.[16] Domitian's reformed weights are calculated from what is known of the important Zemun hoard of AD 98/9.[17]

Under Severus Alexander, most of the British Museum aurei ($N = 55$) clearly belong to Caracalla's reduced standard of 50 to the pound (6.46 grams). But 5 coins show a much lower level, with a median of 5.54 grams. This approximates 58 aurei to the pound (5.57 grams), and the group seems to represent a different weight-standard: the lowest weight for coins of the higher standard is 6.05, outside the lower range of 5.30–5.62 grams. The coins at lower weight occur in AD 226, 227, 231 (2 coins) and 232.[18]

[15] The 9 aurei of AD 204–6 in the British Museum suggest a weight increase at that time, but the samples in Paris, New York and Vienna do not bear this out (weights kindly communicated by the collections concerned).

[16] Nero's weight-reduction is $4\frac{1}{2}$%, not 2% as stated by Sutherland (*RIC* I² 135).

[17] The targets suggested are the closest plausible figures, but true median weights are not available for this hoard, and the median of Carradice's mean averages for individual issues is used instead.

[18] West's tabulation of aurei for this reign, which has a tail of much lighter coins with a point of concentration of approximately 3.24 grams, evidently conflates quinarii (half-aurei) and aurei (West 1941, 133; weights in grains).

Table 15.3 *Coins per pound of metal and nominal gold:silver ratio*

Ruler	Denarii per pound of silver	Aurei per pound of gold	Nominal gold:silver ratio
Augustus	84.95	41	12.07
Tiberius	86.08	41.5	12.05
Claudius	86.08	41.5	12.05
Nero, 54–64	89.38	42	11.75
Nero, 64–8	100.7	44	10.92
Vespasian	103.2	44	10.66
Titus	98.56	41.5	10.53
Domitian, 85–96	96.39	42.25	10.96
Nerva	97.76	42.25	10.80
Trajan, 100–17	102.9	44	10.69
Hadrian	104.6	44	10.52
Antoninus Pius	107.0	44	10.28
Marcus Aurelius	119.9	44	9.17
Commodus, 180–6	134.4	44.5	8.27
Commodus, 187–92	152.3	44.5	7.30
Septimius Severus, 193–8	156.4	44.5	7.11
Septimius Severus, 198–211	169.6	44.5	6.56
Caracalla	192.0	50	6.51
Elagabalus	228.0	50.5	5.54
Severus Alexander	226.8	50	5.51

Note Pure silver is taken to be 98% fine (see p. 223 and n.43). The final column shows the ratio between the figures in the first two, when converted into sesterces (the silver figures on which they are based are usually approximate). Changes within reigns are omitted except where specific dates are shown. For fuller details, see Tables 15.2 and 15.5. Walker 3, 154–5 gives parallel calculations, using approximate weights from *BMCRE* and Bolin.

2.2. GOLD SUMMARY

Compared with the denarius, the aureus underwent relatively little change (Table 15.3). Even so, discreet adjustments began as early as Augustus, and weight had reached 42 to the pound by the early years of Nero. One of the few contemporary statements about coin-weight tells us that the aureus had reached 45 to the pound by Pliny's day. Unfortunately, good surviving coin-evidence from Pliny's time indicates a figure of 44, not 45.[19] The figure in

---

[19] *NH* 33.47. See Duncan-Jones 1987, 249–52: if 45 were right, most coin in both the earliest samples of Nero's aurei, from Utrecht and Pompeii, would be overweight. Thirion (50) saw this also, but took refuge in a different explanation involving a heavier Roman pound. But Pliny's figure cannot be rehabilitated in this way, since assuming a heavier pound would make the denarii in known hoards weigh too little (cf. chapter 13).

the medieval manuscripts of Pliny is evidently either a transmission error or a mistake by Pliny.[20] Nero's gold reduction in AD 64 was only $4\frac{1}{2}$%, compared with his reduction of about 11% in the silver content of the denarius.[21] Domitian briefly reversed the trend with a return to the pre-Neronian weight for three years early in his reign. Domitian's later modified standard lasted until the early years of Trajan, who then evidently returned to Nero's weight of 44 to the pound.[22]

The next significant change was a half-aureus drop to 44.5 under Commodus. This standard was apparently maintained under Septimius Severus. Caracalla made the first decisive devaluation of the aureus, issuing it in AD 215 at a new weight of 50 to the pound, making a reduction of 10%.[23] Caracalla's new standard lasted in essence until the end of our period. But under Severus Alexander, there were also signs of the emergence of a new lower standard of 58 to the pound, a drop greater than the one under Caracalla.

The slow changes in aureus weight, and the more rapid decline in denarius-weight after AD 64 meant a steadily shifting relationship between gold and silver in terms of monetary value. Starting from a steady figure of 1:12 for almost all the Julio-Claudian period, the gold:silver ratio declined until it had almost halved by the late Severan Emperors (see fig. 15.1).[24] The dual decline in weight showed that supplies of both metals had come under pressure. But minting of gold remained much more stable, with the paradoxical result that gold fell in nominal value against silver. Altering the metallic ratio a little at a time did not necessarily provoke any immediate reaction in the market-place. But by the end of the Severan period, if not earlier, payment in gold enjoyed some premium over payment in silver.[25]

[20] Pliny is not an impeccable source here: for a catalogue of his misinformation about Republican coinage, see Burnett 1987, 10–11.

[21] In terms of the metal content of the currency, the gold:silver ratio appears to have fallen in AD 64 from 1:11.75 to 1:10.92. From available co-ordinates, the silver values are (1) 322.8/(3.63 × 97.5/98) = 89.4 denarii to the pound and (2) 322.8/(3.36 × 93.5/98) = 100.7 (for the figures, see Table 15.5). Since Walker's fineness readings are always rounded to the nearest quarter, or more often half of a per cent (and since the weight target in AD 54–64 remains uncertain, see p. 221), these calculations may be imprecise. The earlier silver target might be as high as 90 denarii to the pound, and the later one as low as 100 denarii. If so, the successive gold:silver ratios would be 1:11.67 and 1:11 (HS4,200/360 and HS4,400/400).

[22] Weight-loss analysis of the large Belgian hoard shows that roughly the same standard was in use in AD 69–79, and in 100–70 (after the early years of Marcus Aurelius, the sample becomes too small). Cf. p. 182, Table 13.1.

[23] One of the aurei of AD 215 in the British Museum still shows the earlier standard (Caracalla 148, 7.28 grams). The 12 coins of the new standard range from 6.26 to 6.62 grams. Reduction in aureus weight was briefly anticipated by usurpers of the 190s (see chapter 16, n.2).

[24] Less exact figures are given by Walker, 3.154–5 (up to AD 251–3). The weight ratio between denarii and aurei, which of course changed relatively little, can be seen from West's approximate figures (West 1941, 8, Table A). The traditional ratio between gold and silver of 1:12 has been identified in an Egyptian papyrus of AD 113 (Foraboschi 1988).

[25] Granted the steep decline in the metallic ratio (Table 15.3), anything else would be surprising. CIL XIII 3162 shows payment in gold to an army officer recorded as a privilege in AD 238 (Jones 1974, 195). The relationship between Severan and pre-Severan denarii in circulation was

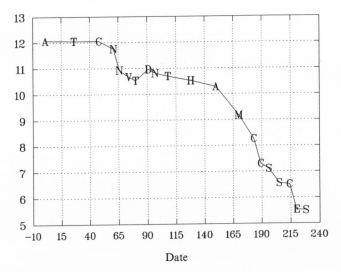

Date

Figure 15.1 The ratio of a pound of gold to a pound of silver in terms of implicit monetary value, Augustus to Severus Alexander: twenty samples from seventeen reigns. (Symbol: Emperor's initial.)

3. THE WEIGHT OF THE DENARIUS

In the late Republic, the weight-standard of the denarius remained relatively stable, although it apparently fell from 82 to 83 coins to the pound at about the time of the Social War.[26] By the Triumviral period the weight had reached 84 to the pound, from Pliny's reference to minting by Antony.[27]

AUGUSTUS.   Under Augustus, there were a series of experiments with striking at different mints, and the denarius was struck at more than one weight-standard. The weight-index used throughout this discussion is the median average.[28]

uneasy: thus the pre-Severan coin in the big Viuz-Faverges hoard from AD 251–3 seems to have very little of the wear which would show that it went on circulating after the 190s (Duncan-Jones 1987, 241). If the market could recognise Severan denarii as being different from earlier coin, willingness to go on exchanging them against gold at par remains unlikely, whatever the occurrence of the old ratio in a short fragment of Dio may mean (55.12.3–5, discussed in Buttrey 1961). About a decade after the steepest fall in the denarius, the local banking monopoly at Mylasa was reinforced by imperial decree; black market currency dealing is clearly implied (AD 209/11; *OGIS* 515).

[26] From unpublished analyses of the big Cosa hoard by the writer.
[27] *NH* 33.132. In the following discussion, reigns of short-lived Emperors are omitted.
[28] Where numerical data are 'normally' distributed, mean and median averages should be the same. Where they are not the same, as in much ancient coin-evidence, the median is the more stable and more reliable measure. Unlike the mean, it is unaffected by the amount of deviation in the most extreme values.

     G.F. Hill recommended the frequency table as a means of establishing original striking-weight, using a wear-factor of 1% (Hill 1924; cf. Babelon 1901, 577 n.4). Much modern work remains influenced by this approach. The frequency table or histogram is a straightforward device for

Table 15.4 *Denarius-weight under Augustus*
Median weight (in grams); samples in brackets

	American Numismatic Society	*BMCRE*
Emerita	3.67 (27)	3.80 (25)
Lugdunum	3.75 (87)	3.75 (60)
Rome	3.84 (108)	3.81 (112)
Spain 1	3.73 (33)	3.69 (23)
Spain 2	3.81 (99)	3.76 (70)

Note: Despite relatively large totals, the two sets of findings are mostly inconsistent, showing discrepancies in the degree of wear. Weights from the American Numismatic Society collection were kindly supplied by Dr W.E. Metcalf.

Big museum samples of Augustan denarii are summarised in Table 15.4.

For cross-sections of coin in circulation, we must turn to the hoards. In a British hoard from Beck Row ending with coin of AD 79, the 22 Augustan denarii have a median weight of 3.60 grams. Larger samples from Membury and Sutton show median weights of 3.63 and 3.67 grams. The Membury hoard ends with coin of Tiberius, and the Sutton hoard in AD 42. However both were presumably deposited after the Claudian conquest in AD 43. If weight-loss was about $\frac{1}{1,600}$ per year, the implied original weights, calculated back to the middle of Augustus's reign, are about 3.81 (Beck Row), 3.80 (Sutton) and 3.75 (Membury).[29] Taking the median of 3.80, the implied striking-weight is 85 to the pound (322.8/3.80 = 84.95). This suggests a slight fall since Antony's level of 84 to the pound. This figure is synthetic, because of the conflicting Augustan weight-targets implied in Table 15.4.

TIBERIUS.   The median weights of coins in 4 British hoards provide a useful regression of weight against date. Accepting the end-dates of the hoards as indicating the date of burial, the weight projected for the mid-point in

showing a weight-distibution. But it cannot reveal or compensate for the underlying degree of wear. The point of concentration can easily move by more than Hill's 1%. For example, even in slow-wearing gold coin, ninety years of circulation makes the peak move by 4% between successive hoard-samples of Neronian aurei (Duncan-Jones 1987, 247, fig.3). For criticism of the frequency table, see also Crawford in Crawford, Millar 1983, 223–4.

The 'corrected' mean figures sometimes used in Walker's weight summaries are unconvincing, and the samples he used contain too much unidentifiable coin-wear to provide a good basis for assessing weight-targets (Walker, 2.46–7; cf. 1.2). A.S. Hemmy's weight figures in *BMCRE* 4, xv–xvi rely too much on conventional wear factors.

[29] For rates of weight-loss, see p. 191, Table 13.11.

Tiberius's reign is 3.754 grams. This argues a striking-weight of 86 to the pound ($322.8/3.754 = 86$).[30]

CLAUDIUS. Little hoard-evidence is available, but the median weight in a British Museum sample of 26 denarii is 3.71 grams, as is the corresponding figure for Tiberius ($N = 31$). A change from the Tiberian standard appears unlikely.[31]

NERO. Nero's coinage before AD 64 also suffers from a lack of hoard-evidence. But the British Museum sample shows a median of 3.60 ($N = 17$). Set alongside the museum samples for Tiberius and Claudius, without allowing for any differences in wear, the implied target is about 89 to the pound ($1/86 \times 3.60/3.71 = 1/88.6$). If the Neronian coin is appreciably less worn, a target of $1/90$ would be possible.[32] The new weight-standard from AD 64, though not explicitly stated, is generally agreed to have been 96 to the pound.[33] This target tallies with the evidence of weight-loss shown in large denarius hoards.[34] Nero's weight-reduction was thus 6–7%.[35]

After Nero, the weight of denarii struck for the Emperor remained more or less stable until the mid-Flavian period. Under TITUS, the standard apparently rose to 93 to the pound, to judge from the sample of 45 coins at La Magura. DOMITIAN reformed weights further, the new standard from AD 82 apparently being 92 to the pound. A target of 92 is implied by the La Magura evidence for the period AD 85–96. Evidence from the period of high fineness between 82 and 85 is very incomplete, but Walker's sample of 14 coins suggests a target of 92.

---

[30] The regression, based on Sutton, Eriswell, Scole and Beck Row, reads: weight = 3.832 − (date × 0.00298); $r^2 = 0.971$. For the view that the Eriswell and Scole hoards were buried as by-products of the Boudiccan revolt of AD 61, see Lind 1992.

[31] Claudius's short-lived predecessor Caligula has left relatively little coin (some bronze was deliberately melted down as part of his *damnatio*, p. 98). The 15 denarii in the British Museum catalogue have a median weight of 3.69 grams. Granted the small sample, there is too little variation to show any decisive difference from the standard of Tiberius and Claudius (and too little to sustain the view that precious-metal weights fell and had to be restored under Claudius, cf. *RIC* I² 118). The four denarii analysed by Walker suggest no obvious change in fineness (the median is 97.5%; 1.14).

[32] Sutherland in *RIC* I² 134 suggests a target of $\frac{1}{89}$ at this point, but bases his calculation on the Boeckh pound, for which see p. 213 above.

[33] For a weight of 96 denarii to the pound, see *MSR* 1.125.

[34] Duncan-Jones 1987, 255.

[35] For Nero's corresponding reduction in gold weight by 4.5%, in sestertius-weight by 4.2%, and in the fineness of the Alexandrian tetradrachm, see Tables 15.2, 15.5, and 15.10. Lo Cascio makes the silver reduction greater by assuming that denarii were still being struck at 84 to the pound up to AD 64 (Lo Cascio 1980, 458). Numismatists have suggested possible technical grounds for Nero's reductions in precious-metal content, such as a rise in the price of gold and silver, a rise in the price of commodities, and even the supposed need to keep in line with existing worn coin, lest Gresham's Law should drive new coin out of circulation (e.g. *BMCRE* I, l; *RIC* I², 134–5). But the sources are quite explicit about Nero's gigantic extravagance, the scale of his need for further funds, and the desperate devices used to find them (cf. chapter 1, n.94). Even without this evidence, production of coin after AD 64 on a scale which marks out this period from almost all others would suggest that the changes were more than a technical adjustment.

Under NERVA the target fell slightly to 93 to the pound. It was apparently about 94 in TRAJAN's first period, AD 98–9 (94.4 is projected at La Magura). But from AD 100, the Neronian standard of 96 seems to have been resumed.

Weights then remained roughly stable for half a century or more. Serious changes took place under COMMODUS, however, with targets of 102 in AD 180–6 and 114 in 187–92, to judge from the Viuz evidence.[36] SEVERUS first returned to Commodus's earlier standard, and then resumed the Neronian weight-standard from AD 198 onwards (using the Viuz-Faverges hoard with its large samples of little-worn Severan coin). The median weight for Severus at Viuz is 3.33 grams. For CARACALLA it is 3.18 in AD 211–14 and 3.205 in 215–17 (N = 44 and 32). This probably suggests a target of 100–101 coins to the pound.

The radiate coin, referred to as the 'Antoninianus', introduced by Caracalla, shows a median weight of 5.055 grams in the Viuz sample for his reign (N = 28).[37] The ratio of radiate to denarius at Viuz is 1:0.634, virtually 7:11. If the denarius was struck at 100 to the pound in 215–7 (see above), this ratio would make the radiate 63.6 to the pound or 5.07 grams, which is compatible with the Viuz median of 5.055.[38] Since its fineness was almost that of the denarius, the radiate yielded a substantial minting profit, accepting that it was tariffed at a face-value of 2 denarii.[39]

Similar manipulations are encountered in later monetary history. For example, in Florence a new *grosso* was introduced in 1345, tariffed at 48 *denari* instead of 30, an increase of 60%, but containing only 45% more silver. The new larger coin was well received nevertheless, and circulated widely.[40]

Under ELAGABALUS, denarius-weight fell appreciably to 106–7 denarii to the pound: at Viuz the median figures are 3.02 in AD 218–19 and 3.00 in 220–2

---

[36] The Viuz hoard has 90 coins struck for Commodus. The same developments are visible in the Magura coins (N = 53), but bigger weight samples would be needed before the point of change could be identified clearly. Weight-standards during this reign were extremely erratic. (For the regressions used to evaluate the pre-Severan averages in these hoards, see Tables 13.3 and 13.4.)

[37] For Julia Domna the Viuz median is 5.265, but this comes from only 8 coins. The 47 radiates of Caracalla in *BMCRE* show a median of 5.04 grams.

[38] In the absence of bigger samples, this finding can only be approximate. But assuming a denarius target of 101 in 215–17 makes the radiate fall below the Viuz median.

[39] See n.48 below. The numismatic logic of thinking the silver radiate a double denarius was clearly put by Mattingly (*BMCRE* 5, xviii): '(1) The ratio of 2 to 1 is obviously simpler and more natural than $1\frac{1}{2}$ or $1\frac{1}{4}$ to 1. (2) The radiate crown differentiates the double piece from the single on both gold and *aes*. Why not then on the silver too? The double piece in gold is of course twice the weight of the single; but the double piece in *aes* (the dupondius) is nothing like twice the weight of the as. The silver follows the bronze in disregarding exact weight, and why not, when it was itself virtually a token coinage?' In this sense, see also Jones 1974, 194; Linant de Bellefonds 1980, 576; Depeyrot, Hollard 1987, 57. For other theories about the reform, arguing for an antoninianus worth $1\frac{1}{4}$ denarii, see Lo Cascio 1984.

[40] 'A conjuring trick – but it worked. Villani commented: "And it was a very handsome coin . . . and had a large circulation in Florence and throughout Tuscany."' (Cipolla 1982, 38; a misprint makes the silver increase 25% instead of 45%). The silver value, 43.6 *denari*, was 9% below the nominal value of the coin.

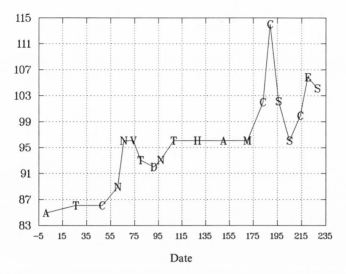

Date

Figure 15.2 The number of denarii struck per pound of metal, Augustus to Severus Alexander: twenty samples from seventeen reigns. (Symbol: Emperor's initial.)

(N = 19 and 28).[41] Under SEVERUS ALEXANDER the weight recovers somewhat to 103–4 denarii to the pound: the Viuz median is 3.09 (N = 125)

The weight pattern overall is shown in fig. 15.2. Figure 15.3 shows weight-accuracy as measured by the coefficient of variation (the standard deviation as a percentage of the mean). The coefficient is below 5 for the first century of the empire; then above 5 from Domitian onwards, reaching new heights under Commodus and the Severi.

4. SILVER FINENESS

4.1. LONG-TERM CHANGE

The Julio-Claudian dynasty lasted nearly a century, from 31 BC to AD 68.[42] For almost all this time the denarius was struck from silver whose purity of 98% approximated that of Roman silver bullion.[43] Although its weight fell slightly, no attempt was made to stretch the metal with alloy until the reign of Nero. Denarii of Nero's first ten years show a fractional decline to 97.5% median

[41] This allows a wear-factor of approximately 0.7% in the denarius figures for Caracalla. At Viuz, Elagabalus's radiate shows a median of 5.16 (N = 16), which is higher than before, but cannot be pressed given the small sample size.

[42] For the technical problems of deriving exact figures for fineness from Walker's non-destructive analyses, see n.46 below.

[43] Three sheets of silver discovered near a Roman mine in Germany showed silver content of 96.32, 96.70 and 97.45% (Willers 1898).

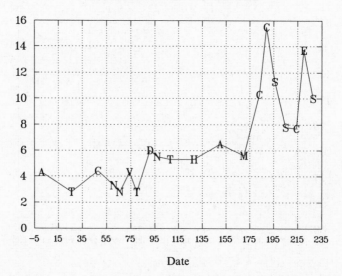

Figure 15.3 Approximate percentage coefficient of variation for denarius-weight (in grams), Augustus to Severus Alexander: twenty samples from seventeen reigns. (Symbol: Emperor's initial.)

fineness, on Walker's reading of a small sample. But the first decisive fall took place in AD 64, when fineness was reduced to about 93.5%, a drop of over 4%.

Under Vespasian the overall level was lowered again, to 91.75%.[44] Titus began to reverse this trend, with an increase to 92.5%. Early in Domitian's reign, full purity of approximately 98% was briefly restored, in the issues of AD 82–5.[45] But after this the Neronian level of 93.5% was resumed. By Trajan's reign, with an overall level of 91.5%, fineness was back to where it had been under Vespasian. The gradual descent continued under Hadrian and Antoninus Pius, with overall levels of 90% and 88%. Then came a much larger deterioration: the overall figure for the reign of Marcus Aurelius is 78%, which had become 74% by the second half of Commodus's reign. Silver-content in the Severan period was little more than half of coin-weight. Overall fineness was apparently 55.5% under Severus, 51% under Caracalla, and about 45% under Elagabalus and Severus Alexander.[46] The changes in fineness are

---

[44] Here most reigns are treated as one, disregarding the internal variations seen in Tables 15.7–15.9. The figures continue to be based on coin struck for the Emperor (for 'non-Emperor' coin, see pp. 240–2).

[45] See Carradice, 142.

[46] Recent destructive analysis of denarii of Gordian III using neutron activation has shown that with heavily debased coin, Walker's surface readings of silver-content (based on X-ray fluorescence spectrometry) can be as much as 12% too high (from forthcoming work by Dr R.F. Bland, kindly communicated by the author; for the problem of surface enrichment, see also Tyler 1975, 10 and Butcher 1992, 42 n.2). If an error of this order is also present in Walker's data for the Severi, that will reinforce the downward trend already obvious from the figures as

Table 15.5 *The denarius: median weight (in grams) and fineness*

Emperor	Target-weight	CVar	N (weight)	Sample	Fineness (Walker data)	CVar
Augustus	3.80	4.3	33	Membury	98.0	1.0
Tiberius	3.75	2.8	36	Membury	98.0	0.7
Claudius	3.75	4.4	31	BMuseum	98.0	0.8
Nero, 54–64	3.63	3.3	17	BMuseum	97.5	0.9
Nero, 64–68	3.36	2.8	19	Magura	93.5	1.2
Vespasian	3.36	4.3	329	Magura	91.25	4.7
Titus	3.47	2.8	45	Magura	92.5	2.9
Domitian, 85–96	3.51	6.0	78	Magura	93.5	0.8
Nerva	3.47	5.5	43	Magura	93.25	0.8
Trajan	3.36	5.3	622	Magura	91.5	4.0
Hadrian	3.36	5.3	528	Magura	90.0	4.8
A. Pius	3.36	6.5	242	Magura	88.0	6.7
M. Aurelius	3.36	5.6	134	Magura	78.5	7.0
Commodus, 180–6	3.16	10.3	40	Viuz	74.5	6.5
Commodus, 187–92	2.83	15.5	50	Viuz	73.4	7.2
Severus, 193–8	3.16	11.3	26	Viuz	64.0	16.2
Severus, 198–211	3.36	7.8	151	Viuz	55.5	11.6
Caracalla	3.23	7.7	76	Viuz	51.0	9.7
Elagabalus	3.05	13.7	47	Viuz	45.5	14.7
S. Alexander	3.10	10.0	125	Viuz	45.0	19.0

Note: Based on coin of the Emperor, from AD 64 onwards normally struck at Rome. For detailed arguments about weight, see pp. 219–23. Median figures for fineness are calculated from Walker's samples used in Tables 15.7–15.9 below. The pre-Severan weight-targets after Nero are calculated from hoard-averages using linear regression (see chapter 13, section 3, and Tables 13.3 and 13.4).
CVar = percentage coefficient of variation.

plotted in fig. 15.4, and the coefficient of variation for fineness in fig. 15.5.

It is clear that weight and fineness were both manipulated in order to produce more coins from a given amount of silver. For the first two centuries of the Empire, the ratio of fineness to weight did not change very much, despite the frequent manipulation of one variable or the other. Percentage fineness as a multiple of denarius-weight mainly stayed within the range 25–7 during this period. But from Marcus Aurelius onwards, fineness changed

they stand. Unfortunately, no other large-scale surveys of silver fineness are available at present. The samples in other published analyses are almost always so small that their results remain statistically uncertain.

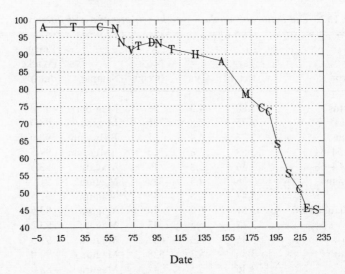

Figure 15.4 Median percentage fineness of denarii struck for the Emperor, Augustus to Severus Alexander: twenty samples from seventeen reigns. (Symbol: Emperor's initial.)

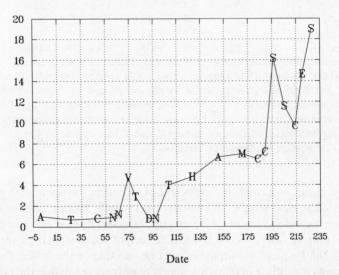

Figure 15.5 Percentage coefficient of variation in denarius fineness, Augustus to Severus Alexander: twenty samples from seventeen reigns. (Symbol: Emperor's initial.)

Table 15.6 *The number of denarii struck per pound of silver*

Emperor	Denarii per pound of silver	Median fineness (%)	Target denarius-weight
Augustus	84.9	98	3.80
Tiberius	86.1	98	3.75
Claudius	86.1	98	3.75
Nero, 54–64	89.4	97.5	3.63
Nero, 64–8	100.7	93.5	3.36
Vespasian	103.2	91.25	3.36
Titus	98.6	92.5	3.47
Domitian, 82–5	92	97.9	3.51
Domitian, 85–96	96.4	93.5	3.51
Nerva	97.8	93.25	3.47
Trajan	102.9	91.5	3.36
Hadrian	104.6	90	3.36
A. Pius	107	88	3.36
M. Aurelius	120	78.5	3.36
Commodus, 180–6	134.4	74.5	3.16
Commodus, 187–92	152.3	73.4	2.83
S. Severus, 193–8	156.4	64	3.16
S. Severus, 198–211	169.6	55.5	3.36
Caracalla	192	51	3.23
Elagabalus	228	45.5	3.05
S. Alexander	226.8	45	3.10

Note: Column 1 is calculated literally from columns 2 and 3. Walker's readings used in column 2 are always rounded by him to the nearest quarter per cent or more often half per cent, reducing any precision possible in column 1.
Source: Table 15.5.

much more than weight. The ratio started to fall rapidly, and by the end of the Severan period, it was less than 15 (fig. 15.6).

The crucial index is the number of denarii struck from a pound of silver, taking both weight and fineness into account (see Table 15.6). At the start of the Empire this was about 85 denarii to the pound, but the denarius fell under Nero from $\frac{1}{89-90}$ of the pound to approximately $\frac{1}{100}$ with the changes in AD 64.[47] After an initial decline under Vespasian, the target recovered to more than $\frac{1}{100}$ under the later Flavians. Trajan let the target fall to $\frac{1}{103}$, and it lost a further 2 points or so under Hadrian and under Antoninus Pius.

The first spectacular change was the fall to $\frac{1}{120}$ under Marcus Aurelius, from $\frac{1}{107}$. This began a rapid slide, and under Commodus a level of $\frac{1}{152}$ was reached,

[47] In fact, the Neronian target may explicitly have been 100 denarii per pound of silver (see n.21 above).

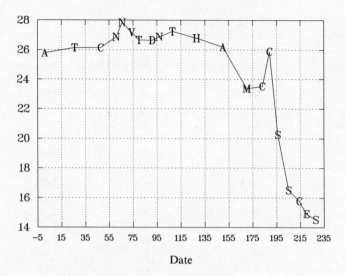

Figure 15.6 Median percentage fineness as a multiple of median denarius-weight (in grams), Augustus to Severus Alexander: twenty samples from seventeen reigns. (Symbol: Emperor's initial.)

declining under the first Severi to about $\frac{1}{170}$ and $\frac{1}{190}$.[48] By the end of the Severan dynasty, the level was about $\frac{1}{226} - \frac{1}{227}$.[49]

Figure 15.7, which is based on Table 15.6, shows the pattern as a whole. A pound of silver was producing twice as many denarii under Severus as it had under Augustus two centuries earlier. By the late Severan period the figure was more than twice what it had been under Antoninus Pius, only seventy years earlier. Thus the pressures were increasing rapidly, and they continued to grow after the Severan period.[50]

4.2. SHORT-TERM CHANGE IN FINENESS

The period between Nero and Trajan marks the transition from pure silver struck at consistent fineness to debased silver with erratic fineness. As a time of experiment and adaptation, this period is worth a closer look. Figure 15.8 shows the main changes in fineness (for the details, see Tables 15.7, 15.8 and 15.9). Nero's initial coin is struck close to 98% fine, almost at par. His

[48] For Caracalla's radiate, Walker's analyses give a median fineness of 50% (N = 35). For a radiate tariffed at 2 denarii, if the target weight was 5.07 grams, its value would be about 255 denarii per pound of silver.

[49] These statistics are based on Walker's figures for fineness as they stand (using median average). As already seen (n.46), Walker's fineness readings for periods of heavy debasement may underrate the degree of debasement, and in that case, the later fractions will be correspondingly smaller.

[50] See Duncan-Jones 1982, 375 and Callu 1969, 256.

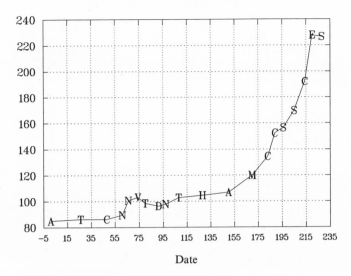

Figure 15.7 The number of denarii struck per pound of silver, Augustus to Severus Alexander: twenty samples from seventeen reigns. (Symbol: Emperor's initial.)

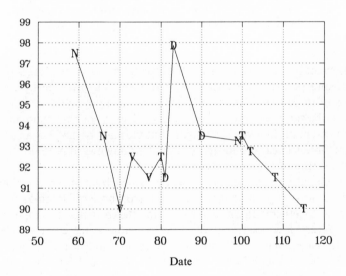

Figure 15.8 Median percentage fineness of the denarius, AD 54–117: fourteen samples from six reigns. (Symbol: Emperor's initial.)

Table 15.7 *Median denarius fineness: coin struck for the Emperor, 31 BC–AD 98*

Emperor	Median	Mean	CVar	N
Augustus	98.0	97.8	1.0	25
Tiberius	98.0	98.1	0.7	7
Claudius	98.0	98.0	0.8	19
Nero, 54–64	97.5	97.3	0.9	13
Nero, 64–8	93.5	93.5	1.2	24
Vespasian, 69–71	90.0	88.6	5.3	37
Vespasian, 72–4	92.5	91.0	4.0	39
Vespasian, 74–9	91.5	90.3	4.3	30
Titus	92.5	92.0	2.9	57
Domitian, 81–2	91.5	90.7	4.1	28
Domitian, 82–5	97.9	98.0	0.9	14
Domitian, 85–96	93.5	93.5	0.8	92
Nerva	93.25	93.1	0.8	37

Note: Based on readings for 'Emperor' coin in Walker's lists (where it can only be identified by catalogue number). Coin from provincial mints is omitted. Overall figures for fineness for reigns subdivided here are given in Table 15.5. CVar = percentage coefficient of variation.

debasement is followed by a further drop. No improvement takes place until the second period of Domitian, who restores full silver purity for a short period of three years. Domitian's fall-back position for the main part of his reign is the same as Nero's debased level. This is roughly maintained under Nerva and in the first years of Trajan. But the main part of Trajan's reign sees a more or less linear decline in fineness. This downward path sets the pattern for the future of the denarius.

The changes in fineness were accompanied by a sharp deterioration in quality control (fig. 15.9). The issues of Nero, those of Domitian from AD 82 onwards, together with those of Nerva and the early part of Trajan's reign all show a very low coefficient of variation, approximately 1%. The earlier Flavian issues, including Domitian's accession coinage, and the later issues of Trajan, show a much higher figure of 4% or more.[51] Such a vivid contrast must reflect some change in the character of coin production. The high level starts at a time of very heavy mint-output and financial crisis in the aftermath of civil war. And it returns, never to disappear, with Trajan's well-known reminting in AD 107 (see fig. 15.5).

[51] Titus forms a small exception, with a figure of 3%, but this is still closer to the upper level.

Table 15.8 *Median denarius fineness: coin struck for the Emperor, AD 98–192*

Emperor	Median fineness	Mean	CVar	N
Trajan, 98–100	93.5	93.2	1.4	33
Trajan, 101–2	92.75	93.0	1.2	22
Trajan, 103–11	91.5	90.3	4.1	120
Trajan, 112–17	90.0	89.4	4.1	100
Hadrian, 117–18	88.5	87.1	5.8	40
Hadrian, 119–28	90.0	88.8	5.2	156
Hadrian, 128–38	90.5	89.6	4.0	169
A. Pius, 138–9	88.5	87.9	4.9	35
A. Pius, 140–4	88.75	87.8	4.7	47
A. Pius, 148–9	89.0	86.7	5.7	21
A. Pius, 150–7	83.25	83.9	7.3	59
A. Pius, 158–61	86.5	84.1	8.7	34
M. Aurelius, 161–5	77.5	78.4	6.7	42
M. Aurelius, 165–9	80.0	79.2	7.9	35
M. Aurelius, 170–4	78.0	78.2	5.8	31
M. Aurelius, 175–9	78.5	80.0	7.7	29
Commodus, 180–3	75.0	76.2	7.2	34
Commodus, 184–7	74.5	75.7	6.1	62
Commodus, 188–92	73.0	73.8	7.1	71

Note: See note on Table 15.7. Coin assigned to the mid-140s by Walker is insecurely dated, and has been omitted.
CVar = percentage coefficient of variation.

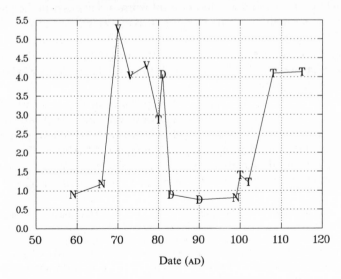

Figure 15.9 Percentage coefficient of variation in denarius fineness, AD 54–117: fourteen samples from six reigns. (Symbol: Emperor's initial.)

Table 15.9 *Median denarius fineness: coin struck for the Emperor, AD 193–235*

Emperor	Median fineness	Mean	CVar	N
Severus, 193–4	79.0	77.8	6.6	25
Severus, 194–6	60.5	63.0	12.8	22
Severus, 196–8	56.5	57.6	10.9	54
Severus, 198–201	56.5	57.7	12.1	43
Severus, 202–8	55.0	55.9	10.5	41
Severus, 209–11	55.75	56.9	12.0	28
Caracalla, 211	54.75	55.8	13.5	14
Caracalla, 212–14	50.5	51.1	5.8	33
Caracalla, 215–17	51.25	51.4	9.5	44
Elagabalus, 218–19	45.0	45.3	9.4	25
Elagabalus, 220–2	46.25	46.9	16.5	52
S. Alexander, 222–4	42.75	43.1	11.8	56
S. Alexander, 225–7	42.0	41.7	21.8	55
S. Alexander, 228–30	47.0	45.2	19.5	53
S. Alexander, 231–5	49.0	49.6	17.7	43

Note: See note on Table 15.7.

5. THE WEIGHT AND FINENESS OF EGYPTIAN SILVER

In Egypt the local precious-metal currency was based on the Alexandrian tetradrachm. The median weight of extant worn specimens is in the region of 13.25 grams, strongly suggesting a target striking-weight of 24 to the Roman pound or 13.45 grams (Table 15.10).[52] An equivalent silver drachm should have 96 coins to the pound. But in rare surviving examples, the silver drachm and didrachm seem to have been struck to a standard $\frac{1}{7}$ lighter (about 112 drachmas to the pound).[53]

Under the Empire, the tetradrachm, which was tariffed at parity with the denarius at least by the early Roman period, was first struck in Tiberius's reign. Its silver-content then was about 15% greater than that of the denarius. But very soon the tetradrachm lost its advantage and fell below the denarius. That made coin of Tiberius an anomaly. None of the second-century tetradrachm hoards reported by Milne contains any coin of Tiberius.[54] It had

[52] Allowing for worn specimens, this approximation to an obvious fraction of the Roman pound of 322.8 grams is close. The higher weights of the last Ptolemaic tetradrachms reported by Walker (1.141–2) presumably belong to a pre-Roman weight-standard.

[53] Five drachms of Claudius show a median weight of 2.96 grams (mean 2.80); 5 didrachms show a median of 5.72 and a mean of 5.66 (weight-lists kindly communicated by Dr A.M. Burnett).

[54] Milne 1933, Table of Hoards. Christiansen surprisingly states that 'according to the hoard evidence, there was no systematic attempt at calling in coin in Egypt before the reign of Commodus' (Christiansen 1988, 1.256).

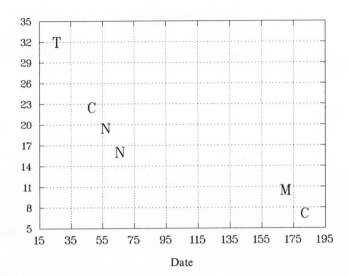

Date

Figure 15.10 Percentage silver fineness of the Alexandrian tetradrachm, AD 14–190: six samples from five selected reigns. (Emperors: Tiberius, Claudius, Nero 1, Nero 2, Marcus Aurelius, Commodus.)

evidently vanished, along with the much finer Ptolemaic coin, in the gigantic reminting of Alexandrian coin under Nero. Nero's mintmasters commemorated Tiberius on tetradrachms produced in AD 66/7.[55]

The median weight of the tetradrachm seems to have remained stable under the Julio-Claudians, probably at a target of 24 to the pound (Table 15.10). By the time of Marcus Aurelius in the 160s it had lost about 7% of its weight, and under Commodus it was down by 10%, suggesting weight-targets of 26 and 27 to the pound (Table 15.10). These falls were bigger than those in the denarius in the period since Nero. Changes in tetradrachm fineness were much more drastic. The decline in fineness between Tiberius and the second period of Nero appears virtually linear, falling from 32% to 16% in a few decades. A century later under Marcus Aurelius and Commodus, fineness had fallen as low as 10% and 7% (fig. 15.10).[56]

The silver-content of individual tetradrachms fluctuated quite erratically, apparently showing a wide gulf between provincial minting standards and

[55] See e.g. Milne 1933, nos. 256–61. Hoards of AD 66–70 are already without any Tiberian coin (Jungfleisch, El Madamud and 'EEF' in the list in Christiansen 1988, 2.92–3; the proportion of Neronian coin in the El Madamud hoard is closer to 100% than to Christiansen's 83%; see Baratte 1974, 82. n.3).

[56] Chemical analyses of much smaller samples by Caley broadly agree with Walker's results, the main variant being a mean fineness of 43.8% for Tiberius, based on 5 coins (Caley 1958). In Walker's denarius:tetradrachm comparisons (1.156), some figures differ from findings elsewhere in his book.

Table 15.10 *Fineness of the Alexandrian tetradrachm and of the denarius*

Reign	Coins per pound (estimated)	Implied target weight (grams)	Median observed weight	Median fineness (%)	Implied target silver weight
Tetradrachm					
Tiberius	24	13.45	13.25	32.0	4.24
Claudius	24	13.45	13.18	22.5	2.97
Nero, AD 57	24	13.45	13.27	19.5	2.59
Nero, 59-67	24	13.45	13.14	16.0	2.10
Marcus Aurelius, 167–9	26	12.42	12.32	10.5	1.29
Commodus	27	11.96	11.97	7.13	0.85

Reign	Denarii per pound of metal	Implied target weight (grams)	Median fineness (%)	Implied target silver weight
Denarius				
Tiberius	86	3.75	98.0	3.68
Claudius	86	3.75	98.0	3.68
Nero, pre-64	89	3.63	97.5	3.54
Nero, 64–68	96	3.36	93.5	3.14
Marcus Aurelius	96	3.36	78.5	2.64
Commodus, 180–6	102	3.16	74.5	2.40
Commodus, 187–92	114	2.83	73.4	2.12

Reign	Tetradrachm	Denarius	Tetradrachm as percentage of denarius
Median silver weight per coin			
Tiberius	4.24	3.68	115.2
Claudius	2.97	3.68	80.7
Nero, 1	2.59	3.42	75.7
Nero, 2	2.10	3.14	66.9
Marcus Aurelius	1.29	2.64	48.9
Commodus	0.85	2.37	35.9

Note: The analysis of tetradrachm fineness and weights is based on data in Walker, 1.143–9 and 2.114–5. The time-periods for Nero, Marcus Aurelius and Commodus are slightly out of alignment, unavoidably making comparisons approximate. For denarius weight and fineness, see Table 15.5.[57]

[57] Caley's chemical readings show mean fineness for Vespasian, Hadrian and Antoninus Pius of 17.3%, 16.7% and 17.0% (N = 8, 4 and 6; see n.56 above). These small discrepancies may be due to sampling error.

those at Rome.[58] From Walker's readings of fineness, the three Julio-Claudian reigns have a coefficient of variation of about 20%, rising drastically by the time of Marcus Aurelius, when the figure approached 40% (fig. 15.11). At Rome by comparison, the coefficient of variation for silver fineness was about 1% under the Julio-Claudians, and a mere 7% under Marcus Aurelius.[59]

6. CHANGE IN THE BRONZE COINAGE

The base-metal coinage, generically called bronze, primarily consisted of sestertii and dupondii (half-sestertii) struck from orichalcum, together with asses (quarter-sestertii) and quadrantes (quarter-asses) struck from copper.[60] Pliny describes orichalcum as a blend of copper and 'cadmea', evidently a form of zinc, which modern analyses show as the main secondary ingredient of

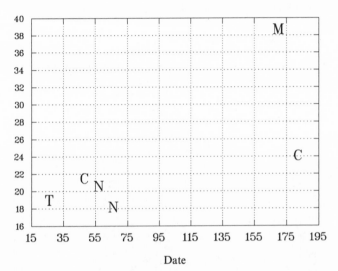

Figure 15.11 Percentage coefficient of variation in fineness of the Alexandrian tetra-drachm, AD 14–190: six samples from five selected reigns. (Emperors: Tiberius, Claudius, Nero 1, Nero 2, Marcus Aurelius, Commodus.)

---

[58] But limitations in the effectiveness of Walker's non-destructive analyses in assessing coins with low silver-content (n.46 above) may affect these findings. Even greater deviations are seen in Tiberian coin in the hoard examined in Milne 1910, whose weights seem aberrant by large amounts.

[59] See Table 15.5. For weight, the Egyptian coefficient of variation is much lower, 4 or 5% under the Julio-Claudians, and 11–17% under Marcus and Commodus (from Walker's specimens).

[60] For asses, see Caley 1964, 97, Table 54. The half-as (semis) and quarter-as (quadrans) were sometimes struck from orichalcum and sometimes (to a higher weight) from copper. Under Nero the orichalcum versions had a significantly lower percentage of zinc than the sestertius (Carter, King 1988, 106, Table 5).

Table 15.11 *Mean zinc percentage in orichalcum coin (sestertii and dupondii)*

Emperor	Mean zinc percentage	Sample
1. Augustus	22.8	10
2. Claudius	20.4	8
3. Nero	15.7	6
4. Galba	19.6	12
5. Vespasian	18.6	94
6. Titus	16.4	40
7. Domitian	15.7	68
8. Nerva	15.3	52
9. Trajan	14.5	355
10. Hadrian	13.0	281
11. A. Pius	12.4	56
12. M. Aurelius	7.0	21
13. Commodus	3.4	11

Note: Figures based on summary analyses of Garonne hoard (Etienne 1984, 378; lines 4–11); and Riederer 1977, 80–81 (lines 1–3, 12–13). Figures from the small Riederer samples in lines 1–3 are approximate: his parallel results for later reigns do not follow the big Garonne sample closely.

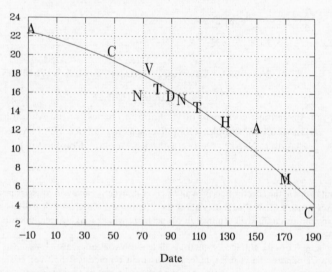

Figure 15.12 Percentage of zinc in orichalcum sestertius coin: twelve selected reigns, 31 BC–AD 192. (Emperors: Augustus, Claudius, Nero, Vespasian, Titus, Domitian, Nerva, Trajan, Hadrian, Antoninus Pius, Marcus Aurelius, Commodus.)

orichalcum coin.[61] This compound required additional smelting processes. The large samples of orichalcum coinage from the Garonne hoard, with smaller museum samples for outlying reigns show that zinc content steadily declined. The pattern is similar in essentials to that for silver coin, with a turning-point under Nero, although the decline is faster for bronze (Table 15.11 and fig. 15.12). Caley suggested that this was partly a snowball effect due to loss of perhaps 10% of the zinc content each time that existing coin was reminted.[62] But reminting would have to be very frequent for this explanation to work. Progressive shortage of zinc is much more likely, especially when the parallel decline in sestertius weight explicitly suggests metal shortage. Sestertius hoards imply target-weights of $11\frac{1}{2}$ to the pound under Claudius, 12 under Vespasian (reflecting a reduction by Nero), $12\frac{1}{4}$ by the middle of Hadrian's reign, $12\frac{1}{2}$ and 12.8 under Antoninus Pius, 13.3 under Marcus Aurelius, and $17\frac{1}{4}$ under Commodus.[63]

[61] Caley 1964, 92–3.   [62] Caley 1964, 99–100.   [63] See p. 189.

16

CONTRAST AND VARIATION IN THE COINAGE

One of the ways in which Roman coinage contrasts most obviously with an industrially produced coinage is its wide variation in weight and metallic composition. Much of this is due to the inherent limitations of Roman techniques of fabrication and production. But there are also some systematic effects which have a wider interest.

1. SILVER FINENESS AND COIN-OUTPUT

The accession of a new Emperor brought pressures to produce new coin in substantial amounts as fast as possible. That is probably why silver fineness tended to sag at the start of a reign. This effect is noticeable at the beginning of several reigns (Table 16.1).

In five of the seven major reigns from Vespasian to Commodus, fineness fell at the accession of the new ruler, and then recovered again later in his reign.[1] This is both a reflection of spending pressures at the start of the reign, and an

Table 16.1 *Comparisons of median fineness before and after accession issues*

Emperor	Date (AD)	Fineness compared with previous issue-period (%)	Fineness compared with next issue-period (%)
Vespasian	69–72	96.2	97.3
Domitian	81–2	98.9	93.5
Trajan	98–9	100.3	100.9
Hadrian	117–18	98.3	98.3
A. Pius	138–9	97.8	99.7
Marcus	161–4	89.6	96.9
Commodus	180–3	95.5	100.7

Note: For fuller information, see Tables 15.7–15.9.

---

[1] The retrospective comparison for Vespasian is with late Neronian coin, and for Domitian with coin of Titus.

Table 16.2 *Fineness and denarius-output under Severus Alexander*

Period (AD)	Coins at Reka Devnia	Coins per year	Median fineness	Fineness sample
222–4	2,269	825	42.75	56
225–7	2,460	820	42.0	55
228–30	1,586	529	47.0	53
231–5	1,181	281	49.0	43

Note: Totals from Reka Devnia by issue and year from *BMCRE* 6.43–83. Fineness data from lists in Walker.

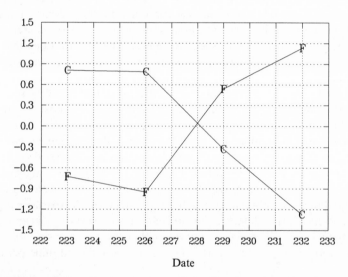

Figure 16.1 Percentage of coin per year at Reka Devnia and median denarius fineness for four periods in the reign of Severus Alexander (standardised values). (C: coin; F: fineness.)

acknowledgement that the mint habitually stretched the available silver when working under pressure. Under Commodus fineness duly fell, but it failed to improve again later in the reign, presumably because of silver shortage. The lowering of aureus-weight by short-lived claimants to the throne such as Didius Julianus and Pescennius Niger expressed the same need to mint more coin than the available supplies of precious metal allowed.[2]

The monetary environment had changed radically by the time of the Severi, and the early issues of Severus, Caracalla and Severus Alexander show no such dip in fineness. Possibly heavy debasement now made standards less

[2] For deviations in the aureus to c.6.80 grams under Julianus and c.6.74 under Niger, see Bland, Burnett, Bendall 1987, 75.

vulnerable. Nevertheless, this period displays another important interrelation between fineness and coin-output. Denarius output declined in successive stages under Severus Alexander, to judge from the large sample at Reka Devnia. The decline was accompanied by significant rises in fineness (Table 16.2). The resulting pattern is shown in fig. 16.1, based on standardised values.

2. MINTING VARIATIONS

2.1. VARIATIONS BETWEEN CONTEMPORARY COIN MINTED FOR DIFFERENT INDIVIDUALS

Although the coin of a given reign is conventionally treated as a single unit even when parts of it were struck for different individuals, analysis of subdivisions where they exist sometimes reveals substantive differences. The differences are normally too slight to indicate major variations in minting policy. But they certainly suggest divisions within the production process, and presumably a division between minting authorities.

The first reign to have major subdivisions is that of Vespasian, with extensive minting for his sons Titus and Domitian for most of the reign. Differences in denarius-weight in this period are summarised in Table 16.3. In almost all cases, the coin of Titus and Domitian is slightly heavier than that of Vespasian. Some of Vespasian's coin was produced in AD 69–72, before minting for Titus and Domitian began. Potentially, this might allow a chronological explanation. But in reality the large samples from La Magura show no difference between the weight of coin struck for Vespasian early in his reign and that struck later on (the median in both cases is 3.11 grams).

Contemporary differences in minting policy are also suggested by figures for fineness.[3] Discrepancies certainly exist in the mid-Antonine period. On

Table 16.3 *Differences in median denarius-weight (in grams) under Vespasian*

| Hoard (date) | Excess over weight of coin of Vespasian (%) | | Titus (N) | Domitian (N) | Vespasian (N) |
	Titus	Domitian			
Magura (196)	+1.3	+2.8	3.15 (30)	3.20 (39)	3.11 (260)
Puriceni (194/5)	+3.3	+3.5	3.10 (12)	3.105 (16)	3.00 (136)
Beck Row (80/5)	+2.4	+3.6	3.40 (7)	3.44 (7)	3.32 (90)
Londonthorpe (153/4)	+1.6	+3.5	3.18 (6)	3.24 (6)	3.13 (24)
L. Brickhill (187)	−4.3	+1.6	2.92 (5)	3.10 (10)	3.05 (69)
Bletchley (183)	+2.6		3.14 (9)		3.06 (29)

[3] Although Walker does not identify coin by individual, identifications can be made from his catalogue numbers.

Table 16.4 *Contemporary differences in median denarius fineness, AD 157–69*

Date	A. Pius (N)	M. Aurelius (N)	L. Verus (N)	Shortfall in Marcus silver content (%)
157–61	86.5 (34)	76.5 (11)	—	−11.6
161–4	—	77.5 (42)	83.0 (20)	−6.4
165–9	—	80.0 (35)	82.0 (32)	−2.4

Note: From Walker's fineness readings.

Table 16.5 *Differences in median denarius-weight (in grams), AD 176–80*

Hoard	Shortfall in coin of Commodus (%)	Marcus (N)	Commodus (N)
La Magura	−2.5	3.28 (19)	3.20 (15)
Viuz Faverges	−3.1	3.335 (14)	3.255 (12)

median average, the denarii struck for Marcus Aurelius between AD 157 and 169 are noticeably more debased than the denarii of Antoninus Pius struck while Marcus was still heir, and more debased than the denarii of Lucius Verus struck after Marcus and Verus had become joint-Emperors. The direction of the differences is consistent, arguing against random variation (Table 16.4).

Later in Marcus's reign, differences in fineness apparently recede, and Walker's data for AD 176–80 show the same median fineness for Marcus and for Commodus (78.5%, N = 29 and 23). But at this point, weight variation apparently took over as the significant variable. Hoard samples suggest differences in median weight between Marcus and Commodus of approximately the order seen under Vespasian (Table 16.5).[4] Here the 'non-Emperor' coin is the lighter of the two.

It is striking that Commodus's lighter denarii in the 170s anticipate his reductions in denarius-weight as Emperor, which were the most important of the whole period (Table 15.5). Equally striking is the fact that the heavier denarii of Titus and Domitian produced in AD 73–9 (Table 16.3) anticipated the increases in denarius-weight made when they were Emperors (Table 15.5).

Divisions in minting authority seem to be suggested here. Although the

---

[4] In the corresponding British Museum samples, a differential is still seen, though smaller than in the hoard samples; the weights show that the British Museum coins are considerably more worn. The median weights are: Commodus 3.16, and Marcus 3.18 (N = 51 and 71).

extant literary tradition offers few clues, a detail in Suetonius apparently assumes divided financial responsibility. He states that when Vespasian had been succeeded by Titus, Domitian (though not himself Emperor) debated at length whether to give a double donative to the soldiers.[5]

2.2. THE RELATIONSHIP BETWEEN FINENESS AND WEIGHT

Walker's data allow weight and fineness to be compared. In any large sample of denarii, weight is inevitably affected by wear, and Walker's second-century specimens show noticeable signs of wear. Although this may blur certain comparisons, their validity as a whole would be undermined only if finer coin was systematically more worn, or vice-versa. But such systematic effects remain unlikely.

Tests of Walker's samples reveal that finer specimens in some coin-issues

Table 16.6 *Comparisons between denarius-weight and fineness: median weight of less fine specimens as a percentage of median weight of finer specimens*

Issue period (AD)	Percentage difference	Correlation (r) between weight and fineness
Nero, 64–8	−3.1%	−0.11
Vespasian, 69–74	+3.8	−0.31
Vespasian, 75–9	+4.1	−0.23
Titus, 79–81	0.0	−0.15
Domitian, 81–2	+3.5	−0.04
Domitian, 85–96	+1.9	−0.22
Nerva, 96–8	+0.2	−0.06
Trajan, 98–102	−2.9	−0.05
Trajan, 112–17	+5.8	−0.50
A. Pius, 149–56	+4.8	−0.34
Commodus, 180–6	+4.8	−0.11
Severus, 198–201	+8.0	−0.25
Elagabalus, 218–22	+25.3	−0.22
S. Alexander, 222–35	+1.4	−0.07

Note: Based on Rome coin struck for the Emperor; samples from Walker. Samples were sorted by fineness, then bisected to give a median weight for finer coin and a median for less fine coin. For coin-totals, see Tables 15.7–15.9.

[5] *Dom.* 2.3.

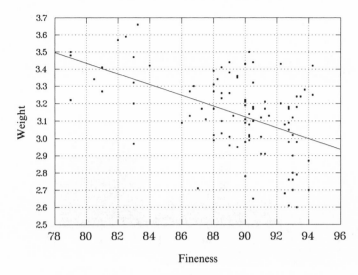

Figure 16.2 Coin-weight (in grams) and percentage fineness in Walker's denarius sample, AD 112–17.

tend to show lower average weight than less fine specimens. Fourteen samples were examined, with the results shown in Table 16.6. The ratio of fineness to weight is unstable in the early period, and it is lowest when overall fineness is high (Nero, Titus, Nerva). But in the century after Trajan's reform of AD 107, the samples show that, on median average, less fine coin weighs about 5% more than finer coin. Figure 16.2 shows an example based on Trajan's coinage in the last five years of his reign (n = 100).

Although this effect is present in most of the samples examined, its meaning remains unclear. If alloy weighed more than silver, that would provide a possible explanation. But the copper mainly used for alloy differed little in specific gravity from silver. If weight was the determining factor, the inverse relationship would presuppose some mechanism which partly compensated for lesser fineness by heavier weight. But on average, heavier specimens still contain more silver than lighter specimens, despite the inverse effect. This, together with the degree of dispersal in fig. 16.2, may argue against there being any deliberate policy. The effect appears to be a by-product of specific metallurgical procedures, which was not necessarily intended.[6]

2.3. PLURAL STANDARDS OF FINENESS

Analysis of Walker's large samples reveals some significant peculiarities of minting practice at Rome.[7] The dispersal seen in the readings of fineness under

[6] Controls on Walker's readings using other techniques remain highly desirable.
[7] Although Walker's samples are many times larger than those in any other published study of fineness, they are usually still too small to sustain reliable year-by-year analyses. His data normally need to be aggregated into larger time-units, as has been done here where possible.

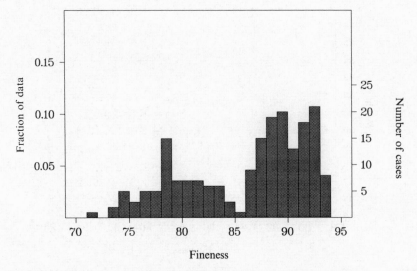

Figure 16.3 Percentage fineness of denarii struck for the Emperor under Antoninus
Pius.

Vespasian and from Trajan onwards grew under the Antonine emperors
(Table 15.5). By the time of Antoninus Pius, the pattern of fineness was
actually bimodal. Part of the denarius output was produced at relatively high
fineness, and part at lower fineness, with a distinct trough between the two (fig.
16.3).

This pattern seems to result from there being different standards in
simultaneous use, rather than oscillation between one year and the next.[8] If
the mint was producing coin at more than one level of fineness, was this
deliberate policy or accident? If deliberate, it might almost suggest a two-tier
system under which better coin went to more privileged recipients. However, if
differences could not readily be detected by eye, that explanation becomes
unconvincing.[9] Other explanations are purely technical. If some workshops
within the mint received less silver, without corresponding reductions in their
production quota, that could lead to some coin being produced at lower
fineness. Alternatively, if some of the raw material was debased coin, and
some of it new bullion, differences in fineness would result, whatever the level
of current debasement.[10] In this context, a limited technical explanation seems
the most likely.

[8] Walker's year-by-year analyses (see n.7) suggest some clusters of high and low fineness within
single years under Antoninus Pius (Walker, 2.50–2).
[9] Compare Kolendo 1980, 170.
[10] This would depend however on the recycled coin being relatively recent. The hypothesis could
perhaps be pursued by full analysis of the composition of less fine coin.

3. UNDERWEIGHT SILVER HOARDS

Analysis of denarius hoards of the second and third centuries shows that in most reigns up to AD 180 coin followed a regularly graded pattern of weight-loss.[11] Linear regressions based on these hoards normally predict unity, in other words zero coin-wear, at dates close to the latest coin in the hoard.

But some hoards show significantly lower coin-weights, in which even the latest coin-groups are well below target. Three 'underweight' hoards come from Egypt (end-date 114/17, N = 265 denarii), La Puriceni in Romania (end-date 194/5, N = 1,157), and Drzewicz Nowy in Poland (final coin 217/18, but main contents end c.192; N = 1,263).[12] In Tables 16.7–16.9 these are compared with other more typical hoards.

Table 16.7 *Egypt (114/17) compared with Londonthorpe (153/4)*

Reign	Londonthorpe			Egypt			Weight-difference (%)
	Median	CVar	N	Median	CVar	N	
Vespasian	3.14	3.1	41	2.86	6.8	23	−8.9
Domitian, 85–96	3.24	4.8	44	3.24	5.1	57	—
Nerva	3.26	4.8	16	3.275	5.0	24	+0.5
Trajan	3.20	5.7	121	2.92	7.1	131	−8.8

Note: CVar = percentage coefficient of variation.

Table 16.8 *Drzewicz Nowy compared with Viuz-Faverges*

Reign	Viuz-Faverges			Drzewicz Nowy			Weight-difference (%)
	Median	CVar	N	Median	CVar	N	
Vespasian	3.085	2.8	24	2.55	7.4	25	−17.5
Trajan	3.22	3.8	62	2.69	9.0	101	−16.3
Hadrian	3.21	5.5	93	2.695	8.6	165	−16.0
A. Pius	3.25	6.3	118	2.70	9.6	178	−16.9
M. Aurelius	3.31	5.7	107	2.73	9.8	121	−17.5
Commodus	3.02	12.8	90	2.455	16.6	80	−18.7

Note: CVar = percentage coefficient of variation.

The most striking difference is seen in Table 16.8. At Drzewicz the coin minted for the Emperor in six major reigns is at least 16% lighter on median average than the corresponding coin at Viuz-Faverges. The shortfall ranges

[11] See pp. 185–6
[12] The Egypt hoard of 300 coins in all (Egypt 1) also contains eastern silver which is excluded from this analysis.

Table 16.9 *La Puriceni (194/5) compared with La Magura (196)*

	La Magura			La Puriceni			Weight-
Reign	Median	CVar	N	Median	CVar	N	difference (%)
Vespasian	3.11	4.3	260	3.0	4.2	136	−3.5
Titus	3.20	2.8	45	3.11	3.1	24	−2.8
Domitian, 85–96	3.29	6.0	78	3.165	6.4	38	−3.8
Trajan	3.19	5.3	621	3.16	6.0	198	−0.9
Hadrian	3.21	5.3	527	3.17	6.5	178	−1.2
A. Pius	3.265	6.5	242	3.11	7.9	140	−4.7
M. Aurelius	3.30	5.6	134	3.19	6.0	72	−3.3
Commodus	3.05	12.4	53	2.87	10.7	24	−5.9

Note: CVar = percentage coefficient of variation.

from 16% for Hadrian to 18.7% for Commodus.[13] It is difficult to account for most of this by wear. There is some graduation of weight between the earliest and the latest coin present in bulk, corresponding to different periods of circulation. The weight gradations can be turned into a linear regression over time.[14] But the regression would take more than three centuries to reach the expected target weight of 3.36 grams (it predicts unity or zero weight-loss in AD 535). The end-date projected in the Puriceni hoard is lower (AD 279) but is still quite unrealistic in view of its actual end-date.[15] Thus second-century wear does not explain the low weights at Drzewicz. And it is unlikely that the coin remained in circulation for several centuries longer, when the latest coin belongs to the early third century.[16]

In these hoards, weights are abnormally low, and this probably has an artificial origin. The samples may be the product of selection, and not ordinary samples of coin subjected to drastically heavy wear. But selection of coin for low weight by private owners is difficult to explain. If hoards of the Principate were mainly army payments, as argued in chapters 5 and 6, the

[13] About 25% of the hoard seems to have disappeared (Krzyzanowska 1976, 85). But even if, for the sake of argument, that missing 25% were entirely made up of heavy specimens, the median weights would be only slightly higher, and the strong contrast with Viuz-Faverges and other 'normal' hoards would still remain.

[14] Regression based on Drzewicz median weights for Vespasian/Trajan/Hadrian/Antoninus.Pius/ Marcus Aurelius: intercept 2.46186, slope 0.0016757, r² = 0.783.

[15] Regression based on Puriceni median weights: intercept 2.9337, slope 0.001526, r² = 0.554.

[16] For hoards outside the empire whose low weight has been ascribed to prolonged circulation, see for example Lind 1988, 209–10. 6,000 out of 7,000 denarii found in Sweden come from the island of Gotland. Most date from between Nero and Commodus. The latest coins are said to be as worn as the earliest; mean weights in the big Hemse hoard are: pre-Trajan 2.83, Trajan 2.83, Hadrian 2.83, Antoninus Pius 2.85, Marcus Aurelius 2.84, Commodus 2.65, post-192, 2.84. Lind suggests that the hoards represent barbarian subsidies paid after AD 200; but other possibilities should not be excluded (see pp. 92–4 above).

low-weight hoards must look like payments in short measure.[17] Possibly the soldier sometimes received less silver than he was entitled to.[18]

In the other hoard comparisons, contrasts are less extreme. The comparison between Puriceni and Magura shows shortfalls of 3–4% with extremes of 0.9% and 5.9%. The comparison between Egypt and Londonthorpe shows a difference of 8% in the reigns of Vespasian and Trajan, but virtual parity in the intervening reigns of Domitian and Nerva (though the underweight Trajanic denarii in Egypt are almost in mint condition).[19] Similarly the weight-difference between Puriceni and Magura falls to 1% or less in two adjacent reigns (Trajan and Hadrian) before it rises again.

Shifting chronological differences of this kind suggest either inefficient sorting for low weight, or pockets of less heavy coin of a certain date within the circulating medium as a whole. Underweight coin was evidently circulating alongside normal coin in the same region. The Puriceni–Magura contrast from across the Dacian frontier is one example. Another is a difference between two Flavian hoards in Britain. At Beck Row, coin struck for Vespasian has a median weight of 3.32 grams, but in the contemporary hoard from Howe, the figure is only 2.96 grams, a shortfall of 11%.[20]

More samples and further study are needed to clarify these questions. But manipulated differences seem likely. Occasional minor fraud within the army is an obvious possibility. But the reign-to-reign variation seen in Table 16.7 also raises the possibility of more general manipulation behind the despatch of particular blocs of coin.[21]

---

[17] See p. 82 n.43.

[18] The Drzewicz hoard comes from outside the empire, and is potentially one of the payments to foreign soldiers discussed on p. 94. The descriptions of this hoard suggest that some of its contents are specimens of very poor quality. In the Egypt hoard on the other hand, the underweight Trajanic denarii are described as being 'in brilliant condition, showing little, if any evidence of circulation' (Appendix 10 no.107).

[19] See previous note. For other Egyptian evidence, note the eccentric hoard of Tiberian tetradrachms described by Milne 1910, whose weights range from 5.54 to 13.52 grams, with some concentration at 7–7.5 grams.

[20] For underweight hoards, see also the denarius hoard from Rinteln (N = 243) ending under Marcus Aurelius (Berger 1990, 220 ff.).

[21] Part of the sample comes from outside the empire (Drzewicz Nowy, La Puriceni); some foreign recruits may have fared worse than those at home. It is worth noticing that solidi used in Byzantine contacts with western Europe and Russia in the sixth and seventh centuries were often lightweight (Hendy 1985, 262; Adelson 1957, 78–103).

APPENDIXES

APPENDIX 1. PAYMENTS OF *CONGIARIA*

1. MODULES

Most known *congiaria* in our period could have been paid in gold coin alone. Typical amounts are HS300, 400 or 600, equalling 3, 4 or 6 aurei. All known payments in the period AD 37–180 share this format.[1] When Marcus Aurelius returned to Rome for a triumph in 177, citizens held up eight fingers to show that they wanted 8 aurei this time.[2]

But there are also periods with a different pattern. From 5 BC to AD 23 most *congiarium* amounts do not equal totals in aurei.[3] And much later, Dio's figure of HS560 (140 drachmas) under Commodus could not have been fully paid in aurei. Any coincidence with periods when little gold was being minted may not be completely accidental.[4]

2. THE SCALE OF SPENDING

For most of the first-century distributions, *congiarium* amounts are indicated by the main literary sources.[5] From Trajan onwards, most reign-totals have to be estimated by extrapolation from surviving co-ordinates. The results are inevitably schematic. The number of *congiaria* per reign in this period is usually shown by coin-legends.[6] The one continuous source, the Chronographer of the year 354, is late and erratic.[7]

Its totals for all the Julio-Claudian Emperors save Nero are understated (Table A.1, final column). The figures for the last three principal reigns also appear too low. The totals for Trajan, Hadrian and Marcus Aurelius appear

---

[1] Listed by Barbieri.
[2] Dio 71.32.1; Barbieri, 853. In the same popular idiom, the Emperor Claudius held up fingers to show how many aurei an arena performance was worth (Suet. *Claud.* 21.5). According to Dio, Marcus paid 200 drachmas (denarii) on this occasion, instead of the gold coins asked for.
[3] Van Berchem 1939, 144–6.
[4] New gold appears to have been scarce from the late 160s onwards (p.132 n.23, and see n.2 above).
[5] See evidence cited by Van Berchem 1939, 141–61; Barbieri reproduces the material more fully
[6] See Barbieri, with careful discussion of numismatic sources which appear to include some forgeries.
[7] T. Mommsen (ed.) *Chron. Min.* 1, 1892, 145–7 (*MGH* 9). For contrasting aspects of this source, cf. Salzman 1990.

Table A.1 *Spending on congiaria, 31 BC–AD 235*
(money amounts in sesterces)

Reign	Congiaria distribution	Per capita cost per reign (estimated)	Per capita cost per reign-year	Total cost per reign-year (million)	Chronographer per capita cost per reign
Augustus	5	1,680	37	9	1,450
Tiberius	4	1,040	45	7	290
Claudius	2	600	44	7	300
Nero	1	400	29	4	400
Vespasian	1	300	32	5	300
Domitian	3	900	60	9	900
Trajan	3	1,500	77	12	2,600
Hadrian	7	3,000	147	22	4,000
A. Pius	9	3,300	146	22	3,200
Marcus	7	3,200	168	25	5,000
Commodus	6	3,360	263	39	3,400
Septimius	6	4,000	226	41	4,400
Caracalla	4	2,400	388	70	1,600
Elagabalus	4	2,400	630	113	1,000
S. Alexander	5	3,000	231	42	2,400
Short reigns					
Caligula	2	600	176	26	290
Nerva	1	(300)	200	30	300
Pertinax	1	400	—	—	600
Macrinus	1	600	513	92	600

Note: For references, see Van Berchem 1939 and Barbieri. For explanation of estimated amounts in the second column, see text below. Figures in the final column are from the Chronographer of the year 354 (n.7 above). The total number of recipients is taken to be 150,000 from AD 14 to 192 (cf. Van Berchem 1939, 29). *Res Gestae* 15 indicates more recipients under Augustus. After AD 192, the total is taken as approximately 180,000 (Dio 76.1.1).

to be seriously exaggerated. Totals for Domitian and for three reigns with one *congiarium* each appear to be correct (Nero, Vespasian, Macrinus), and figures for Antoninus Pius, Commodus and Septimius Severus are approximately correct.

ESTIMATES

TRAJAN. The Chronographer gives a total of HS2,600 for the three distributions of the reign. But Domitian, Hadrian and probably Nerva used a module of HS300 per distribution, and even if the *congiaria* for Trajan's two triumphs paid double, as is possible, the suggested total would not be more than HS1,500.

ANTONINUS PIUS. Pius paid HS400 at his fourth *congiarium* in 145 (*Fasti Ostienses*), but cannot have paid at this rate throughout the reign if the Chronographer is approximately right. His figure of HS3,200 is almost met if the rate is taken to be HS400 from AD145 and HS300 before that date (the result is HS3,300).

HADRIAN.   If the module of HS400 did not become regular until the 140s, Hadrian's module is presumably HS300 throughout the reign, as at the start (*HA*). A reconstruction can then be three double *congiaria* of HS600 (the second, which is 'duplex' in the *HA*, and the two heir-adoptions at the end of the reign) and four normal *congiaria* of HS300, making a total of HS3,000.

MARCUS AURELIUS.   The Chronographer's HS1,600 for the first four *congiaria* suggests a rate of HS400 continuing from the reign of Antoninus Pius. The seventh was HS800 (Dio). The presumed total for seven occasions is HS3,200.

COMMODUS.   Dio gives the rate of his *congiaria* as HS560. Seven payments at this rate cost HS3,360, close to the Chronographer's figure of HS3,400.

SEPTIMIUS SEVERUS.   The third *congiarium*, paid in 202 for the *decennalia*, was HS1,000 (Dio). The standard module was presumably either HS560 as under Commodus, or the figure of HS600 known under Macrinus and Elagabalus. If HS600, the reign-total would be HS4,000.

CARACALLA.   Probably likewise HS600, making the reign-total HS2,400.

ELAGABALUS.   The second *congiarium* was HS600 (Dio), again implying a reign-total of HS2,400 if maintained.

SEVERUS ALEXANDER.   Presumably still HS600, suggesting a reign-total of HS3,000.

The last three reconstructed figures are substantially more than the Chronographer's totals (Table A.1), and they result in unparalleled levels of *congiarium* spending under Caracalla and Elagabalus. Clearly they cannot be pressed hard in the absence of comprehensive evidence. But there are distinct arguments in their favour: (1) The Chronographer's figure of HS1,000 for the four payments by Elagabalus is virtually overturned by Dio's contemporary figure of HS600 for his second payment alone, which is in keeping with the other evidence for this period. And (2) the frequency of *congiaria* certainly increased sharply under Caracalla and Elagabalus (see fig. 5.10), and it is rather unlikely that this was accompanied by a sharp drop in amounts, as the Chronographer's totals would imply.

APPENDIX 2.   THE CHRONOLOGY OF MINTING
UNDER TIBERIUS

The main gold- and silver-output of Tiberius after AD 16 lacks explicit dating. But the gold quinarii are dated, and Giard used them to establish a general chronology of obverse types for the PONTIF MAXIM issues, from which undated gold- and silver types can be assigned by period (thus for gold, see Sutherland 1987B). Giard's typology dates 47% of denarii of the reign to c.AD 31–6, and 31% to c.AD 36–7, in the sample of 101 denarii of Tiberius from the Woodham

Mortimer hoard. Corresponding figures for the Sutton hoard with 51 denarii of Tiberius are 56% and 24%. Both hoards suggest that about four-fifths of denarii struck under Tiberius belonged to the last six or seven years of his reign. In the 36 denarii in the Membury hoard, the proportion of late denarii is even higher: 25 or 70% belong to Giard 4 = *BMCRE* 48 of c.31–6 (Giard 1983, 114 ff.).

For aurei the pattern is somewhat different. Dated by the same means, their absolute peak occurs early, in AD 14–16, with 37% of the coin of the reign, in the sample of 150 illustrated specimens assembled by Giard from all available sources; 23% belong to c.31–6 and 17% to c.36–7. Nevertheless, as a proportion of coin struck between AD 17 and March 37, the gold total in the last 6–7 years is as high as 55%, compared with the 78–80% for denarii (there being no denarii in AD 14–16).

RATIOS BETWEEN EARLY AND LATE COIN-OUTPUT OF TIBERIUS

Taking the end of AD 30 as the junction-point between Giard 3 (c.28–31) and Giard 4 (c.31–6), in the combined denarius samples from Woodham Mortimer and Sutton for AD 17–March 37 (N = 152), 22.4% or 1.6% per year fall in AD 17–30, and 77.6% or 12.5% per year in AD 31–7; the ratio is 7.8 ($\frac{12.5}{1.6}$). In the Giard aureus-sample for the same period (N = 94), 44.7% or 3.2% per year fall in AD 17–30, and 55.3% or 8.9% per year in AD 31–7; the ratio is 2.8 ($\frac{8.9}{3.2}$).

APPENDIX 3.   VARIATIONS IN LAND-TAX IN EGYPT

Looked at in detail, the amount of tax a given piece of land paid in Egypt could be affected by a number of different variables. The most important of these, juridical status, is discussed in chapter 4 (pp. 47–8). Further elements were the agricultural quality of the land, its production-category, and its irrigation-status.

1.   DIFFERENCES DEPENDING ON LAND-QUALITY

Explicit tax-rates for ousiac or estate land ranged from $5\frac{1}{16}$ artabas per aroura to $7\frac{11}{18}$, with no less than 12 intermediate rates, in an early second-century document from the Hermopolite nome.[8] In the Oxyrhynchite nome, a Hadrianic document shows a range for ousiac land from $4\frac{1}{4}$ to $5\frac{7}{25}$, with 9 intermediate rates.[9] These documents also suggest some noticeable regional variation: their median rates for ousiac land are 6.67 (Hermopolite) and 4.78 (Oxyrhynchite), a ratio of 7:5.

[8] *PRyl* 207; Johnson, 504n.
[9] *POxy* 986, AD 131/2; Johnson, 504n.

2. TAX DIFFERENCES BY PRODUCTION–CATEGORY AND LAND-TYPE

The very full land-register for the village of Hiera Nesos in the Arsinoite nome in AD 167 (*PBour* 42) illustrates the effects of how land was watered on how much tax it paid, and different tax-rates for different types of land. The total area described is more than 12,000 arouras, about 34 square kilometres. Land classified as sown (*sporimos*) paid aggregate tax at an average of 4.43 artabas per aroura. Land classified as unflooded (*abrochos*) paid 4.25 artabas per aroura. Thus *sporimos* paid more tax than *abrochos*. The aggregate figures are summarised in Table A.2. The distribution of land-types by watering category shows a clear-cut pattern. Most of the private land (*idiotike*) is *sporimos*, whereas most public land is in the less productive category of *abrochos* (Table A.3).

Table A.2 *Hiera Nesos: tax-rates by production-status and juridical type* (figures in artabas)

	Ousiac	Basilikos	Prosodikos	Idiotike
Sporimos	4.77	6.11	5.80	1.03
Abrochos	3.64	4.99	8.71	1.06

Source: *PBour* 42.

Table A.3 *Hiera Nesos: land-area by production-status and juridical type (%)*

	Ousiac	Basilikos	Prosodikos	Idiotikē	Aggregate
Sporimos	34.7	14.2	30.7	81.5	36.8
Abrochos	65.3	85.8	69.3	18.5	63.2

Source: *PBour* 42.

In Table A.2, sown land (*sporimos*) pays 20–5% more tax than *abrochos* if the land is estate (ousiac) or royal (*basilikos*). Only *prosodikos* or revenue land shows a significant difference the other way; but this category is usually rare, and makes up only a small fraction of the land at Hiera Nesos (5.5%).

3. IRRIGATION-STATUS

Arable land essentially fell into one of three categories: (1) flooded; (2) unflooded but productive; and (3) unflooded and unproductive.[10] Flooded

---

[10] See Westermann 1920–2; Bonneau 1979.

land was called *bebregmenē*, unflooded *abrochos*, and land which was dry (though not by definition unproductive) *chersos*. One early document lays down that the farmers were to leave no field untilled whether unflooded or flooded.[11] But in the Diocletianic tax-lists from Karanis, land which is *abrochos* is also described more graphically as *asporos*, unsown.[12]

Land which was cultivated and taxable in the normal way could be described generically as *homologos*. Land which was uncultivated and outside current tax assessment was called *hypologos*. An Oxyrhynchite tax-schedule of the early third century explains that revision of royal land which is *aphoros* (not tax-yielding) takes place every 3 years, such land being called *hypologos*.[13]

Westermann's short dossier showed land which was unflooded, *abrochos*, as paying *more* than flooded land in the same place. For private land and royal land, the excess amounts are quite small, 6.4%, and 1.66%.[14] For diocesan and ousiac land the excess is 26.4%.[15] Here land which was artificially irrigated pays more tax than land fertilised by the Nile flood.[16] To explain this, Westermann maintained that land with a higher labour-input was taxed more heavily to make the taxpayer cultivate more effectively and produce more from land of this type.

But any such discrimination would have meant that the government conceded revenue on flooded land, a contradiction which Westermann did not resolve. His theory is undermined in any case by substantial evidence which shows an opposite difference. At Hiera Nesos in AD 167, ousiac land paid at a rate 31% higher if sown, *sporimos*, than if unflooded, *abrochos*; and royal land at a rate 22% higher (Table A.2).[17] Only in one minor category, *prosodikos*, is there a big difference the other way (−33%); and for private land, as in Westermann's data, the variant is insignificant (−3%).

APPENDIX 4. ASSESSMENTS OF TAX-REVENUE IN THE SOURCES

The provinces. Plutarch's report of figures published at Pompey's triumph indicates a figure of HS200 million for provincial revenues (*telai*) before Pompey's eastern conquests, and HS340 million after those conquests (*Pompey* 45).[18]

---

[11] *PLond* 256e, Fayum AD 11; Johnson, no. 291, p. 461.   [12] *PCair* Isid 11.
[13] *POxy* 2847.   [14] *PBrux* 1.
[15] *BGU* 84, AD 242/3, from Pelusium in the Arsinoite. Westermann 1921, 172–3.
[16] Cf. Wallace 1938, 358 n.36.
[17] Westermann 1921, 172–4. Wallace (1938, 358) and others who have criticised Westermann's finding seem to have done so without knowing the tax-rates for each production-category at Hiera Nesos (not shown in the summary in *PBour* 42); cf. also El Sayed, El-Ghany 1988.
[18] Cf. Jones 1974, 119, suggesting that the revenues from Sicily, being mainly in kind, may be missing. The different interpretation of Plutarch's figure by Meijer 1990, 18 and others is unconvincing.

Egypt. There are four assessments of total revenue:

1. HS355 million (14,800 talents) and $1\frac{1}{2}$ million artabas of wheat under Ptolemy Philadelphus: Jerome *ad Dan.* 11.5.
2. HS300 million (12,500 talents) under Ptolemy Auletes: Cicero cited by Strabo 17.1.13.
3. HS144 million (6,000 talents), presumably under Ptolemy Auletes: Diodorus 17.52.
4. Twelve times the revenue of Roman Palestine: a speech in Josephus *BJ* 2.386.

The hierarchy between Jerome's figure for Philadelphus and Cicero's total for Auletes is probably plausible. Cicero's evidence is that of a contemporary, but 300 million is a conventional amount which need not have precise meaning (see pp. 16–17 above).[19] A detailed calculation for the Roman period suggests a somewhat lower figure (p. 53 above). The low figure from Diodorus can probably be discounted. Josephus's figure belongs to a rhetorical context. It is very high, making the revenue about HS600 million if Josephus's explicit total for Palestine is accepted (see below).

Gaul. The figure given for the *stipendium* that Caesar imposed on Tres Galliae is HS40 million (Suet. *Iul.* 25). Velleius's claim that Egypt's revenues were slightly less than those from Gaul unconvincingly conflicts with this, though it should include the wealthy Narbonensis as well (2.39; for Narbonensis, cf. Duncan-Jones 1980).

Asia. A passage in Philostratus (*VS* 548) makes procurators complain to the Emperor that with an expenditure of HS28 million (7 million drachmas) on an aqueduct at Alexandreia Troas, the tribute of 500 cities was being spent on a single city. By contrast, Sulla imposed an indemnity of HS480 million (20,000 talents) on Asia in 84 BC, a debt which grew sixfold, thanks to compound interest, over the next 14 years (Plut. *Sulla* 25; *Lucull.* 20; Jones 1974, 119). And Cicero saw the customs dues of Asia as one of the chief sources of state revenue (*de leg. ag.* 2.80). The orders of magnitude are clearly different, and the comparison in Philostratus must be rhetorical exaggeration.

Palestine. A figure of HS48 million (2,000 talents) is given for the revenues of Palestine under Herod Agrippa, in Claudius's time (Josephus *AJ* 19.352, referring to the tetrarchies of Philip and Herod, and the territory of Judaea, Samaria and Caesarea). Figures in Josephus are not always reliable; cf. Broski 1977, 380–1.

Sicily. In the 70s BC when Verres was governor, the wheat tithe was reckoned as 3 million modii (more than twice this amount was officially taken from Sicily at this time, but the rest was paid for by the government). That was worth about HS7.5 million at a basic Sicilian price of HS$2\frac{1}{2}$ per modius (*Verr.* 2.3.174; 194; Jones 1974, 119 n.33; Scramuzza *ESAR* 3.256, 266). The customs-dues and other money taxes must have contributed a sizeable

---

[19] Although Frank's discussions are sometimes useful, he accepts virtually all ancient statements about tax-revenue however much they conflict (*ESAR* 5.51–2 etc.).

amount, presumably implying a total revenue of the order of HS10 million. (Because of early treaty arrangements, eight of Sicily's sixty-five cities, including some of the most important, were not subject to tithe.)

Macedonia. The *stipendium* of Macedonia was set by Aemilius Paullus in the 160s BC at HS2.4 million (100 talents); Plut. *Aem. Paul.* 28; cf. Livy 45.18.7.

Commagene. A Roman province from AD 18 to the reign of Caligula, when Rome's tax-receipts were returned in full as a sum of HS100 million (Tac. *Ann.* 2.56; Suet. *Gaius* 16.3). If Suetonius's figure has any meaning, the revenue for approximately twenty years works out at HS5 million per year.

APPENDIX 5. TAX COMPARISONS WITH MUGHAL INDIA

For taxation in Mughal India, systematic descriptions are available: see Raychaudhuri, Habib 1982. Principal sources are Abu'l Fazl 1595 and Bernier 1914.

Mughal India shows some vivid similarities to what we see in Egypt. The system of land-tax tended to develop from a pro rata system depending on annual assessment of the crop (*kankut*), into a fixed-rate system (*zabt*), where the amount payable depended on modules fixed in advance (Raychaudhuri, Habib 1982, 236). This system was more convenient to collect, but it made few concessions to years of poor harvest. The main concession was one where land was classified as cropless ('nabud', cf. *abrochos* in Appendix 3). But only one-eighth of the sown land could be reclassified in this way.

Lower revenue rates were granted to encourage the cultivation of waste land. There were graduated tax-rates rising to a full rate payable after five years (ibid. 239). There were sometimes concessions about the rate paid by the large landowner, and the system as a whole tended to lay the fiscal burden more heavily on the small cultivator (ibid. 239; compare higher poll-tax rates in the Egyptian countryside, Table 4.5 p. 52).

But some very clear differences are also seen. The method of payment was usually cash, not grain as in Egypt. And the amount taken by tax seems to have been typically half the crop, or even more in fertile areas. The practice of extra charges over and above the basic rate, in itself very reminiscent of practice in Egypt, might add one-quarter to the basic tax. By contrast, the direct tax-burden on the land in Egypt under the Principate is of the order of 20–25%, allowing for the ratio between private and public land.[20] On the other hand, payments on ousiac land, with averages as high as 6 artabas in some cases, and crown land with rents above 4 artabas, represent important categories where the burden in Egypt was comparable to that seen in India.

There are other echoes of Roman experience. In the Deccan, assessment of tax-units had been by the number of ploughs or plough-units (Raychaudhuri,

[20] P. 48.

Habib 1982, 237), a practice widespread in the later Roman Empire, though
going back to a much earlier date (Duncan-Jones 1990, chapter 13). And in
Bengal there was a system of laying a fixed-rate cash contribution on a whole
village (*muqtah*). This echoes the practice sometimes seen in Roman provincial
taxation under the Republic (Duncan-Jones 1990, 188).

APPENDIX 6. HOARDS BELOW THE SAMPLING THRESHOLD

The main analysis is restricted to hoards with a minimum value of HS400
(p. 67 n.2 above). Finds of small amounts run a greater risk of being
incomplete, and where they are incomplete, they may fail to show the true
end-date (see p. 68 n.5 above). The hoard-sample analysed is relatively large
notwithstanding its size-threshold and, for the reason stated, its main
statistical results should be more solidly based than those which use all hoards
irrespective of size.

An additional test-analysis was carried out nevertheless. This augmented
the 230 hoards in the main sample with a further 72 hoards valued between 20
and 99 denarii, taken from Bolin and from regional hoard-lists (20 denarii is
Bolin's size-threshold). The result (fig. Appendix 6.1) shows a very close
correlation between numbers of hoards per reign-year in the enlarged sample,
and those in the original sample (enlarged sample = main sample × 1.316;
$r^2 = 0.979$).

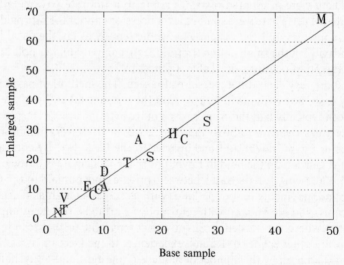

Figure Appendix 6.1 Correlation between hoards in main sample and hoards in
enlarged sample. (Symbol: Emperor's initial.)

APPENDIX 7.   RATES OF DONATIVE

The literary evidence for rates of donative (Table A.4 below) mainly refers to special occasions or special contingencies, and thus offers little guidance to typical rates of payment. The present identification of the main source of coin-hoards (chapter 5) suggests that hoards should offer guidance to donative amounts. But three hidden variables, rank, unit, and the level of generosity on a particular occasion, make it difficult in practice to use them in this way. The largest hoard amounts may suggest undistributed group payments.

For the amounts of donatives in the Republic, see Frank *ESAR* 1.127–37 and Brunt 1988, 262–5. For the Late Empire, see Delmaire 1989, 548–52. The usual rank differentials in the early second century BC were 1:2:3 (Frank, *ESAR* 1. 127–37). For proportioning of donatives to rank by Pompey and Caesar, see Appian *Mith.* 116, and *BC* 2.102 (cf. *BC* 4.100 for rates promised by Brutus and Cassius).

Table A.4 *Donatives and bequests to the troops in literary evidence* (amounts in sesterces)

Amount	Unit	Date (AD)	Source
A. Praetorians			
20,000		161	*HA Marcus* 7.9; Dio 74.8.4
15,000		41	Suet. *Claud.* 10.4
12,000		193	Dio 74.8.4
2,000		64	Tac. *Ann.* 15.72
1,000/2,000		37	Dio 59.2.1
1,000		14	Tac. *Ann.* 1.8; Suet. *Aug* 101
1,000		202	Dio 76.1.1
100 annually		42–54	Dio 60.12.4
B. Other troops			
4,000	Alban legion	AD 218	Dio 78.34.3
1,000	Veterans	29 BC	Augustus *RG* 15.3
1,000	Pannonian legions	AD 196	Dio 46.46.7
500	Urban cohorts	AD 14	Suet. *Aug.* 101
500	Urban cohorts	AD 37	Dio 59.2.3
400	Army in Gaul	AD 40	Suet. *Gaius* 46
300	Legions	AD 14	Tac. *Ann.* 1.8; Suet. *Aug.* 101
300	Legions	AD 37	Dio 59.2.3

Note: Payments after AD 235, *ad hoc* payments during the Civil War of 68–9, and amounts promised and not necessarily paid are not shown.

APPENDIX 8.   PROGRAMS FOR FINDING NEGATIVE BINOMIAL K AND FOR ESTIMATING DIE-POPULATIONS

The coin-populations examined above can be modelled efficiently by the negative binomial distribution. But they differ considerably in configuration, with corresponding differences in the level of negative binomial k (fig. 8.5). Some small differences in the known value of k can still mean large differences in population-size. But k can only be calculated indirectly. Defining it thus requires many trial-and-error calculations from given co-ordinates, or else a table of equivalences running to many pages. But a computer program can perform hundreds of calculating cycles almost instantly, and this removes the need for trial-and-error calculation.

The following programs by the writer, which incorporate the formula for k provided by R.A. Kempton, run on a personal computer in versions of Microsoft Basic such as GW–BASIC, BASICA and N88–BASIC. For Program 1, the user who wishes to check that they have been copied correctly should input dies as 5, coins as 10 and dies expected as 10 (answer: k = 1). To check Program 2, input k as 1, dies as 5, and coins as 10 (answer: dies expected = 10).

The programs can be used with either dies or types. The limits to their use are those of the available techniques for efficient modelling of die-populations, for which simpler methods are generally no substitute (see p. 144 above). Program 1 can be used only when the size of the matrix is already known, as with a well-attested set of numbered dies (Table 10.4, Method B), or the types of some relatively large type-population which have already been effectively catalogued (see data in Table 10.2). The validity of the results will still depend on the size of individual coin samples. But lack of large samples can sometimes be mitigated by averaging the readings from this program for half a dozen smaller samples.

Program 2 uses the value of k for the coin-issue concerned to estimate the total number of dies (or types) from the co-ordinates for dies (or types) and coins in an individual hoard-sample. But it requires the value of k for the coin issue concerned to be already known. Normally that means running program 1 first (for specimen results, see Tables 10.7 and 10.11, and fig. 8.5).

Alternatively, with a relatively large sample, MLP can be used to estimate k by fitting its frequencies (see Ross, Preece 1985, and Table 10.2). This is subject to the standard error of k shown by MLP, which can often be high, although it is relatively low for the Reka Devnia material used in Table 10.2, and for data in Ross, Preece 1985.

PROGRAM 1

10 PRINT "PROGRAM FOR FINDING NEGATIVE BINOMIAL K FROM HOARD CO-ORDINATES"

20 PRINT "HOW MANY DIES (OR TYPES) IN SAMPLE";:INPUT M
30 PRINT "HOW MANY COINS IN SAMPLE";:INPUT N
40 C = M/N
50 IF C > 0.8 THEN PRINT "TOO FEW REPEATED FREQUENCIES;
LARGER SAMPLE NEEDED";: IF C > 0.8 THEN GOTO 200
60 PRINT "HOW MANY DIES (TYPES) EXPECTED";:INPUT D
70 K = 0.05
80 A = D/N
90 B = A * (1 − EXP(− K * LOG(1 + 1/K/A)))
100 IF B < C GOTO 180 ELSE 110
110 K = K/1.11
120 B = A * (1 − EXP(− K * LOG(1 + 1/K/A)))
130 IF B < C GOTO 140 ELSE 160
140 K = K * 1.001
150 GOTO 120
160 PRINT "D/c = ";A;"   d/c = ";B;"   k = ";K
170 GOTO 200
180 K = K * 1.12
190 GOTO 90
200 END

PROGRAM 2

1 PRINT "PROGRAM FOR FINDING TOTAL POPULATION OF DIES (OR
TYPES) FROM HOARD CO-ORDINATES FOR A KNOWN VALUE OF K"
10 PRINT "K = ";:INPUT K
20 PRINT "HOW MANY DIES (TYPES) IN SAMPLE";:INPUT M
30 PRINT "HOW MANY COINS IN SAMPLE";:INPUT N
40 C = M/N
50 A = C − 0.009
60 B = A * (1 − EXP(− K * LOG(1 + 1/K/A)))
70 IF B < C GOTO 180 ELSE 80
80 A = A/1.11
90 B = A * (1 − EXP(− K * LOG(1 + 1/K/A)))
100 IF B < C GOTO 110 ELSE 130
110 A = A * 1.001
120 GOTO 90
130 PRINT "DIES (FORMULA APPROXIMATION) = ";(B * N);" /
     (OBSERVED) = ";M
140 PRINT "K = ";K
150 Z = A * N
160 PRINT "ESTIMATED DIE (TYPE) POPULATION = ";Z
170 GOTO 200
180 A = A * 1.12
190 GOTO 60
200 END

APPENDIX 9. DIE-PRODUCTIVITY IN MEDIEVAL EVIDENCE

1. CASE-STUDIES

A. *Shrewsbury, 1249–50.* A sample of 304 Long Cross pence shows 37 obverse dies and 86 reverse dies. Brand assumes that this population of dies is complete (Brand 1971). But it is unlikely that an original population of 86 dies would be fully revealed by such a small coin sample. Even a relatively low dispersal of about $k = 2$, as in the Crepusius denarii (p. 150 n.23), would give 103 reverses. The amount struck is known to have been £7,167. That would make the output per reverse die 16,700 on average.

The survival-rate is $4\frac{1}{44}$d per £100, i.e. $\frac{1}{5,647}$, from Brand 1971. The example is cited by Stahl (1985, 49), who by applying the Carter formula which assumes that k is close to 2 (cf. Carter 1983) estimates 104 reverse dies. For Chester in 1300 Stewart noted 9 obverse dies from 15 coins (Stewart 1964, 208), whereas Mate has since found from documentary records that there were almost certainly 16 originally (Mate 1969, 209). These three co-ordinates make negative binomial k 3.36 (from Program 1, Appendix 8); but a result from such a small coin sample cannot be pressed.

B. In England under Edward I and Edward II, the respective average number of coins struck per obverse die were 39,031 and 28,187 (ibid., 1969, 209). The norm was apparently 2 reverse dies (trussels) for every obverse die (pile). So for reverse dies, the corresponding gross averages are 19,516 and 14,094.

Looking at some of the figures in more detail, for obverse dies the averages for the royal mints in 1300 are as follows (ibid., 1969, 199):

Chester	21,750
London and Canterbury	23,150
Newcastle	23,155
Exeter	23,220
York and Hull	33,319
Bristol	34,606

The first four figures are tightly grouped around a mid-point of 22,485 ($\pm 4\%$). The two remaining figures have a mid-point 50% higher, 33,963 ($\pm 2\%$). The exact ratio between the two sets is 1:1.51. This appears to be a structured difference, not a random variant. That would imply different target volumes of striking per die. The corresponding reverse-die figures would be 11,243 and 16,982.

C. There are also continuous figures for London and Canterbury for the period 1281–1310 (ibid., 217–18). These can be resolved into a set of small-scale strikings, where the prospective number of obverses was below 60 (Set A), and a second set where the number was over 60 (Set B). Set A accounts for less than 5% of all coins and 3.6% of all dies, and its mean is 47,342 coins per obverse die, with a high coefficient of variation of 36.8% (n = 10). Set B, which accounts for almost all the coin and almost all the dies, has a mean of 33,778, with a lower coefficient of variation of 19.6% (n = 21). For set B the corresponding reverse-die figure is 16,889.

The small-scale strikings in Set A show output levels per die 40% higher on average. If only one coin-denomination was involved, these might indicate that small die-sets were normally worked harder than larger sets.

D. In thirteenth-century France, Louis VIII laid down prices for coin-dies. In conjunction with other figures, they imply targets of 13,278 and 16,830 coins per reverse die (Blancard 1868, 95–104. I owe knowledge of this work to Professor Grierson).

2. IMPLIED MODULES

The implicit reverse-die figures calculated above are as follows:

		Section
1.	11,243 (±4%) Chester, London, Newcastle, Exeter 1300	B
2.	13,278 thirteenth-century France	D
3.	16,700? Shrewsbury 1249–50	A
4.	16,830 thirteenth-century France	D
5.	16,889 London and Canterbury, 21 high-output years, 1281–1310	C
6.	16,982 (±2%) York and Hull, Bristol, 1300	B
7.	23,671 London and Canterbury, 10 low-output years, 1281–1310	C

The most frequent mean figure is in the region of 16,500–17,000 coins per reverse die.

APPENDIX 10.   AUREUS AND DENARIUS HOARDS USED IN THE MAIN ANALYSIS

For the terms of reference, see chapter 5, p. 67 n.2. The hoards summarised are dated by reign or by year, have a minimum value of HS400, and come from within the empire. For smaller hoards, see Appendix 6. For hoards outside the empire, see pp. 92–4. For hoards of Egyptian coin, see pp. 90–2. For reasons of space, isolated Greek drachmas included in denarius hoards are counted under denarii in the few cases where they occur (see pp. 174–5, n.10).

For ease of consultation, hoards have usually been cited from collections, unless discrepancies with the original publication were found. A number of the hoards have not yet appeared in general lists. The sequence is gold, nos. 1–61; mixed hoards, 62–79; silver, 80–230. The remaining hoards cited individually in the text are shown at the end of the list (nos. 231–74).

Zones: A Britain; B West Continent; C Italy; D Danube; E East

Cat. no.	Value (HS)	Site and Zone	Aurei	Den- arii	Rad- iates	Dates	Source
1	19,600	Ambenay B	196	—	—	10 BC	Blanchet, 381
2	1,700	Limoges B	17	—	—	31 BC/ AD 14	CTMAF 1.75
3	20,000	Cherbourg B	200	—	—	15–37	Note p. 267
4	3,700	Bredgar A	37	—	—	41	ASR 22
5	1,400	Este 1 C	14	—	—	44/5	Note p. 267
6	20,000	Contres en Vairais B	200	—	—	41/54	Blanchet, 520
7	3,500	Patras E	35	—	—	46/7	CH 4.106
8	2,800	Benkovac D	28	—	—	41/54	Mirnik, 50
9	3,100	Briatico C	31	—	—	48	Note p. 267
10	7,000	St Georges sur Loire B	70	—	—	51	CTMAF 3.65
11	20,000	Lentilly B	200	—	—	59/60	CTMAF 5.1.53
12	100,000	Langres B	1,000	—	—	68	Blanchet, 114
13	5,000	Utrecht B	50	—	—	69	Thirion, 78
14	500	Caerleon 1 A	5	—	—	74	ASR 62
15	500	Springhead A	5	—	—	75	ASR 60
16	7,500	Cumae C	75	—	—	88	Note p. 267
17	7,300	Monteleone C	73	—	—	81/96	Note p. 267
18	12,000	Nijlen B	120	—	—	81/96	CH 3.142
19	1,800	St Pantaléon les Vignes B	18	—	—	81/96	CTMAF 5.2.28
20	13,000	St Pierre lès Nemours B	130	—	—	81/96	Blanchet, 344 bis
21	11,800	Zirkovci D	118	—	—	92/4	Note p. 268
22	2,000	Clunia B	20	—	—	98	Carradice, 181
23	23,000	Zemun D	230	—	—	98/9	Carradice, 181
24	3,600	Annecy B	36	—	—	103/11	CTMAF 5.2.88
25	4,500	Villeurbanne B	45	—	—	103/11	CTMAF 5.1.61
26	1,500	Buchen B	15	—	—	98/117	Note p. 268
27	4,200	Caesarea E	42	—	—	98/117	Thirion, 80
28	1,600	Emona D	16	—	—	107/11	Carradice, 181
29	2,700	Beograd D	27	—	—	119/20	Mirnik, 53
30	10,000	Coyanca B	100	—	—	123	CH 5.120
31	12,200	Castronovo C	122	—	—	117/38	Regling, 377
32	500	Drobeta D	5	—	—	117/38	CH 7.235
33	7,200	Vidy B	72	—	—	140/4	Carradice, 181–2
34	6,000	Karanis E	60	—	—	156/7	Kunisz, 128
35	900	Aartrijke B	9	—	—	145/61	Thirion, 81
36	16,000	Corbridge A	160	—	—	159/60	ASR 203
37	6,000	La Haye Malherbe B	60	—	—	138/61	CTMAF 4.83
38	37,800	Rome 1 C	378	—	—	165	Thirion, 44
39	36,800	Liberchies B	368	—	—	166	Thirion, passim
40	17,100	Braga B	171	—	—	168	CH 5.126
41	29,800	Vienna 1 D	298	—	—	161/75	FMRÖ 9.85
42	14,400	Italica B	144	—	—	163/9	Note p. 268
43	5,700	Autun B	57	—	—	161/75	Blanchet, 291
44	15,000	Reims 1 B	150	—	—	161/80	Blanchet, 128

Cat. no.	Value (HS)	Site and Zone	Aurei	Denarii	Radiates	Dates	Source
45	8,000	Le Buis B	80	—	—	177	*CTMAF* 1.72
46	6,000	Lyon B	60	—	—	175/80	*CTMAF* 5.1.54
47	2,900	Tobarra B	29	—	—	161/80	Regling, 378
48	29,900	Sakha E	299	—	—	178	Kunisz, 128
49	160,000	Mespelaer B	1,600	—	—	175/80	Blanchet, 678
50	2,700	Cailly B	27	—	—	182	*CTMAF* 4.23
51	160,000	Paris 1 B	1,600	—	—	180/82	Blanchet, 326
52	45,800	Corné B	458	—	—	183/4	*CTMAF* 3.61
53	58,800	Perscheid B	588	—	—	180/92	Thirion, 78
54	20,000	Turkey 1 E	200	—	—	180/92	*CH* 3.156
55	21,200	Troyes B	212	—	—	193	Note p. 268
56	11,800	Brigetio D	118	—	—	196/211	Note p. 268
57	120,000	Paris 2 B	1,200	—	—	193/211	Blanchet, 327
58	50,000	Vertus B	500	—	—	198/211	Blanchet, 144
59	81,200	Belgium B	812	—	—	205	Note p. 268
60	12,900	Le Cannet B	129	—	—	211	Carradice, 182
61	120,000	Karnak E	1,200	—	—	218/20	Kunisz, 130
62	1,780	Dombresson B	1	420	—	55	Note p. 268
63	1,484	Este 2 C	7	196	—	79	Note p. 268
64	1,608	Howe A	12	102	—	87	Normanby, 22
65	4,220	Shap A	19	580	—	81/96	ASR 103
66	540	Thorngrafton A	3	60	—	119/28	ASR 137
67	6,828	Castagnaro C	20	1,207	—	128/34	Carradice, 174
68	12,984	Erla D	103	671	—	134/8	Dembski, 14
69	3,692	Dormagen B	4	823	—	138/61	Blanchet, 743
70	4,268	Acre E	38	117	—	161	*CH* 7.243
71	1,800	Longuenesse B	2	400	—	161/9	*CTMAF* 2.76
72	11,416	Verona C	2	2,804	—	166	Note p. 268
73	6,100	Stockstadt B	7	1,350	—	167	*FMRD* 1.6.67
74	3,484	Rudchester A	16	471	—	168	ASR 242
75	2,232	Barway A	5	433	—	180	ASR 317/317A
76	1,612	Holler B	1	378	—	180/92	Blanchet, 734
77	16,216	Villach D	162	4	—	197	*FMRÖ* 2.3.35
78	4,944	Pré Haut B	9	1,011	—	198/211	Blanchet, 483
79	2,916	Welzheim B	3	654	—	222/35	*FMRD* 2.4.354
80	13,816	Castro do Avarelhos 1 B	—	3,454	—	28 BC	*CH* 6.89
81	2,092	Castro do Avarelhos 2 B	—	523	—	8 BC	*CH* 6.90
82	1,104	Zare C	—	276	—	15 BC	*CH* 2.207
83	1,812	Maillé B	—	453	—	12 BC	*CTMAF* 3.107
84	1,548	Albacete B	—	387	—	2 BC	Note p. 268
85	1,172	Andalucia B	—	293	—	31 BC/ AD 14	*CH* 3.138
86	1,600	Ingrandes B	—	400	—	31 BC/ AD 14	*CTMAF* 3.63
87	1,200	Seiches sur le Loir B	—	300	—	31 BC/ AD 14	*CTMAF* 3.66
88	16,000	Cinto Caomaggiore C	—	4,000	—	AD 15	Note p. 268

Cat. no.	Value (HS)	Site and Zone	Aurei	Denarii	Radiates	Dates	Source
89	55,704	Mans B	—	13,926	—	14/37	Blanchet, 506
90	816	Sutton A	—	204	—	41/2	ASR 28A
91	2,336	Cogeces B	—	584	—	41/54	CH 5.110
92	576	Rheingonheim B	—	144	—	69	Bolin, 336
93	536	Dolni D	—	134	—	69/79	Bolin, 339
94	1,108	Beck Row A	—	277	—	80	ASR 86
95	1,176	Rome 2 C	—	294	—	80	Note p. 268
96	1,484	Aubenton B	—	371	—	80/81	Bolin, 337
97	444	Tekija D	—	111	—	84/5	Mirnik, 52
98	600	Boljetin D	—	150	—	81/06	Mirnik, 50
99	1,344	Draganci D	—	336	—	96/8	Gerov, 148
100	2,400	Junuzlar D	—	600	—	96/8	Gerov, 148
101	1,200	Italy C	—	300	—	100/1	Note p. 268
102	3,084	Gradesnica D	—	771	—	105/11	Gerov, 148
103	788	Lavenhan A	—	197	—	103/11	ASR 120
104	1,600	Gigen D	—	400	—	98/117	Gerov, 149
105	2,200	Lovec D	—	550	—	98/117	Gerov, 149
106	952	Popovo D	—	238	—	98/117	Gerov, 149
107	1,200	Egypt 1 E	—	300	—	114 /17	Note p. 268
108	3,600	Cervena D	—	900	—	119	Gerov, 149
109	420	Volubilis	—	105	—	119/22	Carradice, 174
110	88	Ormskirk A	—	122	—	119/25	ASR 135
111	688	Boston A	—	172	—	119/28	ASR 154
112	5,720	Bazaurt D	—	1,430	—	117/38	Gerov, 149
113	1,860	Flaminda D	—	465	—	117/38	Protase 1, 85
114	628	Garesnica D	—	157	—	117/38	Mirnik, 54
115	3,200	Lipnik D	—	800	—	117/38	Gerov, 149
116	800	Popica D	—	200	—	117/38	Gerov, 149
117	2,400	Slatino D	—	600	—	117/38	Gerov, 149
118	1,208	Tolic D	—	302	—	117/38	Mirnik, 58
119	932	Mont, Mosel B	—	233	—	133/4	Bolin, 345
120	1,140	Eleutheropolis E	—	285	—	134/8	Carradice, 174
121	552	Mallerstang A	—	138	—	134/8	ASR 141
122	712	Swaby A	—	178	—	137/8	ASR 165
123	1,300	Heddernheim B	—	325	—	139	Bolin, 345
124	960	Goljama D	—	240	—	140	Gerov, 150
125	452	Covasint D	—	113	—	138/61	Mihailescu, 115
126	2,056	Razvigorovo D	—	514	—	138/61	Gerov, 150
127	1,680	Londonthorpe A	—	420	—	153/4	ASR 214
128	2,392	Lawrence Weston A	—	598	—	156/7	ASR 215
129	12,808	La Salasuri D	—	3,202	—	158	Carradice, 175
130	468	Wallern D	—	117	—	157/8	FMRÖ 1.2.413
131	2,800	Chichester A	—	700	—	145/61	ASR 276
132	540	Dimbau D	—	135	—	140/4	Mihailescu, 114
133	1,196	Allerton A	—	299	—	161/2	ASR 294
134	3,132	Gradistea D	—	783	—	164	Mihailescu, 120
135	4,948	Mocsolad D	—	1,232	—	164	Bolin, 348
136	3,760	Silistra 1 D	—	940	—	164	Gerov, 151
137	4,572	Tolna Megye D	—	1,143	—	164	Bolin, 348

Cat. no.	Value (HS)	Site and Zone	Aurei	Den- arii	Rad- iates	Dates	Source
138	8,000	Kleinredrichingen B	—	2,000	—	161/9	Blanchet, 803
139	1,900	Nemenikuce D	—	475	—	161/9	Mirnik, 55
140	10,000	Osijek D	—	2,500	—	165	Mirnik, 56
141	2,000	Bezanovo D	—	500	—	166	Gerov, 151
142	416	Mrcevac D	—	104	—	166	Mirnik, 55
143	8,160	Sotin D	—	2,040	—	165/6	Carradice, 176
144	708	Apetlon D	—	177	—	166/7	*FMRÖ* 1.2.293
145	800	Spital D	—	200	—	167	Dembski, 19
146	3,052	Tibodu D	—	753	—	167	Mihailescu, 120
147	440	Carnuntum D	—	110	—	168	Dembski, 17
148	596	Grocka D	—	149	—	168	Mirnik, 54
149	416	Corban B	—	104	—	161/80	Blanchet, 836
150	1,028	Metkovce D	—	257	—	161/75	Bolin, 349
151	900	Riopar B	—	225	—	161/80	Bolin, 350
152	912	Rongeres B	—	228	—	161/80	Blanchet, 545
153	1,840	Draghiceni D	—	460	—	176/80	Protase 2, 182
154	1,028	Frondenberg B	—	257	—	175/7	Note p. 268
155	1,204	Reghin D	—	301	—	175/7	Mihailescu, 121
156	1,180	Caerleon 2 A	—	295	—	177	ASR 316
157	796	Castle Bromwich A	—	199	—	177	ASR 315
158	4,000	Szombathely D	—	1,000	—	176/7	Carradice, 177
159	620	Lydney A	—	155	—	175/80	ASR 338
160	448	Sighisoara D	—	112	—	175/80	Mihailescu, 121
161	5,784	Vienna 2 D	—	1,446	—	175/80	*FMRÖ* 9.87
162	1,476	Edwinstowe A	—	369	—	179	ASR 314
163	1,812	Mezdra D	—	453	—	180	Note p. 268
164	1,280	Girla Mare D	—	320	—	181	*CH* 2.232
165	1,328	Bela Reka D	—	332	—	182	Mirnik, 53
166	2,380	Cephallenia E	—	595	—	180/3	*CH* 2.231
167	668	Kirkby Thore A	—	167	—	180/3	ASR 333
168	1,184	Bletchley A	—	296	—	183	Note p. 268
169	424	Unterammergau D	—	106	—	184	Bolin, 350
170	2,392	Alba Iulia D	—	598	—	185	Mihailescu, 132
171	2,472	Gyulfehervar D	—	618	—	185	Bolin, 350
172	3,132	Larnaka E	—	783	—	180/92	Metcalf 1979
173	2,800	Prelazko D	—	700	—	186	Mirnik, 56
174	3,200	Silly, Orne B	—	800	—	180/92	Bolin, 348
175	716	Briglands A	—	179	—	186/7	ASR 335
176	2,508	Little Brickhill A	—	627	—	187	Tuckett 1992
177	3,604	Sascut D	—	901	—	187	Mihailescu, 282
178	1,272	Barger Compascuum B	—	318	—	187/8	Carradice, 177
179	2,400	Hasanfaka D	—	600	—	180/3	Gerov, 151
180	416	Menden D	—	104	—	193	Bolin, 352
181	460	Miskocz D	—	115	—	193	Bolin, 352
182	1,200	Vaulx B	—	300	—	193	*CTMAF* 5.2.98
183	408	Seidol D	—	102	—	194	Gerov, 152
184	4,636	Borlesti D	—	1,159	—	195	*CH* 2.238
185	1,072	Gt Melton A	—	268	—	195	Chalfont, 70
186	2,556	Handley A	—	639	—	194/5	ASR 380

Cat. eno.	Value (HS)	Site and Zone	Aurei	Den- arii	Rad- iates	Dates	Source
187	1,032	Silchester A	—	258	—	194/5	ASR 362
188	408	Benha E	—	102	—	193/8	CH 7.105
189	8,000	Genas B	—	2,000	—	197	CTMAF 5.1.52
190	600	Belene D	—	150	—	193/211	Gerov, 151
191	460	Dolna Orehovica D	—	115	—	193/211	Gerov, 152
192	4,492	Osterode B	—	1,123	—	193/211	Mihailescu, 152
193	24,000	Silly en Goufran B	—	6,000	—	193/211	Blanchet, 409
194	3,200	Abergele A	—	800	—	201/6	ASR 383
195	6,192	Adamclisi D	—	1,548	—	204	Note p. 268
196	1,360	Vidin D	—	340	—	201/7	Carradice, 179
197	1,092	Zadar D	—	273	—	201/10	Mihailescu, 144
198	5,912	Bristol A	—	1,478	—	208	ASR 385
199	2,616	Muswell Hill A	—	654	—	209	ASR 387
200	11,400	Roussé D	—	2,850	—	211/17	CH 6.115
201	2,108	Wilten D	—	527	—	210/13	Dembski, 27
202	2,000	Darfield A	—	500	—	213	ASR 394
203	608	Egypt 2 E	—	152	—	211/17	Note p. 268
204	608	Enosesti D	—	152	—	211/17	Protase 1, 85
205	800	Silistra 2 D	—	200	—	211/17	Gerov, 152
206	1,044	Syria E	—	251	—	214	Bolin, 352
207	400	Chadwell St Mary A	—	400	—	213/17	ASR 395
208	1,800	Avezé B	—	450	—	218/22	CTMAF 3.20
209	1,500	Dura E	—	376	—	217/22	Bolin, 357
210	5,460	Frincesti D	—	1,365	—	218/22	Protase 2, 182
211	3,840	Kervian en Cameret B	—	960	—	218/20	Note p. 268
212	7,896	Lay B	—	280	847	222	CTMAF 5.1.77
213	9,400	Tell Kalak E	—	2,350	—	222	Carradice, 179
214	948	Emirovo D	—	237	—	224	Gerov, 153
215	448	Vienna 3 D	—	112	—	222/5	Dembski, 26
216	26,052	Rome 3 via Braccianese C	—	6,409	52	222/8	Note p. 268
217	588	Britain A	—	147	—	226	ASR 416
218	2,216	Llanarmon A	—	548	—	227	ASR 426
219	5,116	Akandzilar D	—	1,279	—	222/35	Bolin, 356
220	2,352	Börgend D	—	588	—	222/35	Bolin, 356
221	1,224	Causevo D	—	306	—	222/35	Bolin, 356
222	3,444	Ensiedel B	—	861	—	222/35	Note p. 268
223	2,560	Kempten Lindenberg B	—	640	—	222/35	FMRD 1.7.287
224	2,276	Baden Baden B	—	569	—	222/35	FMRD 2.2.182
225	3,012	Reims 2 B	—	753	—	222/35	Blanchet, 129
226	3,796	Tisa D	—	949	—	229	Protase 2, 182
227	548	Wigan A	—	137	—	228	ASR 422
228	13,104	Colchester A	—	3,062	107	230	ASR 406
229	1,504	St Mary Cray A	—	376	—	222/35	ASR 408
230	4,676	Kirchmatting D	—	1,169	—	231	FMRD 1.2.174

Other hoards and finds cited in the text

231 Arnouville-lès-Gonesses: Turckheim-Pey 1981
232 Bath: Walker 1988
233 Boscoreale: Canessa 1909
234 Budge Row: ASR 69
235 Cologne: *FMRD* 6.1.1
236 Cosa: Buttrey 1980
237 Coventina's Well: Allason-Jones, McKay 1985; Roach Smith 1879
238–9 Cunetio: Besley, Bland 1983
240 Diarbekir: Regling 1931
241 Drzewicz Nowy: Krzyzanowska 1976
242 Elveden: ASR 449
243 Eriswell: ASR 45
244 Falkirk: ASR 415
245 Gare: ASR 530
246 Garonne: Etienne, Rachet and others 1984
247 Guelma: Turcan 1963
248 Hemse: Lind 1981, 2,53
249 La Mafumet: Campo, Richard, von Kaenel 1981
250 La Magura: Mihailescu-Birlibà 1977
251 La Oboroceni: Mitrea, Zaharia 1967
252 La Puriceni: Mihailescu-Birlibà 1972–3
253 Membury: Howgego, King 1992
254 Much Hadham: Bland 1992
255 Nietulisko Male 1: Mitkowa-Szubert 1989
256 Nietulisko Male 2: Mitkowa-Szubert 1989
257 Normanby: Bland, Burnett 1988
258 Pompeii 1812: Regling, 376
259 Pompeii 1957: Pozzi 1958–9
260 Puy-Dieu: Desnier 1985
261 Reka Devnia: Mouchmov 1934
262 Rinteln: Berger 1990, 220
263 Sapte: Bolin, 339
264 Scole: ASR 44
265 Sisak: Jelocnik 1961
266 Snettisham: ASR 202
267 Stein: Bolin, 337
268 Turkey 2: Bendall 1966
269 Utrecht: Thirion, 79–80
270 Vannes: Brenot 1963
271 Viuz-Faverges: Pflaum, Huvelin 1981
272 Vyskovce: Ondrouch 1934
273 Woodham Mortimer: Hobbs 1992
274 York: ASR 57

Notes and supplementary hoard references

3 Cherbourg: D. Lagarde, *RN* 2.2 (1857) 82
5 Este 1: G. Gorini, *RIN* 90 (1988) 149
9 Briatico: G. Riccio, *Per. num.* 2 (1869) 145
16 Cumae: G. Riccio, *Per. num.* 1 (1868) 75
17 Monteleone: F. Gnecchi, *RIN* 5 (1890) 263
21 Zirkovci: E. Toth, *NK* 76–7 (1977–9) 13

26 Buchen: K. Regling, *ZfN* 40 (1930) 68
42 Italica: H. Willers, *NZ* 34 (1903) 29
55 Troyes: H. Huvelin, *RN* 31 (1989) 113
56 Brigetio: L. Barkoczi, B. Sey-Katalin, *NK* 62–3 (1963–4) 1
59 Belgium: unpublished; photographs and weights communicated by Dr A.M. Burnett. Information from Dr J. Van Heesch indicates that the hoard is separate from other deposits.
62 Dombresson: T. Mommsen, *Histoire de la monnaie romaine*, 3 (1875) 50
63 Este 2: A. Prosdocimi, *NSc* (1891) 279
72 Verona: A. Ancona, *RIN* 1 (1881) 229
84 Albacete: L. Villaronga, *Ampurias*, 33–4 (1971–2)
88 Cinto Caomaggiore: anon., *NSc*. 5.2 (1905) 53
95 Rome 1: L.A. Milani, *Mus. ital. ant. class.* 2 (1888) 290
101 Italy: B. Borghesi, *Oeuvres complètes* (Paris) 1 (1862) 214
107 Egypt (Delta): S.H. Weber, *ANSMusN* 54 (1932) 1
154 Frondenberg: K. Regling, *ZfN* 29 (1912) 194
163 Mezdra: D.E. Tachella, *RN* 3.14 (1896) 114
168 Bletchley: M.H. Crawford, *NC* 7.9 (1969) 113. The writer's comparison of the unpublished 'Bletchley' coin-weights with those of the slightly later Little Brickhill hoard found close by (no.176) implies that the hoards are distinct.
176 Little Brickhill; see previous note.
195 Adamclisi: B. Mitrea, *Dacia,* 24 (1980) 374
203 Egypt 2: G. Dattari, *RIN* 16 (1903) 285
211 Kervian: G. Aubin, P. Galliou, *TMon* 1 (1979) 17
216 Private information, Professor E. Lo Cascio.
222 Einsiedel: Christ 1960, 2, 107

BIBLIOGRAPHY

The bibliography lists books and articles cited in the text and appendixes. Books are cited by author, date, title, and place of publication. Standard works such as coin-catalogues and encyclopaedias are omitted. Where available, *Année philologique* abbreviations are used for journals. Some further hoard-publications are cited in Appendix 10.

Abou Yousouf Ya'koub (1921) *Le livre de l'impôt foncier (Kitab el-Kharadj)*, trans. E.Fagnan (Paris)

Abu'l Fazl (1595) *A'in-i Akbari* (ed. H. Blochmann, Calcutta, 1876–7)

Adelson, H.L. (1957) *Lightweight solidi and Byzantine trade during the sixth and seventh centuries* (New York)

Alföldi, M.R. (1958–9) 'Epigraphische Beiträge zur römischen Münztechnik', *SNR* 39, 35–48

Allason-Jones, L., McKay, B. (1985) *Coventina's Well: a shrine on Hadrian's Wall* (Chollerford)

Anderson, M.L., Nista, L. (1990) (edd.) *Radiance in stone: sculptures in colored marble from the Museo Nazionale Romano* (Rome)

Andreau, J. (1974) *Les affaires de Monsieur Jucundus* (Rome)

(1987) *La vie financière dans le monde romain: les métiers de manieurs d'argent* (Rome)

Andreau, J. (1989–90) 'Recherches récentes sur les mines à l'époque romaine', *RN* 6.31, 86–112; 6.32, 85–108

Babelon, E. (1901) *Traité des monnaies grecques et romaines* 1 (Paris)

Bagnall, R.S. (1985) 'Agricultural productivity and taxation in Late Roman Egypt' *TAPhA* 115, 289–308

Bagnall, R.S. Worp, K.A. (1978) *Chronological systems of Byzantine Egypt* (Zutphen) (1980) 'Grain land in the Oxyrhynchite nome' *ZPE* 37, 263–4

Bahrfeldt, M. (1923) *Die römische Goldmünzenprägung während der Republik und unter Augustus* (Halle)

Baratte, F. (1974) 'Un trésor de tetradrachmes neroniens provenant de Madamoud (Egypte)', *RN* 6.16, 81–94

Barnes, T.D. (1984) *Early Christianity and the Roman empire* (London)

Bastianini, G. (1988) 'Il prefetto d'Egitto (30 a.C.–297 d.C.): Addenda 1973–85', *ANRW* 2.10.1, 503–17

Bastien, P. (1967) *Le monnayage en bronze de Postume* (Wetteren) (1988) *Monnaie et donativa au Bas-Empire* (Wetteren)

Bateson, J.D. (1973) 'Roman material from Ireland: a reconsideration', *PRIA* 73 C2, 21–97

Bellen, H. (1976) 'Die Krise der italischen Landwirtschaft unter Kaiser Tiberius, 33 n.Chr.', *Historia* 25, 217–34

Bellinger, A.R. (1949) *The excavations at Dura-Europos; final report, 6: the coins* (New Haven)

Bendall, S. (1966) 'An eastern hoard of Roman imperial silver', *NC* 7.6, 165–70

Berger, F. (1990) *Untersuchungen zu den Fundmünzen der römischen Zeit in Nordwestdeutschland* (diss. Hanover)

Berghaus, P. (1989) 'Funde severischer Goldmünzen in Indien', in H.-J. Drexhage, J. Sunskes (edd.) *Migratio et commutatio: Studien zur Alten Geschichte und deren Nachleben T. Pekáry dargebracht* (St Katharinen) 93–101

Bernhardt, R. (1980) 'Die Immunitas der Freistädte', *Historia* 29, 190–207

Bernier, F. (1914) *Travels in the Moghul empire 1656–68* (London)

Besley, E., Bland, R.F. (1983) *The Cunetio treasure: Roman coinage of the third century AD* (London)

Birley, A.R. (1981A) *The Fasti of Roman Britain* (Oxford)

(1981B) 'The economic effects of Roman frontier policy', in A. King, M. Henig (edd.) *The Roman West in the third century* (Oxford) 39–53

Birley, E.R. (1969) 'Septimius Severus and the Roman army', *Epig. Stud.* 8, 63–82

Blancard, L. (1868) *Essai sur les monnaies de Charles Ier* (Paris)

Blanchet, A. (1900) *Les trésors de monnaies romaines et les invasions germaniques en Gaule* (Paris)

(1936) 'Les rapports entre les dépôts monétaires et les évènements militaires, politiques et économiques', *RN* 4.39, 3–69

Bland, R.F. (1992) *The Chalfont hoard and other hoards* (London) (*CHRB* 9)

Bland, R.F., Aydemir, P. (1991) 'The Haydere hoard and other hoards of the mid-third century from Turkey', in C.S. Lightfoot (ed.) *Recent Turkish coin-hoards and numismatic studies* (Oxford) 91–180

Bland, R.F., Burnett, A.M. (1988) *The Normanby hoard* (London) (*CHRB* 8)

Bland, R.F., Burnett, A.M., Bendall, S. (1987) 'The minting of Pescennius Niger', *NC* 147, 65–83

Bliss, C.I. (1971) 'The aggregation of species within spatial units', in G.P. Patil, E.C. Pielou, W.E. Waters (edd.) *Statistical Ecology* 1 (Philadelphia) 311–35

Boatwright, M.T. (1987) *Hadrian and the city of Rome* (Princeton)

Bodei Giglioni, G. (1974) *Lavori pubblici e occupazioni nell'antichità classica* (Bologna)

Boeckh, A. (1838) *Metrologische Untersuchungen* (Berlin)

Bogaert R. (1987) 'Recherches sur la banque en Egypte gréco-romaine', in Hackens, Marchetti (1987), 49–77

(1988) 'Les opérations en nature des banques en Egypte gréco-romaine', *AncSoc* 19, 213–24

Bolin, S. (1958) *State and currency in the Roman empire to 300 AD* (Stockholm)

Bompaire, M., Turckheim-Pey, S. de (1986) 'Le Trésor de sesterces de Montfalcon (Isère)' *BSFN* 41, 473–6

Bonneau, D. (1979) 'Fiscalité et irrigation artificielle en Egypte à l'époque romaine', in H. Van Effenterre (ed.) *Points de vue sur la fiscalité antique* (Paris) 57–68

Boon, G.C. (1978) 'Les monnaies fausses de l'époque impériale et la valeur des espèces courantes', *Les dévaluations à Rome, 1975* (Rome) 99–106

(1988) 'Counterfeit coins in Roman Britain', in Reece, Casey (1988) 102–88

Botti, F. (1955) 'Le monete alessandrini da El Hibeh nel Museo Egizio di Firenze', *Aegyptus* 35, 245–74

Boulvert, G. (1974) *Domestique et fonctionnaire sous le Haut-Empire romain: la condition de l'affranchi et de l'esclave du Prince* (Paris)

Bove, L. (1979) *Documenti processuali delle Tabulae Pompeianae di Murecine* (Naples)

Bovill, E.W. (1968) *The golden trade of the Moors*[2] (London)

Bowman, A.K. (1967) 'The crown tax in Roman Egypt', *BASP* 4, 59–67
(1985) 'Landholding in the Hermopolite nome in the fourth century', *JRS* 75, 137–63

Bowman, A.K., Thomas, J.D. (1991) 'A military strength report from Vindolanda', *JRS* 81, 62–73

Brand, J.D. (1971) 'The Shrewsbury mint 1249–50', in R.A.G. Carson (ed.) *Mints, dies and currency* (London) 129–50

Braudel, F. (1984) *Civilisation and capitalism* 3 (London)

Braund, D.C. (1984) *Rome and the friendly king: the character of the client kingship* (London)

Breglia, L. (1950) 'Circolazione monetale ed aspetti di vita economica a Pompei', *Pompeiana: Raccolta di studi per il secondo centenario degli scavi di Pompei* (Naples) 41–59

Brenot, C. (1963) 'Le trésor de Vannes (Morbihan)', *RN* 6.5, 159–63

Brenot, C., Loriot, X. (1992) *L'or monnayé III: trouvailles de monnaies d'or dans l'occident romain* (Paris)

Broski, M. (1977) 'The reliability of Josephus', *JJS* 33, 379–84

Brunt, P.A. (1950) 'Pay and superannuation in the Roman army', *PBSR* 18, 50–71
(1980) 'Free labour and public works in Rome', *JRS* 70, 81–100
(1988) *The fall of the Roman Republic* (Oxford)
(1990) *Roman imperial themes* (Oxford)

Bruun, P. (1991) 'The charm of quantitative studies in numismatic research', *Die Münze: Bild, Botschaft, Bedeutung. Festschrift für Maria R. Alföldi* (Frankfurt) 65–83

Burnett, A.M. (1977) 'The authority to coin in the late Republic and early Empire', *NC* 137, 37–83
(1987) *Coinage in the Roman world* (London)

Burnett, A.M., Amandry, M., Ripolles, P.P. (1992) *Roman provincial coinage* 1 (London–Paris)

Burnett, A.M., Craddock, P. (1983) 'Rome and Alexandria: the minting of Egyptian tetradrachms under Severus Alexander', *ANSMusN* 28, 109–18

Burnett, A.M., Plouviez, J., Tuckett, T. (1992) 'Sutton, Suffolk', in Bland (1992) 25–31

Bursche, A. (1989) 'Contacts between the Roman empire and the mid-European Barbaricum in the light of coin finds', in Carradice (1989) 279–88

Butcher, K. (1988) *Roman provincial coins: an introduction to the Greek Imperials* (London)
(1992) 'Rhodian drachmas at Caesarea in Cappadocia', *NC* 152, 41–8
(forthcoming) *Coinage in Roman Syria* (London)

Buttrey, T.V. (1961) 'Dio, Zonaras and the value of the Roman aureus', *JRS* 51, 40–5
(1972) 'A hoard of sestertii from Bordeaux and the problem of bronze circulation in the third century AD', *ANSMusN* 18, 33–58
(1976) 'The denarii of P. Crepusius and Roman Republican mint organization', *ANSMusN* 21, 67–108
(1980) 'Cosa: the coins', *Mem. Amer. Ac. Rome* 34, 9–153
(1991) 'Exchange and circulation at Pergamum in the second century', *NC* 151, iii–xii

Caley, E.R. (1958) 'Chemical composition of Alexandrian tetradrachms', *American*

Numismatic Society: Centennial Publication (New York) 167–80

(1964) *Orichalcum and related ancient alloys* (New York)

Callu, J.-P. (1969) *La politique monétaire des Empereurs romains de 238 à 311* (Rome)

(1983) 'Structure des dépôts d'or au IVᵉ siècle (312–92)', in E. Frézouls (ed.) *Crise et redressement dans les provinces européennes de l'Empire* (Strasbourg) 157–74

Callu, J.-P., Loriot, X. (1990) *L'or monnayé II: la dispersion des aurei en Gaule romaine sous l'Empire* (Juan-les-Pins)

(1992) 'Avant-propos', in Brenot, Loriot, (1992) 21–32

Calzolari, M. (1987) 'Il tesoro di aurei romani scoperto nel territorio di Brescello', *RIN* 89, 43–68

Campbell, B. (1984) *The Emperor and the Roman army, 31 BC–AD 235* (Oxford)

Campo, M., Richard, J.-C., Von Kaenel, H.-M. (1981) *El Tesoro de La Pobla de Mafumet* (Barcelona)

Canessa, C. (1909) 'Le trésor monétaire de Boscoreale', *Le Musée* 6, 259–65

Carradice, I.A. (1983) *Coinage and finances in the reign of Domitian AD 81–96* (Oxford)

(1989) (ed.) *Proceedings of the 10th International Congress of Numismatics, London 1986* (Wetteren)

Carradice, I.A., Cowell, M. (1987) 'The minting of Roman imperial bronze coins for circulation in the East: Vespasian to Trajan', *NC* 147, 26–50

Carson, R.A.G. (1956) 'System and product in the Roman mint', *Essays in Roman history presented to Harold Mattingly* (Oxford) 227–39

Carson, R.A.G., Kraay, C.M. (1978) *Essays presented to Humphrey Sutherland: Scripta Nummaria Varia* (Oxford)

Carter, G.F. (1981A) 'Die-link statistics for Crepusius denarii and calculations of the total number of dies', *PACT* 5, 193–203

(1981B) 'Comparison of methods for calculating the total number of dies from die-link statistics', *PACT* 5, 204–13

(1983) 'A simplified method for calculating the original number of dies from die-link statistics', *ANSMusN* 28, 195–206

Carter, G.F., King, C.E. (1988) 'Zinc content of Neronian semisses and quadrantes and the relative value of zinc and copper in the coin of Nero', *ANSMusN* 33, 91–106

Casey, J. (1986) *Understanding ancient coins* (London)

Casson, L. (1980) 'The role of the state in Rome's grain trade', in J.H. D'Arms, E.C. Kopff (edd.) *The seaborne commerce of ancient Rome* (Rome) 21–33

(1986) 'New light on maritime loans: P.Vindob. G 19792 (= *SB* VI 9571)', in R.S. Bagnall, W.V. Harris (edd.) *Studies in Roman law in memory of A.A. Schiller* (Leiden) 11–17

(1989) *The Periplus Maris Erythraei* (Princeton)

Cesano, S.L. (1925) 'Nuove ripostigli di denari di argento dell'Impero romano', *Att. Mem. Inst. It. Num.* 5, 57–72

(1929) 'Ripostiglio di aurei imperiali rinvenuto a Roma', *BCAR* 57, 5–119

Châlon, G. (1964) *L'Edit de Tiberius Iulius Alexander* (Lausanne)

Chantraine, H., Alföldi, M.R. (1978) *Cohen–RIC Konkordanz* (Bonn)

Christ, K. (1960) *Antike Münzfunde Südwestdeutschlands: Münzfunde, Geldwirtschaft und Geschichte im Raume Baden-Württembergs von keltischer bis in alamannische Zeit* (Heidelberg)

Christiansen, E. (1985) 'The Roman coins of Alexandria (30 BC to AD 296): an inventory of hoards', *CH* 7, 77–140

(1988) *The Roman coins of Alexandria: quantitative studies* (Aarhus)

Cipolla, C.M. (1952) *Mouvements monétaires dans l'État de Milan 1580–1700* (Paris)

(1956) *Money, prices and civilisation in the Mediterranean world from the fifth century to the seventeenth century* (Cincinnati)

(1981) *Before the Industrial Revolution: European society and economy, 1000–1700*[2] (London)

(1982) *The monetary policy of fourteenth-century Florence* (Berkeley)

Clay, T. (1988) 'Metallurgy and metallography in numismatics', *NAC* 17, 341–52

Coale, A.J., Demeny, P. (1983) *Regional model life-tables*[2] (Princeton)

Cope, L.H. (1972) 'The metallurgical analysis of Roman imperial silver and aes coinage', in E.T. Hall, D.M. Metcalf (edd.) *Methods of chemical and metallurgical investigation of ancient coinage* (London) 3–47

Corbier, M. (1985) 'Dévaluations et évolution des prix (Ier–IIIe siècles)' *RN* 6.27, 69–106

(1986) 'Svalutazione, inflazione e circolazione monetaria nel III secolo', in A. Giardina (ed.) *Società romana e Impero tardoantica; istituzioni, ceti, economie* 1, (Bari) 489–533

Crawford, D. (1971) *Kerkeosiris* (Cambridge)

Crawford, M.H. (1968) 'Plated coins – false coins', *NC* 7.8, 55–9

(1969A) 'Coin-hoards and the pattern of violence in the late Republic', *PBSR* 37, 76–81

(1969B) *Roman Republican coin-hoards* (London)

(1970) 'Money and exchange in the Roman world', *JRS* 60, 40–8

(1974) *Roman Republican coinage* (Cambridge)

(1980) 'Economìa imperiale e commercio estero', *Tecnologìa, economìa e società nel mondo romano* (Como) 207–18

(1985) *Coinage and money under the Roman Republic: Italy and the Mediterranean economy* (Cambridge)

Crawford, M.H., Millar, F. (1983) *Sources for ancient history* (Cambridge)

Dattari, G. (1903) 'Appunti di numismatica alessandrina XVI', *RIN* 16, 11–35

Davies, R.W. (1989) *Service in the Roman army* (Edinburgh)

Day, J. (1987) 'The Fisher equation and medieval monetary history', in *The medieval market economy* (Oxford) 108–15

Delamare, F. (1993) *Circulation et usure des monnaies: le frai et ses lois* (Paris)

Delia, D. (1991) *Alexandrian citizenship during the Roman Principate* (Atlanta)

Delmaire, R. (1989) *Largesses sacrées et res privata: l'aerarium impérial et son administration au IVe siècle* (Paris)

Dembski, G. (1977) 'Die antiken Münzschatzfunde aus Österreich', *NZ* 91, 3–64

Demougin, S. (1988) *L'ordre équestre sous les Julio-Claudiens* (Paris)

Depeyrot, G. (1987A) *Le Bas-Empire romain: économie et numismatique* (Paris)

(1987B) 'Numéraire et prix: le rôle des métaux', in Depeyrot, Hackens, Moucharte 1987, 707–29

(1988) 'La durée d'utilisation des solidi romains', *Studia Numismatica Labacensia A. Jelocnik oblata* (Ljublana) 213–17

(1991) *Crises et inflation entre antiquité et Moyen Age* (Paris)

Depeyrot, G., Hackens, T., Moucharte, G., (1987) [1990] (edd.) *Rythmes de la production monétaire de l'antiquité à nos jours, Paris 1986* (Louvain)

Depeyrot, G., Hollard, D. (1987) 'Pénurie d'argent et crise monétaire au IIIe siècle après J.-C.', *Histoire et Mesure* 2.1, 57–85

Desnier, J.-L. (1985) 'Le trésor de Puy-Dieu', *TMon* 7, 33–104

Develin, R. (1971) 'The army pay rises under Severus and Caracalla and the question of annona militaris', *Latomus* 30, 687–95

Domaszewski, A. (1898–1900) 'Zu lateinischen Schriftstellern', *RhM* 54, 311–12

Domergue, C. (1990) *Mines de la péninsule ibérique dans l'antiquité romaine* (Rome)

Downey, G. (1961) *Ancient Antioch* (Princeton)

Drexhage, H.-J. (1986) 'Eselpreise im römischen Ägypten: ein Beitrag zum Binnenhandel' *MBAH* 5.1, 34–48

(1991) *Preise, Mieten/Pachten, Kosten und Löhne im römischen Ägypten bis zum Regierungsantritt Diokletians* (St Katharinen)

Duncan-Jones, R.P. (1964) 'Human numbers in towns and town organisations of the Roman empire: the evidence of gifts', *Historia* 13, 199–208

(1965) 'An epigraphic survey of costs in Roman Italy', *PBSR* 33, 189–306

(1976A) 'The price of wheat in Roman Egypt under the Principate', *Chiron* 6, 241–62

(1976B) 'The size of the modius castrensis', *ZPE* 21, 53–62

(1980) 'The wealth of Gaul', *Chiron* 11, 217–20

(1982) *The economy of the Roman Empire²* (Cambridge)

(1984) 'Problems of the Delphic manumission payments 200–1 BC', *ZPE* 57, 203–9

(1987) 'Weight-loss as an index of coin-wear in currency of the Roman Principate', in Depeyrot, Hackens, Moucharte (1987), 235–54

(1989) 'Mobility and immobility of coin in the Roman Empire', *AIIN* 36, 121–37

(1990) *Structure and scale in the Roman economy* (Cambridge)

(1994) 'Empire-wide patterns in coin-hoards', in C.E. King, D. Wigg (edd.) *Coin-finds and coin use in the Roman world* (Bonn)

Duvignaud, J. (1970) *Change at Shebika: report from a North African village* (London)

Eck, W. (1990) 'Cn. Calpurnius Piso cos. ord. 7 v. Chr. und die lex portorii provinciae Asiae', *EA* 15, 139–45

Einzig, P. (1966) *Primitive money²* (London)

El-Sayed, M., El-Ghany, A. (1988) 'The problem of *abrochos gè* in Roman Egypt', in B.G. Mandaliras (ed.) *Proceedings of the eighteenth International Congress of Papyrology, Athens 1986*, 1 (Athens) 295–9

Engelmann, H., Knibbe, D. (1989) 'Das Zollgesetz der Provinz Asia', *EA* 14, 1–206

Ermatinger, J. (1990) 'The circulation pattern of Diocletian's nummi', *AJN* 2.2, 107–17

Esty, W.W. (1986) 'Estimation of the size of a coinage: a survey and comparison of methods', *NC* 146, 185–215

Esty, W.W., Carter, G.F. (1991–2) 'The distribution of the numbers of coins struck by dies', *AJN* 2.3–4, 165–86

Etienne, R., Rachet, M. and others (1984) *Le trésor de Garonne* (Paris)

Fagerlie, J. (1967) *Late Roman and Byzantine solidi found in Sweden and Denmark* (New York)

Fant, J.C. (1988) 'The Roman Emperors in the marble business: capitalists, middlemen or philanthropists?', in N. Herz, M. Waelkens (edd.) *Classical marble: geochemistry, technology and trade* (Dordrecht–London–Boston) 147–58

(1989A) *Cavum antrum Phrygiae: the organization and operation of the Roman imperial marble quarries* (Oxford)

(1989B) 'Poikiloi lithoi: the anomalous economics of the Roman imperial marble quarry at Teos', in S. Walker, A. Cameron (edd.) *The Greek Renaissance in the Roman Empire: papers from the 10th British Museum Classical Colloquium* (London) 206–17

(1993) 'Ideology, gift and trade: a distribution model for the Roman imperial marbles', in W.V. Harris (ed.) *The inscribed economy* (Rome–Ann Arbor) 145–70

Ferguson, J. (1976) 'China and Rome', *ANRW* 2.9.2, 581–603

Flach, D. (1978) 'Inschriftenuntersuchungen zum römischen Kolonat in Nordafrika', *Chiron* 8, 441–92

Foraboschi, D. (1988) 'Il rapporto oro/argento nel 113 d.C.', *ZPE* 75, 79–80

Foraboschi, D., Gara, A. (1982) 'L'economìa dei crediti in natura', *Athenaeum* 60, 69–83

Forni, G. (1953) *Il reclutamento delle legioni da Augusto a Diocleziano* (Milan)

Frank, T. (1935) 'The financial crisis of 33 AD', *AJPh* 56, 336–41

Frederiksen, M.W. (1966) 'Caesar, Cicero and the problem of debt', *JRS* 56, 128–41
    (1984) *Campania* (London–Rome)

Frere, S.S. (1987) *Britannia³* (London)

Frere, S.S., Wilkes, J.J. (1989) *Strageath: excavations within the Roman fort 1973–1986* (London)

Fulford, M. (1978) 'Coin circulation and mint activity in the later Roman Empire: some economic implications', *AJ* 135, 67–114

Gara, A (1976) *Prosdiagraphomena e circolazione monetaria: aspetti dell' organizzazione fiscale in rapporto alla politica monetaria dell'Egitto romano* (Milan)

Gascou, J. (1989) 'La table budgétaire d'Antaeopolis (P.Freer 08.45 c-d)', *Hommes et richesses dans l'Empire byzantin*, 1 (Paris) 279–314
    (1990) 'Remarques critiques sur "La table budgétaire d'Antaeopolis"', *ZPE* 82, 97–101

Gerasimov, T. (1938) 'Hoard of Roman denarii from Nis [Naissus]', *Bull. Inst. Arch. Bulg.* 12, 427–8 [in Bulgarian]

Gerov, B. (1977) 'Die Einfälle der Nordvölker in den Ostbalkanraum im Lichte der Münzschatzfunde', *ANRW* 2.6, 110–81

Giard, J.-B. (1983) *Le monnayage de l'atelier de Lyon, 43 av. J.-C. à 41 ap. J.-C.* (Wetteren)
    (1985) 'Les jeux de l'imitation: fraude ou nécessité?', *NAC* 14, 231–8

Gibb, H.A.R. (1971) (trans.) *Travels of Ibn Battuta AD 1325–1354*, 3 (Cambridge)

Gnoli, R. (1988) *Marmora romana* (Rome)

Goldsmith, R.W. (1987) *Pre-modern financial systems: a historical comparative study* (Cambridge)

Gordon, C.D. (1949) 'Subsidy in Roman imperial defence', *Phoenix* 3, 60–9

Grant, M. (1955) 'The mints of Roman gold and silver in the early Principate', *NC* 6.15, 39–54

Grierson, P. (1956) 'The Roman law of counterfeiting', in *Essays in Roman history presented to H. Mattingly* (Oxford) 240–61
    (1964) 'Weight and coinage', *NC* 7.4, i–xvii
    (1965) 'The interpretation of coin-finds (I)', *NC* 7.5, i–xvi
    (1968) 'Variations in die-output', *NCirc.* 76, 298–9
    (1979) *Bibliographie numismatique²* (Brussels)

Grosso, F. (1964) *La lotta politica al tempo di Commodo* (Turin)

Gruel, K. (1981) *Le trésor de Trébry* (Paris)

Guey, J., Carcassonne, C. (1978) 'Propos de statistique: quelques échantillons monétaires', *Les dévaluations à Rome, 1975* (Rome) 55–78

Guey, J. (1955–6) 'Trésors de monnaies romaines en Europe orientale (à propos d'un récent article de V.Kropotkine)', *MEFR* 65, 189–216; 66, 139–204

Hackens, T. (1987) 'L'apport de la numismatique à l'histoire économique', in Hackens, Marchetti (1987), 151–69

Hackens, T., Marchetti, P. (1987) (edd.) *Histoire économique de l'antiquité* (Louvain)

Hamilton, E.J. (1934) *American treasure and the price revolution in Spain 1501–1650* (Cambridge, Mass.)

Harrauer, H., Sijpestein, P.J. (1985) 'Ein neues Dokument zu Roms Indienhandel: P.Vindob. G 40822', *Anz. Öst. Ak. Wiss. Phil.-Hist. Kl.* 122, 124–55

Harris, W.V. (1979) *War and imperialism in Republican Rome* (Oxford)

Heil, M. (1991) 'Einige Bemerkungen zum Zollgesetz aus Ephesos', *EA* 17, 9–18

Helly, B. (1991) 'Méthodes de laboratoire, statistique et informatique en numismatique', in T. Hackens and others (edd.) *A survey of numismatic research 1985–1990*, 2 (Brussels) 847–56

Hendy, M. (1985) *Studies in the Byzantine monetary economy c.300–1450* (Cambridge)

Hennig, D. (1967) *Untersuchungen zur Bodenpacht im ptolemäisch-römischen Ägypten* (Munich)

Hill, G.F. (1924) 'The frequency table', *NC* 5.4, 76–85

Hirschfeld, O. (1905) *Die kaiserlichen Verwaltungsbeamten bis auf Diokletian*[2] (Berlin)

Hirth, F. (1885) *China and the Roman Orient* (Leipzig–Munich–Shanghai–Hongkong)

Hobbs, R. (1992) 'Woodham Mortimer, Essex', in Bland (1992) 20–3

Holder, P.A. (1980) *Studies in the auxilia of the Roman army from Augustus to Trajan* (Oxford)

Hombert, M., Préaux, C. (1952) *Recherches sur le recensement dans l'Egypte romaine* (Leiden)

Hopkins, K. (1980) 'Taxes and trade in the Roman empire 200 BC–AD 400', *JRS* 70, 101–25

Howgego, C.J. (1985) *Greek imperial countermarks: studies in the provincial coinage of the Roman empire* (London)

  (1990) 'Why did ancient states strike coin?', *NC* 150, 1–25

  (1992) 'The supply and use of money in the Roman world, 200 BC to AD 300', *JRS* 82, 1–31

Howgego, C.J., King, C.E., (1992) 'Membury, Wiltshire', in Bland (1992) 11–19

Iluk, J. (1985) 'The export of gold from the Roman empire to barbarian countries from the 4th to the 6th centuries', *MBAH* 4.1, 79–102

  (1988) *Ekonomiczne i polityczne aspekty cyrkulacji zlota w Posnym Cesarstwie Rzymskim* (Gdansk)

Jacques, F. (1991) 'Municipia libera de l'Afrique Proconsulaire', *Epigrafia: Actes du Colloque international d'épigraphie latine en mémoire de A.Degrassi* (Rome) 583–606

  (1992) 'Les nobiles exécutés par Septime Sévere selon l'Histoire Auguste: liste de proscription ou énumeration fantaisiste?', *Latomus* 51, 121–44

Jelocnik, A. (1961) 'Najdba argenteusov zgodnje tetrarhije v Sisku', *Situla* 3, 1–92

  (1967) 'Les multiples d'or de Magnence découvertes à Emona', *RN* 6.9, 209–35

Johnson, A.C., West, L.C. (1949) *Byzantine Egypt: economic studies* (Princeton)

Johnson, C. (1956) *The De Moneta of Nicholas Oresme and English mint documents* (London)

Johnson, N.L., Kotz, S. (1969) *Discrete distributions* (New York)

Johnston, A. (1984) 'Greek imperial statistics: a commentary', *RN* 6.26, 240–57

Jones, A.H.M. (1939) 'Civitates liberae et immunes in the East', in W.M. Calder, J. Keil (edd.) *Studies presented to W.H. Buckler* (Manchester) 103–17

  (1960) *Studies in Roman government and law* (Oxford)

  (1964) *The Later Roman Empire 284–602* (Oxford)

(1974) *The Roman economy* (Oxford)

Jones, B.W. (1992) *The Emperor Domitian* (London)

Jonsson, K. (1987) *The new era: the reformation of the late Anglo-Saxon coinage* (Stockholm)

Kaenel, H. von (1986) *Münzprägung und Münzbildnis des Claudius* (Berlin)

Kambitsis, S. (1985) *Le Papyrus Thmouis 1.11 colonnes 68–160* (Paris)

Katzoff, R. (1972) 'Precedent in the courts of Roman Egypt', *ZRG* 89, 256–92

Kehoe, D. (1988) *The economics of agriculture on Roman imperial estates in North Africa* (Göttingen)

Kienast, D. (1990) *Römische Kaisertabelle: Grundzüge einer römischen Kaiserchronologie* (Darmstadt)

Kinns, P. (1983) 'The Amphictionic coinage reconsidered', *NC* 143, 1–22

Klein, M.J. (1988) *Untersuchungen zu den kaiserlichen Steinbrüchen an Mons Porphyrites und Mons Claudianus in der östlichen Wüste Ägyptens* (Bonn)

Kloft, H. (1970) *Liberalitas Principis: Herkunft und Bedeutung* (Vienna)

Kolendo, J. (1980) 'L'arrêt de l'afflux des monnaies romaines dans le barbaricum sous Septime Sévère', *Les dévaluations à Rome, 1978* (Rome) 169–72

Kos, P. (1986) *Monetary circulation in the south-east Alpine region* (Ljubljana)

Kraay, C.M. (1956) *The aes coinage of Galba* (New York)

(1960) 'Two new sestertii of Domitian', *ANSMusN* 9, 109–16

Kromann, A. (1989) 'Recent Roman coin finds from Denmark', in Carradice (1989) 263–74

Kropotkin, V. (1961) *Klady rimskih monet na territorii S.S.S.R.* (Moscow)

Krzyzanowska, A. (1976) *Skarb denarow rzymskich z Drzewicza* (Warsaw)

Kubiak, S. (1979) *Znaleziska monet rzymskich a Mazowsza i Podlasia* (Warsaw)

Kubitschek, W. (1928) *Grundriss der antiken Zeitrechnung* (Munich)

Kunisz, A. (1973) *Katalog skarbów monet rzymskich odkrytych na ziemiach polskich* (Warsaw)

(1983) 'Udzial zlotego pienadza w cyrkulacji na terytorium Egiptu w I–III w n.e.' *Wiadomisci Numizmatyczne* 27, 121–65

(1985) *Znaleziska monet rzymskich z Malopowski* (Warsaw)

Lane, F.C., Mueller, R.C. (1985) *Money and banking in medieval and Renaissance Venice* 1 (Baltimore)

Laser, R. (1980) *Die römischen und frühbyzantinischen Fundmünzen auf dem Gebiet der DDR* (Berlin)

Le Roy, M. (1971) 'Le poids de la livre romaine', *BSFN* 26, 98–9

Levick, B.M. (1976) *Tiberius the politician* (London)

(1987) '"Caesar omnia habet": property and politics under the Principate', *Entretiens Hardt* 33, 187–211

Lewis, N. (1983) *Life in Egypt under Roman rule* (Oxford)

Ligt, L. de (1990–1) 'Demand, supply, distribution. The Roman peasantry between town and countryside; rural monetisation and peasant demand', *MBAH* 9.2, 24–56; 10.1, 33–77

Linant de Bellefonds, X. (1980) 'Un modèle monétaire pour l'économie de l'Empire romain au IIIᵉ siècle de notre ère', *RD* 58, 561–86

Lind, L. (1981) *Roman denarii found in Sweden* (Stockholm)

(1988) *Romerska denarer funna i Sverige* (Stockholm)

(1992) 'Julio-Claudian denarius hoards in Britain: date of deposit', *Florilegium*

Numismaticum: studia in honorem U. Westermark edita (Stockholm) 247–53

Lo Cascio, E. (1978) 'Oro e moneta in età traianea', *AIIN* 25, 75–102

    (1979) 'Carbone, Druso e Gratidiano: la gestione della res nummaria a Roma tra la Lex Papiria e la Lex Cornelia', *Athenaeum* 57, 215–38

    (1980) 'La reforma monetaria di Nerone: l'evidenza dei ripostigli', *MEFRA* 92, 445–70

    (1984) 'Dall'antoninianus al "laureato grande": l'evoluzione monetaria del III secolo nella luce della nuova documentazione di età diocleziana', *Opus* 3, 133–201

Lopreato, P. (1984) 'I pesi ageminati del Museo di Aquileia e il sistema ponderale bizantino', *AAAd* 24, 71–102

Loriot, X. (1988) 'Trouvailles isolées de monnaie d'or romaine dans la province de Rétie (Ier–Ve siècles)', *Studia numismatica Labacensia A. Jelocnik oblata* (Ljubljana) 53–98

Loriot, X., Nony, D. (1982–) *Corpus des trésors monétaires antiques de la France* (Paris)

MacDowall, D.M. (1966) 'The quality of Nero's orichalcum', *Schw. Mzbl.* 16, 101–6

    (1979) *The western coinages of Nero* (New York)

MacMullen, R. (1959) 'Roman imperial building in the provinces', *HSPh* 64, 207–35

    (1984) 'The Roman Emperor's army costs', *Latomus* 43, 571–80

    (1987) 'Tax pressure in the Roman empire', *Latomus* 46, 737–54

Macro, A.D. (1976) 'Imperial provisions for Pergamum', *GRBS* 17, 169–79

Manacorda, D. (1977) 'Il kalendarium Vegetianum e le anfore della Baetica', *MEFRA* 89, 313–32

Mann, J.C. (1983) *Legionary recruitment and veteran settlement during the Principate* (London)

Marquardt, J. (1881–5) *Römische Staatsverwaltung³* (Leipzig)

Mate, M. (1969) 'Coin dies under Edward I and Edward II', *NC* 7.9, 207–18

Mattingly, H. (1926) 'The restored coins of Trajan', *NC* 5.6, 232–78

    (1960) *Roman coins²* (London)

Mattingly, H.B. (1982) 'The management of the Roman Republican mint', *AIIN* 29, 9–46

Meijer, F. (1990) 'The financial aspects of the leges frumentariae of 123–58 BC', *MBAH* 9.2, 14–23

Metcalf, D. (1986) 'The monetary history of the tenth century viewed in the perspective of the eleventh century', in M.A.S. Blackburn (ed.) *Anglo–Saxon monetary history: essays in memory of M. Dolley* (Leicester) 133–55

Metcalf, W.E. (1976) 'Two Alexandrian hoards', *RBN* 122, 65–77

    (1979) 'A Roman hoard from Cyprus', *NC* 139, 26–35

    (1989) 'Rome and Lugdunum again', *AJN* 1, 51–70

    (1993) 'The coinage of Otho and early imperial mint organisation', in A.M. Burnett, M.J. Price (edd.) *Essays in honour of G.K. Jenkins and R.A.G. Carson* (London) 155–60

Mihailescu-Birlibà, V. (1972–3) 'Tezaurul de denari romani imperiali de la Puriceni', *Memoria Antiquitatis* 4–5, 125–230

    (1977) *Tezaurul de La Magura* (Bucharest)

    (1980) *La monnaie romaine chez les Daces orientaux* (Bucharest)

Millar, F. (1977) *The Emperor in the Roman world* (London)

Milne, J.G. (1910) 'Alexandrian tetradrachms of Tiberius', *NC* 4.10, 333–9

    (1933) *Catalogue of Alexandrian coins* (Oxford)

Mirnik, I.A. (1981) *Coin-hoards in Yugoslavia* (Oxford)

Miskimin, H.A. (1984) *Money and power in fifteenth-century France* (New Haven)

(1987) 'Money, the law and legal tender', in Depeyrot, Hackens, Moucharte (1987) 697–705

Mitkowa-Szubert, K. (1989) *The Nietulisko Male hoards of Roman denarii* (Warsaw)

Mitrea, B., Zaharia, E. (1967) 'Tezaurul de La Oboroceni', *Arheologia Moldovei* 5, 82–124

Mocsy, A. (1974) *Pannonia and Upper Moesia* (London)

Mommsen, T. (1875) *Histoire de la monnaie romaine* (Paris)

Montevecchi, O. (1939) 'Ricerche di sociologia nei documenti dell'Egitto greco-romano', *Aegyptus* 19, 11–53

Morrisson, C. and others (1985) *L'Or Monnayé I: Purifications et altérations de Rome à Byzance* (Paris)

Mouchmov, L.A. (1934) *Le trésor de Réka-Devnia (Marcianopolis)* (Sofia)

Mrozek, S. (1987) 'Inopia rei nummariae et l'usure dans l'histoire romaine', in Depeyrot, Hackens, Moucharte (1987) 323–34

Munro, J.H. (1984) 'Mint output, money, and prices in late-medieval England and the Low Countries', in E. van Cauwenberghe, F. Irsigler (edd.) *Münzprägung, Geldumlauf und Wechselkurse* (Trier) 31–122

Müller, J.W. (1981) 'Estimation du nombre originel de coins', *PACT* 5, 157–72

Nash, D.M. (1978) 'Plus ça change: currency in central Gaul from Julius Caesar to Nero', in Carson, Kraay (1978) 12–31

Naville, L. (1920–2) 'Fragments de métrologie classique', *RSN* 22, 42–60, 257–63

Nesselhauf, H. (1964) 'Patrimonium und res privata des römischen Kaisers', *HAC* 1963, 73–93

Nohejlová-Pratová, E. (1955) *Nálezy mincí v Cechách na Morave a ve Slezsku* (Prague)

Ondrouch, V. (1934) *Der römische Denarfund von Vyskovce* (Bratislava)

(1938) *Limes Romanus na Slovensku* (Bratislava)

Patterson, C. (1972) 'Silver stocks and losses in ancient and medieval times', *EcHR* 2.25, 205–35

Pekáry, T. (1959) 'Studien zur römischen Währungs- und Finanzgeschichte von 161 bis 235 n. Chr.', *Historia*, 8, 443–89

Perelli, L. (1975) 'La reforma monetaria di Nerone: una questione di metodo', *RSI* 87, 726–35

Pflaum, H.-G. (1950) *Les procurateurs équestres sous le Haut-Empire romain* (Paris)

(1960) *Les carrières procuratoriennes équestres* (Paris)

Pflaum, H.-G., Huvelin, H. (1981) 'Le trésor de Viuz-Faverges', *TMon* 3, 33–76

Pollard, J.H. (1977) *A handbook of numerical and statistical techniques* (Cambridge)

Pozzi, E. (1958–9) 'Tesoretto di età flavia da Pompei', *AIIN* 5–6, 211–30

Preston, H. (1983) 'Roman Republican coin-hoards: an age correction and other comments', *AIIN* 30, 83–93

Protase, D. (1966) *Problema continuitatii in Dacia in lumina arheologici si numismaticii* (Bucharest)

(1980) *Autohtonii in Dacia: I Dacia Romana* (Bucharest)

Raschke, M.G. (1978) 'New studies in Roman commerce with the East', *ANRW* 2.9.2, 604–1361

Rathbone, D. (1990) 'Villages, land and population in Graeco–Roman Egypt' *PCPhS* 216, 103–42

(1991) *Economic rationalism and rural society in third-century Egypt: the Heroninos archive and the Appianus estate* (Cambridge)

(1993) 'Egypt, Augustus and Roman taxation', *Cahiers du Centre Glotz* 4, 81–112

Raychaudhuri, T., Habib, I. (1982) (edd) *Cambridge Economic History of India* 1 (Cambridge)

Rea, J. (1982) 'PLond Inv 1562 verso: market taxes in Oxyrhynchus', *ZPE* 46, 191–209

Reece, R. (1974) 'Numerical aspects of Roman coin-hoards in Britain', in R. Reece, J. Casey (edd.) *Coins and the archaeologist* (Oxford) 78–94

(1981) 'The "normal" hoard', *PACT* 5, 299–308

(1987A) *Coinage in Roman Britain* (London)

(1987B) 'Coin-finds and coin-production', in Depeyrot, Hackens, Moucharte (1987) 333–41

(1991) *Roman coins from 140 sites in Britain* (Cirencester)

Reece, R., Casey, J. (1988) (edd.) *Coins and the archaeologist*[2] (London)

Reekmans, T. (1977) 'La politique économique et financière des autorités dans les Douze Césars de Suétone', *Historiographia antiqua: Commentationes Lovanienses in honorem W. Peremans* (Louvain) 265–314

Regling, K. (1931) 'Der Schatz römischer Goldmünzen von Diarbekir (Mardin)', *Blätter für Münzfreunde* 66, 353–81

Riederer, J. (1974) 'Metallanalysen römischer Sesterzen', *JNG* 24, 73–98

Roach Smith, C. (1879), 'Discovery of altars, coins, etc., near the site of Procolitia, on the site of the Roman Wall', *NC* n.s.19, 85–91

Robathan, D.M. (1942) 'Domitian's Midas touch', *TAPhA* 79,130–44

Robertson, A.S. (1956) 'The numismatic evidence of Romano-British coin-hoards', *Essays in Roman history presented to H. Mattingly* (Oxford) 262–85

(1978) 'The circulation of Roman coins in N. Britain: the evidence of hoards and site-finds from Scotland', in Carson, Kraay (1978) 186–216

(1982) 'The Falkirk (1933) hoard of over 1900 denarii: a review in the light of recent research', in S. Scheers (ed.) *Studia P. Naster oblata* 1 (Louvain) 207–26

(1993) 'Finds of Roman imperial coins in Britain from Near Eastern and Eastern mints: the evidence of Romano-British coin hoards', in A.M. Burnett, M.J. Price (edd.) *Essays in honour of G.K. Jenkins and R.A.G. Carson* (London) 229–40

(forthcoming) *An inventory of Romano-British coin-hoards* (London)

Robinson, E.S.G. (1960) 'Some problems in the later fifth-century coinage of Athens', *ANSMusN* 9, 1–15

Rodewald, C. (1976) *Money in the age of Tiberius* (Manchester)

Rogers, P.M. (1984) 'Domitian and the finances of state', *Historia* 33, 60–78

Rogers, R.S. (1947) 'The Roman Emperors as heirs and legatees', *TAPhA* 78, 140–58

Roncière, C.M. de la (1973) *Un changeur florentin du Trecento: Lippo di Fede del Sega* (Paris)

Ross, G.J.S. (1980) *Maximum Likelihood Program* (Rothamsted)

Ross, G.J.S., Preece, D.A. (1985) 'The negative binomial distribution', *The Statistician* 34, 323–36

Roueché, C. (1984) 'Acclamations in the Later Roman Empire: new evidence from Aphrodisias', *JRS* 74, 181–99

Roxan, M.M. (1981) 'The distribution of Roman military diplomas', *Epig. Stud.* 12, 265–86

Sainte Croix, G.E.M. de (1981) *The class struggle in the ancient Greek world* (London)

Salama, P., Callu, J.-P. (1990) 'L'approvisionnement monétaire des provinces africaines au IVe siècle', *L'Afrique dans l'Occident romain, 1987* (Rome) 91–115

Salzman, M. (1990) *On Roman time* (Berkeley)

Sartre, M. (1991) *L'Orient romain: provinces et sociétés provinciales en Méditerranée orientale d'Auguste aux Sévères (31 avant J-C–235 après J-C)* (Paris)

Sasianu, A. (1980) *Moneda antica in vestul si nord-vestul Romaniei* (Oradea)

Scheidel, W. (1992) 'Inschriftenstatistik und die Frage des Rekrutierungsalters römischer Soldaten', *Chiron* 22, 281–97

Schmidt-Dick, F. (1987) 'Konkordanz zwischen erster und zweiter Auflage von RIC Band 1', *LNV* 3, 395–542

Sellwood, D. (1963) 'Some experiments in Greek minting technique', *NC*, 7.3, 217–31

Sey-Katalin, B. (1986) 'A Keceli eremlet', *Kumania* 9, 27–71

Shaw, S.J. (1962) *The financial and administrative organization and development of Ottoman Egypt* (Berkeley)

Sijpestein, P.J. (1987) *Customs duties in Roman Egypt* (Zutphen)

Smith, R.E. (1972) 'The army reforms of Septimius Severus', *Historia* 21, 481–501

Snyder, W.F. (1964) 'Nero's birthday in Egypt and his year of birth', *Historia* 13, 503–6

Soraci, R. (1974) *L'opera legislativa e amministrativa dell'Imperatore Severo Alessandro* (Catania)

Speidel, M.A. (1992) 'Roman army pay scales', *JRS* 82, 87–106

Speidel, M.P. (1973) 'The pay of the auxilia', *JRS* 63, 141–7

    (1984) 'The Roman army in Asia Minor: recent epigraphical discoveries and research', *Roman army studies* 1 (Amsterdam) 273–300

    (1985) 'Furlough in the Roman army', *YClS* 28, 283–93

    (1987) 'The rise of the mercenaries in the third century', *Tyche* 2, 191–201

Spooner, F.C. (1956) *L'économie mondiale et les frappes monétaires en France 1493–1680* (Paris)

    (1972) *The international economy and monetary movements in France 1493–1725* (Cambridge, Mass.)

Stahl, A.M. (1985) *The Venetian Tornesello: a medieval colonial coinage* (New York)

Stam, A.J. (1987) 'Statistical problems in ancient numismatics', *Statistica Neerlandica* 41, 151–73

Stauffenberg, A. Schenk Graf von (1931) *Die römische Kaisergeschichte bei Malalas* (Stuttgart)

Stewart, B.H.I.H. (1964) 'Second thoughts on medieval die output', *NC* 7.4, 293–303

Strack, P.L. (1937) *Untersuchungen zur römischen Reichsprägung des 2. Jahrhunderts, 3* (Stuttgart)

Suchodolski, S. (1981) 'Encore le poids de la livre romaine: réconstruction du poids de l'unité pondérale d'aprés les monnaies', *PACT* 5, 122–30

Sutherland, C.H.V. (1937) *Coinage and currency in Roman Britain* (Oxford)

    (1985) 'Spanish bullion supplies AD 68–9', *NAC* 14, 239–42

    (1987A) *Roman history and coinage 44 BC–AD 69* (Oxford)

    (1987B) 'The Pontif Maxim aurei of Tiberius', *NAC* 16, 219–27

Sutherland, C.H.V., Olcay, N., Merrington, K.E. (1970) *The cistophori of Augustus* (London)

Swiderek, A. (1960) *La propriété foncière privée dans l'Egypte de Vespasien, et sa technique agricole d'après PLond 131 recto* (Warsaw)

    (1971) 'The land register of the Phernouphitou toparchy in the Mendesian nome', *JJP* 16–17, 31–44

Syme, R. (1971) *Emperors and biography: studies in the Historia Augusta* (Oxford)

    (1979) 'The imperial finances under Domitian, Nerva and Trajan', in *Roman papers*

I (Oxford) 1–17

(1988) 'Clues to testamentary adoption', in *Roman papers* 4 (Oxford) 159–73

(1991) 'Marriage ages for senators', in *Roman papers* 6 (Oxford) 233–46

Szilágyi, J. (1963) 'Prices and wages in the western provinces of the Roman empire', *AAntHung* 11, 325–89

Taylor, L.R. (1961) 'Freedmen and freeborn in the epitaphs of imperial Rome', *AJPh* 82, 113–32

Thirion, M. (1972) *Le trésor de Liberchies* (Brussels)

Thomas, J.D. (1978) *'Epigraphai* and indictions in the reign of Diocletian', *BASP* 15, 133–45

Thomas, J.D., Davies, R.W. (1977) 'A new military strength-report on papyrus', *JRS* 67, 50–61

Thomasson B. (1984) *Laterculi praesidum* I (Göteborg)

Thordeman, B. (1948) 'The Lohe hoard', *NC* 7.8, 188–204

Thornton, M.K., Thornton R.L. (1989) *Julio-Claudian building programs: a quantitative study in political management* (Wauconda)

Todd, M. (1985) 'The Falkirk hoard of denarii: trade or subsidy?', *PSAS* 115, 229–32

Torelli, M. (1982) *The typology and structure of Roman historical reliefs* (Ann Arbor)

Tuckett, T. (1992) 'Bletchley, Buckinghamshire', in Bland (1992) 50–64

Turcan, R. (1963) *Le Trésor de Guelma* (Paris)

Turckheim-Pey, S. de (1981) 'Le Trésor d'Arnouville-lès-Gonesse', *TMon* 3, (1981), 17–31

Turner, P. (1989) *Roman coins from India* (London)

Tylecote R.F. (1986) *The prehistory of metallurgy in the British Isles* (London)

Tyler, P. (1975) *The Persian Wars of the third century* AD *and Roman imperial monetary policy* AD *253–68* (Wiesbaden)

Ungaro, L. (1985) 'Il ripostiglio della Casa delle Vestali, Roma 1899', *BNum* 4, 45–160

Van Berchem, D. (1939) *Les distributions de blé et d'argent à la plèbe romaine sous l'Empire romain* (Geneva)

Van Gansbeke, P. (1955) 'Les trésors monétaires d'époque romaine en Belgique', *RBN* 101, 5–44

Van Hengel C. (1982) 'Wear of silver coins', *Jaarboek voor Munt- en Penningkunde* 69, 139–45

Vermeule, C.C. (1953–4) 'Some notes on ancient dies and coining methods', *NCirc* 61, 397–402, 447–52, 499–504; 62, 1–6, 53–8

Veyne, P. (1979) 'Rome devant la prétendue fuite de l'or: mercantilisme ou politique disciplinaire?', *Annales(ESC)* 34, 211–44

(1990) *La société romaine* (Paris)

Volk, T.R. (1986) 'Scientific techniques in numismatics: the application of computers', in M.J. Price (ed.) *A survey of numismatic research 1978–1984* (London) 1041–76

(1987) 'Mint-output and coin-hoards', in Depeyrot, Hackens, Moucharte (1987) 141–221

Waggoner N.M. (1979) 'Lifetime tetradrachms of Alexander struck at Babylon', in O. Mørkholm, N.M. Waggoner (edd.) *Essays in memory of Margaret Thompson* (Wetteren) 269–80

Walker, D.R. (1976–8) *The metrology of the Roman silver coinage* (Oxford)

(1980) 'The silver content of the Roman Republican coinage', in D.M. Metcalf, W.M. Oddy (edd.) *Metallurgy in numismatics*, I (London), 55–72

(1988) 'The Roman coins', in B. Cunliffe (ed.) *The temple of Sulis Minerva at Bath*

(Oxford) 281–338

Wallace, S.L. (1938) *Taxation in Egypt from Augustus to Diocletian* (Princeton)

Watson, G.R. (1969) *The Roman soldier* (London)

Weaver, P.R.C. (1972) *Familia Caesaris* (Cambridge)

Weber, E. (1976) *Peasants into Frenchmen: the modernisation of rural France, 1870–1914* (Stanford)

Weinstock, S. (1971) *Divus Julius* (Oxford)

West, L.C. (1941) *Gold and silver standards in the Roman empire* (New York)

West, L.C., Johnson, A.C. (1944) *Currency in Roman and Byzantine Egypt* (Princeton)

Westermann, W.L. (1920) 'The uninundated lands in Ptolemaic and Roman Egypt I', *CPh* 15, 120–37

(1921) 'The uninundated lands in Ptolemaic and Roman Egypt II', *CPh* 16, 169–88

(1922) 'The dry land in Ptolemaic and Roman Egypt', *CPh* 17, 21–36

(1925) 'Hadrian's decree on renting state domain land in Egypt', *JEA* 11, 155–67

Wielowiejski, J. (1980) 'Der Einfluss der Devaluation des Denars auf die Annahme römischer Münzen durch die hinter der Donau ansässigen Völker' *Les dévaluations à Rome, 1978* (Rome) 155–67

Wierschowski, L. (1984) *Heer und Wirtschaft: das römische Heer der Prinzipatszeit als Wirtschaftsfaktor* (Bonn)

Wilkinson, L. (1988), *SYSTAT 4.1/SYGRAPH 1.1.* (Evanston, Ill.)

Willers, H. (1898) 'Römische Silberbarren mit Stempeln', *NZ* 30, 211–35

Wilson, A.J.N. (1966) *Emigration from Italy in the Republican age of Rome* (London)

Wolters R. (1990–1) 'Zum Waren- und Dienstleistungsaustausch zwischen dem römischen Reich und dem Freien Germanien in der Zeit des Prinzipats: eine Bestandsaufnahme', *MBAH* 9.1, 14–44; 10.1, 78–131

Woolf, G. (1990) 'Food, poverty and patronage: the significance of the epigraphy of the Roman alimentary schemes in early imperial Italy', *PBSR* 58, 197–228

Worp, K.A. (1991) 'Remarks on weekdays in late antiquity occurring in domestic sources', *Tyche* 6, 221–30

Zijlstra, J.S.A. (1967) *De delatores te Rome tot aan Tiberius' regering* (Leiden)

INDEX

For named coin hoards, the number in italic refers to the list on pp. 261–8. For the few hoards below not in that list, references are given in the notes.